China's Economic Rise

Sangaralingam Ramesh

China's Economic Rise

Lessons from Japan's Political Economy

palgrave
macmillan

Sangaralingam Ramesh
Department for Continuing Education
University of Oxford
Oxford, UK

ISBN 978-3-030-49810-8 ISBN 978-3-030-49811-5 (eBook)
https://doi.org/10.1007/978-3-030-49811-5

This Palgrave Macmillan imprint is published by the registered company Springer Nature Switzerland AG.
The registered company address is: Gewerbestrasse 11, 6330 Cham, Switzerland

Preface

This book is the fourth in a series of books by me which explores the economic and political rise of China and its consequences for China and the rest of the world. The first books of the series encompassed the two volumes of 'China's Lessons for India'. In Volume 1, The Political Economy of Development, the emphasis was on evaluating the economic and political past of China and the economic reform programme which started in 1978. In Volume 2, The Political Economy of Change, the emphasis was on how the economic reform programme impacted on the Chinese economy effecting its rise to become the world's second largest economy by 2011 as well as its transition from a manufacturing-based economy to a knowledge economy. At this moment in time, the Chinese economy faces one of two future trajectories which also have historical precedents. The first of these historical precedents is the one in which China follows the path followed by Great Britain after it became the first country in the world to industrialise in the eighteenth century, subsequently building an empire. This potential future for China is explored in the third book of the series, 'The Rise of Empires—The Political Economy of Innovation'. On the other hand, the purpose of this book, the fourth in the series, is to explore the second historical precedent which the Chinese economy will follow, that of Japan after the Meiji restoration of 1868. In this case, just as China started to reform its economy from 1978, Japan started its reforms in earnest after the Meiji Restoration of 1868. This book will show that there are economic, political and military similarities between the rise of modern Japan today and the rise of contemporary China, and what it may face in years to come. In this context, this book will be useful reading for academics, politicians, the general public and for anyone interested in one of China's possible future trajectories.

Japan's rise to statehood through the Kamakura Period (1185 AD to 1333 AD) to the Tokugawa Period (1600 AD to 1868 AD) was quite unremarkable. And for all of this time, China was the centre of the universe and Japan its vassal state. Japan itself was secluded for over 200 years during the Tokugawa Period when all foreigners were expelled from Japan. However, Japan's seclusion from the rest of the world was ended with the arrival off the coast of Japan of US, Russian and British warships. As a result of which western nations won trade concessions as well as other benefits from the Tokugawa Bakufu in the mid-nineteenth century. Japan at that time, compared to the United States and Britain, was underdeveloped and technologically backward especially in the military sphere. However, Japan had already gone through proto-industrialisation before the British had in the late eighteenth century. Nevertheless, whereas British proto-industrialisation led to rapid technological development and industrialisation proper, this did not happen in the case of Japan. This is probably because Japan did not have increasing demand for its manufactured goods from overseas colonies whilst domestic producers faced increasing costs of production due to rising wages, as was the case of Great Britain. The arrival of the British in Japan in particular must have stirred intense debates in the Tokugawa Bakufu about the choices of either being colonised or rapidly industrialising and becoming militarily capable of defending Japan's borders. This is particularly true in the context of the use of superior military force against the Chinese Qing imperial court by the British to win trade and territorial concessions in order to further their domestic prosperity through enforced trade. At this time, unlike the Chinese, the Japanese realised that in order for their country, their society and culture to survive the ravages of becoming colonised, they would have to modernise extremely fast. The Tokugawa Shogunate and Bakufu were incapable and perhaps unwilling to take the policy steps required to safeguard Japan's sovereignty. It was for this reason that the Tokugawa Shogunate and Bakufu were replaced by a constitutional monarchy based on multi-party democratic politics as a result of the Meiji Restoration of 1868.

Historically when countries have undergone rapid economic development, increasing disparities between the rich and the poor and economic crises have arisen. The historical trend has been a shift away from democracy, a mixed economic system encompassing free market forces, government intervention and the use of private capital towards bureaucratic fascism. This was the case of Japan at the end of the 1920s and early 1930s and Germany in the 1930s. The result was a rise in nationalism, racial self-awareness of the peoples of these countries, a rush to militarism and inevitably global military conflict. Herein lies the juxtaposition between economic activity and human behaviour. In this case, negative economic activity resulting in increasing income disparities as well as increasing deprivation in society leads to the rise of populism, and the democratic system becomes the mechanism which facilitates the rise of autocracy. The issues which the contemporary world economy faces have been seen before specifically in the 1930s. Then globalisation and global trade came to a stuttering halt with economic crises in several countries most prominently associated with the Wall Street Crash of 1929. As western economies began to suffer the economic consequences of the crash, particularly associated with rising unemployment, increasing income disparities and social deprivation, they turned to protect their economies with the use of tariffs to make Japanese goods more expensive and domestically produced goods cheaper in comparison. The British Empire decided at the imperial economic conference in Ottawa in 1932 to impose tariffs on Japanese manufactured goods including textiles which were beginning to displace British and Canadian goods due to their relative cheapness.[1] However, this made the economic situation worse and led to military conflict. But the Japanese economy began to grow in the 1930s because of its militarily planned nature. This situation has comparisons with contemporary global economics. In this case, the Global Financial Crisis of 2008 can perhaps be compared to the Wall Street Crash of 1929. The global and national economic crises which followed both of these economic events were similar in nature, increasing income disparities and increasing social deprivation. Both events were due to the fault of the poor regulation financial system which was being driven by the webs of human intrigue and avarice. However, the big difference between these two triggers of economic crisis was that the global and national economic impact of the Global Financial Crisis was mitigated, and it did not cause a Great Depression as the Wall Street Crash of 1929 did. Indeed, the negative economic effects of the Global Financial Crisis of 2008 were mitigated by

[1] Miners, N. (2002), Industrial development in the colonial empire and the imperial economic conference at Ottawa 1932, 30:2, 53–76, DOI: https://doi.org/10.1080/03086530208583141.

a globally co-ordinated economic policy response which involved the use of expansionary monetary and fiscal policies in association with unorthodox monetary policies such as Quantitative Easing. Nevertheless, national debt-to-GDP ratios were indicating the unsustainability of the debt such that governments such as that of the United Kingdom in 2010 began an austerity policy in order to bring debt and government borrowing down to sustainable levels. However, contemporary global debt has increased by 50% in comparison to its levels in 2008–2009.[2] Moreover, Eurozone government and household debt is also higher in 2019 than was the case a decade ago.[3] Furthermore, while debt is cheap, firms have accumulated debt in order to increase equity returns.[4] But at the moment, it is difficult to pinpoint the trigger/s of the next financial crisis, at least in the long term. Although the heart of any potential financial crisis could lie with the Chinese economy in which unsustainable local government debt as well as the debt of state-owned enterprises has built up over several years. If China's economic growth continues to fall in subsequent years and/or it adopts a floating exchange rate mechanism, then these could serve as possible triggers for domestic economic stagnation and a potential global economic crisis in the context of the Great Depression of the 1930s. Nevertheless, currently the US economy seems to be in good shape because economic growth is taking place at a sustained and consistent level, and housing debt has fallen since the crisis.[5] In the short term, firms may be able to manage debt repayments because interest payments remain low and dividend payments can be cut.[6] However, if unemployment begins to rise as a result of an economic crisis, then this may lead to payment defaults by households. But in the United States, mortgage-related household debt is at its lowest since 2008, although sub-prime auto loans are increasing.[7] Nevertheless, in contrast to the levels of sub-prime mortgage loans in 2008, the value of the sub-prime auto loans is comparatively

[2] Fletcher, L. (2019), Global debt – when is the day of reckoning? https://www.ft.com/content/949d08da-462d-11e9-a965-23d669740bfb.

[3] Fletcher, L. (2019), Global debt – when is the day of reckoning? https://www.ft.com/content/949d08da-462d-11e9-a965-23d669740bfb.

[4] Ibid.

[5] Ibid.

[6] Ibid.

[7] Tett, G. (2019), Driven to default: what's causing the rise in sub-prime auto loans? https://www.ft.com/content/1ce6d32e-4520-11e9-b168-96a37d002cd3.

smaller at $300 billion.[8] Moreover, the size of Eurozone household debts is at its lowest levels since 2006.[9] This reduces the risk of big Eurozone loan defaults due to either rising unemployment or rising interest rates. However, the main concerns seem to lie with the status of the Chinese economy and other emerging economies. In China's case, the property market is cooling as the Chinese economy has begun to slow from its double-digit growth rates.[10] As Chinese property developers find it difficult to offload new developments, they begin to slash prices and profits and revenues fall. At the same time, in 2019 Chinese property developers face debt repayments amounting to $55 billion.[11] Despite the fact that the growth of the Chinese economy has slowed to its lowest level in thirty years, Chinese property developers increased their US-related bond debt by $19 billion in the first two months of 2019.[12] Public sector debt in other developing countries is also a major concern where such debt now accounts for 50% of GDP.[13] This is the highest level in nearly fifty years.[14] Furthermore, while 80% of developing countries have increased public debt over the last five years, the number of developing economies with high risk, unsustainable debt has increased to thirty-two.[15] More worrying is that the source of debt is not just Chinese lending but also lending by other countries and multilateral institutions.[16]

In the case of the European Union (EU), the free movement of labour, one of the economic pillars of the European Union, caused additional competition for jobs and public service provision in the United Kingdom. Moreover, the influx of workers from the former Soviet Bloc countries which joined the EU in 2004, the EU-8 which included Poland and

[8] Ibid.

[9] Romei, V. (2019), Eurozone household debt falls to lowest levels since 2006, https://www.ft.com/content/3cbbf5f8-1a41- 11e9-9e64-d150b3105d21.

[10] Dunkley, E. (2019), Jiayuan crash underscores China property risks, https://www.ft.com/content/b5560666-1a37-11e9-b93e-f4351a53f1c3.

[11] Dunkley, E. (2019), Jiayuan crash underscores China property risks, https://www.ft.com/content/b5560666-1a37-11e9-b93e-f4351a53f1c3.

[12] Weinland, D. (2019), China's property developers binge on record dollar debt, https://www.ft.com/content/e8ff4e1a-3fe3-11e9-9bee-efab61506f44.

[13] Callan, P., Bendary, B., and Sequeira, Y. (2019), Emerging markets face a new debt crisis: Chinese lending is not the only cause, https://www.ft.com/content/4fd4e6ac-440a-11e9-b168-96a37d002cd3.

[14] Ibid.

[15] Ibid.

[16] Ibid.

Hungary,[17] acted to lower the wages of UK skilled and semi-skilled workers.[18] In association with the Coalition government's austerity policies, the lowering of wages would have contributed to the growing poverty in British society and the increased economic deprivation. This would have led to a resurgent national identity which would have resulted in the people of Britain voting to leave the European Union in the June 2016 Referendum, by a winning margin of 3.8%.[19] Those who voted to leave the EU represented 51.9% of those who voted, while those who voted to remain in the EU comprised 48.1% of a total electorate of 46,501,241 eligible UK voters.[20] Thus, the majority in favour of leaving the EU may have arisen because of either the Coalition government's economic austerity policies or the influx of cheap labour from the EU. Child poverty in the United Kingdom has also increased due to low economic growth and cuts in welfare benefits by the government.[21] Moreover, working-class UK families are increasingly having to rely on charities in order to meet their basic needs.[22] In America, Donald Trump was voted into office as President in November 2016 with a promise to 'make America great again'. His election victory may have resulted because of increasing inequality in America due to the loss of manufacturing jobs caused by the economic rise of China. In an effort to bring jobs back to America, President Trump has imposed tariffs on cheap Chinese goods just as the United States did to Japanese goods in 1932. In the European Union, economic stagnation following the Global Financial Crisis has given way to far right governments in Poland, Hungary, the Czech Republic and Italy.[23] In Germany, the far right has been gaining a popular mandate in elections, and in

[17] Portes, J. (2017), Immigration and the UK-EU relationship, IN The Economics of UK-EU Relations: From the Treaty of Rome to the Vote for Brexit, Campos, N., Coricelli, F. (Eds), Palgrave Macmillan.

[18] Clarke, H., Goodwin, M., and Whiteley, P. (2017), Brexit: Why Britain Voted To Leave The European Union, Cambridge University Press, Cambridge.

[19] Withnall, A. (2016), EU referendum results in full: Brexit campaign secures victory by 4 points, https://www.independent.co.uk/news/uk/politics/brexit-eu-referendum-final-result-leave-campaign-secures-official-lead-a7099296.html.

[20] Ibid.

[21] Wright, R. (2019), Child poverty set to hit record levels, says think tanks, https://www.ft.com/content/0e26447c-3455-11e9-bb0c-42459962a812.

[22] Rovnick, N. (2019), UK working poor increasingly rely on charities for basic needs, https://www.ft.com/content/f6c2dd6e-343a-11e9-bd3a-8b2a211d90d5.

[23] Camus, J., and Lebourg, N. (2017), Far-Right Politics in Europe, The Belknap Press of Harvard University Press, Cambridge, Massachusetts.

France, the far right has been momentarily seen off by promises of better things to come from an enfeebled Emmanuel Macron. This is all at a time when countries are not experiencing sufficient levels of economic growth. For example, China's economic growth is slowing from its historic levels of the first decade of the twenty-first century. The imposition of tariffs on Chinese goods is clearly negatively impacting on Chinese economic growth. As a result, many Chinese firms have begun to freeze recruitment and instead relying on unpaid internships to maintain their staffing levels. Simultaneously many if not all Chinese families are investing heavily in their children's future by spending a lot of money on their education in order to acquire a foreign education. At the same time, China is enhancing its military power by increasing training and investing in and introducing new technologies. China's leaders take for granted that the South China Sea is its own backyard and that the breakaway province of Taiwan must be re-joined to the motherland. At the same time, children in China are taught about the atrocities committed by the Japanese in the invasion of China in the 1930s. Just as in Japan there was an antagonism against foreigners and the foreign powers, can the same thing be said of China today? Furthermore, the rapid ascent of the Chinese economy since 1978 has fuelled a national pride which has lent itself to increasing nationalism. This is exactly the same thing which happened to Japan in the decades which followed the Meiji Restoration of 1868. And from an economics perspective, the contemporary Chinese economy is beginning to experience difficulties which are particularly associated with the imposition of tariffs by the United States. The rate of Chinese factory output growth, a measure of the country's manufacturing sector, year on year in January 2019 grew at its lowest level since 1995.[24] Similarly, just as the Chinese economy is struggling to create jobs, the Japanese economy of the 1930s was unable to create enough jobs for an increasing population. Moreover, while the Japanese had been building and technologically upgrading their military capacity since 1868, China has begun to do this in a big way only in the last decade or so. Unfortunately, contemporary China has some of the characteristics of post-Meiji Japan—rising nationalism, increasing militarisation, a potentially impending economic crisis and millions still living in poverty in the rural parts of the country. If, indeed, China today is on the same economic, political and military trajectory as post-Meiji Japan, then

[24] Wildau, G. (2019), Chinese factory-output growth slows to weakest on record, https://www.ft.com/content/a2c7edf8-45fb-11e9-b168-96a37d002cd3.

its policy makers must turn the country away from this trajectory to conflict and human suffering. Rather, China today is at a place where it can benefit humanity and return to its place as the centre of the universe. But in order to achieve this it must turn away from the negativity of nationalism and militarism and instead embrace humanity and its neighbours in benevolence. Today's rivals were ancient friends, and today India and China must return to their ancient status. In fact, 2020 will be marking the beginning of the Asian century as from that date the value of Asian economies will be bigger than the rest of the world combined.[25] In terms of purchasing power parity, China is already the world's largest economy and India the third.[26]

Japan had begun the process of modernising its economy in the mid-nineteenth century because of a fear of colonisation by the western powers. However, this modernisation did not take off until the Meiji Restoration of 1868 in which the Shogun and a military government of a decentralised Japan were replaced by a constitutional monarchy based on a democratic system of government. Japanese society and economy then developed according to a twin-track approach. One track favoured the use of market forces, private capital and government support in order to rapidly modernise and industrialise the Japanese economy in association with an educational system which still favoured traditional Japanese values. The second track involved developing Japanese institutions along western lines and improving Japan's military capacity by increased manpower and technological ability. At the same time the rising urban middle classes and the availability of a relatively free press gave way to increasing individualism and a strong democratic system based on party politics. However, an ever-present and growing undercurrent in Japan was the antagonism against the western powers because of unfair treaties and constraints upon Japan's military capacity, as well as increasing income disparities between the well off and the less well off. The growing undercurrent sentiment in Japan was becoming stronger in the 1920s and the early 1930s such that liberalism and multi-party politics were being swept away by rising militarism and nationalism towards bureaucratic fascism. This it was felt would be able to more efficiently allocate economic resources, especially social goods, which could help to alleviate poverty, and income disparity, in

[25] Romei, V., and Reed, J. (2019), The Asian Century is Set to Begin, https://www.ft.com/content/520cb6f6-2958-11e9-a5ab-ff8ef2b976c7.

[26] Ibid.

Japanese society. The transition to bureaucratic fascism was made easier through the destabilising effect of an economic crisis in Japan in the 1920s and in the 1930s which was only made worse by the imposition of tariffs by the western powers, notably the United States, on Japanese exports in 1932. Japanese military aggression, notably against China in the 1930s, led to sanctions being imposed by the United States. These developments contributed directly to the Japanese bombing of US warships based at Pearl Harbor on 7 December 1941. Moreover, Japanese politicians of the first three decades of the twentieth century were unable to formulate the optimal economic policy in order to resolve the economic crises which had been developing. This was because policies had to be diluted in order to achieve a compromise to facilitate agreement amongst multi-party politicians in the Japanese parliament, the 'Diet'. This is similar to what is happening in the UK Parliament with regard to Brexit. While China does not have the problem of having to dilute economic policy, it does have a multitude of other factors which could easily contribute to a large-scale economic crisis. These factors include huge provincial government debts and the property bubble in major urban centres, most notably Shanghai and Beijing. Property prices are so high that people simply have to work in order to pay their rent with little money left to enjoy anything else.

In the light of what has been previously discussed, China has the same ingredients—nationalism, militarism, income disparities, social deprivation and economic crisis—in a hostile global environment in which tariffs are being imposed on Chinese goods, and Chinese firms are placed under intense scrutiny, as was Japan in the first decades of the twentieth century. Furthermore, the distribution of income in Japan in the 1920s as well as in the 1930s was unfair.[27] This may have led to the undermining of the democratic system of governance and the imposition of the command economy by the military. Like Japan in the decades following the Meiji Restoration of 1868, China took its first steps along the same path with the market-oriented economic reforms of 1978. Since then China has industrialised in the context of manufactured goods, to become the world's second largest economy. Although it may be the world's largest economy in PPP terms. But this has, like the Japan of the 1920s and the 1930s, been at the expense of growing income inequality between China's

[27] Minami, R. (1998), Economic development and income distribution in Japan: an assessment of the Kuznets hypothesis, Cambridge Journal of Economics, 22, pp. 39–58.

regions and its peoples.[28] It is, therefore, important that the Chinese government instigates and implements policies to mitigate the unequal distribution of income in Chinese society to prevent the political and social instability which Japan experienced in the 1920s and the late 1930s. Moreover, China's economic growth is also experiencing a downturn, but only time can tell how severe that will be or not. In this case, the purpose of this book is to determine where Japan went wrong and how China can learn from that experience in order to build a better future for itself and the rest of humanity. This analysis will primarily be based on Japanese economic and political development as a state over time, and the policies which were followed by successive governments in the decades which followed the Meiji Restoration of 1868. At this time, Japan having embraced economic and political reform went onto industrialise at the start of the Meiji Restoration of 1868. At the same time, Japan's history of government by the military, the Bakufu, under the command of an all-powerful Shogun lent itself to the start of militarisation at the same time. As the Japanese economy developed after WW1, economic crises were not managed sufficiently well enough. The result was that income disparities between Japan's rural and urban populations increased. The poor were in the ranks of the military, and increasing disparities between the rich and the poor led to military control of the Japanese economy which became a military command economy after the mid-1930s. Today, China stands on ground upon which Japan stood in the first decades of the twentieth century. Disparities in income between the urban rich and the rural poor are ever omnipresent. Due to this and the exploitation of workers, some Chinese have become fervent supporters of neo-Marxism. The danger is that it is not the old who are turning against the Chinese capitalist state but the young, the young educated, who see the suffering of their young countrymen and women.[29] Now that China's economic engine has begun to slow, the situation of the poor and the issue of the divide between China's rural poor and its urban rich become ever more critical. At the same time China has been modernising its military forces. Economically, tariffs have been imposed by the United States on Chinese exports, and

[28] Shi, L., Sato, H., and Sicular, T. (2013), Rising Inequality in China, IN Rising Inequality in China: Challenges to a Harmonious Society, Shi, L., Sato, h., and Sicular, T. (Eds), Cambridge University Press, Cambridge.

[29] Yang, Y. (2019), Inside China's Crackdown on Young Marxists,' https://www.ft.com/content/fd087484-2f23-11e9-8744-e7016697f225.

Chinese firms are under attack by western governments due to security fears.[30] For example, Huawei, a Chinese mobile and telecommunications company, is being sidelined from western government contracts and tenders because of fears that it is controlled by the Chinese state. And, if Huawei technology is used in western countries' telecommunications infrastructure, then China would be able to use such infrastructure to gather data which it could use to its military advantage in the event of a conflict. It is for this reason that western governments, the United States, the countries of Europe, New Zealand and Australia, are disinterested in doing business with Chinese firms. Unfortunately, this will only cause resentment in China against foreigners. A similar thing happened to a developing Japan at a time in the nineteenth century when the same western governments were imposing unfavourable treaties on Japan. And in the latter part of the twentieth century, Japan was being blamed for the economic misfortunes of the western economies, just as China is being blamed today. Similarities between Japan's economic reform and rise and the China of today abound. The question remains whether China will be able to find a way to become a peaceful and harmonious country and neighbour or will it fail and embroil the world in another war. Will history repeat itself? Whether or not it does, economic crisis will always occur as it did to a resurgent Japan, by now a superpower, in 1989. The economic crisis Japan experienced from 1989 onwards may also happen to contemporary China.

Oxford, UK — Sangaralingam Ramesh

References

Callan, P., Bendary, B., and Sequeira, Y. (2019), Emerging markets face a new debt crisis: Chinese lending is not the only cause, https://www.ft.com/content/4fd4e6ac-440a-11e9-b168-96a37d002cd3.

Camus, J., and Lebourg, N. (2017), Far-Right Politics in Europe, The Belknap Press of Harvard University Press, Cambridge, Massachusetts.

Clarke, H., Goodwin, M., and Whiteley, P. (2017), Brexit: Why Britain Voted To Leave The European Union, Cambridge University Press, Cambridge.

Dunkley, E. (2019), Jiayuan crash underscores China property risks, https://www.ft.com/content/b5560666-1a37-11e9-b93e-f4351a53f1c3.

[30] Ram, A. (2019), Huawei lashes Out at US 'Political Campaign', https://www.ft.com/content/458f173c-2fa9-11e9-ba00-0251022932c8.

Fletcher, L. (2019), Global debt – when is the day of reckoning? https://www.ft.com/content/949d08da-462d-11e9-a965-23d669740bfb.

Minami, R. (1998), Economic development and income distribution in Japan: an assessment of the Kuznets hypothesis, Cambridge Journal of Economics, 22, pp. 39–58.

Miners, N. (2002), Industrial development in the colonial empire and the imperial economic conference at Ottawa 1932, 30:2, 53–76, DOI: https://doi.org/10.1080/03086530208583141.

Portes, J. (2017), Immigration and the UK-EU relationship, IN The Economics of UK-EU Relations: From the Treaty of Rome to the Vote for Brexit, Campos, N., Coricelli, F. (Eds), Palgrave Macmillan.

Ram, A. (2019), Huawei lashes Out at US 'Political Campaign', https://www.ft.com/content/458f173c-2fa9-11e9-ba00-0251022932c8.

Romei, V., and Reed, J. (2019), The Asian Century is Set to Begin, https://www.ft.com/content/520cb6f6-2958-11e9-a5ab-ff8ef2b976c7.

Romei, V. (2019), Eurozone household debt falls to lowest levels since 2006, https://www.ft.com/content/3cbbf5f8-1a41-11e9-9e64-d150b3105d21.

Rovnick, N. (2019), UK working poor increasingly rely on charities for basic needs, https://www.ft.com/content/f6c2dd6e-343a-11e9-bd3a-8b2a211d90d5.

Shi, L., Sato, H., and Sicular, T. (2013), Rising Inequality in China, IN Rising Inequality in China: Challenges to a Harmonious Society, Shi, L., Sato, h., and Sicular, T. (Eds), Cambridge University Press, Cambridge.

Tett, G. (2019), Driven to default: what's causing the rise in sub-prime auto loans? https://www.ft.com/content/1ce6d32e-4520-11e9-b168-96a37d002cd3.

Weinland, D. (2019), China's property developers binge on record dollar debt, https://www.ft.com/content/e8ff4e1a-3fe3-11e9-9bee-efab61506f44.

Wildau, G. (2019), Chinese factory-output growth slows to weakest on record, https://www.ft.com/content/a2c7edf8-45fb-11e9-b168-96a37d002cd3.

Withnall, A. (2016), EU referendum results in full: Brexit campaign secures victory by 4 points, https://www.independent.co.uk/news/uk/politics/brexit-eu-referendum-final-result-leave-campaign-secures-official-lead-a7099296.html.

Wright, R. (2019), Child poverty set to hit record levels, says think tanks, https://www.ft.com/content/0e26447c-3455-11e9-bb0c-42459962a812.

Yang, Y. (2019), Inside China's Crackdown on Young Marxists,' https://www.ft.com/content/fd087484-2f23-11e9-8744-e7016697f225.

Acknowledgement

I would like to thank Wyndham Hacket Pain, Editor (Economics), Palgrave Macmillan, London, and Tula Weis, Executive Editor, Palgrave Macmillan, New York, for all their invaluable help in getting this book published. I would also like to thank the library service at University College London, where the idea for this book was formulated in May 2019 and where writing of the book began in August 2019.

Contents

1 Introduction: The Rise of a Nation 1

2 The Kamakura Period (1185–1333): Emergence of Military Government: The Bakufu 35

3 The Muromachi Period (1333–1568) and the Azuchi–Momoyama Period (1568–1600) 71

4 The Tokugawa Period (1600–1868): Isolation and Change 101

5 The Meiji Period (1868–1912): Industrialisation and Democratisation 135

6 The Taisho Period (1912–1926): Transition from Democracy to a Military Economy 173

7 The Showa Period (1926–1989): War and the Emergence of a Modern Japan 211

8 The Heisei Period (1989–2019): Economic Stagnation and the Rise of China 251

9 Conclusion: Lessons for Contemporary China 281

Index 297

CHAPTER 1

Introduction: The Rise of a Nation

Chinese Chronicles

The earliest known writings inclusive of Japan, the Chinese chronicles before 700 AD, refer to Japan as 'Wa' which was composed of one hundred conflicting states.[1] The earliest of such records, which can be dated to 57 AD, notarised the names of chieftains and other polities in the archipelago.[2] The Chinese chronicles also mention the tributary missions between the chieftains of Japan and the Chinese Han and Wei courts.[3] Reference was also made to Han colonies in Korea.[4] These included Lelang and Daifang.[5] The reference made by the Chinese Chronicles to the conflicting states in Japan could have been due to a population explosion which necessitated the need for more land for intensive agriculture following the emergence of the Yoyoi culture on the island of Kyushu. Archaeological evidence from around this time does suggest an increase in defensive settlements; and skeletons with evidence of damage due to the

[1] Diamond, J. (1998), In Search of Japanese Roots, Discover, http://discovermagazine.com/1998/jun/japaneseroots1455/

[2] Barnes, G. (2007), State Formation in Japan, Emergence of a 4th Century Ruling Elite, Routledge, London.

[3] Ibid.

[4] Ibid.

[5] Walker, H. (2012), East Asia: A New History, Author House, Bloomington.

S. Ramesh, *China's Economic Rise*,
https://doi.org/10.1007/978-3-030-49811-5_1

impact with projectiles.[6] Nevertheless, which of the Wa states was the most powerful is indeterminate. This is because one Chinese chronicle written between 280 AD and 297 AD refers to it as 'Yamaichi', while another Chinese chronicle written 150 years later refers to it as 'Yamadai'.[7] It is difficult to determine if they were the same states, different or whether they existed at all. An alternative theory which has been put forward is that an entirely different entity existed, the state of Kyushu, one of whose princes invaded the Kinai-Yamato area becoming the first Emperor of Japan, Jimmu.[8] The early Chinese writings are the only literary evidence of early Japanese history, because either no Korean or Japanese literary evidence exists or survived prior to the early eighth century AD. The first Japanese literary evidence of Japanese history did not arrive until 712 BC, with the emergence of the first tangible Emperor from whom the current Emperor can claim to be a direct descendant. In this case, it is evident that literary influences developed much earlier in China than they did in either Korea or Japan. The early Chinese literary sources suggest that there was a significant diffusion of cultural influences from both Korea and China, with Korea as a conduit, to the peoples of the islands of Japan.[9] However, Chinese influence was more significant over the Japanese archipelago; and the legitimacy of the titles of Japanese chieftains was somewhat dependent on recognition by the imperial Chinese court.[10] But the legitimacy of Japanese polity ended in 631 AD when the Tang Emperor absolved the Japanese from having to pay annual tribute to the Tang Court.[11]

Palaeolithic, Jomon and Yayoi Periods

Until 13,000 years ago the Japanese islands were part of continental Asia, but as the ice age ended and glaciers melted, sea levels rose, flooding the land bridges across which ancient animals, including *Homo Erectus* and

[6] Diamond, J. (1998), In Search of Japanese Roots, Discover, http://discovermagazine.com/1998/jun/japaneseroots1455/

[7] Toro, T. (1983), The Kyushu Dynasty: Furuta's Theory on Ancient Japan, Japan Quarterly, Vol. 30, p. 4.

[8] Ibid.

[9] Diamond, J. (1998), In Search of Japanese Roots, Discover, http://discovermagazine.com/1998/jun/japaneseroots1455/

[10] Holcombe, C. (2001), The Genesis of East Asia, 221BC–907AD, University of Hawaii Press, Honolulu.

[11] Ibid.

Homo Sapiens, had crossed over from Asia to Japan half a million years previously.[12] The earliest Palaeolithic stone tools found in the Japanese islands were at a site called Takamori in Miyagi Prefecture, dated to be as 500,000 years old.[13] The stone tools found at Takamori are of a similar age to the stone tools found at the Zhoukoudian in China.[14] At the latter site, a remarkable number of *Homo Erectus* fossils were also found. The presence of land bridges which connected the islands of Japan to the Asian mainland may have facilitated the movement of *Homo Erectus* populations from China to Japan during the mid to the late Pleistocene period.[15] The latter period ranges from 125,000 years to 10,000 years ago.[16] Dynamic changes in human evolution were taking place during that time.[17] *Homo Sapiens*, having evolved in Africa, were moving out of Africa to colonise other continents.[18] Where the Japanese islands were once connected to mainland Asia, this facilitated the movement of hominid species like *Homo Erectus* and *Homo Sapiens* to Japan. The land bridges to the Japanese islands from continental Asia are best associated as starting from either the Korean peninsula, Siberia and/or Sakhalin.[19] Nevertheless, no archaeological evidence has been found which can shed led light on the physique of the early *Homo Erectus* population of Japan or to provide sufficient grounds to infer that these early populations were the root of future Japanese populations.[20] However, the skeletal remains found on the island of Okinawa, the so-called Minatogawa remains, do provide an insight into the physique of the first Palaeolithic inhabitants of Japan 17,000 years

[12] Diamond, J. (1998), In Search of Japanese Roots, Discover, http://discovermagazine.com/1998/jun/japaneseroots1455/

[13] Kazumichi, K. (2001), The Japanese as an Asia-Pacific Population, IN Multicultural Japan, Palaeolithic to Postmodern, Denoon, D., Hudson, M., McCormack, G., and Morris-Suzuki, T. (Eds), Cambridge University Press, Cambridge.

[14] Ibid.

[15] Ibid.

[16] Gowlett, J., and Dunbar, R. (2011), A Brief Overview of Human Evolution, IN Early Human Kinship, from Sex to Social Reproduction, Allen, N., Callan, H., Dunbar, R., and James, W. (Eds), Wiley-Blackwell, Oxford.

[17] Kaifu, Y., and Fujita, M. (2012), Fossil Record of Early Modern Humans in East Asia, Quaternary International, Vol. 248, pp. 2–11.

[18] Ibid.

[19] Naumann, N. (2000), Japanese Prehistory, The Material and Spiritual Culture of the Jomon Period, Harrassowitz Verlag, Wiesbaden.

[20] Kazumichi, K. (2001), The Japanese as an Asia-Pacific Population, IN Multicultural Japan, Palaeolithic to Postmodern, Denoon, D., Hudson, M., McCormack, G., and Morris-Suzuki, T. (Eds), Cambridge University Press, Cambridge.

ago.[21] Analysis of the cranium of the Minatogawa population indicates similarities with populations in southern China, 30,000 BC, and to north China, 10,000 BC.[22] However, the mainland Japanese population during the Holocene period were different in form and structure from the Minatogawa people.[23] The Holocene period covers the time period from the present to 11,000 years ago.[24] Nevertheless, stone tools have been found in the south of Kanto which may be older than 30,000 years in age.[25] The technology used to produce the stone tools is unique to Japan, although some examples have been found in Australia.[26] The technology itself was reflected by the use of edge grinding to produce sharp stone blades which were then fixed to wooden handles to produce axe like stone tools.[27] Archaeological evidence suggests that knowledge of the technology moved from Kanto to Honshu and then on to Kyushu.[28]

As sea levels began to rise at the end of the last ice age, the Japanese islands, Kyushu, Shikoku, Honshu and Hokkaido, became cut off from the rest of humanity, and the cut-off populations on the islands developed on their own for some time. However, throughout Japan's history, the three plains in Japan's geographical topography were important to its development.[29] These plains include the Kanto plain encompassing Tokyo Bay, the Nobi plain encompassing Ise Bay and the Kinai plain encompassing Osaka Bay. While all three plains house the greatest population concentrations in the islands of Japan due to their fertile nature, the Kanto plain is by far the largest of the three plains encompassing 5000 square miles.[30] As these three plains are the most fertile regions in Japan, the three plains are of historical importance in the story of Japan's rise as a nation. This is because agricultural production would be substantive in

[21] Ibid.

[22] Ibid.

[23] Kaifu, Y., and Fujita, M. (2012), Fossil Record of Early Modern Humans in East Asia, Quaternary International, Vol. 248, pp. 2–11.

[24] Giraud, R. (2004), Geologic Hazards of Monroe City, Sevier County, Utah, Special Study 110, Utah Geological Survey, US.

[25] Oda, S., and Keally, C. (1992), The Origin and Early Development of Axe-Like and Edge-Ground Stone Tools in the Japanese Palaeolithic, IPPA Bulletin, Vol. 12, pp. 23–31.

[26] Ibid.

[27] Ibid.

[28] Ibid.

[29] Sansom, G. (1959), A History of Japan to 1334, Stanford University Press, Stanford, California.

[30] Ibid.

these regions whose possessors would be bestowed with great wealth and power.[31] This would to some extent explain the migration of peoples from the southwest of Japan to eastern Japan, through its central region.[32] It would therefore follow that the development of Japan's cultural, social, political and economic development would be influenced by the possession and the competition for possession of these lands. This is evidenced by the fact that throughout Japan's long history, all three plains have contributed to it in some way or another. For example, in distant time, the Nobi plain was the seat of the food goddess, the plain of Kinai housed the commercial centre of Osaka and the ancient royal capital of Kyoto, while the plain of Kanto houses the strategically important Tokyo Bay which also was the seat of feudal power.[33]

While there is insufficient evidence to conjecture that there was a Palaeolithic culture in Japan,[34] it is logical to deduce that animals including humans must have had to live there after the disappearance of the land bridges. Moreover, it would be reasonable to conclude that the Minatogawa population would have also expanded to the main islands of Japan.[35] Nevertheless, archaeological evidence does suggest that a Neolithic culture did exist on the Japanese islands. The climate proved to be beneficial to plant and animal ecosystems, and as result, the Neolithic people of Japan, the Jomon, were best placed to thrive and to innovate. The Jomon culture prevailed between 14,000 BC and 2500 BC.[36] The early Jomon populations may have evolved from the beings similar to those who occupied the Minatogawa site because the early Jomon remains found in coastal and mountain areas are similar to the remains found at Minatogawa.[37] Thus, it would be safe to conclude that the early Jomon population

[31] Ibid.

[32] Ibid.

[33] Ibid.

[34] Kidder, J. (1954), A Reconsideration of the 'Pre-Pottery' Culture of Japan, Artibus Asiae, Vol. 17, No. 2, pp. 135–143.

[35] Kazumichi, K. (2001), The Japanese as an Asia-Pacific Population, IN Multicultural Japan, Palaeolithic to Postmodern, Denoon, D., Hudson, M., McCormack, G., and Morris-Suzuki, T. (Eds), Cambridge University Press, Cambridge.

[36] Matsui, A., and Kanehara, M. (2006), The Question of Prehistoric Plant Husbandry during the Jomon Period in Japan, World Archaeology, Vol. 38, No. 2, pp. 259–273, DOI: 10.1080/00438240600708295

[37] Kazumichi, K. (2001), The Japanese as an Asia-Pacific Population, IN Multicultural Japan, Palaeolithic to Postmodern, Denoon, D., Hudson, M., McCormack, G., and Morris-Suzuki, T. (Eds), Cambridge University Press, Cambridge.

inherited the physical characteristics of the mid to late Pleistocene period.[38] However, by the latter half of the Jomon period, evolution seems to have played its part in changing the physique of the inhabitants of Japan.[39] Human fossil remains were more abundant as the Jomon had begun to use shell mounds to bury their dead. As a result, it was possible for anthropologists and archaeologists to discern that the Jomon had become taller, with robust limb bones, and had more moderate tooth wear in comparison to their ancestors of the mid-late Pleistocene.[40] However, the people of the Jomon culture were strikingly dissimilar to modern Japanese people in several ways.[41]

There were two main innovations which resulted from the Jomon culture. The first of these innovations was pottery, with Japanese pottery being the oldest known in the world, made in Japan nearly 13,000 years ago in Kyushu, the southernmost of the Japanese islands, spreading northwards to reach the northern most of the Japanese islands, 7000 years ago.[42] However, more up to date analysis suggests that the Neolithic Jomon culture of Japan produced the world's oldest pottery at between 10,750 BC and 10,000 BC.[43] The latter date coincides with the emergence of the Jomon culture on the island of Honshu.[44] The word 'Jomon' is associated with the rope pattern found on pottery made during the time of that culture.[45] The earliest pottery found was on the island of Kyushu.[46] This may suggest that the Jomon culture existed there too, perhaps by migrating from Honshu. However, it is probable that Jomon culture extended throughout the islands of Japan, from Hokkaido to Okinawa.[47] But Jomon culture flourished predominantly on the main island in the

[38] Ibid.

[39] Ibid.

[40] Ibid.

[41] Ibid.

[42] Diamond, J. (1998), In Search of Japanese Roots, Discover, http://discovermagazine.com/1998/jun/japaneseroots1455/

[43] Karan, P. (2005), Japan in the 21st Century, Environment, Economy and Society, The University Press of Kentucky, Lexington, Kentucky.

[44] Richardson, H. (2005), Life in Ancient Japan, Crabtree Publishing Company, New York.

[45] Ibid.

[46] Irapta, A., and Duka, C. (2005), Introduction to Asia: History, Culture and Civilisation, Rex Book Store, Manila.

[47] Matsui, A., and Kanehara, M. (2006), The Question of Prehistoric Plant Husbandry during the Jomon Period in Japan, World Archaeology, Vol. 38, No. 2, pp. 259–273, DOI: 10.1080/00438240600708295

districts of Kanto and Tohuku.[48] There was also a high population density in the mountainous areas of Chubu, but a sparsely populated area of western Japan which was covered by evergreen forest.[49] Although there was a tendency for the population to flourish in regions where there was a big availability of nuts, such as in Southern Hokkaido.[50] The Jomon diet of nuts probably proved to be the cause for the need to find something to hold them in. Pottery provided an answer. The invention of pottery in Japan proved to be revolutionary because food could now be combined and cooked; and food could be stored. The implication of this is that people could be consistently fed; and they could maximise the accumulation of the nutritional value of food. The hunter-gatherers of Japan were then better able to exploit the natural abundance of the Japanese ecosystem far better than possible before the arrival of intensive agricultural techniques nearly 10,000 years later.[51] However, while there is no archaeological evidence to suggest that the Jomon were anything but hunter-gatherers, they may have not been exclusively so.[52] This is because although the Jomon did not use metal tools, they may have used wooden and stone tools to plant chestnut trees and grow millet grain to make bread at around 2500 BC.[53] Indeed, there is archaeological evidence to suggest that the Jomon culture was a hybrid of a hunter-gatherer existence as well as small-scale *in-situ* agricultural production.[54] But, in this case the Jomon may simply just have been 'managing' their forestry resources.[55] It was only after 2500 BC that the agricultural production of food sources became a

[48] Matsui, A., and Kanehara, M. (2006), The Question of Prehistoric Plant Husbandry during the Jomon Period in Japan, World Archaeology, Vol. 38, No. 2, pp. 259–273, DOI: 10.1080/00438240600708295

[49] Koyama, S. (1978), Jomon Subsistence and Population, Senri Ethnological Studies 2.

[50] Matsui, A., and Kanehara, M. (2006), The Question of Prehistoric Plant Husbandry during the Jomon Period in Japan, World Archaeology, Vol. 38, No. 2, pp. 259–273, DOI: 10.1080/00438240600708295

[51] Diamond, J. (1998), In Search of Japanese Roots, Discover, http://discovermagazine.com/1998/jun/japaneseroots1455/

[52] Karan, P. (2005), Japan in the 21st Century, Environment, Economy and Society, The University Press of Kentucky, Lexington, Kentucky.

[53] Richardson, H. (2005), Life in Ancient Japan, Crabtree Publishing Company, New York.

[54] Matsui, A., and Kanehara, M. (2006) The Question of Prehistoric Plant Husbandry during the Jomon Period in Japan, World Archaeology, Vol. 38, No. 2, pp. 259–273, DOI: 10.1080/00438240600708295

[55] Bleed, P., and Matsui, A. (2010), Why Didn't Agriculture Develop in Japan? A Consideration of Jomon Ecological Style, Niche Construction, and the Origins of Domestication, Journal of Archaeological Method and Theory, Vol. 17, pp. 356–370.

predominant feature of the local economy in Japan, with the mass migration of wet rice farmers from Korea or China.[56] This represented the start of the Yayoi period. The beneficial exploitation of the land led to a population explosion in which a few thousand people became hundreds of thousands of individuals.[57] However, in order to better understand the transition from the semi-agrarian economy of the Jomon culture to the agrarian economy of the Yayoi culture, it is necessary to consider changes in the environment, settlement for subsistence, ceremonial practices as well as the location of a specific craft or trade at a specific site.[58] The Sannai Maruyama archaeological site is best placed to provide evidence of the decline of Jomon culture in its Middle Period.[59] This occurred between 4800 BC and 4050 BC.[60] The plant-based remains at the site indicate that the site went into decline at a time when subsistence specialisation in plant food, such as chestnuts, had occurred.[61] The settlement may have become smaller as the population declined because the food consumed had less nutritional content than the food types which had been consumed before.

The discovery of the oldest pottery in the world in Japan caused some contradictions to be overturned.[62] The first of these contradictions was that hunter-gatherers, which the Japanese of that time were, could not innovate. Nevertheless, the invention of pottery would allow the population of the time to become more sedentary leading to a fall in the hunter-gatherer existence.[63] The second contradiction to be overturned was that innovation could only occur in large populations and that it could not occur in small isolated populations, which would be an apt description for the categorisation of the population of Japan during that time. The second

[56] Matsui, A., and Kanehara, M. (2006) The Question of Prehistoric Plant Husbandry during the Jomon Period in Japan, World Archaeology, Vol. 38, No. 2, pp. 259–273, DOI: 10.1080/00438240600708295

[57] Diamond, J. (1998), In Search of Japanese Roots, Discover, http://discovermagazine.com/1998/jun/japaneseroots1455/

[58] Habu, J. (2008), Growth and Decline in Complex Hunter-Gatherer Societies: A Case Study from the Jomon Period Sannai Maruyama Site, Japan.

[59] Ibid.

[60] Oh, C. (2011), Cosmogonical Worldview of Jomon Pottery, Sankeisha Co., Ltd., Aichi, Japan.

[61] Habu, J. (2008), Growth and Decline in Complex Hunter-Gatherer Societies: A Case Study from the Jomon Period Sannai Maruyama Site, Japan.

[62] Diamond, J. (1998), In Search of Japanese Roots, Discover, http://discovermagazine.com/1998/jun/japaneseroots1455/

[63] Ibid.

innovation or diffuse of innovation again occurred on the island of Kyushu, nearest Korea, in 200 BC. This second innovation can be associated with the emergence of the use of the first metal tools and intensive agriculture with crop irrigation, cultivation and animal husbandry, especially that of the pig.[64] This signified a transition from the original Jomon culture of Kyushu to the emergent Yoyoi culture, with intensive agriculture taking another three centuries to spread north to Honshu.[65] The Yoyoi Period, 200 BC to 300 AD, was then a time of simultaneous change from the use of stone tools and the gathering of food to intensive agriculture and metallurgy.[66] It was also a period of time which in many ways can be compared to the Meiji Period several centuries later for two reasons.[67] Firstly, while in Yoyoi Period small isolated settlements became unified showing tangible signs of state formation, this actually did occur during the Meiji Period.[68] Secondly, while in the Yoyoi Period there was rapid technological change, the same is true of the Meiji Period when Japan went through a process of rapid industrialisation.[69] In this case, during the Yoyoi Period, intensive agriculture and husbandry, the weaving of cloth from a single thread using a spindle whorl and the emergence of the metal and glass industries facilitated increasing specialisation of labour and the development of a class structure.[70] Furthermore, pottery was seen to have more use value rather than an ascetic value, allowing for it to be produced in greater quantity.[71] However, despite advances in technology and the increased specialisation of labour, goods such as bronze mirrors, iron weapons and tools as well as glass ornaments still had to be imported from central China.[72] At the time, Han Dynasty China was the contemporary civilisation of Yoyoi Period Japan.[73] Therefore, the contemporary Han

[64] Ibid.

[65] Ibid.

[66] Kanaseki, H., and Sahara, M. (1976), The Yoyoi Period, Asian Perspectives, Vol. 19, No. 1.

[67] Ibid.

[68] Keene, D. (2002), Emperor of Japan, Meiji and his World, 1852–1912, Columbia University Press, New York.

[69] Ibid.

[70] Ibid.

[71] Kitagawa, J. (1987), On Understanding Japanese Religion, Princeton University Press, Princeton, New Jersey.

[72] Kanaseki, H., and Sahara, M. (1976), The Yayoi period, Asian Perspectives, Vol. 19, No. 1.

[73] Walker, H. (2012), East Asia: A New History, AuthorHouse, Bloomington, Indiana.

Dynasty China was more technologically advanced than the Yoyoi culture of Japan.

The Japanese are very similar genetically and in physical appearance to Koreans.[74] This would suggest that the Japanese are relatively recent arrivals to Japan because insufficient time has passed in order for them to become more distinct from the peoples of their closest neighbours, the Koreans and the Japanese. However, if the Japanese are genetically like the Koreans and perhaps even to the Han Chinese, then it would logically follow that the Japanese language would also be closely related to the Chinese and the Korean languages just as the English language is related to other continental European languages such as French and German.[75] But the paradox is that the Japanese language is dissimilar from the Korean and the Chinese languages, suggesting that its roots are much older than the emergence of the Japanese people themselves.[76] Nevertheless, the Japanese language has been grouped with Korean, Turkic and Mongolic languages in the Altaic set of languages because of resemblances in grammar and a common word order in the context of subject–object–verb.[77] However, the Japanese language differs from the other Altaic languages with regard to sound system use of prefixes, the use of few consonants and a choice of open syllables.[78] In this regard, Japanese would more resemble the languages originating from Taiwan, the Austronesian group.[79] It could just be that the Japanese language is a hybrid of the Altaic and Austronesian group of languages. Nevertheless, to resolve the language paradox, four distinct theories have emerged.[80] The first theory contends that the Japanese people emerged from early ice age peoples who had colonised the islands of Japan well before 20,000 BC. According to the second theory, the Japanese people descended Asiatic nomads who reached Japan by moving through the Korean peninsula in the fourth century, although remaining distinctive from the Koreans themselves. The third theory

[74] Diamond, J. (1998), In Search of Japanese Roots, Discover, http://discovermagazine.com/1998/jun/japaneseroots1455/

[75] Ibid.

[76] Ibid.

[77] Jandt, F. (2004), Intercultural Communication: A Global Reader, Sage Publications, London.

[78] Ibid.

[79] Ibid.

[80] Diamond, J. (1998), In Search of Japanese Roots, Discover, http://discovermagazine.com/1998/jun/japaneseroots1455/

contends that the Japanese are the descendants of Korean paddy field rice cultivators of the fifth century BC. The final theory contends, on the other hand, that the Japanese people emerged from the mixing of pre-ice age settlers, Asiatic nomads and Korean invaders. Despite the existence of these theories, the earliest Japanese chronicles from the eighth century BC suggest a fairy tale beginning for the Japanese people.[81] According to this legend the birth of the world coincided with the creation of the islands of Japan.[82] The island of Ono-goro-jima was the first land to be created from the drips of brine from the sword of the God Izanagi after it emerged from the cosmic ocean.[83] The remaining islands of Japan as well as the forces of nature were then created through the union of the God Izanagi and the Goddess Izanami.[84] The most prominent of these forces of nature or Kami was the Sun Goddess Amaterasu.[85] It was the great-great grandson of Amaterasu, Jimmu, who became according to the legend the first emperor of Japan in 660 BC.[86] This legend, fairy tale would become the foundation of the divine status of the Emperor and his legitimacy in the rule of the Japanese people.[87] However, before Amaterasu became the divine founder of the imperial family, worship had revolved around several sun deities.[88] Furthermore, a legend such as this may also belie the root of the perception by the Japanese of Japan's unique linguistic and cultural heritage as a homogenous people which required a unique and complex process of development giving them a superior status in comparison to other peoples and civilisations.[89] This would allow for a beneficial interpretation of archaeological evidence whenever such evidence is open to interpretation. An example of this would be the movement of people and objects between

[81] Ibid.

[82] Cornille, C. (1999), Nationalism in New Japanese Religions, Nova Religio: The Journal of Alternative and Emergent Religions, Vol. 2, No. 2, pp. 228–244.

[83] Ibid.

[84] Ibid.

[85] Ibid.

[86] Diamond, J. (1998), In Search of Japanese Roots, Discover, http://discovermagazine.com/1998/jun/japaneseroots1455/

[87] Cornille, C. (1999), Nationalism in New Japanese Religions, Nova Religio: The Journal of Alternative and Emergent Religions, Vol. 2, No. 2, pp. 228–244.

[88] Takeshi, M. (1978), Origin and Growth of the Worship of Amaterasu, Asian Folklore Studies, Vol. 37, No. 1, pp. 1–11.

[89] Diamond, J. (1998), In Search of Japanese Roots, Discover, http://discovermagazine.com/1998/jun/japaneseroots1455/

the Korean peninsula and the islands of Japan between 300 and 700 AD.[90] The Japanese would believe that this was a result of the Japanese conquest of Korea, while the Koreans would believe the opposite.[91] However, despite the legend, Japan is geographically unique.[92] For example, whereas the island of Britain is only 22 miles from its nearest continental neighbour France, the nearest islands of Japan to continental Asia are located 110 miles further away; and Japan is at least 480 miles away from mainland China.[93] The seas surrounding Japan are also treacherous for a safe crossing by any potential invaders. The Okhotsk Current and the Black Stream flow towards the shores of Japan in a north to south direction.[94] Furthermore, while the winter monsoon blows towards Japan, the summer monsoon moves from the southwest to the northeast.[95] This would make sea navigation and sea-based travel through the China Sea from China very difficult if not impossible. The difficulty for ships of crossing and of staying in tact even upon reaching Japanese waters can be evidenced by the experience of the Mongols in the thirteenth century AD. It was at this time that the grandson of Genghis Khan, Khubilai Khan, the Emperor and founder of the Yuan Dynasty of China, sent ships in 1274 AD and 1281 AD to invade the islands of Japan. However, while the fleet of 1274 AD turned back to Korea due to bad weather, it could have been either a practice run or a scouting mission for the 1281 AD invasion.[96] While the invasion ships of 1274 AD returned to their home ports, the two fleets which sailed from Korea and the Yangtze River Basin made landings in Japan.[97] The two fleets were meant to meet and make a coordinated landing and attack. But while the fleet from Korea landed in Hakata Bay, the second fleet landed in Imari Bay. Hakata Bay is present-day Fukuoka[98] on the island of Kyushu, and Imari Bay is present-day

[90] Ibid.

[91] Ibid.

[92] Ibid.

[93] Ibid.

[94] Sansom, G. (1959), A History of Japan to 1334, Stanford University Press, Stanford, California.

[95] Ibid.

[96] Clements, J. (2010), The Samurai, The Way of Japan's Elite Warriors, Constable & Robinson Ltd., London.

[97] Delgado, J. (2008), Khubilai Khans Lost Fleet, In Search of a Legendary Armada, University of California Press, Berkeley.

[98] Delgado, J. (2010), Kamikaze: History's Greatest Naval Disaster, The Bodley Head, London.

Takashima[99] on the island of Honshu. After two weeks of battle, when the Japanese were about to be defeated, an ocean storm destroyed 4400 Mongol ships killing 100,000 Mongol warriors effectively saving Japan from invasion.[100] Moreover, the terrain of the Japanese islands also makes it difficult to conquer. In this case, 80% of Japan's landmass is mountainous and unsuitable for agriculture. But the 14% of land suitable for agriculture is fertile enough, supported by a wet temperate climate with heavy rainfall, to support a very significantly sized population.[101]

Kofun Period (250 AD to 538 AD)

Since this period in Japanese history there has been no change in the genetic make-up of the people of Japan.[102] In this case, the modern Japanese morphology developed from and shares parallels with north east Asians, from the Korean Peninsula, who migrated to the Japanese islands during the emergence of the Yayoi culture. During the Kofun period the building of burial tombs to house the remains of the dead elite was characteristic.[103] In fact the Kofun period represented a time in which the ancient world saw the biggest monument construction projects of the time, including the tomb of the fifth century ruler Nintoku.[104] The latter was reputedly the sixteenth Emperor of Japan as reported in the early Japanese chronicles, of the eighth century AD, whose chronology would place him under 'legendary time'.[105] When Nintoku succeeded his father, he shifted his capital to Osaka.[106] Nintoku's reign also emphasised the

[99] Ibid.

[100] Delgado, J. (2008), Khubilai Khans Lost Fleet, In Search of a Legendary Armada, University of California Press, Berkeley.

[101] Diamond, J. (1998), In Search of Japanese Roots, Discover, http://discovermagazine.com/1998/jun/japaneseroots1455/

[102] Kazumichi, K. (2001), The Japanese as an Asia-Pacific Population, IN Multicultural Japan, Palaeolithic to Postmodern, Denoon, D., Hudson, M., McCormack, G., and Morris-Suzuki, T. (Eds), Cambridge University Press, Cambridge.

[103] Tsude, H. (1990), Chiefly Lineages in Kofun-Period Japan: Political Relations between Centre and Region, Antiquity, Vol. 64, pp. 923–931.

[104] Kaner, S. (2011), The Appropriation of Religious Power By The Tomb-Builders of the Kofun Period (AD 250–710), Oxford University Press, Oxford.

[105] Metevelis, P. (1993), A Reference Guide to the 'Nihonshoki' Myths, Asian Folklore Studies, Vol. 52, No. 2, pp. 383–388.

[106] Takokoshi, Y. (2004), The Economic Aspects of the History of the Civilisation of Japan, George Allen & Unwin Ltd, London.

acquisition of knowledge from Korea and China by employing ethnic Chinese and Koreans, and making the latter officials through a naturalisation process.[107] Moreover, the acquisition of Korean prisoners during military expeditions to Korea and their repatriation to Japan further facilitated the diffusion of knowledge about Korea and China back to Japan.[108] One hundred years after the collapse of the Chinese Han dynasty, the Chinese colonies in the north of Korea had been overrun and Korea itself had become consolidated into three separate kingdoms, Koguryo, Paekche and Silla.[109] The first of these three kingdoms had connections with southern Manchuria and the Yellow Sea region, respectively, with the last kingdom being the most powerful of the three.[110] It was the appeal to Japan by the Kingdom of Paekche for military assistance against incursions which gave the Japanese the cause to militarily incur into Korea.[111]

The use of tombs, known as keyhole tombs, was present in the Yayoi period as well as in the Kofun period.[112] However, what makes each period distinct and the Kofun period the successor to the Yayoi period is that in the former period the level of exchanges and interactions between people was much greater than it was in the latter period. This was only facilitated by the development of social complexity during the Yayoi Period. It was this which facilitated the evolution of the first recognisable state on the Japanese archipelago during the Kofun Period.[113] The Kofun period is, therefore, known as the period of state formation.[114] Other characteristic features of the Kofun period include the use of haniwa or fired clay images in detailed funeral rites.[115] The close relationship between the peoples of the Korean peninsula and the islands of Japan is supported by archaeological

[107] Ibid.

[108] Ibid.

[109] Beasley, W. (1999), The Japanese Experience: A Short History of Japan, University of California Press Berkeley and Los Angeles, California.

[110] Ibid.

[111] Ibid.

[112] Kazumichi, K. (2001), The Japanese as an Asia-Pacific Population, IN Multicultural Japan, Palaeolithic to Postmodern, Denoon, D., Hudson, M., McCormack, G., and Morris-Suzuki, T. (Eds), Cambridge University Press, Cambridge.

[113] Mizoguchi, K. (2013), The Archaeology of Japan from the Earliest Rice Farming Villages to the Rise of the State, Cambridge University Press, New York.

[114] Tsude, H. (1990), Chiefly Lineages in Kofun-Period Japan: Political Relations between Centre and Region, Antiquity, Vol. 64, pp. 923–931.

[115] Ortolani, B. (1995), The Japanese Theatre, From Shamanistic Ritual to Contemporary Pluralism, Princeton University Press, Princeton.

evidence of burial tombs and haniwa on the Korean peninsula as well.[116] This may also dignify the movement of peoples from the Korean peninsula to the islands of Japan as well as a diffusion of its culture. This introduced many new things into the life of the Japanese, such as the production of ceramics in kilns, horse riding, writing and eventually Buddhism.[117]

The tombs were more concentrated in the jurisdictions of the contemporary prefectures of Nara and Osaka than in either Kyoto, Okayama or Hyogo prefectures.[118] It is due to the concentration of burial tombs in the contemporary prefectures of Osaka and Nara that this region is referred to as the Central Court in comparison to the other regions in western Honshu.[119] The Central Court was denoted by different names in different time periods.[120] In the fourth century it was known as the Miwa Court, and in the fifth century, it was known as the Kawachi Court. The form of governance exercised during the Miwa court was based on a ritual authority derived from a religious cult associated with Queen Himiko.[121] The latter was a Shaman Queen who ascended the throne at the age of fourteen, unifying and ruling large parts of Japan from 180 AD to 248 AD with her capital in the city of Yamatai.[122] Queen Himiko's power depended on her Shamanic ability in performing rituals with offerings to the spirits and the gods such that the people would prosper.[123] The religious practices recreated a set of values which were associated with wealth, respect for others and oneself, morality, affection, enlightenment and wealth.[124] These values enabled a primitive form of governance by codifying people's behaviours according to a social hierarchy. This view of a system of governance based on ritual practices during the Miwa Court is supported by the writers of the eighth century Japanese chronicles as well as by archaeological

[116] Imamura, K. (1996), Prehistoric Japan: New Perspectives on Insular East Asia, University of Hawaii Press, Honolulu.

[117] Ibid.

[118] Tsude, H. (1990), Chiefly Lineages in Kofun-Period Japan: Political Relations between Centre and Region, Antiquity, Vol. 64, pp. 923–931.

[119] Ibid.

[120] Ibid.

[121] Barnes, G. (2007), State Formation in Japan, Emergence of a 4th Century Ruling Elite, Routledge, London.

[122] Hosak, M., and Lubeck, W. (2006), The Big Book of Reiki Symbols, Lotus Press, Twin Lakes, WI, USA.

[123] Ibid.

[124] Barnes, G. (2007), State Formation in Japan, Emergence of a 4th Century Ruling Elite, Routledge, London.

evidence.[125] Some scholars assert that during the period of the Miwa Court and the Kawachi Court, there was a radical political transformation of the centre, its relationship with the regions and within the regions themselves.[126] The transition from the Miwa Court to the Kawachi Court in the Middle Kofun period, 400 AD to 475 AD, essentially involved a change in the nature of burial goods from bronze mirrors and bead stones to iron tools and weaponry.[127] The transition from the Middle Kofun period to the Late Kofun period, 475 AD to 710 AD, necessitated a transition from the Kawachi Court to the Yamato Court in the fifth century AD, the time at which many scholars consider the birth of a unified Japanese state. The factors which proved essential to this were the long-held cultural concepts of Kami and Uji.[128] These two concepts emerged from Japan's pre-history in the third century AD when Japan lacked literacy and a cohesive and coherent political system.[129] However, awareness of Kami and Uji allowed for state formation. The former referred to the spirit of the universe which contextually includes deities, royalties and unexplained natural phenomenon, whereas the latter refers to a clan.[130] The Uji or clan is held together by the Uji Chieftain whose authority is derived from the Uji Kami.[131] In the fourth century AD, the Yamato Uji began to militarily assert itself over the other Uji of the Japanese islands, while claiming descent from the Sun Goddess Amaterasu.[132] Thus, the Japanese imperial institution of Emperor, which would continue into the twenty-first century, had been formed by the fifth century AD.[133]

[125] Kaner, S. (2011), The Appropriation of Religious Power by the Tomb-Builders of the Kofun Period (AD 250–710), Oxford University Press, Oxford.

[126] Tsude, H. (1990), Chiefly Lineages in Kofun-Period Japan: Political Relations between Centre and Region, Antiquity, Vol. 64, pp. 923–931.

[127] Barnes, G. (2007), State Formation in Japan, Emergence of a 4th Century Ruling Elite, Routledge, London.

[128] Takayama, K. (1998), Rationalisation of State and Society: A Weberian View of Eraly Japan, Sociology of Religion, Vol. 59, No. 1, pp. 65–88.

[129] Ibid.

[130] Ibid.

[131] Ibid.

[132] Ibid.

[133] Ibid.

Asuka Period (538 AD to 710 AD)

During the Asuka Period at the start of the sixth century AD, the knowledge and the practice of Buddhism flowed to Japan from India via China and Korea.[134] However, this only encompassed part of the knowledge diffusion from China and Korea to Japan. For example, cultural and scholarly knowledge also diffused to Japan from China and Korea including architectural knowledge and the knowledge of Chinese written language.[135] The latter began to be incorporated into the Japanese language. Prince Shotoku, the Regent, was so influenced by Confucianism and Buddhism that he proposed a constitutional government as well as other political reforms in 604 AD.[136] Shotoku was Prince Regent to the Empress Suiko, 592 AD to 628 AD, governing Japan as a statesman as well as a warrior.[137] He defeated the Mononofu and ruled Japan according to Buddhist doctrine.[138] In early Japanese history the Mononofu were defined as courageous warriors, well trained and able to use weapons.[139]

The development of the constitution in Japan should be seen in contrast to western civilisation where in England in 1215 the notion of a constitution was forced upon King John by the nobility, but in the case of sixth century AD Japan, a constitution was prepared by a noble man, Prince Shotoku himself.[140] Shotoku is believed to have implemented Japan's first imperial laws in the sixth century AD as well as writing the seventeen articles of the constitution of a centralised Japanese state which emphasised the need to achieve and maintain societal harmony and not discord.[141] However, the codification and the enforcement of laws were

[134] Alt, M., Yoda, H., and Joe, M. (2012), Japan Day by Day, Wiley & Sons Inc., New Jersey, USA.

[135] Ibid.

[136] Ibid.

[137] Tanaka, F. (2003), Samurai Fighting Arts: The Spirit and the Practice, Kodansha International, Tokyo.

[138] Ibid.

[139] Musashi, M. (2010), The Complete Book of Five Rings, Tokitsu, K. (Ed), Shambhala Publications Inc., Boston, Massachusetts, USA.

[140] Maruta, Y. (1980) The Management of Innovation in Japan: The Tetsuri Way, Research Management, Vol. 23, No. 1, pp. 39–41, DOI: 10.1080/00345334.1980.11756587.

[141] Sakamoto, T. (1980), Japanese History, International Society for Educational Information Press, Tokyo.

secondary to an emphasis on moral and spiritual values.[142] Furthermore, Shotoku's constitution was merely a synthesis of continental Asian religious thought and its institutions with traditional Japanese cultural and social values.[143] The principles of the constitution laid out in its articles the need for debate and wise counsel in the process of taking decisions as well as the importance of teamwork based on the dignity and equality of the individual.[144] These ideals were in keeping with the traditional Japanese cultural value of the achievement of societal harmony, and the Buddhist belief that the primary goal of society should be the removal of interpersonal conflict.[145] Moreover, according to traditional Japanese cultural belief, the right of the individual should be superseded to the good of society, in other words disputes were unproductive while societal harmony was productive in achieving the needs of society.[146] Thus, Shotoku believed that everyone should be able express their views in an environment in which a spirit of harmony permeated discussion.[147] As Shotoku can be regarded to be a Confucian scholar, the values of Confucianism were also reflected in the constitution.[148]

Prince Shotoku, 572 AD to 621 AD,[149] also sent Japanese scholars to China to study Buddhism as well as starting a programme of Buddhist temple building in 607 AD, and establishing a spy network called the Shinobi.[150] Furthermore, Shotoku encouraged the use of chopsticks for

[142] De Bary, WT. (1988), East Asian Civilisations: A Dialogue in Five Stages, Harvard University Press, Cambridge, Massachusetts.

[143] De Bary, WT. (1995), The Constitutional Tradition in China, Journal of Chinese Law, Vol. 9, p. 7.

[144] Sakamoto, T. (1980), Japanese History, International Society for Educational Information Press, Tokyo.

[145] Nakamura, H. (1969), A History of the Development of Japanese thought from AD 592 to AD 1868, Kokusai Bunka Shinkokai, Tokyo.

[146] Callister, R., and Wall, J. (1997), Japanese Community and Organisational Mediation, Journal of Conflict Resolution, Vol. 41, No. 2, pp. 311–328.

[147] Bhatta, C. (2005), Leadership Excellence: The Asian Experience, Asia-Pacific Business Review, Vol. 1, No. 1.

[148] Durlabhji, S. (1993). The Influence of Confucianism and Zen on the Japanese organization. In Durlabhji, S. & Marks, N. (Eds.), Japanese Business: Cultural Perspectives, State, University of New York Press, Albany, New York.

[149] Kimio, I. (1998), The Invention of Wa and the Transformation of the Image of Prince Shotoku in Modern Japan, IN Mirror of Modernity: Invented Traditions of Modern Japan, Vlastos, S. (Ed), University of California Press, Berkeley.

[150] Alt, M., Yoda, H., and Joe, M. (2012), Japan Day by Day, Wiley & Sons Inc., New Jersey, USA.

eating food, as it would be more hygienic and the Japanese would appear less barbaric.[151] Before the introduction of chopsticks, food in Japan was either eaten using one's hands or by using leaves.[152] In the spirit of Buddhist enlightenment, Shotoku also engaged in enterprise for social relief by providing facilities to help the poor and the destitute within Buddhist temples.[153] For example, the Shitenno-Ji Temple in Osaka was established by Shotoku; and it housed areas specially reserved for the reception of the poor and to cure the sick without charge.[154]

The cultural knowledge exchange between China, the world's most advanced civilisation at that time, and the peoples of the Japanese islands facilitated the diffusion of the knowledge of chopsticks from China to Japan. The use of chopsticks for eating food was in vogue in Japan at the time.[155] Historically, Prince Shotoku has been held to be a symbol of Japanese nationalism, and great emphasis was placed on this in the context of Japan's perceived superiority over China during the 1930s' occupation of Manchuria.[156] However, in this case the principles by which Japan should have been led as laid down by Shotoku in the sixth century AD had become lost with the advent of Shintoism which eventually led Japan into World War 2.[157]

Nara Period (710 AD to 794 AD)

The Nara Period takes its name from the imperial capital of Nara which was founded in 710 AD. However, in 784 AD, the Emperor Kammu ordered the construction of a new capital at Nagaoka, but after ten years of construction, he once again ordered that the capital should be moved

[151] Seligman, L. (1994), The History of Japanese Cuisine, Japanese Quarterly, Vol. 41, No. 2.

[152] Ibid.

[153] Bhatta, C. (2005), Leadership Excellence: The Asian Experience, Asia-Pacific Business Review, Vol. 1, No. 1.

[154] Ibid.

[155] Ibid.

[156] Kimio, I. (1998), The Invention of Wa and the Transformation of the Image of Prince Shotoku in Modern Japan, IN Mirror of Modernity: Invented Traditions of Modern Japan, Vlastos, S. (Ed), University of California Press, Berkeley.

[157] Maruta, Y. (1980) The Management of Innovation in Japan: The Tetsuri Way, Research Management, Vol. 23, No. 1, pp. 39–41, DOI: 10.1080/00345334.1980.11756587.

to Kyoto.[158] The latter stayed as Japan's imperial capital until 1869 when the Meiji Emperor shifted it to Edo which became to be known as Tokyo.[159] It is thought that the Emperor Kammu may have ordered the move of the imperial capital away from Nara due to the growing influence of Buddhist institutions and clergy there on the imperial house.[160] The shift of the imperial capital from Nara seems coincidental with the timing of the Dokyo incident in which the Buddhist monk Dokyo charmed the Empress Shotoku into giving him more political and religious power.[161] This can be seen as an attempt by the Buddhist clergy of Nara to replace imperial power with a sovereign whose power base would be Buddhist theocracy.[162] However, with the death of the Empress Shotoku, the monk Dokyo lost the basis of his power and was no longer a threat to the imperial hegemony over Japan. Nevertheless, Nara remained a hotbed of Buddhist Monasticism and therefore a threat to imperial power.[163] It was for this reason that the imperial capital was eventually moved to Kyoto where a new form of Buddhist monasticism developed, the Tendai Sect, which was more favourable and loyal to legitimising the divinity of the Emperor and imperial power.[164]

The century which encompasses the Nara Period starts with the period which includes the Jinshin Revolt of 672 AD as well as the period at which the Imperial capital was moved from Nara in 784 AD.[165] It was a period in which the contemporary practices of T'ang China were imported, copied and implemented by the Japanese aristocracy in the embryonic Japanese state. The Nara Period in Japanese history was a time in which the Japanese aristocracy imitated the contemporary developments and practices of T'ang China with regard to culture, religion, institutions and military practice. In this case, during the Nara Period, the Japanese aristocracy focused on bringing Japanese cultural and political norms to comparable

[158] Toby, R. (1985), Why Leave Nara?: Kammu and the Transfer of the Capital, Monumenta Nipponica, Vol. 40, No. 3, pp. 331–347.

[159] Ibid.

[160] Tucker, J. (2000), Nation Building, IN Encyclopedia of Monasticism, Routledge, London.

[161] Ibid.

[162] Ibid.

[163] Ibid.

[164] Ibid.

[165] Brown, D. (1993), The Cambridge History of Japan: Volume 1, Ancient Japan, Cambridge University Press, Cambridge.

T'ang levels in three respects.[166] Firstly, there was an emphasis on the development of Shinto and Buddhist rights and rituals which would serve to legitimise the divine nature of imperial rule and the power of the Emperor. Secondly, there was a focus on the building of contemporary T'ang style capitals to politically legitimise imperial power over the emergent centralised Japanese state. Lastly, T'ang style governmental administrative procedures were put in place so that the people and the use of the land could be more efficiently controlled. However, the knowledge of the principles of Chinese governance was brought to Japan by Japanese scholars who had already spent twenty-five years in China.[167] It was these scholars whose knowledge of contemporary Chinese governance helped with the development and the implementation of the Taika Reform in 645 AD.[168] The Taika Reform involved the opening up of Japan to Chinese T'ang dynasty Confucianism, technology and institutions including government bureaucracy and temples.[169] As a result, the Confucian values of sincerity, harmony, faithfulness, loyalty and benevolence were introduced to Japan.[170] The Taika Reform is often viewed as one of the pivotal occasions in Japanese history alongside the Meiji Restoration of 1868 and the American occupation of Japan after World War 2.[171] As the centralised Japanese government institutions, imitated from T'ang Dynasty China, began to develop and grow, there was a need for more educated bureaucrats to run them.[172] As a result a university was established in Nara to train bureaucrats based on Confucian values. University examinations revolved around a test of knowledge of the Confucian classics, the laws of the state which were based on Confucian principles and the capability to apply and use Confucian theory to resolve real world problems.[173] While it was easier for the sons of aristocracy to enter the government bureaucracy,

[166] Ibid.

[167] Mason, R., and Caiger, J. (2011), History of Japan: Revised Edition, Tuttle Publishing.

[168] Ibid.

[169] Zhu, Z. (2000), Cultural Change and Economic Performance: An Interactionistic Perspective, International Journal of Organisational Analysis, Vol. 8, No. 1, pp. 109–126.

[170] Morishima, M. (1982). Why has Japan "Succeeded"? Western Technology and the Japanese Ethos. Cambridge: Cambridge University Press.

[171] Zhu, Z. (2000), Cultural Change and Economic Performance: An Interactionistic Perspective, International Journal of Organisational Analysis, Vol. 8, No. 1, pp. 109–126.

[172] Mason, R., and Caiger, J. (2011), History of Japan: Revised Edition, Tuttle Publishing.

[173] Ibid.

promotion was based on merit in the context of attainment in scholarly exams.[174]

Following the death of Emperor Tenjin, there was a war of succession to the imperial throne between Prince Oama and Prince Omoto which culminated at the Battle of Jinshin in 672 AD.[175] Prince Oama won and ascended the imperial throne as Emperor Tenmu. In that capacity Tenmu wanted to cement his legitimacy and did so by facilitating the publication of the Kojiki in 712 AD and the Nihon Shoki in 720 AD.[176] The Kojiki chronicled negotiations between China and Japan but did not discuss Buddhism.[177] On the other hand, the Nihon Shoki detailed events in chronological order; and it was written in classical Chinese.[178] Moreover, while the Nihon Shoki showed an acceptance of Chinese norms in Japanese civilisation, the Kojiki was written using a mythological Japanese framework.[179] From this perspective, the writing of the Kojiki can be thought of as an attempt to maintain Japanese influence at a time when Chinese norms and culture were pervading into an ancient and traditional Japanese society.[180] Due to the advancement of Japanese society, it is inevitable that its forward looking embrace with the real world would hold the Nihon Shoki more to heart than the Kojiki.

Heian Period (794 AD to 1185 AD)

The Heian Period can be divided into three sub-periods, the early Heian (794 AD–967 AD), the Mid or Fujiwara Heian (967 AD to 1068 AD) and the late Heian (1068 AD to 1185 AD).[181] The Heian Period was an epoch in which there were innovations in the arts as well as in literature, the solidification of aristocratic rule in the capital Kyoto and the evolution

[174] Ibid.

[175] Kazuo, M. (2006), Ancient Japan and Religion, IN Nanzan Guide To Japanese Religions, Swanson, P., and Chilson, C. (Eds), University of Hawaii Press, Honolulu.

[176] Ibid.

[177] Ibid.

[178] Ibid.

[179] Kazuo, M. (2006), Ancient Japan and Religion, IN Nanzan Guide To Japanese Religions, Swanson, P., and Chilson, C. (Eds), University of Hawaii Press, Honolulu.

[180] Ibid.

[181] Meyer, M. (2009), Japan: A Concise History, Rowman & Littlefield Publishing Inc., New York.

of court partisanship and religious institutions.[182] However, central rule from the imperial capital, Osaka, brought challenges from the provinces which brought doubt to the belief that central rule was best.[183] This may have been why central government and a central bureaucracy, which also encompassed the land owning aristocracy in the Heian Period, went through a process of decentralisation.[184] This was evidenced by the loss of control over two types of human labour.[185] The first associated with agricultural production and the second with the provision of a centrally commanded military force. Over the course of the tenth century AD, there was an increase in the fragmentation of agricultural land over which government could collect taxes as well as an increase in the number of 'private' armies.[186] The aristocracy took advantage of the lapse of central control over the provinces by claiming suzerainty in their own name, but on behalf of the Emperor, over the lands which they held.[187] The usurping of power away from the Emperor and the imperial court was further evidenced by the rise of the permanent regency especially during the late Heian Period. While the Regent was titular in nature, his only prerogative being to provide consorts to the royal household to produce heirs to the throne, it became monopolised by a single clan, the northern Fujiwara.[188] The emergence of the Regent signalled a period in which the holder of authority and the power to disperse it became separated.[189] This was also a feature of land ownership and possession in the eleventh and twelfth centuries AD, in which case a member of the aristocracy associated with the imperial court may have owned the land, but possession of the land was in the hands of a custodian in a perpetual hereditary agency.[190] In a

[182] Adolphson, M., and Kamens, E. (2007), Between and Beyond Centers and Peripheries, IN Heian Japan: Centers and Peripheries, Adolphson, M., Kamens, E., and Matsumoto, S. (Eds), University of Hawaii Press, Honolulu.

[183] Ibid.

[184] Kiley, C. (1974), Estate and Property in the Late Heian Period, IN Medieval Japan: Essays in Institutional History, Hall, J., and Mass, J. (Eds), Stanford University Press, Stanford, California.

[185] Ibid.

[186] Ibid.

[187] Ibid.

[188] Kiley, C. (1974), Estate and Property in the Late Heian Period, IN Medieval Japan: Essays in Institutional History, Hall, J., and Mass, J. (Eds), Stanford University Press, Stanford, California.

[189] Ibid.

[190] Ibid.

similar fashion, the institution of the Fujiwara dynasty can be seen to have possessed the assets which were under the ownership of the imperial dynasty.[191] This incentivised political factionalism and battles between factions to gain possession, because possession meant power. Factionalism also gave way to the institution of property rights due to the perceived weakness of the central state to be able to distribute rewards to the factions on a fair basis.[192] The emergence of the institution of property rights occurred because factions which lost out by not winning a political argument, perhaps because some factions were not as strong as others, were sweetened by the grant of property which was frequently in the form of land.[193] A characteristic feature of this behaviour was that once the right to ownership of land had been given to a faction by the Regent, by the central government, it could not be rescinded.[194] However, despite its diminished capacity, the central state still retained the ability to act as an institution by which important assets such as food stocks and a military force could be garnered.[195] The exercise of judgement by the state as to which assets were garnered and how factions should be rewarded and compensated reflected its judicial capacity rather than its administrative one. Nevertheless, the judicial authority of the central state was weak and Japanese society was not presented with stability and peace. In such an environment, the central government was ill placed to enforce claims on resources such as land.[196] This judicial void was filled by the temples, and the monasteries, which being exempt from tax, had the financial and human resources to enforce claims on land ownership and to settle disputes.[197] In return parties to claims would sign over a percentage of future harvests to the monasteries as compensation.[198]

The period encompassing 794 AD to 894 AD represents a time which saw the emergence of a unique Japanese cultural identity which resulted from the process of the assimilation of cultural, political, economic,

[191] Ibid.
[192] Ibid.
[193] Ibid.
[194] Ibid.
[195] Ibid.
[196] Adolphson, M., and Ramseyer, J. (2009), The Competitive Enforcement of Property Rights in Medieval Japan: The Role of Temples and Monasteries, Journal of Economic Behavior and Organisation, Vol. 71, pp. 660–668.
[197] Ibid.
[198] Ibid.

religious, military and institutional knowledge from T'ang dynasty China.[199] The importation, adoption, assimilation and transformation of Chinese T'ang dynasty norms had an impact on the development of Japanese society, culture and civilisation thereafter.[200] Indeed, some of the transformed practices, in Politics, Economics, language and society, which emerged during the ninth century AD in Japan lasted until the end of the Heian period, whilst others lingered on to the end of the Tokugawa period; and some practices especially in written and spoken Japanese and Politics last to this day.[201] For it was in the ninth century AD that the spoken Japanese language was transformed with the reduction in the number of vowels from eight to five and reduction in the number of consonants to a comparable level to those in use today.[202] The writing system also changed from one which was based on the Mana system of the Nara period to the newly devised Kana syllabary system.[203] The innovation of the Kana syllabary system led to the emergence of a graphical writing style which consisted of Japanese syllabary and Chinese characters.[204]

Conclusion

Ancient Japan, perhaps due to the very long distance of the archipelago from the Asian mainland, remained a primitive society even as far back as 400 AD. However, the period 200 BC to 300 AD had seen the transition from the aboriginal hunter-gatherer culture to the Yoyoi culture. The latter emerged as a consequence of the migration of farmers to the Japanese island of Kyushu, where it was first seen to emerge on the Japanese archipelago, from the Korean peninsula. Over the coming five centuries, the Yoyoi culture would sweep across the whole of the Japanese islands pushing the Jomon culture into isolated pockets, today represented by the Ainu minority. The transition from the Jomon culture to the Yoyoi culture was a technological transformation comparable to the Meiji period after 1868 when Japan began to emerge as an industrialised power. In this case, the Yoyoi culture represented the emergence of agriculture and animal

[199] Kato, S. (1997), A History of Japanese Literature, From the Man'Yoshu to Modern Times, Curzon Press Ltd., Richmond, Surrey.

[200] Ibid.

[201] Ibid.

[202] Ibid.

[203] Ibid.

[204] Ibid.

husbandry as a source of food, rather than that represented by the hunter-gatherer existence on its own. Furthermore, the spindle whorl was used to weave cloth from a single thread; and the glass and the metal industries emerged. Nevertheless, while the specialisation of labour was able to develop, a class structure also developed as a result. But technological innovation was in its infancy in Japan at the time, and items such as bronze mirrors, iron weapons and tools as well as glass ornaments still had to be imported from China.

Written Japanese sources, about Japan's culture and history, did not emerge until 712 AD, and the knowledge of ancient Japanese matters before these times was documented by Chinese scholars of the Han and the Wei imperial courts. As the imperial Chinese court influence expanded into north Korea, it began to get close to the periphery of the islands of Japan. The first knowledge gained by the imperial Chinese court of ancient Japan was through the contact between its north Korean colonies and Korean tribesmen who inhabited the islands which were towards the Japanese side of the Korean peninsula.[205] However, it was not until 57 AD, comparable in time to the occasion in which Julius Caesar brought the Roman legions to Britain, that the Chinese received more robust information on the state of Wa (referring to an embryonic Japan) when a messenger from Wa visited the Eastern Han (25 AD to 220 AD) Court.[206] Nevertheless, the next most intimate contact between the imperial Chinese court of Wei (220 AD to 265 AD) and Japan did not occur until 240 AD when a Chinese official became the first of his kind to step on Japanese soil.[207] From the time of the court of Wei to the Tang dynasty (618 AD to 907 AD), the exchange of embassies between the Chinese court and the rulers of Japan allowed for an exchange of knowledge between the two cultures. However, the levels of cultural, economic, political, technological and literacy were far higher in ancient China at any period than in a comparable one in ancient Japan. As a result China was more innovative than Japan which remained backward in comparison.

Japanese historical records or chronicles did not emerge until the early part of the eighth century AD, with the Kojiki in 712 AD and the Nihon

[205] Wang, Z. (2005), Ambassadors from the Islands of Immortals, China-Japan Relations in the Han-Tang Period, University of Hawaii Press, Honolulu.

[206] Wang, Z. (2005), Ambassadors from the Islands of Immortals, China-Japan Relations in the Han-Tang Period, University of Hawaii Press, Honolulu.

[207] Ibid.

Shoki in 720 AD. The Kojiki, while ignoring the Buddhist influence on Japanese civilisation, chronicled negotiations between China and Japan, but at the same time also elucidating Japanese history based on a mythological framework, for example the Sun Goddess Amaterasu. On the other hand, the Nihon Shoki showed an acceptance of the impact of Chinese norms on Japanese civilisation; and was written in classical Chinese, detailing events in Chronological order. In a historical context, the Nihon Shoki was relied more upon than the Kojiki in future centuries to better understand ancient Japan, due to its realism. Despite the late arrival of Japanese literacy and scholarship, even in a Chinese context, the nascent Japanese state had emerged in the fourth century AD. This was in the context of the rise of the Yamato Uji which dominated the leadership of the Japanese islands over the other Uji. However, the rise to power of the Yamato Uji was not a spontaneous one, but one which was spread over the fourth century AD to the eighth century AD. It was in the Nara period that the imperial court established the first permanent imperial capital at Nara, to the south of Kyoto.[208] It was a capital city which was modelled on the Chinese capital.[209] By the sixth century AD, the Yamato clan had not only imported Buddhism and Confucianism into Japan from China but made Buddhism the official state religion of Japan.[210] This was mainly under the auspices of Prince Shotoku, the Prince Regent to the Empress Suiko, 592 AD to 628 AD. Shotoku ruled Japan as a statesman and a warrior, proposing political reforms and a constitutional government in 604 AD. With regard to constitutional government and political reform, Shotoku proposed and implemented a seventeen-page constitution, which was based on Confucian thinking emphasising social harmony, moral and spiritual values. During Shotoku's period of governance, not only was there an inflow of knowledge about Buddhist and Confucian thinking from China to Japan but also Chinese written characters also began to enter the Japanese language. Following the development of agriculture and animal husbandry during the Yoyoi Culture, the Kofun Period (300 AD to 700 AD) also saw the increased use of iron tools in

[208] Ishibashi, K. (2004), Status of Historical Seismology in Japan, Annals of Geophysics, Vol. 47, No. 2/3.

[209] Ibid.

[210] Fukase-Indergaard, F., and Indergaard, M. (2008), Religious Nationalism and the Making of the Modern Japanese State, Theory & Society, Vol. 37, pp. 343–374.

agriculture.[211] This allowed the farmers of the time to dig and plant seeds deeper into the soil, allowing for the crops to draw more nutrients from the soil. In conjunction with well-maintained irrigation channels, this led to not only an expansion of arable land but also to a higher yield of crops.[212] Moreover, the use of iron knives allowed farmers to harvest genetically identical crops with shots and heads attached than would have been possible with stone-based knives.[213] As a result of this advancement in agriculture, household wealth increased as did the population level; and as a result, the class strata in society also increased. In this case, the Yamato Emperor was able to unleash social, economic and political reforms, known jointly as the Taika Reforms in 645 AD.[214] These reforms would, it was hoped, contribute to Japan becoming a centralised state in the mould of China.[215] By the eighth century AD, when the Yamato clan had established their control over central Japan, they introduced elements of the indigenous animistic religion, Shintoism, into Buddhism.[216] The Yamato chieftain, claiming descent from the Sun Goddess Amaterasu, became known as 'Emperor' and gave rise to the imperial line from which the current Japanese emperor is also drawn from.[217] Furthermore, in 701 AD, a legal system known as the Ritsuryo, which encompassed both civil and criminal code, became established across the whole of Japan except for Hokkaido which had not yet become integral to Japanese territory.[218] Under the Ritsuryo, planning related to agriculture—re-zoning of the size of paddy fields, the reclamation of paddy fields, changes to irrigation canals, were all under the control of the central government.[219] A diet of rice and other grains went hand in hand with Buddhism, a religion which did not encourage consumption of meat, as a result of which animal

[211] Ito, M., and Hiraizumi, K. (2008), Agriculture in Japan, IN Encyclopaedia of the History of Science, Technology, and Medicine in Non-Western Cultures, Selin, H.(ed), 2nd Edition, Springer.

[212] Ibid.

[213] Ibid.

[214] Ibid.

[215] Ibid.

[216] Ibid.

[217] Ibid.

[218] Ito, M., and Hiraizumi, K. (2008), Agriculture in Japan, IN Encyclopaedia of the History of Science, Technology, and Medicine in Non-Western Cultures, Selin, H. (Ed), 2nd Edition, Springer.

[219] Ibid.

husbandry was shunned.[220] This trend in the convergence of farming, cuisine and religion continued until the end of World War 2. However, as private territories of the aristocrats and the temples began to emerge in the middle Heian period, 794 AD to 1192 AD, the centrally administered Ritsuryo system began to weaken.[221] Landowners and farmers began to supply their own tools, as well as reclaiming swampy land for agriculture at their own initiative. Both had been under the jurisdiction of the central government during the time in which the Ritsuryo legal system was in force.[222] As landowners and farmers became more wealthy, they armed themselves and their followers, and gradually over time, under their powerful leaders, these autonomous armed groups came to be known as Samurai.[223] Fighting between different Samurai bands resulted two powerful Samurai bands emerging in the twelfth century AD, the Genji and the Heishi.[224] In the resulting civil war between these two bands, the Genji won and gained national dominance. Thus, at the start of the Kamakura period, 1192 AD to 1333 AD, the dominant Samurai group, the Genji, ruled over Japan.

References

Adolphson, M., and Kamens, E. (2007), Between and Beyond Centers and Peripheries, IN Heian Japan: Centers and Peripheries, Adolphson, M., Kamens, E., and Matsumoto, S. (Eds), University of Hawaii Press, Honolulu.

Adolphson, M., and Ramseyer, J. (2009), The Competitive Enforcement of Property Rights in Medieval Japan: The Role of Temples and Monasteries, Journal of Economic Behavior and Organisation, 71, pp. 660–668.

Alt, M., Yoda, H., and Joe, M. (2012), Japan Day by Day, Wiley & Sons Inc., New Jersey.

Barnes, G. (2007), State Formation in Japan, Emergence of a 4th Century Ruling Elite, Routledge, London.

Beasley, W. (1999), The Japanese Experience: A Short History of Japan, University of California Press Berkeley and Los Angeles, California.

Bhatta, C. (2005), Leadership Excellence: The Asian Experience, Asia-Pacific Business Review, Vol. 1, No. 1.

[220] Ibid.
[221] Ibid.
[222] Ibid.
[223] Ibid.
[224] Ibid.

Bleed, P., and Matsui, A. (2010), Why Didn't Agriculture Develop in Japan? A Consideration of Jomon Ecological Style, Niche Construction, and the Origins of Domestication, Journal of Archaeological Method and Theory, 17, pp. 356–370.

Brown, D. (1993), The Cambridge History of Japan: Volume 1, Ancient Japan, Cambridge University Press, Cambridge.

Callister, R., and Wall, J. (1997), Japanese Community and Organisational Mediation, Journal of Conflict Resolution, Vol. 41, No. 2, pp. 311–328.

Clements, J. (2010), The Samurai, The Way of Japan's Elite Warriors, Constable & Robinson Ltd., London.

Cornille, C. (1999), Nationalism in New Japanese Religions, Nova Religio: The Journal of Alternative and Emergent Religions, Vol. 2, No. 2, pp. 228–244.

De Bary, WT. (1988), East Asian Civilisations: A Dialogue in Five Stages, Harvard University Press, Cambridge, Massachusetts.

De Bary, WT. (1995), The Constitutional Tradition in China, Journal of Chinese Law, Vol. 9, No. 7.

Delgado, J. (2008), Khubilai Khans Lost Fleet, In Search of a Legendary Armada, University of California Press, Berkeley.

Delgado, J. (2010), Kamikaze: History's Greatest Naval Disaster, The Bodley Head, London.

Diamond, J. (1998), In Search of Japanese Roots, Discover, http://discoverma-gazine.com/1998/jun/japaneseroots1455/

Durlabhji, S. (1993). The Influence of Confucianism and Zen on the Japanese Organization. In Durlabhji, S. & Marks, N. (Eds.), Japanese Business: Cultural Perspectives, State, University of New York Press, Albany, New York.

Fukase-Indergaard, F., and Indergaard, M. (2008), Religious Nationalism and the Making of the Modern Japanese State, Theory & Society, 37, pp. 343–374.

Giraud, R. (2004), Geologic Hazards of Monroe City, Sevier County, Utah, Special Study 110, Utah Geological Survey.

Gowlett, J., and Dunbar, R. (2011), A Brief Overview of Human Evolution, IN Early Human Kinship, From Sex to Social Reproduction, Allen, N., Callan, H., Dunbar, R., and James, W. (Eds), Wiley-Blackwell, Oxford.

Habu, J. (2008), Growth and Decline in Complex Hunter-Gatherer Societies: A Case Study from the Jomon Period Sannai Maruyama Site, Japan.

Holcombe, C. (2001), The Genesis of East Asia, 221BC–07AD, University of Hawaii Press, Honolulu.

Hosak, M., and Lubeck, W. (2006), The Big Book of Reiki Symbols, Lotus Press, Twin Lakes, WI.

Imamura, K. (1996), Prehistoric Japan: New Perspectives on Insualr East Asia, University of Hawaii Press, Honolulu.

Irapta, A., and Duka, C. (2005), Introduction to Asia: History, Culture and Civilisation, Rex Book Store, Manila.

Ishibashi, K. (2004), Status of Historical Seismology in Japan, Annals of Geophysics, Vol. 47, No. 2/3.
Ito, M., and Hiraizumi, K. (2008), Agriculture in Japan, IN Encyclopaedia of the History of Science, Technology, and Medicine in Non-Western Cultures, Selin, H. (Ed), 2nd Edition, Springer.
Jandt, F. (2004), Intercultural Communication: A Global Reader, Sage Publications, London.
Kaifu, Y., and Fujita, M. (2012), Fossil Record of Early Modern Humans in East Asia, Quaternary International, Vol. 248, pp. 2–11.
Kanaseki, H., and Sahara, M. (1976), The Yoyoi Period, Asian Perspectives, Vol. 19, No. 1.
Kaner, S. (2011), The Appropriation of Religious Power By The Tomb-Builders of the Kofun Period (AD 250–710), Oxford University Press, Oxford.
Karan, P. (2005), Japan in the 21st Century, Environment, Economy and Society, The University Press of Kentucky, Lexington, Kentucky.
Kato, S. (1997), A History of Japanese Literature, From the Man'Yoshu to Modern Times, Curzon Press Ltd., Richmond, Surrey.
Kazumichi, K. (2001), The Japanese as an Asia-Pacific Population, IN Multicultural Japan, Palaeolithic to Postmodern, Denoon, D., Hudson, M., McCormack, G., and Morris-Suzuki, T. (Eds), Cambridge University Press, Cambridge.
Kazuo, M. (2006), Ancient Japan and Religion, IN Nanzan Guide To Japanese Religions, Swanson, P., and Chilson, C. (Eds), University of Hawaii Press, Honolulu.
Keene, D. (2002), Emperor of Japan, Meiji and his World, 1852–1912, Columbia University Press, New York.
Kidder, J. (1954), A Reconsideration of the 'Pre-Pottery' Culture of Japan, Artibus Asiae, Vol. 17, No. 2, pp. 135–143.
Kiley, C. (1974), Estate and Property in the Late Heian Period, IN Medieval Japan: Essays in Institutional History, Hall, J., and Mass, J. (Eds), Stanford University Press, Stanford, California.
Kimio, I. (1998), The Invention of Wa and the Transformation of the Image of Prince Shotoku in Modern Japan, IN Mirror of Modernity: Invented Traditions of Modern Japan, Vlastos, S. (Ed), University of California Press, Berkeley.
Kitagawa, J. (1987), On Understanding Japanese Religion, Princeton University Press, Princeton, New Jersey.
Koyama, S. (1978), Jomon Subsistence and Population, Senri Ethnological Studies 2.
Maruta, Y. (1980) The Management of Innovation in Japan: The Tetsuri Way, Research Management, Vol. 23, No. 1, pp. 39–41, DOI: https://doi.org/10.1080/00345334.1980.11756587.
Mason, R., and Caiger, J. (2011), History of Japan: Revised Edition, Tuttle Publishing.

Matsui, A., and Kanehara, M. (2006) The Question of Prehistoric Plant Husbandry During the Jomon Period in Japan, World Archaeology, Vol. 38, No. 2, pp. 259–273, DOI: https://doi.org/10.1080/00438240600708295.
Metevelis, P. (1993), A Reference Guide to the 'Nihonshoki' Myths, Asian Folklore Studies, Vol. 52, No. 2, pp. 383–388.
Meyer, M. (2009), Japan: A Concise History, Rowman & Littlefield Publishing Inc., New York.
Mizoguchi, K. (2013), The Archaeology of Japan from the Earliest Rice Farming Villages to the Rise of the State, Cambridge University Press, New York.
Morishima, M. (1982), Why has Japan "Succeeded"? Western Technology and the Japanese Ethos, Cambridge University Press, Cambridge.
Musashi, M. (2010), The Complete Book of Five Rings, Tokitsu, K. (Ed), Shambhala Publications Inc., Boston, Massachusetts.
Nakamura, H. (1969), A history of the development of Japanese thought from AD 592 to AD 1868, Kokusai Bunka Shinkokai, Tokyo.
Naumann, N. (2000), Japanese Prehistory, The Material and Spiritual Culture of the Jomon Period, Harrassowitz Verlag, Wiesbaden.
Oda, S., and Keally, C. (1992), The Origin and Early Development of Axe-Like and Edge-Ground Stone Tools in the Japanese Palaeolithic, IPPA Bulletin, Vol. 12, pp. 23–31.
Oh, C. (2011), Cosmogonical Worldview of Jomon Pottery, Sankeisha Co., Ltd., Aichi, Japan.
Ortolani, B. (1995), The Japanese Theatre, From Shamanistic Ritual to Contemporary Pluralism, Princeton University Press, Princeton.
Richardson, H. (2005), Life in Ancient Japan, Crabtree Publishing Company, New York.
Sakamoto, T. (1980), Japanese History, International Society for Educational Information Press, Tokyo.
Sansom, G. (1959), A History of Japan to 1334, Stanford University Press, Stanford, California.
Seligman, L. (1994), The history of Japanese Cuisine, Japanese Quarterly, Vol. 41, No. 2.
Takayama, K. (1998), Rationalisation of State and Society: A Weberian View of Early Japan, Sociology of Religion, Vol. 59, No. 1, pp. 65–88.
Takeshi, M. (1978), Origin and Growth of the Worship of Amaterasu, Asian Folklore Studies, Vol. 37, No. 1, pp. 1–11.
Takokoshi, Y. (2004), The Economic Aspects of the History of the Civilisation of Japan, George Allen & Unwin Ltd., London.
Tanaka, F. (2003), Samurai Fighting Arts: The Spirit and the Practice, Kodansha International, Tokyo.
Toby, R. (1985), Why Leave Nara?: Kammu and the Transfer of the Capital, Monumenta Nipponica, Vol. 40, No. 3, pp. 331–347.

Toro, T. (1983), The Kyushu Dynasty: Furuta's Theory on Ancient Japan, Japan Quarterly, Vol. 30, p. 4.
Tsude, H. (1990), Chiefly Lineages in Kofun-Period Japan: Political Relations between Centre and Region, Antiquity, Vol. 64, pp. 923–931.
Tucker, J. (2000), Nation Building, IN Encyclopedia of Monasticism, Routledge, London.
Walker, H. (2012), East Asia: A New History, Author House, Bloomington, Indiana.
Wang, Z. (2005), Ambassadors from the Islands of Immortals, China-Japan Relations in the Han-Tang Period, University of Hawaii Press, Honolulu.
Zhu, Z. (2000), Cultural Change and Economic Performance: An Interactionistic Perspective, International Journal of Organisational Analysis, Vol. 8, No. 1, pp. 109–126.

CHAPTER 2

The Kamakura Period (1185–1333): Emergence of Military Government: The Bakufu

Introduction

The Heian period (794 AD to 1185 AD) was the period in Japanese history prior to the Kamakura period.[1] The Heian period began with the founding of the imperial capital of Kyoto in 794 AD, from which date Japan was under the control of the aristocracy, notably the Fujiwara family.[2] However, there developed a governance system in which the private institutions controlled by the aristocracy competed with the central government for control of both land and of its people.[3] This dual system of governance worked well for the first few centuries, but was severely tested in the twelfth century. In this case, the Office of the Retired Emperor (ORE) worked with the Taira Clan to govern Japan. The Taira Clan were responsible for protecting the land owned by the ORE.[4] However, in 1156 AD a dispute arose regarding the imperial succession, and while the succession was championed by the Taira Clan, it was opposed by the Minamoto Clan. Thus, it was in 1156 AD that the first battle, the Hogen

[1] Shultz, E. (1999), Ch'oe Ch'unghon and Minamoto Yoritomo, Japan Review, No.11, pp.31–53.

[2] Ibid.

[3] Cameron, G. (1974), The Structure of the Heian Court: Some Thoughts on the Nature of 'Familial Authority in Heian Japan, IN Medieval Japan: Essays in Institutional History, Hall, J., and Mass, J.(Eds), Stanford University Press, 1974.

[4] Shultz, E. (1999), Ch'oe Ch'unghon and Minamoto Yoritomo, Japan Review, No.11, pp.31–53.

S. Ramesh, *China's Economic Rise*,
https://doi.org/10.1007/978-3-030-49811-5_2

no ran, occurred between the Taira Clan and the Minamoto Clan. This was followed by another battle in 1160 AD, the Heiji no ran. Both the Hogen no ran and the Heiji no ran were won by the Taira Clan, with the Minamoto Clan defeated. These victories increased the status of the Taira Clan as well as that of their leader Taira Kiyomori who was propelled into the highest echelons of power. Kiyomori would eventually become Prime Minister or Dajodaijin, in this capacity sharing power with the ORE.[5] Kiyomori also facilitated the marriage of his daughter to the Crown Prince, ensuring that his young grandson would become Emperor.[6] As Prime Minister, Kiyomori implemented the same policies which had been a success under the Fujiwara.[7] However, the sharing of power with the ORE ended in 1179 AD when Kiyomori and the Taira Clan became the holders of state power in Japan.[8] This involved the arrest of the Emperor which resulted in an imperial Prince calling clans opposed to the Taira Clan to rise up and to restore the throne. But in 1179 AD, Minamoto Yoritomo was living in the plain of Kanto, having married Hojo Masako.[9] Yoritomo know of his noble-military heritage and his descent from a ninth century Emperor.[10] It was not until 1183 AD that Yoritomo received the official imperial seal of approval to defend it and Japan from the rule of Kiyomori and the Taira Clan.[11] Then it was not until 1184 AD that the imperial court gave Yoritomo approval to set up a military government or Bakufu in Kyoto. And it was not until 1185 AD, when the Taira had finally been defeated at the Battle of Dannoura, that Yoritomo was able to establish the Bakufu in Kamakura and in the process giving rise to the birth of the Kamakura Period. At the heart of the Kamakura was the legacy it left for the future of Japan. Following the civil war, the Gempei War between the Taira Clan and the Minamoto Clan, Japan was left with a military government which became known as the Shogunate. The imperial court and the

[5] Ibid.

[6] Mass, J. (1974), Warrior Government in Early Medieval Japan, Yale University Press, New Haven.

[7] Shultz, E. (1999), Ch'oe Ch'unghon and Minamoto Yoritomo, Japan Review, No.11, pp.31–53.

[8] Ibid.

[9] Shultz, E. (1999), Ch'oe Ch'unghon and Minamoto Yoritomo, Japan Review, No.11, pp. 31–53.

[10] Ibid.

[11] Mass, J. (1974), Warrior Government in Early Medieval Japan, Yale University Press, New Haven.

Emperor in Kyoto had been reduced to a religious role in Japanese society. In this case, the Kamakura Period left two strands for the future development of Japan.[12] The first strand draws on Japan's traditional conservative values bound into imperial tradition. The second strand is the reformist agenda of the Shogunate which directly impacts on the first strand. However, Yoritomo as Shogun and the leader of the Bakufu was also able to draw upon the legacy of the Heian Period in which the dual system of governance between the nobility and the central government had arisen.[13] Yoritomo made use of the Heian Period dual system of governance, by side lining the aristocracy and the Emperor to religious duties in Kyoto while running the country from his powerbase in Kamakura as Shogun. This title, Yoritomo, was bestowed by the imperial court in 1192 AD recognising his authority as head of the Bakufu or military government of Japan. However, while the Bakufu nominally had more power than the imperial court, both systems of power charted their own course until there was a conflict between the two in 1221 AD when the Bakufu finally won its ascendancy over the Emperor and the imperial court.

The aftermath of the Gempei War of 1180 AD to 1185 AD left several problems for the founding father, Minamoto Yoritomo, of the Kamakura Bakufu to solve.[14] The first problem was to bring peace and stability to the country. The second problem was to strike a balance between the needs of the aristocracy in the imperial capital of Kyoto and the needs of the rising class of warriors in Japan's provinces.[15] The third problem was how to enrich but control the warriors who had helped to facilitate the victory for Yoritomo while achieving a balance with the aristocracy and the imperial court in Kyoto. To achieve a solution to these problems at the same time, Yoritomo devised two key innovative solutions.[16] Firstly, the administrative structure of the country was split in such a way that the imperial court in Kyoto and the Bakufu would have responsibility for managing different areas of interest to the Japanese economy. In this case, the Bakufu would be responsible for its own citizens, whereas the imperial court in Kyoto

[12] Auriti, G. (1950), Heroic Japan of the Past, East and West, Vol.1, No.2, pp.74–76.

[13] Shultz, E. (1999), Ch'oe Ch'unghon and Minamoto Yoritomo, Japan Review, No.11, pp. 31–53.

[14] Mass, J. (1979), The Development of Kamakura Rule, 1180–1250, A History with Documents, Stanford University Press, Stanford, California.

[15] Ibid.

[16] Ibid.

would be responsible for matters associated with land rights.[17] Furthermore, Bakufu warrior or officer types were either the Shugo or the Jito. The main business of the Bakufu was to resolve legal disputes which revolved around the Jito.[18] In order to achieve a resolution of legal disputes, the Bakufu developed a robust legal system which was to become the second key innovation of the Kamakura period.[19] Legal problems arose with the Jito because while they were administrators for the Bakufu and enjoyed certain privileges income, a home and authority, they were immune from the disciplinary authority of those who administered the land, the Shoen.[20] However, the Bakufu would have encouraged lawlessness in the country from its own officials and warriors had it not accepted and adjudicated legal complaints brought against them by offended parties.[21] Therefore, the application of the principle of impartiality and the utilisation of a robust judicial system represented the cornerstone of governance for the Kamakura Bakufu.[22] However, the state of this governance was impacted in 1221 AD with the Jokyu War. This was especially in the context of the dual administrative structure of Kyoto and the Bakufu as well as the judiciary system.[23] Moreover, the Jokyu War also resulted in the unequal distribution of warriors between the west and the east of Japan, and the landowning elite gaining an upper hand over the aristocracy and the imperial court in Kyoto.[24] The death of Minamoto Yoritomo led to a decline in the fortunes of the Minamoto clan.[25] The third Minamoto Shogun was assassinated and replaced as Regent by a member of the Hojo clan.[26] The latter realised that the title of Shogun 'belonged' to the Minamoto clan and did not use it but in its place used the title of Regent. In this case, the Shogun was now in between the imperial court and the Regent from the Hojo clan and as a result was a puppet to the Hojo clan who maintained their grip on the Regency until the end of the Kamakura period in 1333

[17] Ibid.

[18] Ibid.

[19] Ibid.

[20] Ibid.

[21] Ibid.

[22] Ibid.

[23] Mass, J. (1979), The Development of Kamakura Rule, 1180–1250, A History with Documents, Stanford University Press, Stanford, California.

[24] Ibid.

[25] Turnbull, S. (1977), The Samurai: A Military History, RoutledgeCurzon, Abingdon, Oxon.

[26] Ibid.

AD.[27] The military government of Japan was then under the direct control of the Hojo Regency from 1203 AD to 1333 AD, the period encompassing the years 1274 AD and 1281 AD in which the Mongols of the Yuan dynasty of China tried to invade and conquer Japan.[28]

The Gempei War and the Beginnings of the Shogunate

The transition from the late Heian period (794 AD to 1185 AD) to the Kamakura period saw an increase in the denigration and diffusion of centralised political authority away from the imperial court and the military government to the warrior class.[29] In contrast to the governance processes unleashed in the Kamakura period, from earlier times in Japan's history since the time of the Yamato confederation, the opposite has been true. In other words, the power associated with governance in Japan had always been more centralised.[30] Moreover, the same is also true of China, where there was a shift away from a diffused power governance model to a centralised governance model as the country transitioned from Chou polity to Ch'in and Han dynasties.[31] In ancient China the shift from Shang rule to that of the Chou occurred at about 1000 BC.[32] At this time, religion and government were so intertwined that they were indistinguishable.[33] After 200 years of the Chou conquest, a feudal polity emerged in which religious and political authority became feudalised.[34] In Chou China, the political authority of the ruler lay on a religious foundation; and it was this which enabled feudalism to be strong.[35] The relationship between the Chou ruler and his kinsmen, the feudal lords, was also of a religious nature

[27] Ibid.

[28] Blomberg, C. (1994), The Heart of the Warrior: Origins and Religious Background of the Samurai System in Feudal Japan, Routledge, London.

[29] Friday, K. (2010), The Futile Paradigm: In Quest of Feudalism in Early Medieval Japan, History Compass, 8/2, pp.179–196.

[30] Ibid.

[31] Friday, K. (2010), The Futile Paradigm: In Quest of Feudalism in Early Medieval Japan, History Compass, 8/2, pp.179–196.

[32] Coulborn, R. (1958), The State and Religion: Iran, India and China, Volume 1, Issue 1, pp.44–57.

[33] Ibid.

[34] Ibid.

[35] Schwartz, B. (1985), The World of Thought In Ancient China, The Belknap Press of Harvard University Press, Cambridge, Massachusetts.

based on the worship of the ancestor.[36] Ch'in rule following that of the Chou lasted only until 207 BC.[37] Following Ch'in rule, the Han dynasty became the first to implement a universal legal system which was to have a long-term impact on Chinese civilisation.[38] It was during the Han dynasty that written contracts not only had moral but also legal significance.[39] The Han policies and regulations continued to be impacted by Ch'in regulations.[40] The last 200 years of Han rule witnessed the continuing development of institutions of the law as well as the increase in the influence of noble families.[41] A similar situation would arise in Heian period Japan, when the rise of the nobility and the Taira Clan would throw Japan into a civil war, from which a powerful military government would emerge.

The Gempei War, Japan's civil war, began in 1180 AD due to the increasing autocratic rule of the Taira Clan leader, Kiyomori, and because the leader of the opposing warrior-based clan, Minamoto Yoritomo, believed that a prince who could have become Emperor was left out of the succession.[42]

The *Heike Monogatari* is a twelfth century Japanese poem which tells the story of the battle of the Gempei War between the aristocratic Taira Clan and the warrior like Minamoto clan.[43] It was originally written at around the time of the Jokyu War of 1221 AD.[44] However, over the course of time, several variants of the text emerged.[45] The first and oldest of these variants was written in the Kambun style and was very similar to Chinese script, being written between 1218 AD and 1221 AD.[46] The second variant, the *Yashiro Heike Monogatari*, written between 1242 AD and 1300 AD was written in Japanese, but with Chinese characters from the katakana

[36] Ibid.

[37] Scogin, H. (1990), Between Heaven and Man: Contract and the State in Han Dynasty China, 63 S. Cal. L. Rev. 1325

[38] Ibid.

[39] Ibid.

[40] Ibid.

[41] Ibid.

[42] Fouladi, A. (2017), The Spirit of the Samurai: The Kamakura Bafuku, The Rise of the Bushido, and their role in Diplomacy, Vol.4, No.1.

[43] Butler, K. (1969), The Heike Monogatari and the Japanese Warrior Ethic, Harvard Journal of Asiatic Studies, Vol.29, pp.93–108.

[44] Butler, K. (1969), The Heike Monogatari and the Japanese Warrior Ethic, Harvard Journal of Asiatic Studies, Vol.29, pp. 93–108.

[45] Ibid.

[46] Ibid.

phonetic script.[47] The third variant is known as the Kamakura Heike text, written in Japanese using the Katakana script between 1300 AD and 1340 AD.[48] The Kamakura Heike text is an expanded and more detailed account of the Heike written just before 1221 AD.[49] However, the best variant of the Heike Monogatari is the last one, the Kakuichi text of 1371 AD because it integrates aspects of the second Yashiro version and the third Kamakura version of the Heike text.[50] By comparing passages of script between the different versions, it is possible to develop a very good appreciation of the development of warrior ethics over time.[51] Moreover, in some way it provides a guide for the development of Japanese society in subsequent years.[52] The narrative of the Heike Monogatari of the battles which took place during the Gempei War and the descriptions of the conduct and behaviour of the warriors would serve as a benchmark for them until the twentieth century.[53] However, whether the depiction of the battles in the Heike Monogatari is a true and accurate reflection of the actual battles is unknown.[54] Nevertheless, the commonly found values of the period such as loyalty to one's lord, sacrificing one's life for that of the lord and dying rather than surrendering in the face of a superior foe are all reflected in the narrative of the Heike Monogatari.[55]

The Gempei War from 1180 AD to 1185 AD changed the nature of the role of the bushi or samurai in Japan.[56] Moreover, the result of the war impacted on the nature of the political economy of Japan for the consecutive centuries.[57] This is because warriors or samurai from a common class had risen above the ruling aristocracy to establish a feudalistic society

[47] Ibid.

[48] Ibid.

[49] Ibid.

[50] Ibid.

[51] Ibid.

[52] Ibid.

[53] Reischauer, E., and Fairbank, J. (1960), A History of East Asian Civilisation, Vol.1:East Asia: The Great Tradition, Houghton Miffin Company, Boston.

[54] Butler, K. (1969), The Heike Monogatari and the Japanese Warrior Ethic, Harvard Journal of Asiatic Studies, Vol.29, pp.93–108.

[55] Ibid.

[56] Blomberg, C. (1994), The Heart of the Warrior: Origins and Religious Background of the Samurai System in Feudal Japan, Routledge, London.

[57] Ibid.

based on a manorial system.[58] This overturned an aristocratic, centrally administered society which had begun following the Taika Reforms of 645 AD.[59] The feudalistic society which emerged as a result of the establishment of the Kamakura Bakufu in 1185 AD lasted until the Meiji restoration of 1868 AD. During the intervening time period, while the fundamentals of feudalism remained unchanged, it developed and matured before going into terminal decline in the time leading up to and beyond the beginning of the Meiji Period in 1868 AD.[60] However, the development of the Japanese Navy born from the competition between Russia and Great Britain for control of the Pacific brought feudalism to an end.[61] This was because a strong and modern navy could not be developed without strong central control by government as opposed to the decentralisation of feudalism.[62] The continuance of feudalism would not allow for the establishment of a strong and modern Japanese navy for a number of reasons. Firstly, decentralised control would mean that local lords would continue to hold the loyalty of men. Secondly, a feudal existence would tie these men to a lift as tenant farmers and thus depriving the navy of the manpower it would need. Therefore, there was an urgent need to abolish feudalism not only to build a strong and modern navy but also to build a strong centralised nation state which did not have any divided loyalties.[63] Thus, the feudalistic society with its roots in the emergence of the Kamakura Bakufu several centuries before the Meiji Restoration was brought to an end by it.

The Minamoto clan had emerged as the dominant clan in Japan as a result of the war, hailing from its eastern provinces or Kanto region.[64] The eastern part of the Japanese archipelago had always been home to people possibly tougher than they were in the rest of Japan. This may be why it was disengaged from the rest of Japan and why in the latter part of the twelfth century the Kamakura Bakufu came to be established there

[58] Yanaga, C. (1930), Source Materials in Japanese History: The Kamakura Period: 1192–1333, Journal of the American Oriental Society, Vol.59, No.1, pp.38–55.

[59] Ibid.

[60] Ibid.

[61] Feldman, A. (1945), The Origin of the Japanese Navy, The Historian, Vol.8, Issue 1, P.62.

[62] Ibid.

[63] Ibid.

[64] Blomberg, C. (1994), The Heart of the Warrior: Origins and Religious Background of the Samurai System in Feudal Japan, Routledge, London.

allowing for the divorce of power and authority from its symbolism in Kyoto.[65] But the rise of the Minamoto Clan had been due to its military success in the Early Nine Years War and the Late Three Years War.[66] The military fame the Minamoto Clan gained from their victories won respect from local warlords in the Eastern provinces, who duly gave their land to the Clan which in the process became its retainers.[67] But the Eastern provinces were far from the centre of political power in the imperial capital of Kyoto. However, at the same time, the Taira clan had become more closely aligned with the kuge or the court nobility.[68] The leader of the Taira clan, Taira Kiyomori, was not only the grandfather of the Emperor Antoku, but he also held high ministerial office.[69] In fact when Taira Kiyomori was appointed Prime Minister to the imperial court , relatives and retainers were also given government posts, with the Taira Clan going on to possess estates across half of Japan in Kanto and in the Western provinces.[70] Kanto and the Western provinces were also closer to the centre of political power in Kyoto, giving the Taira Clan an advantage over the Minamoto Clan. In this case, the Taira Clan could call on their military forces more quickly than the Minamoto Clan to impose their will on Kyoto and thus Japan. However, the House of Taira, the Heike, was defeated at the Battle of Dannoura by the House of Minamoto in March or April 1185 AD.[71] The warriors of the Minamoto Clan were simply stronger than those of the Taira Clan. It was at the Battle of Dannoura that the nine-year-old Emperor Antoku was killed, reportedly because his grand-mother, sensing defeat for the Heike, drowned herself and her grandson.[72] Moreover, samurai loyal to the Emperor who did not take their own lives were thrown into the sea by the Genji.[73] On the other hand, one theory suggests that the Heike forces which survived the Battle of Dannoura fled in many different directions because Heike settlements were later to be found in

[65] Yasusuke, M. (1984), Le Society as of Civilization, Journal of Japanese Studies, Vol. 10, No. 2.

[66] Takekoshi, Y. (2016), Rise and Fall of Taira and Minamoto Clans, Taylor & Francis Group.

[67] Ibid.

[68] Blomberg, C. (1994), The Heart of the Warrior: Origins and Religious Background of the Samurai System in Feudal Japan, Routledge, London.

[69] Ibid.

[70] Takekoshi, Y. (2016), Rise and Fall of Taira and Minamoto Clans, Taylor & Francis Group.

[71] Martin, J. (1993), The Samurai Crab, Terra, Vol.31, No.4.

[72] Martin, J. (1993), The Samurai Crab, Terra, Vol.31, No.4.

[73] Ibid.

different parts of Japan.[74] However, it may also be the case that the remnants of the Taira Clan fled to settle on the Amami Gunto islands, the islands facing Japan from Okinawa.[75] Nevertheless, the Amami Islands have only been part of Japan since the seventeenth century, and before this, the islands were a part of the Ryukyu Kingdom, which had its own king and paid tribute to China.[76] Before the Battle of Dannoura, the Heike forces, samurai, wives, children and their servants had fled, taking all of their valuables, from the imperial capital of Kyoto to Dannoura via Yashima.[77] The Heike ships at Dannoura were not only seaworthy but also had a large capacity for carrying passengers and cargo.[78] The Heike ships were needed for trade with China, and Taira Kiyomori, the leader of the Heike, had intended to develop trade links with China by moving the capital from Kyoto to Hyogo.[79] However, this was not to be. But it was one of the reasons which drove more warriors to fight for the Minamoto Clan than the Tiara Clan.[80] This is because trade with China had given Japan a trade surplus and the inflow of coins from China to Japan was high. As a result, prices were being driven up in Japan making the cost of living for warriors also very high. It was because of this that the warriors opposed increased trade with China and the relocation of the capital from Kyoto to Hyogo. Another reason why more warriors joined the Minamoto Clan than the Tiara Clan was that the latter offered warriors firmer tenures which followed them, in comparison to the less favourable court preferment offered by the Tiara Clan.[81] Therefore, the success of the Minamoto Clan against the Tiara Clan in the war of 1181 AD to 1185 AD was due to increased warrior support for the reasons outlined than for any other factor. The civil war of 1181 AD to 1185 AD between the Minamoto Clan and the Taira Clan followed defeats for the former by the latter in 1156

[74] Sakamaki, S. (1967), The Heike: From Defeat at Dannoura to a Golden Age in Ryukyu? The Journal of Asian Studies, Vol.27, Issue 1, pp.115–122.

[75] Haring, D. (1952), Amami Gunto: Forgotten Islands, Far Eastern Survey, Vol.21, No.16, pp.170–172.

[76] Ibid.

[77] Sakamaki, S. (1967), The Heike: From Defeat at Dannoura to a Golden Age in Ryukyu? The Journal of Asian Studies, Vol.27, Issue 1, pp.115–122.

[78] Ibid.

[79] Ibid.

[80] Steenstrup, C. (1991), A History of Law in Japan Until 1868, E.J.Brill, Leiden, The Netherlands.

[81] Ibid.

AD and 1160 AD.[82] The Battle of Dannoura was important in the context that it ended the age of the courtiers and established the age of the military under the Shogun lasting in some form until the Meiji restoration of 1868 AD.[83]

The most prominent samurai or bushi families were descended from the kuge and in some cases from royal princes.[84] In the traditional Japan of the time, the younger sons of the aristocracy did not stand to gain wealth through family inheritances as this was solely a vehicle for enriching the eldest son. Therefore, the only way in which the younger sons of the aristocracy could better themselves economically was in the provinces, far from the court, where they could live as part of the landed gentry while at the same time maintaining a local militia for the protection of themselves and their property.[85] The local militia were needed to contain attacks by rebellious local chieftains, pirates and the indigenous Ainu.[86] As such overtime, the landed gentry became the samurai or the bushi. When the bushi were required to perform guard duty in the imperial capital, they were looked down upon by the kuge as rural rustics. This pattern of behaviour remained true until the Gempei War by which, through their victory over the kuge under the leadership of Minamoto Yoritomo, the bushi or the samurai gained political power and cultural influence.[87] The Gempei War was essentially a conflict which started in 1180 between the Taira Clan and a coalition of samurai families from the Kanto region, eastern Japan, under the leadership of Minamoto Yoritomo.[88] Life at the imperial court did not change as much as a result of the defeat of the kuge in the Gempei War. Nevertheless, the big change was that the balance of political power had shifted away from the kuge to the samurai. Yoritomo established his warrior government or Bakufu at his stronghold of Kamakura on Japan's east coast.[89] One of the policy features of the first Bakufu government was that

[82] Steenstrup, C. (1991), A History of Law in Japan Until 1868, E.J.Brill, Leiden, The Netherlands.

[83] Martin, J. (1993), The Samurai Crab, Terra, Vol.31, No.4.

[84] Ibid.

[85] Blomberg, C. (1994), The Heart of the Warrior: Origins and Religious Background of the Samurai System in Feudal Japan, Routledge, London.

[86] Ibid.

[87] Ibid.

[88] Ikegami. E. (1995), The Taming of the Samurai: Honorific Individualism and the Making of Modern Japan, Harvard University Press, Cambridge, Massachusetts.

[89] Blomberg, C. (1994), The Heart of the Warrior: Origins and Religious Background of the Samurai System in Feudal Japan, Routledge, London.

it tried to ensure that the simple life of the provincial bushi or samurai, which had made the outcome of the Gempei War in their favour, was maintained.[90] In this case, the Bakufu under Yoritomo established a set of laws, which later became codified into a legal code, which placed constraints on the daily life of the bushi.[91] To a large extent the codification of laws to control the bushi formed the cornerstone of the stability and the peace of the Tokugawa period.[92] Moreover, the laws which regulated the behaviour of the samurai and which later became codified also fully reflected the teachings of Confucius and Mencius over time.[93] As a result, a system of ethics known as the Bushido developed between the sixteenth and the twentieth centuries. The Bushido system of ethics simply reflects the ways in which a noble warrior should behave, exhibiting filial piety and loyalty.[94] Parts of the Bushido system of ethics were codified into feudal law during the Tokugawa period.[95] Over time the daily lives of the samurai and the kuge had become separated.[96] And the downfall of the Taira clan may have been because of their attempts to bring the samurai and the kuge closer together.[97] However, the Bakufu would be brought to an end eventually in 1868 AD by a coalition of forces which included low-ranking samurai, the kuge and the prominent western clans with the financial support of the rich merchants of Osaka and Kyoto.[98]

[90] Blomberg, C. (1994), The Heart of the Warrior: Origins and Religious Background of the Samurai System in Feudal Japan, Routledge, London.

[91] Ibid.

[92] Ibid.

[93] Nitobe, I. (2012), Bushido—Samurai Ethics and the Soul of Japan, Dover Publications INC, Mineola, New York.

[94] Ibid.

[95] Ibid.

[96] Blomberg, C. (1994), The Heart of the Warrior: Origins and Religious Background of the Samurai System in Feudal Japan, Routledge, London.

[97] Ibid.

[98] Norman, E. (2000), Japan's Emergence as a Modern State: Political and Economic Problems of the Meiji Period, UBC Press, Vancouver, Toronto.

Jokyu War and Kamakura Institutions

In 1221 AD, the imperial forces of the retired Emperor Gotoba attempted to take back power from the Kamakura Bakufu in what became known as the Shokyu no ran conflict.[99] However, the Bakufu were able to react quickly in order to defeat the imperial forces.[100] Once defeated a proportion of the defeated imperial forces moved to Kyushu, to where the Bakufu deported its undesirables.[101] This reflects that lack of a mandate for the Bakufu's political grip on Kyushu which was not as strong as it was in other parts of Japan.[102] It was from the shores of northern Kyushu that Japanese raids were launched against southern Korean ports in 1223 AD. The trigger for this was a shortage of food which had resulted from a drought in the summer of 1222 AD.[103] However, no such raids had occurred during the Heian period. The reason is that following the suspension of missions to Tang China in 894 AD, the Japanese had lost knowledge about seafaring and were unable to navigate the seas.[104] Nevertheless, by the twelfth century AD, the Japanese were acquiring knowledge on ship building techniques and sea navigation from the Chinese Song merchants who had travelled from China to Japan to trade.[105] It was from the year 973 AD that Song merchants had begun to make voyages to Japan.[106] At this time, Japanese shipping technology was primitive, such that the Japanese temples which sent missions to the Chinese imperial court had to rely on Chinese and Korean merchant ships for transport.[107] The Koreans also helped the Japanese to develop sea going vessels which could not only carry more cargo but which could also

[99] Hazard, B. (1967), The Formative Years of the Wako, Monumenta Nipponica, Vol.22, No.3/4, pp.260–277.

[100] Ibid.

[101] Hazard, B. (1967), The Formative Years of the Wako, Monumenta Nipponica, Vol.22, No.3/4, pp.260–277.

[102] Ibid.

[103] Ibid.

[104] Ibid.

[105] Katsumi, M. (1961), International Relations Between the 10th and 16th Centuries and the Development of the Japanese International Consciousness, Acta Asiatica, No. 2, pp. 85–86.

[106] So, B., and Su, J. (2000), Prosperity, Region, and Institutions in Maritime China: The South Fukien Pattern, 946–1368, Harvard University Asia Center, Harvard University Press, Cambridge, Massachusetts.

[107] Hane, M., and Perez, L. (2015), Premodern Japan: A Historical Survey, Westview Press.

be steered more easily.[108]Furthermore, during the Heian period, many Korean emigrants who had left the Korean peninsula were highly educated and were thus able to facilitate technology transfer between Korea and the Japanese mainland.[109]

The international sea trade of China had expanded rapidly from the Tang to the Song periods. [110] Through this process of the expansion of sea trade, the port of Quanzhou in Fujian province became a centre in which goods from other parts of the world could be found. The incentive for the people of Fujian to turn to the sea to make their living was because the province is mountainous and thus the land is not suitable for intensive agriculture.[111] As a result, the people of Fujian province became very proficient at ship building, especially during the Song period.[112] The Ryukyu Islands, near Japan, were also deficient in natural resources such that the people living there also had to resort to international trade to sustain their economy.[113] However, it was not until 1372 AD that the newly established Ming Dynasty had formal diplomatic relations with one of the kingdoms of Okinawa which is one of the islands forming the Ryukyu oceanic archipelago. The starting point for these chains of islands is located below Kyushu, which is a south facing island of the Japanese mainland.[114] The Ming court provided the Ryukyu islanders with cash, goods, ships and ship repair facilities in exchange for the foreign merchandise which they would bring back to the Ming court in return.[115]

The renaissance in Japanese seafaring in the twelfth century occurred at an opportune time when the warriors of southern Korea were fighting the Mongols from conquering their lands especially between the period 1218 AD and 1260 AD.[116] The use of fighting men to fight the Mongols in Korea meant that there would be less resistance from there to Japanese raiders.[117] In the transition from the Heian Period to the Kamakura Period,

[108] Ibid.

[109] Ibid.

[110] Sakamaki, S. (1964), Ryukyu and Southeast Asia, Volume 23, Issue 3, pp.383–389.

[111] Sakamaki, S. (1964), Ryukyu and Southeast Asia, Volume 23, Issue 3, pp.383–389.

[112] Ibid.

[113] Ibid.

[114] Walker, R. (2014), Okinawa and the Ryukyu Islands, Tuttle Publishing.

[115] Ibid.

[116] Katsumi, M. (1961), International Relations Between the 10th and 16th Centuries and the Development of the Japanese International Consciousness, Acta Asiatica, No. 2, pp. 85–86.

[117] Henthorn, W. (1963), Korea, the Mongol Invasions, Leiden, passim.

the Japanese people had been through devastating civil wars through which they had lost the moral and social values of the former period, becoming more aggressive and footloose in the context of the latter period.[118] In this case, ordinary peasants and fishermen joined roaming leaderless warriors in pursuing lawless activities, in the face of a Bakufu which was unable to restrain them in Kyushu at least. Further economic difficulties towards the end of the Kamakura period, under the regency of Hojo Yasutoki and his successors, led to the coastal residents of Japan turning to marauding southern Korean ports. These economic difficulties were caused by the growing indebtedness of Kamakura military retainers in the Kanto plain, unfavourable climatic conditions causing famine as well as disease and epidemics.[119] At the same time, the Daimyos of the Bakufu were imposing heavy taxes on the peasants and expecting payment in coins.[120] This would have imposed sufficient economic pressure on the peasants for them to take up marauding. The policies of the Bakufu were in the hands of Hojo Regent who maintained power and authority, which would have been in the hands of the Shogun, by appointing Hojo family members to the key governmental posts.[121] The Shogun had become a puppet in the hands of the Hojo Regent and, after 1219 AD, even ceased to be a member of the Minamoto family.[122] Having crushed the imperial prerogative to regain power in 1221 AD, the Hojo Regent through the Bakufu established its own authority by implementing the Joei Code in 1232 AD.[123] This structure of governance defined the duties of the stewards and the military governors who had been appointed to administrate the confiscated lands of the imperial court following the war of 1221 AD.[124] The Joei Code was in itself the codification of the laws relating to the behaviour of the warrior.[125] However, while the focus of the Joei Code was impartial dispute resolution, mainly land disputes, it was based only

[118] Hazard, B. (1967), The Formative Years of the Wako, Monumenta Nipponica, Vol.22, No.3/4, pp.260–277.

[119] Ibid.

[120] Hazard, B. (1967), The Formative Years of the Wako, Monumenta Nipponica, Vol.22, No.3/4, pp.260–277.

[121] Schirokauer, C., Brown, M., Lune, D., Gay, S. (2013), A Brief History of Chinese and Japanese Civilisations, Wadsworth Cengage Learning.

[122] Ibid.

[123] Ibid.

[124] Ibid.

[125] Ibid.

on a few regulations.[126] When these regulations were not sufficient to resolve a dispute, the fall back solution was to use common sense.[127] The first written laws in Japan had been the Taika Reform of 646 AD and the Taiho Code of 702 AD.[128] By the tenth century AD, these laws had homogenised into a set of unwritten Japanese law.[129] However, while the laws of the Taika Reform of 646 AD and the Taiho Code of 702 AD were Chinese laws in origin but adapted to Japanese needs, the Joei Code of 1232 AD embodied the spirit of Japanese feudalism.[130] Moreover, the laws of the Shogunate which followed the Kamakura period in the Muromachi period and the later Tokugawa period reflected the Joei Code of 1232 AD.[131] Moreover, land disputes were just as prevalent in the Muromachi period and the Tokugawa period as it was in the Kamakura period.[132] The Joei Code proved to be distinctly Japanese because it formed the institutional basis of the Bakufu military government.[133] In this way, the Joei Code was distinct from the T'ang Chinese influences on Japanese legal code of the Nara and Heian periods.[134]

In twelfth and thirteenth century Japan, economic life was organised through institutions such as the shoen system of land holding.[135] In fact the most common form of property ownership in Japan was known as the shoen and can literally mean 'estate'.[136] The Ritsuryo system was used to create the shoen through legal means.[137] Nengu (rent) was received by shoen landowners from the shoen as a form of profit.[138] However, the

[126] Ibid.

[127] Ibid.

[128] Burks, A. (2011), The Government of Japan, Routledge, Abingdon, Oxon.

[129] Ibid.

[130] Ibid.

[131] Ibid.

[132] Burks, A. (2011), The Government of Japan, Routledge, Abingdon, Oxon.

[133] Varley, H. (1969), Reviewed Work: Studies in The Institutional History of Early Modern Japan by John W.Hall and Marius Jansen, Harvard Journal of Asiatic Studies, Vol.29, pp. 324–327.

[134] Ibid.

[135] Susumu, I. (1990), The Decline of the Shoen System, IN The Cambridge History of Japan, Volume 3, Medieval Japan, Yamamura, K. (Ed), Cambridge University Press, Cambridge, United Kingdom.

[136] Frohlich, J. (2003), Land Administration in Medieval Japan; Ito no sho in Chikuzen Province, 1131–1336, History, Vol.88, No.

[137] Hayami, A. (2015), Japan's Industrious Revolution: Economic and Social Transformations in the Early Modern Period, Springer, Tokyo.

[138] Ibid.

collection of nengu did not correlate with any obligation of the shoen landowner to either protect the residents or manage the holdings.[139] Furthermore, with regard to nengu collection, the shoen landowner had no right of enforcement.[140] In this case, the collection of the nengu relied upon the enforcement powers of the Ritsuryo government.[141] The Ritsuryo economy depended on the Ritsuryo legal system which was drawn from the Legalist and Confucian traditions of Tang China.[142] Moreover, the Ritsuryo economy extended from the start of the tenth century to the middle of the seventh century, the period encompassing the Taika reform.[143] The latter involved more centralised and bureaucratic control of the nascent Japanese state through rule of the Emperor which was very similar to the nature of governance in China.[144] So, at the time there was the imitation of Chinese political institutions by the Japanese.[145]

The shoen hierarchy of land tenure in the late Heian period (794 AD to 1185 AD) consisted of, from bottom to top, the shomin (cultivators), the ryoshu, shoke or shokan (managers) and then the ryoke and the honke.[146] However, the structure of the traditional shoen system of land tenure was changed following the Jokyu War in 1221 AD by Minamoto Yoritomo, the founder of the Kamakura Bakufu.[147] Yoritomo added an additional layer to the shoen hierarchy by creating the roles of military governor (Shugo) and the military estate steward (Jito).[148] The Jito and Shugo were the key elements of the Kamakura Bakufu's links with the Japanese country side as well as forming the backbone of Kamakura civil

[139] Ibid.

[140] Ibid.

[141] Ibid.

[142] Dean, M. (2002), The Japanese Legal System, Cavendish Publishing Ltd, London.

[143] Yamamura, K. (1974), The Decline of the Ritsuryo System: Hypotheses on Economic and Institutional Change, The Journal of Japanese Studies, Vol. 1, No.1, pp. 3–37.

[144] Dean, M. (2002), The Japanese Legal System, Cavendish Publishing Ltd, London.

[145] Ibid.

[146] Sato, E. (1974), The Early Development of the Shoen, IN Medieval Japan: Essays in Institutional History, Hall, J., and Mass, J. (Eds), Stanford University Press, Stanford, California.

[147] Susumu, I. (1990), The Decline of the Shoen System, IN The Cambridge History of Japan, Volume 3, Medieval Japan, Yamamura, K. (Ed), Cambridge University Press, Cambridge, United Kingdom.

[148] Ibid.

administration.[149] Before establishing the Shugo and the Jito as the key elements of his administrative structure, Yoritomo had established the Samurai Dokoro in 1180 AD to perform a similar function, though it was geographically limited due to the extent of the Kamakura regime at that time. The Jito were sent in large numbers to 'colonise' western and central Japan, the locations of the uprising, from Kanto and Kamakura.[150] However, even after the revolt, the Bakufu respected the imperial court's traditional authority over shoen who were not warriors as well as over land tax.[151] Nevertheless, even before the revolt, the Bakufu also respected Heian institutions such as the prestige of the imperial court and its control over tax lands and the non-warrior shoen.[152] But following the revolt, the Bakufu made changes to the Heian system to increase its control and to maintain the stability of Japan. The new shoen hierarchical layer and roles were created in order to manage the land confiscated from the nobles and warriors who had rebelled against the Kamakura Bakufu in the Jokyu War of 1221 AD.[153] This represented a shift towards a feudalistic structure in which those who worked the land did so for the benefit of the warrior-nobility. Furthermore, the appointment of the Shugo and the Jito to manage privately owned land was intended by the Kamakura Bakufu to be additional support to the political authority and land rights of the private landlords and not as a mechanism to replace them.[154] However, in reality the Jito were doing more than they were remitted to do by the Kamakura Bakufu in terms of just maintaining the flow of income and services to the private land owner.[155] Nevertheless, the Jito system was also used to reward the vassals of the Kamakura Bakufu such as the Gokenin, or the

[149] Shultz, E. (1999), Ch'oe Ch'unghon and Minamoto Yoritomo, Japan Review, No.11, pp.31–53.

[150] Lieberman, L. (2009), Strange Parallels Southeast Asia in Global Context, c.800–1830, Volume 2: Mainland Mirrors: Europe, Japan, China, South Asia and the Islands, Cambridge University Press, Cambridge.

[151] Ibid.

[152] Ibid.

[153] Susumu, I. (1990), The Decline of the Shoen System, IN The Cambridge History of Japan, Volume 3, Medieval Japan, Yamamura, K. (Ed), Cambridge University Press, Cambridge, United Kingdom.

[154] Susumu, I. (1990), The Decline of the Shoen System, IN The Cambridge History of Japan, Volume 3, Medieval Japan, Yamamura, K. (Ed), Cambridge University Press, Cambridge, United Kingdom.

[155] Ibid.

independent military lords.[156] The latter who owed their allegiance to Yoritomo and the Bakufu because of the political and economic benefits would gain from the relationship.[157] In addition to the Gokenin, the Kamakura Bakufu also had lower ranking retainer relationships with the Zoshiki and the Bugyonin.[158] Both were of common origins and worked with Yoritomo from the start of his rule in 1180 AD.[159] Another major difference between the Gokenin and the Zoshiki and the Bugyonin was that the latter two did not own land and depended for their incomes on the treasury of the Shogun.[160] Yoritomo would use the Zoshiki and the Bugyonin to place pressure on the vassals of the Kamakura regime to protect regime interests, to transport tribute from vassals to the regime and finally as a surveillance network.[161] Through this network, Yoritomo was able to control the Gokenin to ensure that Kamakura, the Shogun and the Bakufu were the centre of political authority in Japan. However, the Shoguns who followed Yoritomo were less successful at restraining the independence of the Gokenin who took advantage of their Jito role to achieve greater freedom from the Bakufu.[162] This may have been because the power of the Shogun had been supplanted by the Hojo Regent who was supposed to guide him.[163] On the other hand, Yoritomo had developed a network of governance which allowed him to govern outside the imperial framework, establishing the political legitimacy of the Kamakura Bakufu by being able to do so. But greater control of Japan meant that the Kamakura Bakufu and Yoritomo had to give the Gokenin greater local autonomy to manage their lands and people.[164] Therefore, Yoritomo and the Kamakura Bakufu were never able to fully control Japan. Moreover, even though the power of the imperial court was waning in the ascendancy

[156] Shultz, E. (1999), Ch'oe Ch'unghon and Minamoto Yoritomo, Japan Review, No.11, pp.31–53.

[157] Ibid.

[158] Ibid.

[159] Ibid.

[160] Ibid.

[161] Ibid.

[162] Ibid.

[163] Shackley, M. (1986), Arms and the Men;14th Century Japanese Swordsmanship Illustrated by Skeletons from Zaimokuza, near Kamakura, Japan, World Archaeology, 18:2, pp.247–254.

[164] Shackley, M. (1986), Arms and the Men;14th Century Japanese Swordsmanship Illustrated by Skeletons from Zaimokuza, near Kamakura, Japan, World Archaeology, 18:2, pp.247–254.

of the Kamakura Bakufu, the court aristocracy and religious institutions maintained their political influence as well as land tenures in central and western Japan.[165] Furthermore, religious institutions were interested in having a stable income from their land holdings. In this case, these religious institutions were interested in efficient rent collection, land cultivation and the maintenance of records.[166]

In addition to establishing the Shugo and the Jito as the central elements of the Kamakura Bakufu's civil administration, Yoritomo also established the 'House Chancellery' or Mandokoro and the 'Board of Enquiry' or the Monchuju.[167] Through the auspices of the Mandokoro, Yoritomo was able to issue decrees to the people in the same way it had been done in the Heian Period by the Fujiwara and the ORE.[168] On the other hand, the Monchuju formed the framework of the Kamakura Bakufu's legal system.[169] However, in order to better understand the extent of institutional development in the Kamakura period, it is important to consider not only political, economic and social changes but also religious ones.[170] In this case, Buddhism became a religion accessible to the masses, the peasants, farmers and the warriors rather than being a religion of the aristocracy as it was during the Heian period and beyond.[171] Therefore, it has become possible to recognise the 'New Buddhism' of the Kamakura period with the 'Old Buddhism' of the Heian and the Nara periods.[172] However, the subtle difference between the 'Old Buddhism' and the 'New Buddhism' lies with the fact that the latter is associated with five sects and five founders associated with twelfth and thirteenth century Japan.[173] The five founders associated with the 'New Buddhism' of the Kamakura period began their careers as Tendai monks in an environment in which Hongaku

[165] Frohlich, J. (2003), Land Administration in Medieval Japan; Ito no sho in Chikuzen Province, 1131–1336, History, Vol.88, No.1.

[166] Ibid.

[167] Shackley, M. (1986), Arms and the Men;14th Century Japanese Swordsmanship Illustrated by Skeletons from Zaimokuza, near Kamakura, Japan, World Archaeology, 18:2, pp.247–254.

[168] Ibid.

[169] Ibid.

[170] Foard, J. (1980), In Search of a Lost Reformation: A Reconsideration of Kamakura Buddhism, Japanese Journal of Religious Studies, Vol.7, No.4, pp.261–291.

[171] Ibid.

[172] Ibid.

[173] Ibid.

thought was popular.[174] Hongaku thought is thought which is reflective of that of the Buddha.[175] The evidence for the impact of Hongaku thought on the contextual thinking of the five founders in terms of religion is based on similarities between Hongaku thought and their thought.[176] These similarities included the importance of faith, the universal accessibility to Buddhism for people from all walks of life and the chance for saving the souls of even the most evil people.[177] The feature of Tendai Hongaku thought which allowed it to align itself very closely with the Kamakura identity of the lowly warrior being able to govern over the aristocracy was the ideal that everyone was capable of achieving enlightenment.[178] There is also some relationship between Buddhist ethics and the code of conduct of the warrior. This is discoursed in the 'Heike Monogatari', an epic poem written around the time of the end of the Heian period and the beginning of the Kamakura period between the twelfth and the thirteenth centuries.[179] The 'Heike Monogatari' is an epic poem which chronicles the battles between the Minamoto Clan and the Tiara Clan culminating in the defeat of the latter by the former and the start of the Kamakura period in 1185. The leader of the Tiara Clan, Kiyomori, is evil in the poem. And the code of conduct depicted in the poem deviates from that in real life.[180] For example, in real life, the warrior is expected to show loyalty to his lord, benevolence, loyalty, wisdom, courage and a disdain for saving one's own life.[181] But in the poem there is some interpretation as to the extent of the warrior's loyalty to the lord, which should be more reflective of real life when circumstances change, then the loyalty of the warrior may also change. Another feature of the 'Heike Monogatari' is that it favours the Buddhism associated with the 'Greater Vehicle' which was more prevalent in China and Japan than the Buddhism of the 'Lesser Vehicle' which focuses on the idea of the historical Buddha rather than on a religious

[174] Stone, J. (1995), Medieval Tendai Hongaku Thought and the New Kamakura Buddhism: A Reconsideration, Japanese Journal of Religious Studies, Vol.22, No.1/2, pp.17–48.

[175] Ibid.

[176] Ibid.

[177] Ibid.

[178] Ibid.

[179] Joseph, H. (1976), The 'Heike Monogatari': Buddhist Ethics and the Code of the Samurai, Folklore, Vol.87, No.1, pp.96–104.

[180] Ibid.

[181] Ibid.

ideology being prevalent in a country such as Sri Lanka.[182] The Buddhism of the 'Greater Vehicle' associates itself with the worship of the half-Buddhas or Bodhisattvas, which are seen to allow all of humanity to achieve salvation.[183] However, the Amidist Sect which was prominent at the time of the writing of the 'Heike Monogatari' believed that man was too evil and corrupt to get off the wheel of life.[184] The Sect believed that the only way out of this situation and to attain salvation was to pray to the Amida Buddha and to sincerely request salvation at the time of death.[185] But, ultimately karma also plays a role in salvation, and it is the bad karma brought upon the Taira Clan by the deeds of its leader Kiyomori, for example imprisoning the Emperor, which led to its downfall at the hands of the Minamoto Clan.

Contemporary China: The Song and the Yuan Dynasty and the Shogunate

The Kamakura period (1185 AD to 1333 AD) encompasses the periods of the Song Dynasty (960 AD to 1279 AD) and the Yuan Dynasty (1271 AD–1368 AD) of China. The changes which were taking place in Song Dynasty China facilitated cultural and economic exchanges between Japan and China.[186] Moreover, in traditional regional China, temples and shrines played a key role in the daily lives of people.[187] The same was also true in Japan. The level of cultural and economic exchanges between Japan and China increased as did trade during the Song Dynasty. Prior to the Song period, the system of trade which was characteristic of China's economic engagement with other states was tributary trade.[188] In this case, tributary

[182] Joseph, H. (1976), The 'Heike Monogatari': Buddhist Ethics and the Code of the Samurai, Folklore, Vol.87, No.1, pp.96–104.

[183] Ibid.

[184] Ibid.

[185] Ibid.

[186] Schottenhammer, A. (2010), Preface, IN Trading Networks in Early Modern East Asia, Harrassowitz Verlag, Wiesbaden.

[187] Takashi, S. (2010), The Structure of Regional Society as Seen from Local Historical Documents: Focusing on the Southeastern Shoreline Areas, Song to Ming, IN Trading Networks in Early Modern East Asia, Schottenhammer, A. (Ed), Harrassowitz Verlag, Wiesbaden.

[188] Chan, K. (2008), Foreign Trade, Commercial Policies and The Political Economy of the Song and the Ming Dynasties of China, Australian Economic History Review, Vol.48, No.1.

trade fulfilled two purposes which included the facilitation of international trade and the maintenance of a world order under the hegemony of China and its imperial court. Tribute was paid by vassal states to the Chinese imperial court in terms of goods, with the imperial court sending to the vassal states goods of perhaps a higher value.[189] The vassal states paid tribute to the imperial court out of fear that the imperial court would resort to force to take the vassal state itself through the use of its bigger army and navy.[190] However, by the time of the Song Dynasty, China's power had shifted politically and economically from the north of the country to its south and south-east.[191] This geographical shift was towards the open sea. Therefore, there was now no longer a reliance on the silk road for trade but a shift towards maritime trade from ports on the coastal regions. These ports included Guangzhou, Quanzhou, Xiamen, Fuzhou and Hangzhou, ports which would be forcibly opened as treaty ports in the nineteenth century by the Europeans [192] There were significant shipping innovations which occurred in the Song period.[193] These innovations allowed for more efficient sailing and better and bigger ships to be built. But although China produced twice as much pig iron in 1078 AD as did England in the seventeenth century,[194] ships were for the most part still made from wood. However, it was just not innovations in shipping which favoured increased maritime trade. In this case, Song Dynasty policies also favoured the growth of Chinese trade with the then known world. In fact, the Song state was surrounded by hostile states and therefore needed revenues to maintain a strong military presence. These revenues could not be reliant on agriculture because not enough revenue would be raised. The required levels of revenue could only be raised through growing international maritime trade. Song merchant and navy ships navigated sea routes to Africa,

[189] Ibid.

[190] Chan, K. (2008), Foreign Trade, Commercial Policies and The Political Economy of the Song and the Ming Dynasties of China, Australian Economic History Review, Vol.48, No.1.

[191] Ibid.

[192] Veeck, G., Pannell, C., Smith, C., and Huang, Y. (2011), China's Geography: Globalisation and the Dynamics of Political, Economic and Social Change, Rowman & Littlefield Publishers INC, London.

[193] Ibid.

[194] Fairbank, J., and Goldman, M. (1998), China: A New History, Belknap Press, Cambridge, MA.

the Middle East, South Asia and to India.[195] The trade of porcelain, silk and tea with the Middle East and precious woods, Tung oil and spices in the east was lucrative.[196] Therefore, Song Dynasty policies focused on increasing China's trade with the rest of the world and on increasing productivity within the Song economy.[197] The policies implemented by the Song government to increase productivity and trade included the provisioning of the infrastructure necessary for trade such as ports and warehouses, liberal tax policies to incentivise merchants, career advancement for officials and institutions to document and monitor trade as well as to collect tax efficiently.[198] Increased maritime trade resulted in the tax revenues of the imperial court quadrupling between the latter part of the eleventh century and the mid-twelfth century.[199]

It was during the Song Dynasty that coins from China began to flow into Japan.[200] Moreover, it was during the Song Dynasty that there occurred several financial innovations which eased the way in which payment could be made for goods and services.[201] Promissory notes such as the Yanyin, Jiaoyin and Chayin, whose value was guaranteed by either precious metals or expensive goods, were used as a means of payment.[202] Similarly, the Huizi represented paper notes.[203] The value of the Huizi was also founded on currency reserves which were precious metals rather than

[195] Veeck, G., Pannell, C., Smith, C., and Huang, Y. (2011), China's Geography: Globalisation and the Dynamics of Political, Economic and Social Change, Rowman & Littlefield Publishers INC, London.

[196] Ibid.

[197] Chan, K. (2008), Foreign Trade, Commercial Policies and The Political Economy of the Song and the Ming Dynasties of China, Australian Economic History Review, Vol.48, No.1.

[198] Chan, K. (2008), Foreign Trade, Commercial Policies and The Political Economy of the Song and the Ming Dynasties of China, Australian Economic History Review, Vol.48, No.1.

[199] Levathes, L. (1994), When China Ruled the Seas: The Treasure Fleet of the Dragon Throne, 1405–1433, Simon & Schuster, New York.

[200] Segal, E. (2011), Coins, Trade, and the State: Economic Growth in Early Medieval Japan, Harvard University Asia Center.

[201] Liu, W. (2015), The Chinese Market Economy 1000–1500, State University of New York Press, Albany.

[202] Ibid.

[203] Gernet, J. (1996), A History of Chinese Civilisation, Cambridge University Press, Cambridge.

low value bronze coins.[204] Nevertheless, Sichuan silver was used as the reserve to support the value of the paper money used there, the Qianyin.[205] The Huizi became the common currency used for trade in Song Dynasty China by the mid-twelfth century, retaining its nominal value for in excess of six decades.[206] The promissory notes and paper money used to facilitate trade were in addition to the use of bronze coins and other precious metals.[207] Song merchants were able to benefit financially by using promissory notes and paper money to engage in long distance trade because they did not incur the transactions costs associated with having to transport large amounts of low worth coins.[208] The growth in the types of the means of payment was necessary because of the dramatic increase in urban consumption during the Song period.[209] This increase in urban consumption also facilitated the expansion of markets in Song Dynasty China.[210] However, in the move from the Song Dynasty to the Ming Dynasty, the state lost its control over the issuance of paper money.[211] The result was that people began to lose their trust in the value of paper money.[212] This, in combination with the reluctance of the state to issue coins in large quantities, resulted in silver being predominant in terms of value.[213]

[204] Von Glahn, R. (2013), Cycles of Silver in Chinese Monetary History, IN The Economy of Lower Yangzi Delta in Late Imperial China: Connecting money, markets and institutions, So, B. (Ed), Routledge, London.

[205] Ibid.

[206] Gernet, J. (1996), A History of Chinese Civilisation, Cambridge University Press, Cambridge.

[207] Liu, W. (2015), The Chinese Market Economy 1000–1500, State University of New York Press, Albany.

[208] Guanglin, L. (2015), Market Integration in China, AD 960–1644, IN A History of Market Performance: From Ancient Babylonia to the Modern World, Spek, R., Leeuwen, B., and Zanden, J. (Eds), Routledge, London.

[209] Liu, W. (2015), The Chinese Market Economy 1000–1500, State University of New York Press, Albany.

[210] Liu, W. (2015), The Chinese Market Economy 1000–1500, State University of New York Press, Albany.

[211] Guanglin, L. (2015), Market Integration in China, AD 960–1644, IN A History of Market Performance: From Ancient Babylonia to the Modern World, Spek, R., Leeuwen, B., and Zanden, J. (Eds), Routledge, London.

[212] Ibid.

[213] Ibid.

Monetisation facilitated the re-establishment of markets and economic activity to increase.[214] Nevertheless, markets were prevalent in Japan between 650 AD and 800 AD but became less visible between the ninth and the eleventh centuries.[215] The ensuing demonetisation of the Japanese economy may have occurred because of the increasing scarcity of copper from which coins had been made.[216] This may help to understand why the economy returned to barter trade, but demonetisation may not explain why markets also disappeared.[217] But in the twelfth century as the pace of monetisation continued, markets began to appear throughout Japan and commercial activity increased.[218] However, although the pace of monetisation increased in Japan, towards the end of the Heian Period and the early Kamakura Period, the Bakufu stopped the circulation of new Song copper coins in a bid to prevent inflation.[219] Nevertheless, in 1226 the Bakufu replaced cloth as the standard measure of value with copper coinage, and in 1242, a Japanese merchant vessel returned from Song China with a cargo of copper coins equivalent in volume and value to the annual minting of copper coins in China.[220] Thus, monetisation and the increased commercial activity in Song China had a causal impact on the economy of Bakufu economy.[221] But the significant outflow of copper coinage between Song China and Japan was causing deflationary pressures which led the Song government to ban the export of copper coinage to Japan.[222] The export of rice from Japan to Song China as exchange for copper coins may have also reduced the amount of rice in Japan for consumption.[223] However, despite these problems through the Hojo Regency and towards the late Kamakura Period of the early fourteenth century, commercial activity in Bakufu Japan increased significantly.[224] As such Kamakura, the

[214] Segal, E. (2011), Coins, Trade, and the State: Economic Growth in Early Medieval Japan, Harvard University Asia Center.

[215] Ibid.

[216] Ibid.

[217] Ibid.

[218] Ibid.

[219] Shoji, K. (1988), Japan and East Asia, IN The Cambridge History of Japan: Volume 3 Medieval Japan, Yamamura, K. (Ed), Cambridge University Press, Cambridge.

[220] Ibid.

[221] Ibid.

[222] Shoji, K. (1988), Japan and East Asia, IN The Cambridge History of Japan: Volume 3 Medieval Japan, Yamamura, K. (Ed), Cambridge University Press, Cambridge.

[223] Ibid.

[224] Ibid.

seat of the Bakufu, would become the destination for many Chinese goods whose trail from Song China to Kamakura would pass a transport network which encompassed the port of Hakata, the Seto Inland Sea and Kyoto.[225]

The expansion of markets in Japan may have been due to the diffusion of the increased economic activity from Song Dynasty China, which, as discussed earlier, was experiencing increasing monetisation, increasing commercialisation and market expansion. However, trade between China and Japan had existed and continued to do so even when official ties between the two countries were severed in the late ninth century AD at a time during which the T'ang Dynasty was declining rapidly.[226] In this case, Japanese merchants continued to trade with China from the port of Hakata on Kyushu; and the imperial court maintained soldiers there to control the import trade and to ensure that the aristocracy of Kyoto could still have access to luxury goods.[227] As the Taira Clan was rising to prominence in the late Heian Period and when Taira Kiyomori seized power after 1159 AD, they monopolised the lucrative private merchant trade between China and Japan.[228] At the same time that the Song lost territory in northern China due to invaders, having to move their capital from Kaifeng in the north to Hangchow in the south, the Taira were gaining an upper hand in the control of Japanese trade.[229] However, Song Dynasty China was very different from T'ang Dynasty China from which the Japanese had based their reforms a few hundred years earlier.[230] Despite being surrounded by hostile states, the Song civilisation of southern China was innovative and highly commercial, perhaps representing the height of Chinese civilisation at the time.[231] The increase in commercial activity led to rising incomes with access to more food leading to an increase in population. This was due to an agricultural revolution in which a combination of efficient irrigation and the use of a high yielding variety of rice, originally from what is now Vietnam, allowed for more crops to be produced.[232]

[225] Ibid.

[226] Varley, P. (2000), Japanese Culture, University of Hawai'i Press, Honolulu.

[227] Ibid.

[228] Ibid.

[229] Ibid.

[230] Ibid.

[231] Ramesh, S. (2018), The Rise of Empires: The Political Economy of Innovation, Palgrave Macmillan.

[232] Ho, P. (1956), Early-Ripening Rice in Chinese History by Ping-Ti Ho, The Economic History Review, New Series, Vol.9, No.2, pp.200–218.

Thus, because the population grew quite dramatically under the Song, the Song represented a period in which there was a rapid growth and expansion of cities. The closer contact between peoples and increasing incomes would mean that there would be a growth in innovation. Scholarly activity also increased with the development of philosophy, art, religion and the printing of books.[233] During the time of the Southern Song, 1127 AD to 1279 AD, Zen monks would write poetry and read canonical texts in different monasteries.[234] In fact, the Japanese Five Mountains Zen institution developed through the collaboration of Chinese and Japanese Zen monks, with the Chinese Zen monks having the biggest influence having been active in the latter part of the Song Dynasty period.[235] The Japanese monk's favourite religious works were by the Chinese Zen monk Ching-sou Chu-chien (1164 AD to 1246 AD).[236] Moreover, Chinese monks not only visited Japan during the Kamakura period but also enjoyed the patronage of the Kamakura Bakufu.[237] The Five Mountains Zen institution consisted of the state-sponsored 300 monasteries and the 3000 sub-temples in Japan which emerged in the early part of the Kamakura Period as a result of the introduction of Zen teachings into Japan from China by Chinese monks.[238] The Five Mountains Zen institution then reached its peak through the Gozan system with the support of the Shoguns of the Ashikaga Period through the fourteenth century and the first part of the fifteenth century.[239] One of the legacies left behind by the medieval Kamakura Five Mountains Zen institution was its literature, the *Gozan Bungaku*, which consisted of poetry written in Chinese by Japanese monks.[240] However, in addition to religious works, other texts dealing with the organisation and the policies of the Bakufu were also written by its officials.[241] The most famous of these works was the 'Azuma Kagami'

[233] Varley, P. (2000), Japanese Culture, University of Hawai'i Press, Honolulu.

[234] Parker, J. (1999), Zen Buddhist Landscape Arts of Early Muromachi Japan (1336AD–1573AD), State University of New York Press, Albany.

[235] Ibid.

[236] Ibid.

[237] Ibid.

[238] Collcutt, M. (1981), Five Mountains: The Rinzai Zen Monastic Institution in Medieval Japan, Harvard University Press, Cambridge, Massachusetts.

[239] Ibid.

[240] Kabanoff, A. (2000), Ikkyu and Koans, IN The Koan: Texts and Contexts in Zen Buddhism, Heine, S., and Wright, D. (Ed), Oxford University Press, Oxford.

[241] Yanaga, C. (1939), Source Materials in Japanese History: The Kamakura Period:1192–1333, Journal of the American Oriental Society, Vol.59, No.1, pp.38–55.

which means 'The Mirror of Eastern Japan'.[242] This was a partly historical documentation of the emergence of the Kamakura Bakufu from the raising of his army by Yoritomo to overthrow the power of the Taira Clan to 1226 AD.[243] The objective of writing the 'Azuma Kagami' as a historical study of past achievements was to use it as the basis for future planning.[244] However, while the 'Azuma Kagami' covers everything from religious practice, the economy, the literature to the arts and customs and tastes at Kamakura, it does not consider any of these factors in the imperial capital of Kyoto.[245]

As discussed previously, during the period encompassing the Southern Song, there were also innovations in ship building and in navigation. Whereas during the T'ang dynasty Arabs and Persians sailed in their ships to China, in the Song Dynasty, ships were built in China which were not only very big, but also had waterproof compartments, stern post rudders to allow the ship to change direction, several masts and movable sails to enable changing wind direction and power to be easily harnessed as the ships engine.[246] Song navigation of ships was also the most advanced for its time, incorporating the use of the magnetic compass, star charts and up to date knowledge of sea currents and the directions and seasonality of the winds.[247] Commercialisation and trade between Song China and Japan facilitated the diffusion of scholarly and cultural knowledge and technical innovation from Song China to Japan.[248] The growth of scholarly activity in religion, philosophy, history, geography and medicine in Song China in association with printing resulted in book production in large volumes.[249] As a result of the cultural contact between Japan and Song China, the aristocracy of the late Heian Period in Japan believed that having large numbers of printed Chinese books in their possession represented a status symbol. This diffusion of knowledge was greatly facilitated by the Song desire to increase trade not only with Japan but with other regions, and

[242] Ibid.

[243] Ibid.

[244] Ibid.

[245] Ibid.

[246] Findlay, R., and O'Rourke, K. (2007), Power and Plenty: Trade, War and the World Economy in the Second Millennium, Princeton University Press, Princeton.

[247] Ibid.

[248] Varley, P. (2000), Japanese Culture, University of Hawai'i Press, Honolulu.

[249] Ibid.

the Taira clan's monopoly on trade in Japan.[250] However, although the Song was actively promoting trade with the specific purpose of increasing tax revenues for the state, trade was hindered because of the Song activity of requisitioning merchant ships for military purposes.[251]

Commercial and cultural exchange with Song China created prosperity for Japan and those who monopolised this exchange. However, by the late twelfth century the vassals of the Kamakura Shogunate were significantly indebted to money lenders such that they were losing their lands.[252] To facilitate their high living, the Daimyos needed to spend more and more money, such that they eventually had to resort to borrowing. This affected the capacity of the vassals to contribute to military needs of the Shogunate. This resulted in the Shogunate passing a Debt Relief Law in 1297 AD.[253] The growing indebtedness of the Kamakura vassals may indicate that there was a transition from a 'gift economy' to a 'profit-oriented economy'.[254]

Conclusion

The shift from the Heian Period to the Kamakura Period represented a major change in the dynamics of Japanese social and political organisation. In this case, this shift represented a shift from an aristocratic society to a feudalistic one with a greater military orientation. Perhaps the seeds of Japanese militarism, which would see it defeat Russia, occupy China and become embroiled in a futile world war in the early part of the twentieth century, were laid in the emergence of the Kamakura period and in periods thereafter. Furthermore, the impact of the transition from an aristocratic to a feudalistic society would have a huge impact on Japanese social, economic and political development for centuries with no major change occurring until the Meiji Restoration of 1868. The political change was represented by a shift away from the centralisation of state power to decentralisation in which the Kamakura Bakufu devolved power to local regional war lords or Daimyos. The social change was due to the implementation of feudalism which featured a class structure composed of samurai,

[250] Varley, P. (2000), Japanese Culture, University of Hawai'i Press, Honolulu.

[251] Findlay, R., and O'Rourke, K. (2007), Power and Plenty: Trade, War and the World Economy in the Second Millennium, Princeton University Press, Princeton.

[252] Segal, E. (2011), Coins, Trade, and the State: Economic Growth in Early Medieval Japan, Harvard University Asia Center.

[253] Ibid.

[254] Ibid.

aristocrats, clergy, farmers, peasants, merchants and outcasts in descending order. The merchants were placed at the lower end of this hierarchical order as they were perceived to exist for only making money. With increasing monetisation and the need for coinage by the Bakufu and its Daimyos for paying the samurai and their lavish lifestyles meant that the merchants of Osaka, Kyoto and Edo (Tokyo) became wealthy by acting as intermediaries between farmers and the state apparatus. In effect the merchants 'converted' measured quantities of rice into coinage. Increasing trade with China also brought about market expansion in Japan. The regulation of economic activity through dispute resolution became more Japanese with the first indigenous codification of Japanese law with the implementation of the Joei Code in 1232 AD. The Joei Code was different from the Japanese legal codes of the Nara and Heian periods because it was not influenced by Chinese practice of the time. The other structures put in place by Yoritomo at the beginning of the Kamakura period included the Shugo, the Jito, the Mandokoro and the Monchuju. The Shugo conducted the legal affairs of the Bakufu.[255] These affairs would include interviewing witnesses, enforcing court orders, calling defendants and announcing court judgements, for example.[256] On the other hand, the Jito managed land for its owners with no direct authority over the owner.[257] The Mandokoro was used by the Bakufu to issue orders and decrees to the people. While the Monchuju was the structural framework of the legal system of the Kamakura Bakufu.

The rule of the Kamakura Bakufu and the Hojo Regent came to an end in July 1333 AD when the military forces of the Emperor Go-Daigo stormed their stronghold at Kamakura.[258] One argument for the demise of the Kamakura Bakufu was that the Mongol invasions of 1274 AD and 1281 AD required significant investment in military capacity and defences by the Bakufu that the Bakufu became weaker.[259] However, at the same time it has been noted that as the Kamakura period progressed, the vassals

[255] Mass, J. (1995), The Kamakura Bakufu, IN Warrior Rule in Japan, Jansen, M. (Ed), Cambridge University Press, Cambridge.

[256] Ibid.

[257] Ibid.

[258] Shackley, M. (1986), Arms and the Men;14th Century Japanese Swordsmanship Illustrated by Skeletons from Zaimokuza, near Kamakura, Japan, World Archaeology, 18:2, pp.247–254.

[259] Frohlich, J. (2003), Land Administration in Medieval Japan; Ito no sho in Chikuzen Province, 1131–1336, History, Vol.88, No.1.

of the Bakufu became more and more indebted. And having used their lands as collateral for the loans from money lenders, inability to pay back the loans meant that the land was forfeited to the money lenders. The loss of their lands deprived the vassal Daimyos of the tax revenue from tenant farmers and agriculture. This would mean that the Daimyos would have been unable to pay the wages of the samurai and, therefore, unable to raise the military forces required by the Bakufu for its defence. Furthermore, the indebtedness of the Bakufu Daimyos meant that unpaid samurai and their other retainers had to find in income by other means. These other means included raiding southern Korean ports. However, the sad state of affairs contrasts with the late Heian Period and the start of the Kamakura Period. In this case, the increasing commercialisation and monetisation which was an economic feature of the contemporary Song civilisation of the time had spill over effects on the Japanese economy of the late Heian and subsequent Kamakura Period. In the late Heian Period, the rise of the Taira Clan in Japan favoured more trade between Song China and Japan. To a great extent, this trade was monopolised by the Taira Clan. In the Kamakura Period, this trade was a feature of the flow of goods from Hakata to Kyoto and then on to Kamakura. Increasing monetisation, through the import of copper coins from China, also became a feature of the Japanese economy. The diffusion of economic activity through trade and monetisation from Song China facilitated the expansion of markets in Kamakura Japan. However, the diffusion effects were not limited to just economic activity. Increasing income levels within certain groups in both countries allowed for increased scholarly activity, particularly in religion and poetry. But the spill over effects occurred from China to Japan. Japanese monks learnt from Chinese monks, and poetry in Japanese monasteries and temples were written in Chinese. However, in addition to religious works and poetry, the Kamakura period also produced other prominent works of Japanese literature. These included the 'Heike Monogatari' and the 'Azuma Kagami'. The former is a poem which details the battles between the Minamoto Clan and the Tiara Clan at the end of the Heian Period and the beginning of the Kamakura Period. While the 'Azuma Kagami' is a semi-official text written by Bakufu officials which details the structural organisation and the policies of the Bakufu.

The Kamakura Period came to an end in 1333. The Kamakura Bakufu had been weakened by its expenditure and efforts to defend Japan against the Mongol invasions.[260] And the Emperor Go-Daigo wanted to take back the sovereign power over Japan of the imperial court from the Shogun and the Bakufu. Once the Kamakura Bakufu had been defeated militarily, the government was transferred back to Kyoto in what became known as the short-lived Kemmu Restoration of 1333 to 1336.[261] However, this was followed by the establishment of two rival courts in the Nambokucho Era from 1336 to 1392 when one of the Emperor's generals rebelled. There then followed the ascendancy of the Ashikaga Shoguns from 1392 to 1568, in a period of stability for Japan in the Muromachi or Ashikaga Period.[262]

References

Auriti, G. (1950), Heroic Japan of the Past, East and West, Vol.1, No.2, pp.74–76.

Blomberg, C. (1994), The Heart of the Warrior: Origins and Religious Background of the Samurai System in Feudal Japan, Routledge, London.

Burks, A. (2011), The Government of Japan, Routledge, Abingdon, Oxon.

Butler, K. (1969), The Heike Monogatari and the Japanese Warrior Ethic, Harvard Journal of Asiatic Studies, Vol.29, pp.93–108.

Cameron, G. (1974), The Structure of the Heian Court: Some Thoughts on the Nature of 'Familial Authority' in Heian Japan, IN Medieval Japan: Essays in Institutional History, Hall, J., and Mass, J. (Eds): Stanford University Press, 1974.

Chan, K. (2008), Foreign Trade, Commercial Policies and The Political Economy of the Song and the Ming Dynasties of China, Australian Economic History Review, 48, 1.

Collcutt, M. (1981), Five Mountains: The Rinzai Zen Monastic Institution in Medieval Japan, Harvard University Press, Cambridge, MA.

Coulborn, R. (1958), The State and Religion: Iran, India and China, 1, 1, pp.44–57.

Deal, W. (2006), Handbook to Life in Medieval and Early Modern Japan, Oxford University Press, Oxford.

Dean, M. (2002), The Japanese Legal System, Cavendish Publishing Ltd, London.

[260] Deal, W. (2006), Handbook to Life in Medieval and Early Modern Japan, Oxford University Press, Oxford.

[261] Shackley, M. (1986), Arms and the Men;14th Century Japanese Swordsmanship Illustrated by Skeletons from Zaimokuza, near Kamakura, Japan, World Archaeology, 18:2, pp.247–254.

[262] Ibid.

Fairbank, J., and Goldman, M. (1998), China: A New History, Belknap Press, Cambridge, MA.
Feldman, A. (1945). The Origin of the Japanese Navy, The Historian, Vol.8, Issue 1, P.62.
Findlay, R., and O'Rourke, K. (2007), Power and Plenty: Trade, War and the World Economy in the Second Millennium, Princeton University Press, Princeton.
Foard, J. (1980), In Search of a Lost Reformation: A Reconsideration of Kamakura Buddhism, Japanese Journal of Religious Studies, Vol.7, No.4, pp.261–291.
Fouladi, A. (2017), The Spirit of the Samurai: The Kamakura Bakufu, The Rise of the Bushido, and their role in Diplomacy, Vol.4, No.1.
Friday, K. (2010), The Futile Paradigm: In Quest of Feudalism in Early Medieval Japan, History Compass, 8/2, pp.179–196.
Frohlich, J. (2003), Land Administration in Medieval Japan; Ito no sho in Chikuzen Province, 1131–1336, History, Vol.88, No.1
Gernet, J. (1996), A History of Chinese Civilisation, Cambridge University Press, Cambridge.
Guanglin, L. (2015), Market Integration in China, AD 960–1644, IN A History of Market Performance: From Ancient Babylonia to the Modern World, Spek, R., Leeuwen, B., and Zanden, J. (Eds), Routledge, London.
Hane, M., and Perez, L. (2015), Premodern Japan: A Historical Survey, Westview Press.
Haring, D. (1952), Amami Gunto: Forgotten Islands, Far Eastern Survey, Vol.21, No.16, pp.170–172
Hayami, A. (2015), Japan's Industrious Revolution: Economic and Social Transformations in the Early Modern Period, Springer, Tokyo.
Hazard, B. (1967), The Formative Years of the Wako, Monumenta Nipponica, Vol.22, No.3/4, pp.260–277.
Henthorn, W. (1963), Korea, the Mongol Invasions, Leiden, passim
Ho, P. (1956), Early-Ripening Rice in Chinese History by Ping-Ti Ho, The Economic History Review, New Series, Vol.9, No.2, pp.200–218.
Ikegami. E. (1995), The Taming of the Samurai: Honorific Individualism and the Making of Modern Japan, Harvard University Press, Cambridge, Massachusetts.
Joseph, H. (1976), The 'Heike Monogatari': Buddhist Ethics and the Code of the Samurai, Folklore, Vol.87, No.1, pp.96–104.
Kabanoff, A. (2000), Ikkyu and Koans, IN The Koan: Texts and Contexts in Zen Buddhism, Heine, S., and Wright, D. (Ed), Oxford University Press, Oxford.
Katsumi, M. (1961), International Relations Between the 10th and 16th Centuries and the Development of the Japanese International Consciousness, Acta Asiatica, No. 2, pp. 85–86.
Levathes, L. (1994), When China Ruled the Seas: The Treasure Fleet of the Dragon Throne, 1405–1433, Simon & Schuster, New York.

Lieberman, L. (2009), Strange Parallels Southeast Asia in Global Context, c.800–1830, Volume 2: Mainland Mirrors: Europe, Japan, China, South Asia and the Islands, Cambridge University Press, Cambridge.

Liu, W. (2015), The Chinese Market Economy 1000–1500, State University of New York Press, Albany.

Martin, J. (1993), The Samurai Crab, Terra, Vol.31, No.4.

Mass, J. (1974), Warrior Government in Early Medieval Japan, Yale University Press, New Haven.

Mass, J. (1979), The Development of Kamakura Rule, 1180–1250, A History with Documents, Stanford University Press, Stanford, California.

Mass, J. (1995), The Kamakura Bakufu, IN Warrior Rule in Japan, Jansen, M. (Ed), Cambridge University Press, Cambridge.

Norman, E. (2000), Japan's Emergence as a Modern State: Political and Economic Problems of the Meiji Period, UBC Press, Vancouver, Toronto.

Nitobe, I. (2012), Bushido—Samurai Ethics and the Soul of Japan, Dover Publications INC, Mineola, New York.

Parker, J. (1999), Zen Buddhist Landscape Arts of Early Muromachi Japan (1336AD—1573AD), State University of New York Press, Albany.

Ramesh, S. (2018), The Rise of Empires: The Political Economy of Innovation, Palgrave Macmillan.

Reischauer, E., and Fairbank, J. (1960), A History of East Asian Civilisation, Vol.1: East Asia: The Great Tradition, Houghton Miffin Company, Boston.

Sakamaki, S. (1964), Ryukyu and Southeast Asia, Volume 23, Issue 3, pp.383–389.

Sakamaki, S. (1967), The Heike: From Defeat at Dannoura to a Golden Age in Ryukyu? The Journal of Asian Studies, Vol.27, Issue 1, pp.115–122.

Sato, E. (1974), The Early Development of the Shoen, IN Medieval Japan: Essays in Institutional History, Hall, J., and Mass, J. (Eds), Stanford University Press, Stanford, California.

Schirokauer, C., Brown, M., Lune, D., Gay, S. (2013), A Brief History of Chinese and Japanese Civilisations, Wadsworth Cengage Learning.

Schottenhammer, A. (2010), Preface, IN Trading Networks in Early Modern East Asia, Harrassowitz Verlag, Wiesbaden.

Schwartz, B. (1985), The World of Thought in Ancient China, The Belknap Press of Harvard University Press, Cambridge, Massachusetts.

Scogin, H. (1990), Between Heaven and Man: Contract and the State in Han Dynasty China, 63 S. Cal. L. Rev.1325.

Segal, E. (2011), Coins, Trade, and the State: Economic Growth in Early Medieval Japan, Harvard University Asia Center.

Shackley, M. (1986), Arms and the Men;14th Century Japanese Swordsmanship Illustrated by Skeletons from Zaimokuza, near Kamakura, Japan, World Archaeology, 18:2, pp.247–254.

Shoji, K. (1988), Japan and East Asia, IN The Cambridge History of Japan: Volume 3 Medieval Japan, Yamamura, K. (Ed), Cambridge University Press, Cambridge.

Shultz, E. (1999), Ch'oe Ch'unghon and Minamoto Yoritomo, Japan Review, No.11, pp.31–53.

So, B., and Su, J. (2000), Prosperity, Region, and Institutions in Maritime China: The South Fukien Pattern, 946–1368, Harvard University Asia Center, Harvard University Press, Cambridge, Massachusetts.

Steenstrup, C. (1991), A History of Law in Japan Until 1868, E. J. Brill, Leiden, The Netherlands.

Stone, J. (1995), Medieval Tendai Hongaku Thought and the New Kamakura Buddhism: A Reconsideration, Japanese Journal of Religious Studies, Vol.22, No.1/2, pp.17–48.

Susumu, I. (1990), The Decline of the Shoen System, IN The Cambridge History of Japan, Volume 3, Medieval Japan, Yamamura, K. (Ed), Cambridge University Press, Cambridge, United Kingdom.

Takashi, S. (2010), The Structure of Regional Society as Seen from Local Historical Documents: Focusing on the Southeastern Shoreline Areas, Song to Ming, IN Trading Networks in Early Modern East Asia, Schottenhammer, A. (Ed), Harrassowitz Verlag, Wiesbaden.

Takekoshi, Y. (2016), Rise and Fall of Taira and Minamoto Clans, Taylor & Francis Group.

Turnbull, S. (1977), The Samurai: A Military History, RoutledgeCurzon, Abingdon, Oxon.

Varley, H. (1969), Reviewed Work: Studies in The Institutional History of Early Modern Japan by John W. Hall and Marius Jansen, Harvard Journal of Asiatic Studies, Vol. 29, pp. 324–327.

Varley, P. (2000), Japanese Culture, University of Hawai'I Press, Honolulu.

Veeck, G., Pannell, C., Smith, C., and Huang, Y. (2011), China's Geography: Globalisation and the Dynamics of Political, Economic and Social Change, Rowman & Littlefield Publishers INC, London.

Von Glahn, R. (2013), Cycles of Silver in Chinese Monetary History, IN The Economy of Lower Yangzi Delta in Late Imperial China: Connecting money, markets and institutions, So, B. (Ed), Routledge, London.

Walker, R. (2014), Okinawa and the Ryukyu Islands, Tuttle Publishing.

Yamamura, K. (1974), The Decline of the Ritsuryo System: Hypotheses on Economic and Institutional Change, The Journal of Japanese Studies, Vol. 1, No.1, pp.3–37.

Yanaga, C. (1930), Source Materials in Japanese History: The Kamakura Period: 1192–1333, Journal of the American Oriental Society, Vol.59, No.1, pp.38–55.

Yasusuke, M. (1984), Le Society as of Civilization, Journal of Japanese Studies, Vol. 10, No. 2.

CHAPTER 3

The Muromachi Period (1333–1568) and the Azuchi–Momoyama Period (1568–1600)

Introduction

The rise to prominence of the Ashikaga Clan runs parallel with the Muromachi Period (1333 AD to 1568 AD) in Japanese history.[1] However, taking power and authority from the imperial court in Kyoto was not to be straightforward. It was in 1336 AD that Ashikaga Takauji invaded Kyoto but was driven back by the imperial forces of the Emperor Godaigo, commanded by Kitabatake Akiie.[2] However, Takauji was not to be beaten. He retreated to the island of Kyushu where he regrouped his forces and strengthened his position as leader. Takauji then returned to Kyoto in the summer of 1336 AD whereupon he faced the forces of the Emperor.[3] Takauji made victory certain by gaining the support of local peasant leaders and their warriors through the promise of vassal status.[4] All of the peasant families to which the peasant leaders and their warriors belonged were from the Nishigaoka area, and included the Kawashima, the Terado and the Daini clans.[5] The imperial court was split between a northern and a

[1] Kleiner, F. (2009), Gardner's Art Through the Ages: A Global History, Thomson-Wadworth, United Kingdom.

[2] Gay, S. (1986), The Kawashima: Warrior Peasants of Medieval Japan, Harvard Journal of Asiatic Studies, Vol. 46, No. 1, pp. 81–119.

[3] Ibid.

[4] Ibid.

[5] Ibid.

S. Ramesh, *China's Economic Rise*,
https://doi.org/10.1007/978-3-030-49811-5_3

southern dynasty between 1333 AD and 1392 AD.[6] But, the Emperor Godaigo attempted a coup named the Kemmu Restoration between 1334 AD and 1336 AD. The Kemmu Restoration was an attempt by the Emperor Godaigo to usurp political power away from the Shogun in order to assert his own personal rule.[7] The precedent upon which the Emperor Godaigo based the Kemmu Restoration was imperial restoration enacted by the Chinese Han Emperor Guangwu's Jianwu Restoration, in 25 AD, of the Eastern Han Dynasty.[8] However, the military strength of the Ashikaga Shogun proved too much for the forces of the imperial court.[9] In this case, the emperor fled to Yoshino; and it fell upon the third Ashikaga Shogun to settle the dispute between northern and southern dynasties by agreeing a compromise through which each dynasty would take turns with regard to the accession to become Emperor.[10] However, the northern dynasty continued to maintain its control over the accession, the compromise being unachievable, until the power of the Ashikaga Shoguns ended in 1573 AD.[11]

The Muromachi Period can be regarded as one of the periods in Japanese history which has been repeatedly misinterpreted.[12] In this case, the Muromachi Period had been the transition from the classical Heian Period (781 AD to 1191 AD) to a pre-modern Japan during the Tokugawa period.[13] However, the early interpretations of the Muromachi Period viewed Japanese development in the context of a cultural enlightenment accompanied by weak political structures and declining institutional capability.[14] In contrast to this view the Muromachi Period represented a time in which there were developments in Japanese institutions taking place through political and social changes.[15] Firstly, there was a deepening of the

[6] Dumoulin, H. (2005), Zen Buddhism: A History: Volume 2 Japan, World Wisdom, Bloomington, Indiana, US.

[7] Howland, D. (1996), Borders of Chinese Civilisation, Geography and History at Empire's End, Duke University Press, Durham & London.

[8] Ibid.

[9] Gay, S. (1986), The Kawashima: Warrior Peasants of Medieval Japan, Harvard Journal of Asiatic Studies, Vol. 46, No. 1, pp. 81–119.

[10] Ibid.

[11] Ibid.

[12] Hall, J. (1977), The Muromachi Age in Japanese History, IN 'Japan in the Muromachi Age', Hall, J., and Takeshi, T. (Ed), University of California Press, Berkeley.

[13] Ibid.

[14] Ibid.

[15] Ibid.

economic exploitation of the peasants by the samurai class, who were at the same time fighting amongst each other to extend their borders.[16] For example, in the year 1342 AD, the Muromachi Bakufu implemented the Gozan Josselsu system.[17] This was a way in which monasteries were organised.[18] And between 1339 AD and 1343 AD, the Shoin-Zukuri residential style replaced the Shinden-Zukuri residential style.[19] The Shoin-Zukuri was a new architectural and landscape design style introduced during the Muromachi Period into Japan which remained relatively unchanged until the introduction of western style architecture.[20] In the Shinden-Zukuri style, the landscape was defined and enclosed by buildings.[21] However, in the Shoin-Zukuri style, the main buildings were in the front with the main gardens in the back, with a degree of seclusion and privacy.[22] In the Shinden-Zukuri style, the gardens had been an area of semi-public recreation.[23] Another feature of Japanese gardens which changed during the Muromachi Periods was that ponds became smaller, becoming either fish pools or reflection pools.[24] At the same time, there were also prevailing moral values such as suffering in life would allow for either the attainment of the status of a bodhisattva upon death or to be reincarnated as Amida.[25] A bodhisattva is someone who only has value in spirituality, not in material things, in taking the path to enlightenment and Buddhahood.[26] On the

[16] Allinson, J., and Anievas, A. (2009) The uses and misuses of uneven and combined development: an anatomy of a concept, Cambridge Review of International Affairs, Vol. 22, No. 1, pp. 47–67, https://doi.org/10.1080/09557570802680132.

[17] Yamamura, K. (1988), Introduction, IN The Cambridge History of Japan, Volume 3, Medieval Japan, Yamamura, K. (Ed), Cambridge University Press, Cambridge.

[18] Collcutt, M. (1981), Five Mountains: The Rinzai Zen Monastic Institution in Medieval Japan, Harvard University Press, Cambridge, Massachusetts.

[19] Yamamura, K. (1988), Introduction, IN The Cambridge History of Japan, Volume 3, Medieval Japan, Yamamura, K. (Ed), Cambridge University Press, Cambridge.

[20] Pregill, P., and Volkman, N. (1999), Landscapes of the Rising Sun: Design and Planning in Japan, IN Landscapes in History: Design and Planning in the Eastern and Western Traditions, John Wiley & Sons, INC, New York.

[21] Ibid.

[22] Ibid.

[23] Ibid.

[24] Ibid.

[25] Ruch, B. (1992), Coping with Death: Paradigms of Heaven and Hell and the Six Realms in Early Literature and Painting, IN Flowering Traces: Buddhism in the Literary and Visual Arts of Japan, Sanford, J., LaFleur, W., and Nagatomi, M. (Eds), Princeton University Press, Princeton.

[26] Shantideva (2008), The Way of the Bodhisattva, Shambhala, Boston & London.

other hand, Amida refers to the awakening of the spiritual qualities of human beings and not their divinity.[27] However, although moral values were prominent during the Muromachi Period, there was a decline in the favour for traditional religions such as Esoteric Buddhism or Pure Land.[28] Nevertheless, there was a surge in the fervour for Zen Buddhism.[29] The difference between Zen Buddhism and the Pure Land Faith was that while the latter emphasised the power of Amida, the former emphasised strict discipline and responsibility at a personal level.[30] Zen Buddhism appealed to the Samurai elite whose personal behaviour was guided by the values of courage and personal control.[31] Moreover, if the Samurai elite had knowledge of Chinese Zen Buddhism, then this would only serve to fulfil their elevated status in society as few in Japanese society possessed such knowledge.[32] During the Muromachi Period, the geographical focus on Zen Buddhism shifted from Kamakura to Kyoto as the Muromachi Bakufu became based there in 1338 AD.[33] Other notable events also occurred during the Muromachi period.[34] The Battle of Shijo Nawate occurred in 1348 AD. It was a battle between the Northern and the Southern Court of Emperors for supremacy in Japan; and the Northern Court was victorious.[35] It was during the course of this battle that Kusunoki Masatsura was killed. Masatsura was a General loyal to the imperial house of the southern Japanese court; and he was defeated in battle by the forces of the Shogun.[36]

In the Muromachi Japan of the fifteenth century, the tea ceremony became formalised, and the Machi-gumi or communal organisations for internal security arose. And renga, a form of Japanese poetry,[37] became

[27] Yokota, J. (2000), Understanding Amida Buddha and the Pure Land Buddhism, Horota, D. (Eds), State University of New York, Albany.

[28] Kleiner, F. (2009), Gardner's Art Through the Ages: A Global History, Thomson-Wadworth, United Kingdom.

[29] Ibid.

[30] Ibid.

[31] Ibid.

[32] Ibid.

[33] Yamamura, K. (1988), Introduction, IN The Cambridge History of Japan, Volume 3, Medieval Japan, Yamamura, K. (Ed), Cambridge University Press, Cambridge.

[34] Ibid.

[35] Conlan, T. (2011), Nonbokucho Wars (1331–1392), The Encyclopedia of War, Wiley Online Library.

[36] Saito, H. (1912), A History of Japan, Kegan Paul, Trench, Trubner & Co, Ltd.

[37] Shirane, H. (2012), Traditional Japanese Literature: An Anthology, Beginnings to 1600, Columbia University Press, New York.

favoured by all classes of Japanese society.[38] There were also famines in 1431 AD and 1459 AD, the beginning of tally trade, the selling of goods on credit with written documentation being held by the buyer and the seller, with Korea and Ming China in 1418 AD and 1433 AD respectively. And while control by the Shogun had been a dominant feature of governance during the Muromachi Period, this ended abruptly in 1441 AD with the assassination of Shogun Yoshinori which occurred in association with the Ko-ikki disturbance.[39] This relates to the Ikki attacking money lenders and pawn brokers with the purpose of getting debts owed cancelled.[40] The Ikki was made up of Shinto priests, Buddhist monks, local nobles and peasant farmers.[41] The mistake made by Yoshinori was that he tried to control the power of the military governors or Shugo and was assassinated by one of them.[42] Yoshinori is recognised as being the last strong Ashikaga Shogun, and the role of Shogun deteriorated during the remainder of the Muromachi Period, although the Bakufu continued to thrive.[43] It was towards the end of the Muromachi Period that the European ships began to arrive in Asia. In this case, the Portuguese were the first Europeans to arrive in sixteenth century Japan, landing on the main island of Kyushu in 1543 AD.[44] Their arrival and the arrival of ships from other European countries in the subsequent future would present a threat to Japan as it ushered in the Tokugawa Period (1600 AD to 1868 AD). But the Tokugawa Shogunate would close Japan to all foreigners for over 200 years in order to keep it safe from the European threat. However, the Europeans, their ships and their military power returned to Japanese shores in the mid-nineteenth century. And the Tokugawa Shogunate was faced with the choices of either opening up Japan to trade and commerce with the barbarians, as the Japanese perceived the Europeans to be, or to be colonised by them. As a result of choosing the

[38] Yamamura, K. (1988), Introduction, IN The Cambridge History of Japan, Volume 3, Medieval Japan, Yamamura, K. (Ed), Cambridge University Press, Cambridge.

[39] Ibid.

[40] Turnbull, S. (1996), The Samurai: A Military History, Routledge, London.

[41] Tsang, C. (2007), War and Faith: Ikko Ikki in Late Muromachi Japan, Harvard University Asia Center.

[42] Schirokauer, C., Brown, M., Lurie, D., and Gay, S. (2013), A Brief History of Chinese and Japanese Civilisations, Wadsworth CENGAGE Learning.

[43] Ibid.

[44] Yamamura, K. (1988), Introduction, IN The Cambridge History of Japan, Volume 3, Medieval Japan, Yamamura, K. (Ed), Cambridge University Press, Cambridge.

former and having unfavourable treaties imposed upon them by the Europeans and the Americans, the national feeling ensured that the Tokugawa Shogunate and Bakufu could not survive. In this case, Japan had to undergo political reform, economic reform, cultural reform and industrialisation in order to make it a strong country capable of defending its borders against foreign aggressors.

Institutions of the Muromachi Age

The Muromachi Period was at its height during the time of the Shogun Yoshimitsu.[45] This Shogun was the third of the Muromachi Period, and he favoured autocratic rule in such a way that it was respected by the Shugo.[46] This was in contrast to the two subsequent Shoguns who favoured delegated rule under the Kanrei-Yoriai System.[47] Yoshimitsu's tenure as Shogun was between 1368 AD and 1394 AD; and having resigned as Prime Minister in 1395 AD, he became a Buddhist monk.[48] In this case, it is evident that Yoshimitsu favoured Buddhism over Japan's indigenous religion, Shintoism.[49] His favouritism of Buddhism as well as his leanings towards the ways of the Ying and the Yang, which originated in China and is still prevalent there, suggests a disdain for Japan's Shinto religion.[50] The Yang relates to positive energy, and the Yin relates to negative energy.[51] To achieve a harmonious existence between heaven and earth, a person must be able to achieve a balance between the Ying and the Yang.[52] Yoshimitsu's disdain for Shintoism, to which the imperial court and the Emperor were deeply attached, and his embracement of Buddhism are indicative of his attempt to circumvent, undermine and supplant the imperial lineage to his

[45] Takokoshi, Y. (2004), The Economic Aspects of the History of Civilisation of Japan, 2nd Edition, Routledge, London.

[46] Hall, J. (1995), The Muromachi Bakufu, IN Warriors in Japan, Jansen, M. (Ed), Cambridge University Press, Cambridge.

[47] Ibid.

[48] Akira, I., and Yamamura, K. (1992), Not for Lack of Will or Wile: Yoshimitsu's Failure to Supplant the Imperial Lineage, The Journal of Japanese Studies, Vol. 18, No. 1, pp. 45–78.

[49] Ibid.

[50] Ibid.

[51] Wang, R. (2012), Yinyang: The Way of Heaven and Earth in Chinese Thought and Culture, Cambridge University Press, Cambridge.

[52] Ibid.

own benefit.[53] The undermining of the Japanese Emperor and the imperial court was to some extent achieved by Yoshimitsu seeking a strong alignment with China, culturally and religiously as well as through tally trade.[54] Chinese cultural intrusions at this time included the introduction of Chinese Ming Dynasty script into the Japanese language.[55] Perhaps, by embracing China in this way, Yoshimitsu was trying to denigrate the authority of the Japanese Emperor by lowering his status to that of 'King of Japan', a title given by the Chinese imperial court to the ruler of a vassal state. Moreover, Yoshimitsu's attitude was also shared by the Kuge.[56] In Japanese society, the Kuge was represented by the organisation of the civil nobility.[57]

During his tenure as Shogun, Yoshimitsu also managed to entwine the governance structures and the institutions of the Japanese imperial court with that of the Bakufu. Therefore, Court officials were integrated into the Shogunate, becoming subject to the Shogun, and institutions were either newly established or changed from their previous nature.[58] Furthermore, the times of the Shogun Yoshimitsu were also ones in which the nobility and the Court became poorer as their land and property holdings had been reduced up to at least one tenth of what it had been in previous times.[59] However, following the death of Yoshimitsu in 1408 AD, his son Yoshimochi began to undo the work of Yoshimitsu by making appointments based only on merit and tradition.[60] This had the effect of separating the governance structures and the institutions of the Japanese court and that of the Bakufu.[61] Bakufu officials would be appointed by merit and court officials on the basis of tradition. Therefore, in the Muromachi Period, the foundations of a modern Japan were continuing

[53] Akira, I., and Yamamura, K. (1992), Not for Lack of Will or Wile: Yoshimitsu's Failure to Supplant the Imperial Lineage, The Journal of Japanese Studies, Vol. 18, No. 1, pp. 45–78.

[54] Ibid.

[55] Ibid.

[56] Ibid.

[57] Kiley, C. (1982), The Imperial Court As a Legal Authority in the Kamakura Age, IN Court and Bakufu in Japan, Essays in Kamakura History, Mass, J. (Ed), Stanford University Press, Stanford, California.

[58] Takokoshi, Y. (2004), The Economic Aspects of the History of Civilisation of Japan, 2nd Edition, Routledge, London.

[59] Ibid.

[60] Akira, I., and Yamamura, K. (1992), Not for Lack of Will or Wile: Yoshimitsu's Failure to Supplant the Imperial Lineage, The Journal of Japanese Studies, Vol. 18, No. 1, pp. 45–78.

[61] Ibid.

to be laid as in previous times. However, in this context the Muromachi Period was not anything new to Japanese civilisation in its own right.[62]

Land tenure also experienced rapid changes during the Muromachi Period. Before the period, land ownership under the Shoen system dating from the mid-eleventh century AD had lain with the nobility as well as with religious institutions such as monasteries and temples.[63] The Shoen proprietors of the land determined who lived on the land, who tilled the land and who paid tax. However, the monopoly of the nobility and religious institutions over land tenure via the Shoen system began to denigrate significantly by the middle of the fifteenth century.[64] But this shift of land ownership and management to powerful local warriors had already gotten under way during the civil war stage which had occurred at the start of the Muromachi Period, between the northern and the southern courts.[65] Nevertheless, it was during the Kamakura Bakufu period that local provincial warriors known as Koku-Jin had been appointed by the Bakufu to look after the land in cases where the appropriate Shoen proprietor had been absent and unable to perform his duties.[66] This transition in land tenure occurred at the same time as another trend. This was related to land which had been forest or waste land before being brought into cultivation for the first time.[67] In this case, the management of the land was left in the hands of local people who had previously worked for the Shoen Proprietors.[68] By the end of the fifteenth century, the Shoen proprietors had signed contracts with local warriors to manage their land for them.[69] However, the contracts were more in the favour of the local warriors than the Shoen proprietors. So, the contracts actually represented a sort of transfer of ownership of the land from the Shoen proprietors to the local warlords.[70] At an institutional level the shift in land tenure from the

[62] Takokoshi, Y. (2004), The Economic Aspects of the History of Civilisation of Japan, 2nd Edition, Routledge, London.

[63] Nagahara, Y. (1981), Daimyo and Kandaka System, IN Japan Before Tokugawa: Political Consolidation and Economic Growth, 1500–1650, Hall, S., Nagahara, K., and Yamamura, K. (Eds), Princeton University Press, Princeton, New Jersey.

[64] Ibid.

[65] Ibid.

[66] Ibid.

[67] Ibid.

[68] Ibid.

[69] Ibid.

[70] Nagahara, Y. (1981), Daimyo and Kandaka System, IN Japan Before Tokugawa: Political Consolidation and Economic Growth, 1500–1650, Hall, S., Nagahara, K., and Yamamura, K. (Eds), Princeton University Press, Princeton, New Jersey.

nobility and religious institutions to the local warriors represented a shift of power from the nobility and the imperial court to the local warriors and the Bakufu. However, despite the loss of land tenure of religious institutions, Zen priests were consulted by the Bakufu.[71] This was because Zen had been made an official religion of the Muromachi Shogunate as Zen was in favour with the Ashikaga Shoguns.[72] But, Zen priests may not have had large land holdings anyway. The shift of power was emphasised by the fact that the local warriors and the Bakufu had a greater capacity to raise tax revenues, pay warriors and thus were in a stronger position to raise armies than were the nobility. However, this transformation in land tenure also gave local Daimyos greater power to break away from the Bakufu. Nevertheless, the Bakufu managed this situation almost successfully by devolving power to the local Daimyos but in turn demanding loyalty from them at the threat of military enforcement if required.

The Muromachi Bakufu and Shogunate inherited the legal code embedded in the Joei Shikimoku from the Kamakura period.[73] The Joei Shikimoku was a list of legal precedents which had occurred as a result of cases being brought before a Shogunal court and upon which judgements had been made.[74] It was on the basis of the precedents in the Joei Shikimoku that new rules were to be formulated.[75] In this case, while the Ashikaga Shoguns recognised the prevailing authority of the Joei, they added supplementary edicts to it.[76] One of the major additions to be made to the Joei Shikimoku was the Kenmu Shikimoku by Shogun Ashikaga Takauji in 1336 AD.[77] It was formulated on the basis of seventeen articles, supplemented by edicts and legal rules.[78] The roots of the Kenmu Shikimoku were in the 'Constitution' written by Prince Shotoku in the

[71] Mitchelhill, J. (2003), Castles of the Samurai: Power and Beauty, Kodansha International.

[72] Ibid.

[73] Deal, W. (2006), Handbook to Life in Medieval and Early Modern Japan, Oxford University Press, Oxford.

[74] Steenstrup, C. (1991), A History of Law in Japan Until 1868, E.J. Brill, Leiden, The Netherlands.

[75] Ibid.

[76] Ibid.

[77] O'Haley, J. (2016), Law's Political Foundations, Rivers, Rifles, Rice and Religion, Edward Elgar Publishing, Cheltenham, United Kingdom.

[78] Ibid.

seventh century AD.[79] Prince Shotoku ruled as regent during the reign of Empress Suiko, his aunt.[80] Shotoku recognised the emergence of the Japanese national consciousness and embraced the traditional Shinto Japanese religion. However, he also promoted the religious cultural influences from imperial China and India, the Tao of Confucianism and the Buddhist Dharma respectively.[81] It is apparent that Shotoku was a follower of the policies of Emperor Wen Ti of Sui Dynasty China who reigned from 581 AD to 604 AD.[82] The Emperor Wen Ti initially favoured Buddhism and Confucianism as well as Taoism, but to a lesser extent than the others, as his tools to unify northern China.[83] However, he later turned to Buddhism as the means with which to unify the Sui Dynasty.[84] Moreover, Yang Jian had been a high ranking bureaucrat in the Northern Zhou Dynasty but by usurping power he was able to defeat the Ch'I dynasty, unify northern China and become the Emperor Wen Ti, through the usurpation of power in the Northern Zhou Dynasty in which he had been a high ranking bureaucrat, northern China became unified.[85] Although Buddhism had been the tool by which the Sui Dynasty had become unified, during the T'ang Dynasty, it fell out of favour with Taoism taking the role of state religious ideology.[86] Moreover, the Emperor most closely identified with Taoism during the T'ang Dynasty was Wutsung (841 AD to 846 AD).[87] The displacement of Buddhism by the Taoists now meant that Buddhists were economically persecuted with their land and valuables being expropriated by the state.[88] However, by the time of the Sung

[79] Steenstrup, C. (1991), A History of Law in Japan Until 1868, E.J. Brill, Leiden, The Netherlands.

[80] Kitagawa, K. (1974), The Japanese 'Kokutai' (National Community) History and Myth, History of Religions, Vol. 13, No. 3, pp. 209–226.

[81] Ibid.

[82] Ibid.

[83] Ibid.

[84] Slatyer, W. (2014), Life/Death Rhythms of Capitalist Regimes – Debt Before Dishonour, Timetable of World Dominance 1400 to 2100 AD, Part 1: Historical Ruler Cycles, Partridge Publishing, Singapore.

[85] Yamashita, M., and Lindesay, W. (2007), The Great Wall: From Beginning to End, Sterling Publishing, New York.

[86] Slatyer, W. (2014), Life/Death Rhythms of Capitalist Regimes – Debt Before Dishonour, Timetable of World Dominance 1400 to 2100 AD, Part 1: Historical Ruler Cycles, Partridge Publishing, Singapore.

[87] Ibid.

[88] Ibid.

Dynasty, elements of Buddhism and Taoism had become embedded into Confucian ideology.[89] Some in the literature take the view that the rigid application of neo-Confucianism by the Chinese state to its policies after the thirteenth century AD acted as a constraint on the development of Chinese culture until the twentieth century.[90]

Despite the changes in the nature of the adoption of state ideology following the end of the Sui Dynasty, during its time the mix of adoption of Taoism, Buddhism and Confucianism gave the Emperor an almost divine status which was formalised by the use of religious symbols.[91] The divine status of the Emperor in the Chinese context was transposed into the Japanese context by Prince Shotoku in the writing the 'Seventeen Article Constitution'.[92] In this case in the ensuing years, the principle of the Tao became synonymous with the authority of the Emperor but secondary to it.[93] This was perhaps because the Emperor was a direct descendant of the sun goddess coming to be regarded as akitsu-kami.[94] In this case, the role of the Emperor was more of a religious one, his power and authority on earth being exercised and delegated to a regent who would over the years transform into the Shogun. The separation of religious and political powers between the Emperor and the Regent, developed in the seventh century AD, based on Shinto-Confucian principles came to be known as the 'Ritsuryo State'.[95] This formed the corner stone of governance of the Japanese state in the ensuing centuries until the Meiji Restoration when there was a major upheaval in both Japanese governance and institutions.

The previous discussion suggests that Chinese cultural influences on the development of institutions in Japan continued to be strong during the Muromachi Period. Furthermore, as previously discussed, the roots of the Kenmu Shikmoku, an addition to the Joei made during the Muromachi Period and written by the Shogun Ashikaga Takauji, lay in Prince Shotoku's 'Constitution'. This was based on contemporary Chinese practices. The Constitution dictated the ideal behaviours and attitudes which should

[89] Ibid.

[90] Ibid.

[91] Wright, A. (1957), The Formation of Sui Ideology, IN Chinese Thought and Institutions, Fairbank, J. (Ed), University of Chicago Press, 1957, Chicago.

[92] Kitagawa, K. (1974), The Japanese 'Kokutai' (National Community) History and Myth, History of Religions, Vol. 13, No. 3, pp. 209–226.

[93] Ibid.

[94] Ibid.

[95] Ibid.

prevail amongst Japan's warrior class.[96] Moreover, the seventeen articles of the 'constitution' covered diverse subjects ranging with a narrow focus to personal habits while at a broader level dealing with how subjects should be treated by the ruler.[97] In addition to the Kenmu Shikmoku, the Muromachi Period was notable in its contribution to the development of Japan's legal code with the implementation of the renza and the enza.[98] These formed the principles of joint community responsibility for criminal behaviour by a community member.[99] The premise of the renza and the enza was that crime could be reduced and even prevented if punishment was not restricted to the committer but was equally applicable to the community in which he/she resided. Therefore, there was an incentive for the members of the community to ensure that troublesome individuals were kept in check.[100] Just as the enza and the renza were aimed at crime prevention, the Muromachi Bakufu also established a policy, the Kenka Ryoseibai, which would act as a disincentive for disputes to remain unresolved. In this case, according to the Kenka Ryoseibai, both parties to a dispute would be held equally accountable.[101] So in the case of a land dispute between two Daimyos, if the dispute could not be settled mutually between the Daimyos, then the ownership of the disputed land would be transferred to the Muromachi Bakufu.[102]

Following the Onin War (1467 AD to 1477 AD) which resulted because of disagreements amongst the ruling families about Shogunal succession, the central authority of the Muromachi Bakufu collapsed by the mid-fifteenth century.[103] This disintegration in the central governance of Japan meant that it became impossible for a central legal system, the supplemented Joei Shikmoku, to be equally applicable to the whole of Japan. In this case, the local laws of the Daimyos supplanted the centrally applicable Joei Shikmoku allowing for a variation in the application of a legal structure between one part of Japan and another part of Japan. The local legal codes of the Daimyos were known as the Bunkokubo codes, but

[96] Deal, W. (2006), Handbook to Life in Medieval and Early Modern Japan, Oxford University Press, Oxford.

[97] Ibid.

[98] Ibid.

[99] Ibid.

[100] Ibid.

[101] Ibid.

[102] Ibid.

[103] Ibid.

though variable from one domain to another, still depended on their legitimacy by having the Joei Shikimoku as the legal foundation.[104] The local legal codes of the Daimyos regulated the behaviour of people residing in their domains. Elements of the local legal code may have been dedicated to the rights of commoners to cultivate the land or the rights of people living in a domain to travel in and out of it.[105] However, as the Muromachi period came to an end and the Azuchi–Momoyama Period began, the end of the Muromachi Shogunate meant that Japan was entering into a new period of lawlessness and even local Daimyo laws were difficult to administer for any length of time.[106] This was because of the lack of a strong central government, the Daimyos would fight each other such that domains would not be in the hands of one Daimyo for long.[107] However, during these 'dark' times in which there was an unstable and variable legal code throughout Japan, the Samurai relied upon a code of honour, the Bushi Code, as a means of self-regulation amongst themselves.[108] Nevertheless, in general during the Azuchi–Momoyama Period, there was widespread criminal activity as well as the widespread abuse of land rights.[109] However, the symbols of strength, power and authority during this period were the castles of the Samurai.[110] The three to four decades of instability during the Azuchi–Momoyama Period were brought to an end in 1600 AD with the start of the longest period of stability and economic development in Japanese history, the start of the Tokugawa Period in which Tokugawa Ieyasu was able to re-establish the central control over Japan by the Shogunate.[111] As such the Tokugawa Bakufu implemented a new national system of legal codification which developed as Japanese society also developed.[112] In the Muromachi Period, in addition to the supplementation of the Joei, other institutional changes also took place. For example, the Mandokoro or the Administrative Council[113] took

[104] Ibid.
[105] Ibid.
[106] Ibid.
[107] Ibid.
[108] Ibid.
[109] Ibid.
[110] Mitchelhill, J. (2003), Castles of the Samurai: Power and Beauty, Kodansha International.
[111] Ibid.
[112] Ibid.
[113] Hall, J. (1995), The Muromachi Bakufu, IN Warrior Rule in Japan, Jansen, M. (Ed), Cambridge University Press, Cambridge.

responsibility for the Monchujo. The latter had been set up in the house of the founder of the Kamakura Bakufu, Minamoto no Yoritomo, in the twelfth century AD.[114] The function of the Monchujo was the recording of decisions made by Yoritomo in the cases brought before him.[115] In this case, the function of the Board of Enquiry was brought to the level of record keeping.[116] Furthermore, while the post of deputy military governor, the Shugodai, had been in existence during the Kamakura Period, it became a formal part of the administrative structure of the Ashikaga Shogunate during the Muromachi Period.[117] The Shugodai was subordinate to the Shugo, the military governors, and lived in the provinces in their place. This is because as far back as the latter part of the thirteenth century, the Shugo were only in the province of their jurisdiction for a little time.[118] And in this case, their deputies, the Shugodai, had to take up a semi-permanent residence in the provinces on their behalf. The other institutional changes which occurred during the Muromachi Period were that tandai or the regional deputies of the Bakufu were placed in locations of strategic importance to the Bakufu including Kyushu and north-western Honshu.[119]

Muromachi Commerce, Trade and the Imjin War

During Muromachi times, there were both internal and external Japanese trade.[120] Furthermore, the nature of this trade was that it was either official, semi-official or unofficial and legal or illegal.[121] At the start of the Muromachi Period in the fourteenth century, trade was semi-official, although by the fifteenth century, it had become official trade.[122] However, this official trade was tribute or kango trade with Japanese acquiescence as a vassal state of China which was in turn recognised as the centre of the

[114] Lu, D. (1997), Japan: A Documentary History, M.E. Sharpe, New York.

[115] Ibid.

[116] Deal, W. (2006), Handbook to Life in Medieval and Early Modern Japan, Oxford University Press, Oxford.

[117] Ibid.

[118] Ibid.

[119] Ibid.

[120] Lidin, O. (2002), Tanegashima: The Arrival of Europe in Japan, Nordic Institute of Asian Studies, Monograph Series, No. 90.

[121] Ibid.

[122] Ibid.

world. This ideology came into being during the Shogunate of Yoshimitsu, the third Shogun.[123] Under his auspices, tributary status was re-established with Ming China.[124] Moreover, between 1401 AD and 1547 AD, Muromachi Japan sent a total of nineteen trade missions to Ming China.[125] However, the tribute trade was discontinued under the Shogunate of Yoshimochi, the fourth Shogun, after whom the trade was restarted during the Shogunate of Yoshinori, the sixth Shogun.[126] Nevertheless, in the transition from one Shogun to another, trade was not singly undertaken on behalf of the state but also for the benefit of temples and Daimyos.[127] Moreover, the control of trade began to be dominated by two clans, the Hosokawa and the Ouchi, using their harbours at Sakai and Hakata to send ships to the Chinese port of Ning-Po.[128] At the time, Ning-Po was China's chief port, housing both a trading office as well as an inn for foreigners.[129] The tax on imported goods at Ning-Po was then sent to Nanking, via the trading office.[130] Enormous profits were being made by Japanese merchants, fifty years before the Shogun Yoshiharu, under the Shogun Yoshimasa such that overtrading was taking place merely to secure the profits.[131] The overtrading may have resulted in the unnecessary trading of resources with China which could have been put to better use in Japan. In this case, the Shogun Yoshimasa temporarily stopped trading activities between Japan and China. In later times when Japan was ruled by the Shogun Yoshiharu, Ning-Po was the site of much mercantile trading activity when trade between Japan and China was resumed. However, at the start of the sixteenth century AD, incidents began to occur at the port of Ning-Po, giving way to piracy which brought tribute trade to an end by the mid-sixteenth century AD, remaining closed for the remainder of the Ming dynasty.[132] The troubles at Ning-Po began with the arrival of a Buddhist monk, sent by the Shogun Yoshiharu and an envoy sent by the

[123] Ibid.

[124] Batten, B. (2003), To The Ends of Japan, Premodern Frontiers, Boundaries and Interactions, University of Hawai'I Press, Honolulu.

[125] Ibid.

[126] Lidin, O. (2002), Tanegashima: The Arrival of Europe in Japan, Nordic Institute of Asian Studies, Monograph Series, No. 90.

[127] Ibid.

[128] Ibid.

[129] Ibid.

[130] Ibid.

[131] Ibid.

[132] Ibid.

Ouchi family.[133] The Ouchi family envoy seized the Shogun's envoy and razed Ning-Po to the ground, murdering its Chinese governor in the process.[134] The Ouchi family were out of the 'jurisdiction' of the Shogun, and there was nothing he could do in order to exact retribution. Moreover, the Ming Emperor also sought to exact retribution on the Ouchi family in 1531 AD by sending a squadron of warships to Tsushima.[135] However, the fleet was forced to disperse upon engagement at Tsushima through the intervention of the Ouchi deputy high constable. It would not be till 1548 AD that friendly relations would be restored between China and Japan following the despatch of an envoy to the Ming Court by the Ouchi family as well the despatch of a Buddhist monk from Muromachi.[136] Following the reconciliation between the Ming Court and Muromachi Japan, a smaller amount of maritime trade in comparison to previous times began to take place between the two countries. By mutual consent, the number of trading vessels was limited to 3 and the crew of each vessel was set at a limit of 300.[137] Moreover, tallies were also issued, establishing the amount of goods which could be exported and imported by the two countries. However, by the mid-sixteenth century, the complexion of Chinese trade had begun to change with the arrival of the first of the Europeans, the Portuguese.[138] In this case, there must have been some reduction in the volume of trade between China and Japan as a result of Chinese–European trade. After the death of the shogun Yoshimoto, there was an increasing attempt to unify Japan by the Oda clan and its head, Oda Nobunaga.[139] The latter was not inclined to facilitate reopening and increasing trade with China, despite having a love of Chinese things. By 1562, Oda Nobunaga had signed a treaty with the founder of the Tokugawa Shogunate, Tokugawa Ieyasu.[140] It was Ieyasu who set in stone the institutional role of the Shogunate for it endured after his death in

[133] Kikuchi, D. (2018), Japanese History, Books on Demand.

[134] Ibid.

[135] Ibid.

[136] Ibid.

[137] Ibid.

[138] Wills, J., Cranmer-Byng, J., Peterson, W., and Witek, J. (2011), China and Maritime Europe, 1500–1800, Trade, Settlement, Diplomacy and Missions, Cambridge University Press, Cambridge.

[139] Ibid.

[140] Pitelka, M. (2016), Spectacular Accumulation, Material Culture, Tokugawa Ieyasu and Samurai Sociability, University of Hawai'I Press.

1616 AD until the Meiji Restoration in 1868 AD.[141] However, also towards the end of the sixteenth century, Toyotomi Hideyoshi was also intent on invading Korea and China.[142] Hideyoshi was a Daimyo who wanted to be Shogun as well as unify Japan.[143]

Under Nobunga, Hideyoshi had been General Hashiba Hideyoshi.[144] However, because of his tactical brilliance and skill in siege warfare, the Emperor had bestowed upon him the surname of Toyotomi.[145] Upon the death of Nobunga in 1582, not only did Hideyoshi avenge his death but he also continued the process of the pacification and the reunification of Japan.[146] Nevertheless, Hideyoshi was also intent on conquering neighbouring Korea and Ming China. For Hideyoshi, the conquest of Korea and China was merely an extension of the project of the national reunification of Japan.[147] However, there may also have been an economic need for Japan to control Korea in the context of acquiring Korean resources. This reason for Japan's invasion of Korea may be pertinent especially because of Korean efforts to stem trade with Japan in the sixteenth century, leading to cutting off ties with the Muromachi Bakufu at one point.[148] This may have been due to Japanese violence towards the Koreans at the three open Korean ports, Japanese identity fraud regarding trading permits and Japanese piracy.[149] In this case, Hideyoshi sent an army of 150,000 to 200,000 men from Japanese Kyushu to Korean Pusan in May 1592 with the intention of conquering the Korean Peninsula before China proper.[150] But in the long term Hideyoshi was unable to conquer Korea or China,

[141] Sadler, A. (1978), Shogun: The Life of Tokugawa Ieyasu, Tuttle Publishing, Tokyo.

[142] Hanson, V., and Curtis, K. (2010), Voyages in World History, Volume 1: To 1600, Wadsworth, Boston, USA.

[143] Ibid.

[144] Rockstein, E. (1993), Strategic and Operational Aspects of Japan's Invasion of Korea, 1592–1598, AD-A266 906, The United States Naval War College.

[145] Ibid.

[146] Ibid.

[147] Manji, K. (2015), The Imjin Waeran: Contrasting the First and the Second Invasions of Korea, IN The East Asian War, 1592–1598: International Relations, Violence and Memory, Lewis, J. (Ed), Routledge, London.

[148] Robinson, K. (2015), Violence, trade and impostors in Korean-Japanese Relations, 1510–1609, IN The East Asian War, 1592–1598: International Relations, Violence and Memory, Lewis, J. (Ed), Routledge, London.

[149] Ibid.

[150] Hawley, S. (2014), The Imjin War: Japan's Sixteenth-century Invasion of Korea and Attempt to Conquer China, Conquistador Press.

because by acting together both countries were stronger than the Japanese militarily. However, in the short term, the Japanese warriors were able to occupy the capital Seoul and to overrun much of the country within three months of landing.[151] The reason for the Japanese success was that the Japanese warriors were more experienced at waging warfare domestically than the Korean warriors. Furthermore, the Japanese warriors were also at the edge technologically in comparison to their Korean counterparts, having acquired muskets from the Portuguese.[152] However, the entry into the war of the fleet of Turtle ships under the command of the Korean Admiral Yi turned the tide in the favour of Korea.[153] The Turtle ships had decks covered by a curved iron roof which also housed long metal spikes which prevented Japanese warriors from boarding.[154] Moreover, the Turtle ships also had cannon and firearms with which they were able to decimate the Japanese fleet.[155] Furthermore, the Korean ships were split into an upper and a lower deck. The latter housed the oarsmen who powered the ships and the former housed the fighting men.[156] In July 1592 AD, Admiral Yi destroyed 120 Japanese ships at the Battle of Hansan along with the 100,000 warriors which these ships were carrying.[157] Later in 1592 AD, Yi's fleet was able to destroy a further 133 Japanese ships.[158] As a result, the land-based Japanese army may have experienced shortages of men and materials because the Japanese fleet was unable to efficiently resupply it. Moreover, the Korean fleet was able to reign supreme over the sea lanes and thus able to engage and destroy Japanese vessels. The Koreans were more technologically advanced than the Japanese at sea, while the Japanese were more technologically advanced in terms of having muskets and better swords than either the Koreans or the Chinese.[159] The Koreans, monks, civilian militia and remnants of government forces subsequently began to

[151] Perez, L. (2013), Japan at War: An Encyclopedia, ABC-CLIO, Oxford, UK.

[152] Ibid.

[153] Ibid.

[154] Ibid.

[155] Ibid.

[156] Jacob, F. (2017), Technological Spatialities: Then Impact of geography and Technology during the Imjin War (1592–

1598), IN War and geography: The Spatiality of Organised Mass Violence, Danielsson, S., and Jacob, F. (Eds), Verlag Ferdinand Schoningh GmbH & Co, Paderborn.

[157] Perez, L. (2013), Japan at War: An Encyclopedia, ABC-CLIO, Oxford, UK.

[158] Ibid.

[159] Jacob, F. (2017), Technological Spatialities: Then Impact of geography and Technology during the Imjin War (1592–1598), IN War and geography: The Spatiality of Organised

wage a guerrilla campaign against the occupying Japanese, and they were aided by the arrival of soldiers from the Ming Court in China.[160] The first batch of Chinese soldiers arrived in August 1592 AD. These soldiers represented a force of 5000 men under the command of General Zhao Chengxun.[161] By this time the imperial Korean Court had fled further inland on the Korean peninsula to Yalu, before raising a call to the Ming Court for military support against the Japanese onslaught. However, the force of men under General Chengxun was not sufficient in number to thwart the Japanese offensive. This was particularly because of the deadly musket fire power reigning upon the Ming troops from the Japanese. In this case, the Ming Court realised that it itself was vulnerable to invasion by the Japanese.[162] In this case, the Ming Court despatched a further 35,000 of its soldiers to the Korean peninsula under the command of General Li Rusong, who had recently returned to China following an offensive against the Mongols.[163] Not only was Li Rusong an experienced soldier having fought in over 100 battles, but he was also the eldest son of the most prominent and favoured Ming generals of the times, General Li Chengliang.[164] The latter was well known for eliminating the threat to the Ming Court by the mutiny of Pubei and Liu Dongyang.[165] Pubei was a Mongol leader who had joined the Ming army in the North-East and, together with his men and a Chinese officer named Liu Dongyang, plotted a mutiny against the Ming and its officials in the context of not having been paid, back pay.[166] Thus, the Li family were not only militarily oriented but were closely linked to Korea by claiming heritage from it.[167] The

Mass Violence, Danielsson, S., and Jacob, F. (Eds), Verlag Ferdinand Schoningh GmbH & Co, Paderborn.

[160] Perez, L. (2013), Japan at War: An Encyclopedia, ABC-CLIO, Oxford, UK.

[161] Jacob, F. (2017), Technological Spatialities: Then Impact of geography and Technology during the Imjin War (1592–
1598), IN War and geography: The Spatiality of Organised Mass Violence, Danielsson, S., and Jacob, F. (Eds), Verlag Ferdinand Schoningh GmbH & Co, Paderborn.

[162] Ibid.

[163] Ibid.

[164] Swope, K. (2009), A Dragon's Head And a Serpents Tail, Ming China and the First Great East Asian War, 1592–1598, University of Oklahoma Press, Norman.

[165] Ibid.

[166] Lorge, P. (2005), War, Politics and Society in Early Modern China, 900–1795, Routledge, New York.

[167] Swope, K. (2009), A Dragon's Head And a Serpents Tail, Ming China and the First Great East Asian War, 1592–1598, University of Oklahoma Press, Norman.

despatch to Korea of General Li Rusong signalled the concern of the Ming Court for its own safety from Japanese invasion at the time. In addition to sending troops to bolster Korean defences and counter offensives, the Ming Court was also concerned with its own coastal defences.[168] Like the Japanese, the Ming also had access to musket and cannon. And in order to strengthen coastal defences, the Ming despatched regular troops from Nanjing in order to assist local troops and militia with the mounting of cannon along coastal areas.[169] However, strengthening China's coastal defences were not the only strategy employed by the Ming to defend China from a Japanese onslaught. Others included the building of ships fitted with mounted cannons and three barrelled guns, and the use of long spears to maim and kill the enemy as well as smoke to blind them.[170] Furthermore, an additional 40,000 to 50,000 troops were to be sent to coastal port cities in the north-east of China in order to guard them from Japanese attack.[171]

As a result of the combined strength of the Ming troops and the Korean guerrillas, by May 1593 AD, the Japanese were forced back to the southern coastal areas of Korea.[172] However, as the Japanese were withdrawing from Seoul, they engaged oncoming Chinese troops at the Battle of Pyokchegwan which the Chinese and the Koreans lost.[173] However, this was only a temporary setback because the Japanese lost a subsequent battle at the Korean stronghold at Haengju.[174] A second Japanese invasion of the Korean peninsula followed in 1597 AD following the breakdown in negotiations between the two sides.[175] However, on this occasion the Koreans were better prepared to ward off the Japanese threat. Nevertheless, when Hideyoshi died in 1598 AD, two things happened. Firstly, the Japanese military were withdrawn from the Korean peninsula. And secondly, there was a conflict between Japan's Daimyos for control of the

[168] Ibid.

[169] Ibid.

[170] Ibid.

[171] Ibid.

[172] Perez, L. (2013), Japan at War: An Encyclopedia, ABC-CLIO, Oxford, UK.

[173] Rockstein, E. (1993), Strategic and Operational Aspects of Japan's Invasion of Korea, 1592–1598, AD-A266 906, The United States Naval War College.

[174] Ibid.

[175] Perez, L. (2013), Japan at War: An Encyclopedia, ABC-CLIO, Oxford, UK.

Shogunate. Tokugawa Ieyasu won this conflict and went on to establish the Tokugawa Shogunate.[176]

The difficulties of trading with China posed problems for the Japanese economy, at the time. Perhaps, it was partly due to economic problems in Japan that Hideyoshi wanted to conquer not only Korea but also China. Japanese economic problems arose because Japan depended on China for its currency, Chinese copper coins, and without trade the Japanese economy was being deprived of its money supply. Without money a sophisticated trading economy was not possible, and this constrained the growth and development of a sophisticated Japanese urban economy.[177] Goods could not be traded conveniently by using money as a medium of exchange, but only through barter. The effect of this would be to increase merchant's costs as well as to lower their profits as the market would have shrunk. This was because of the inability to trade over long distances as this would have required a substantial number of goods to be transported over long distances for barter, incurring substantial transport costs. And, Japan did not begin to mint its own currency until the latter part of the fifteenth century AD.[178] Therefore, in order to make up for the shortfall of currency in Japan, once tribute trade had come to an end, private trade took its place.[179] Previously, private trade had been stopped because the Shogun Yoshimitsu had been granted the title of 'King of Japan' by the Ming Court of China; and only tributary trade between Ming China and the Muromachi Bakufu had been permitted. The cessation and the prevention of private trade was a means by which the Shogun Yoshimitsu could control the Daimyos, who without the ability to trade would not be able to accumulate wealth and power.[180] Moreover, the lack of private trade and only tributary trade may have facilitated the acknowledgement by the Daimyos of the sovereignty and the power of Yoshimitsu as Shogun.[181] But, when private trade itself had been forbidden, trade was no more and piracy and pillage prevailed with copper Chinese coins being in

[176] Ibid.

[177] Lidin, O. (2002), Tanegashima: The Arrival of Europe in Japan, Nordic Institute of Asian Studies, Monograph Series, No. 90.

[178] Ibid.

[179] Ibid.

[180] Kang, E. (2016), Diplomacy and Ideology in Japanese-Korean Relations – From the 15th to the 18th century, St Martin's Press INC, NYC.

[181] Ibid.

great demand.[182] However, Muromachi Japan was able to stop the piracy in the fifteenth century AD at the request of not only the Yi dynasty of Korea but also at the behest of Ming dynasty China.[183] But piracy increased in the sixteenth century AD especially in the East China Sea, with the pirates being mainly Chinese rather than Japanese.[184] This is evidenced in some way by the fact that when Ming China enforced a ban on foreign travel by the Chinese in 1567 AD, piracy in the East China Sea began to decline.[185] This decline was in conjunction with actions taken in Japan in the late sixteenth century AD by Toyotomi Hideyoshi, the Japanese overlord, to tackle piracy[186] When the Shogun Yoshimitsu died, his son Yoshimochi discontinued a number of his father's policies.[187] In this case, Yoshimochi shunned the imperial Chinese court, gave more power to the Daimyos and also stopped the tally trade with China.[188]

In his time, Ashikaga Yoshimitsu who was the third Shogun during the Muromachi Period, from 1358 AD to 1408 AD, favoured the Noh theatre and Zeami.[189] The plays of the Noh theatre and the Zeami style of writing the plays are named after the fourteenth century AD Muromachi era playwright Zeami Motokiyo.[190] Sarugaku was the style of play rendition before the Noh theatre took root in 1374 AD.[191] While earlier in Zeami's career, the Yamato Sarugaku was influential on his work, later on in his career, the Omi Sarugaku became more important.[192] However, of the Yamato Sarugaku troupes, only the Hosho and the Takeda troupes survived into the twentieth century AD and beyond. It was in the year

[182] Lidin, O. (2002), Tanegashima: The Arrival of Europe in Japan, Nordic Institute of Asian Studies, Monograph Series, No. 90.

[183] Batten, B. (2003), To the Ends of Japan, Pre-modern Frontiers, Boundaries and Interactions, University of Hawai'i Press, Honolulu.

[184] Ibid.

[185] Lidin, O. (2002), Tanegashima: The Arrival of Europe in Japan, Nordic Institute of Asian Studies, Monograph Series, No. 90.

[186] Ibid.

[187] Kang, E. (2016), Diplomacy and Ideology in Japanese-Korean Relations – From the 15th to the 18th century, St Martin's Press INC, NYC.

[188] Ibid.

[189] Keene, D. (2003), Yoshimasa and the Silver Pavilion: The Creation and the Soul of Japan, Columbia University Press, New York.

[190] Hare, T. (1968), Zeami's Style: The Noh Plays of Zeami Motokiyo, Stanford University Press, Stanford, California.

[191] Ibid.

[192] Ibid.

1374 AD that Ashikaga Yoshimitsu, the seventeen-year-old Shogun, visited the troupe of Zeami's father Kannami.[193] Zeami was twelve years old at the time.[194] For some reason, perhaps at the insistence of a member of the Shogun's entourage, an aspect of how the play was usually conducted was changed. In this case, as leader of the troupe, Kannami played the role of Okina, whereas traditionally this role had always been played by the oldest troupe member.[195] Moreover, the orientation of Sarugaku also changed from having a religious overtone to just a purely entertainment one.[196] And, for the first time in the history of dramatic Japanese art, the troupe led by Kannami gained the support of the Shogun.[197] Nevertheless, despite his patronage of the theatre, Yoshimitsu gained notoriety and earned the hatred of his countrymen through the ages for accepting the title of 'King of Japan' from the Chinese imperial court. This acknowledgement was a formal recognition that Japan was a vassal state of the Chinese imperial court.[198]

Conclusion

The Muromachi Period in Japanese economic and political history was one in which there were social and political changes which contributed towards the development of institutions in Japan. It was during the early Muromachi Period in 1342 that the Gozan Josselsu System of monastery–temple organisation was firmly established. Moreover, between 1339 and 1343, the Shoin-Zukuri residential system replaced the traditional Shinden-Zukuri residential style. In this case, the main house was located at the front and private secluded gardens to the back. Furthermore, while moral standards were upheld, there was a decline in Esoteric Buddhism and shift in favour towards Zen Buddhism. The latter was favoured by the Samurai elite because of its emphasis towards personal control and courage. The geographical focus of Zen Buddhism also shifted away from Kamakura to Kyoto where the Muromachi Bakufu was based. However, the strong central governance of Japan based upon the Shogun ended

[193] Ibid.
[194] Ibid.
[195] Ibid.
[196] Ibid.
[197] Ibid.
[198] Keene, D. (2003), Yoshimasa and the Silver Pavilion: The Creation and the Soul of Japan, Columbia University Press, New York.

with the assassination of Shogun Yoshinori in 1441 AD. Central control of Japan was further reduced in the aftermath of the Onin War which was a civil war which lasted for ten years from 1467 AD. As a result, to maintain some control over the country, the Bakufu devolved power to the local Daimyos to keep them from rebelling. However, although local legal codes varied from the rule of one Daimyo to another, they remained a variant of the Joei Shikimoku.

The Muromachi Period was at its height between 1368 AD and 1394 AD during the tenure of the Shogun Yoshimitsu who favoured Buddhism rather than Japan's indigenous Shinto religion. Because the latter lay at the religious authority of the Emperor, any shift towards Buddhism would undermine that authority and this is what Yoshimitsu wanted in order to further the power of the Bakufu. Yoshimitsu also achieved this by bringing together the governance structures and the institutions of the Bakufu and the imperial court. To some extent he achieved this by bringing court officials under his control. At the same time by bringing court officials under his control, Yoshimitsu also extended his power over the nobility by reducing their land holdings to a tenth of what they previously had, making them poorer. This would reduce the capacity of the nobility to wage war against the Bakufu by using their wealth to raise an army. However, following the death of Yoshimitsu in 1408 AD, his son Yoshimochi undid much of his work by making appointments based on merit and tradition. This had the effect of separating the governance structures of the Bakufu and the Court. Nevertheless, the control of land by the nobility through the Shoen System began to decline through the fifteenth century AD. Such was the case that by the end of the fifteenth century AD, the nobility as Shoen proprietors of the land had given control of the land to local warriors on a contractual basis. The legal code was also extended during the Muromachi Period by supplementing the Joei Shikimoku from the Kamakura Period. One of the additions made to the Joei Shikimoku was the Kenmu Shikmoku by the Shogun Ashikaga Takauji. The roots of the Kenmu Shikmoku are to be found in the 'Constitution' written by Prince Shotoku in the seventh century AD. The 'Constitution' resembled the religious and philosophical ideas of the sixth/seventh century Sui Dynasty China. And, in this context the 'Constitution' elaborated on the ideal behaviours and attitudes which should prevail amongst Japan's warrior class. In addition to the Kenmu Shikmoku, the legal code was further extended during the Muromachi Period with the implementation of the renza and the enza. These extended the punishment of the committer of a crime to his local community as well. Furthermore, under the Kenka Ryoseibai, if land disputes could not be resolved by the disputing parties, then the result would be that land ownership was transferred to the Bakufu.

During the mid-fifteenth century AD, the economically prosperous regions of the world in Asia as well as other parts of the known world experienced an economic recession which was severe in nature.[199] The typical characteristics of this recession were represented by a fall in inter-state trade, a fall in individual and state wealth as well as a fall in productivity.[200] However, by the second half of the fifteenth century AD, most parts of the global economy had begun to recover.[201] In the fifteenth century AD, China had been the engine of the global economy. Any changes in this engine would therefore have impacted on that economy. Such changes may have been brought about by a change in China's leadership. Indeed, this is what happened at the start of the fifteenth century AD when the Emperor Chengzu ascended to the imperial throne. Chengzu rejuvenated the power base of the imperial house to such an extent that his reign became known as another founding of the Ming Dynasty.[202] In rejuvenating the imperial house, Chengzu's reign featured increased government expenditure on infrastructure projects, military campaigns and the financing of maritime trade. The infrastructure projects were associated with the shift of China's imperial and governmental capital from Nanjing to Beijing.[203] The military campaigns were associated with wresting control of more territory from the Mongols, the Koreans as well as the Vietnamese.[204] The financing of maritime trade was associated with facilitating more trade with other parts of Asia as well as with Africa. This last aspect of increased expenditure by the Ming is better illustrated in the context of the six maritime voyages of Admiral Zheng He.[205] The means

[199] Atwell, W. (2002), Time, Money, and the Weather: Ming China and the 'Great Depression' of the Mid-Fifteenth Century, The Journal of Asian Studies, 61, No. 1, pp. 83–113.

[200] Ibid.

[201] Ibid.

[202] Farmer, E. (1976), Early Ming Government: The Evolution of Dual Capitals, Cambridge: Harvard University Press.

[203] Atwell, W. (2002), Time, Money, and the Weather: Ming China and the 'Great Depression' of the Mid-Fifteenth Century, The Journal of Asian Studies, 61, No. 1, pp. 83–113.

[204] Ibid.

[205] Ibid.

of the acquisition of the financial resources by the Ming court required to finance the various activities discussed previously occurred due to two interconnected reasons.[206] Firstly, Chengzu was able to restore peace and stability to China. Secondly, favourable climatic conditions facilitated an increase in agricultural productivity which in turn boosted agricultural tax revenues for the Ming. Finally, there was an increase in the monetary base caused by an expansion in the supply of paper money, copper coins and precious metals such as silver. The increase in the quantity of silver in the economy was caused by the court-authorised increase in mining activities. However, despite the increased state-led mining of silver, significant amount of the precious metal was flowing into the hands of private citizens rather than to the state.[207] This was primarily because private citizens believed more in the value of un-minted silver than they did in the government-backed paper currency as a medium of exchange.[208] This was evident because the Ming government put in place regulations which required the use of paper currency and copper coins for buying and selling rather than measured quantities of un-minted silver.[209] Nevertheless, whereas the monetary base had been expanding in Ming China, it had begun to contract amongst China's trading partners who were losing stocks of precious metals in order to pay for the Chinese imports of ceramics and silk. In this case, in the fifteenth century AD, silk textiles and raw silk were not only valuable exports for China, but a large amount could be transported at a low cost because of the low weight of silk.[210] The loss of precious metals was experienced mostly in Europe and the Middle Eastern region.[211] However, China's impact on the global economy became denigrated due to the policies followed by the Emperor Yingzong (1436–1449 AD and 1457–1465 AD). Yingzong implemented four policies which were essentially the opposite of those policies eschewed by the Emperor Chengzu.[212] Firstly, the mining of precious metals was reduced

[206] Ibid.

[207] Ibid.

[208] Ibid.

[209] Zhang, T. (1974), Ming dynastic history, 28 vols. Beijing: Xinhua.

[210] Atwell, W. (2002), Time, Money, and the Weather: Ming China and the 'Great Depression' of the Mid-Fifteenth Century, The Journal of Asian Studies, 61, No. 1, pp. 83–113.

[211] Day, J. (1979), The Great Bullion Famine of the Fifteenth Century, Past and Present, Vol. 79, pp. 3–54.

[212] Ibid.

with mines being closed, mine inspectors being recalled to Beijing and mining quotas being cut. Secondly, in the 1430s AD, maritime trading activities were stopped. With this Chinese shipping activities of all types, including the voyages of Zheng He, came to an end. Thirdly, the financial support for tributary trade was taken away. And, lastly the allocated annual spending of the imperial court was reduced. In addition to these factors, there were also other features of the economic stagnation which Ming China experienced in the 1430s. These features were associated with a decline in the productivity of remaining mines, loss of mines due to inability to hold north Vietnam as well as instability in the frontier region of south western China.

The three to four decades of instability during the Azuchi Momoyama Period was brought to an end in 1600 AD with the start of the Tokugawa period and the start of the longest period of stability and economic development in Japanese history. For it was during the Tokugawa Period that Tokugawa Ieyasu was able to re-establish the central control of Japan by the Shogunate. However, the last decade of the sixteenth century AD also encompassed the Imjin War, 1592 AD to 1598 AD, initiated by Oda Nobunaga's protégé Toyotomi Hideyoshi. The latter led Japan to wage war against Korea to gain control of its resources on the way to doing the same to Ming China. However, the combined strength of Korean forces and Ming Chinese reinforcements was sufficient enough to eventually drive away Japanese forces. The Imjin War was truly the world's first East-Asian War.

References

Akira, I., and Yamamura, K. (1992), Not for Lack of Will or Wile: Yoshimitsu's Failure to Supplant the Imperial Lineage, The Journal of Japanese Studies, Vol. 18, No. 1, pp. 45–78.

Allinson, J., and Anievas, A. (2009) The uses and misuses of uneven and combined development: an anatomy of a concept, Cambridge Review of International Affairs, Vol. 22, No. 1, pp. 47–67, https://doi.org/10.1080/09557570802680132.

Atwell, W. (2002), Time, Money, and the Weather: Ming China and the 'Great Depression' of the Mid-Fifteenth Century, The Journal of Asian Studies, Vol. 61, No. 1, pp. 83–113.

Batten, B. (2003), To The Ends of Japan, Premodern Frontiers, Boundaries and Interactions, University of Hawai'i Press, Honolulu.

Collcutt, M. (1981), Five Mountains: The Rinzai Zen Monastic Institution in Medieval Japan, Harvard University Press, Cambridge, Massachusetts.

Conlan, T. (2011), Nonbokucho Wars (1331–1392), The Encyclopedia of War, Wiley Online Library.

Day, J. (1979), The Great Bullion Famine of the Fifteenth Century, Past and Present, Vol. 79, pp. 3–54.

Deal, W. (2006), Handbook to Life in Medieval and Early Modern Japan, Oxford University Press, Oxford.

Dumoulin, H. (2005), Zen Buddhism: A History: Volume 2 Japan, World Wisdom, Bloomington, Indiana, US.

Farmer, E. (1976), Early Ming Government: The Evolution of Dual Capitals, Cambridge: Harvard University Press.

Gay, S. (1986), The Kawashima: Warrior Peasants of Medieval Japan, Harvard Journal of Asiatic Studies, Vol. 46, No. 1, pp. 81–119.

Hall, J. (1977), The Muromachi Age in Japanese History, IN 'Japan in the Muromachi Age', Hall, J., and Takeshi, T. (Ed), University of California Press, Berkeley.

Hall, J. (1995), The Muromachi Bakufu, IN Warriors in Japan, Jansen, M. (Ed), Cambridge University Press, Cambridge.

Hanson, V., and Curtis, K. (2010), Voyages in World History, Volume 1: To 1600, Wadsworth, Boston, USA.

Hare, T. (1968), Zeami's Style: The Noh Plays of Zeami Motokiyo, Stanford University Press, Stanford, California.

Hawley, S. (2014), The Imjin War: Japan's Sixteenth-century Invasion of Korea and Attempt to Conquer China, Conquistador Press.

Howland, D. (1996), Borders of Chinese Civilisation, Geography and History at Empire's End, Duke University Press, Durham & London.

Jacob, F. (2017), Technological Spatialities: Then Impact of geography and Technology during the Imjin War (1592–1598), IN War and geography: The Spatiality of Organised Mass Violence, Danielsson, S., and Jacob, F. (Eds), Verlag Ferdinand Schoningh GmbH & Co, Paderborn.

Kang, E. (2016), Diplomacy and Ideology in Japanese-Korean Relations – From the 15th to the 18th century, St Martin's Press INC, NYC.

Keene, D. (2003), Yoshimasa and the Silver Pavilion: The Creation and the Soul of Japan, Columbia University Press, New York.

Kikuchi, D. (2018), Japanese History, Books on Demand.

Kiley, C. (1982), The Imperial Court As a Legal Authority in the Kamakura Age, IN Court and Bakufu in Japan, Essays in Kamakura History, Mass, J. (Ed), Stanford University Press, Stanford, California.

Kitagawa, K. (1974), The Japanese 'Kokutai' (National Community) History and Myth, History of Religions, Vol. 13, No. 3, pp. 209–226.

Kleiner, F. (2009), Gardner's Art Through the Ages: A Global History, Thomson-Wadworth, United Kingdom.
Lidin, O. (2002), Tanegashima: The Arrival of Europe in Japan, Nordic Institute of Asian Studies, Monograph Series, No. 90.
Lorge, P. (2005), War, Politics and Society in Early Modern China, 900–1795, Routledge, New York.
Lu, D. (1997), Japan: A Documentary History, M.E. Sharpe, New York.
Manji, K. (2015), The Imjin Waeran: Contrasting the First and the Second Invasions of Korea, IN The East Asian War, 1592–1598: International Relations, Violence and Memory, Lewis, J. (Ed), Routledge, London.
Mitchelhill, J. (2003), Castles of the Samurai: Power and Beauty, Kodansha International.
Nagahara, Y. (1981), Daimyo and Kandaka System, IN Japan Before Tokugawa: Political Consolidation and Economic Growth, 1500–1650, Hall, S., Nagahara, K., and Yamamura, K. (Eds), Princeton University Press, Princeton, New Jersey.
O'Haley, J. (2016), Law's Political Foundations, Rivers, Rifles, Rice and Religion, Edward Elgar Publishing, Cheltenham, United Kingdom.
Perez, L. (2013), Japan at War: An Encyclopedia, ABC-CLIO, Oxford, UK.
Pitelka, M. (2016), Spectacular Accumulation, Material Culture, Tokugawa Ieyasu and Samurai Sociability, University of Hawai'I Press.
Pregill, P., and Volkman, N. (1999), Landscapes of the Rising Sun: Design and Planning in Japan, IN Landscapes in History: Design and Planning in the Eastern and Western Traditions, John Wiley & Sons, INC, New York.
Robinson, K. (2015), Violence, trade and impostors in Korean-Japanese Relations, 1510–1609, IN The East Asian War, 1592–1598: International Relations, Violence and Memory, Lewis, J. (Ed), Routledge, London.
Rockstein, E. (1993), Strategic and Operational Aspects of Japan's Invasion of Korea, 1592–1598, AD-A266 906, The United States Naval War College.
Ruch, B. (1992), Coping with Death: Paradigms of Heaven and Hell and the Six Realms in Early Literature and Painting, IN Flowering Traces: Buddhism in the Literary and Visual Arts of Japan, Sanford, J., LaFleur, W., and Nagatomi, M. (Eds), Princeton University Press, Princeton.
Sadler, A. (1978), Shogun: The Life of Tokugawa Ieyasu, Tuttle Publishing, Tokyo.
Saito, H. (1912), A History of Japan, Kegan Paul, Trench, Trubner & Co, Ltd.
Schirokauer, C., Brown, M., Lurie, D., and Gay, S. (2013), A Brief History of Chinese and Japanese Civilisations, Wadsworth CENGAGE Learning.
Shantideva (2008), The Way of the Bodhisattva, Shambhala, Boston & London.
Shirane, H. (2012), Traditional Japanese Literature: An Anthology, Beginnings to 1600, Columbia University Press, New York.
Slatyer, W. (2014), Life/Death Rhythms of Capitalist Regimes – Debt Before Dishonour, Timetable of World Dominance 1400 to 2100 AD, Part 1: Historical Ruler Cycles, Partridge Publishing, Singapore.

Steenstrup, C. (1991), A History of Law in Japan Until 1868, E.J. Brill, Leiden, The Netherlands.
Swope, K. (2009), A Dragon's Head and a Serpents Tail, Ming China and the First Great East Asian War, 1592–1598, University of Oklahoma Press, Norman.
Takokoshi, Y. (2004), The Economic Aspects of the History of Civilisation of Japan, 2nd Edition, Routledge, London.
Tsang, C. (2007), War and Faith: Ikko Ikki in Late Muromachi Japan, Harvard University Asia Center.
Turnbull, S. (1996), The Samurai: A Military History, Routledge, London.
Wang, R. (2012), Yinyang: The Way of Heaven and Earth in Chinese Thought and Culture, Cambridge University Press, Cambridge.
Wills, J., Cranmer-Byng, J., Peterson, W., and Witek, J. (2011), China and Maritime Europe, 1500–1800, Trade, Settlement, Diplomacy and Missions, Cambridge University Press, Cambridge.
Wright, A. (1957), The Formation of Sui Ideology, IN Chinese Thought and Institutions, Fairbank, J. (Ed), University of Chicago Press, 1957, Chicago.
Yamamura, K. (1988), Introduction, IN The Cambridge History of Japan, Volume 3, Medieval Japan, Yamamura, K. (Ed), Cambridge University Press, Cambridge.
Yamashita, M., and Lindesay, W. (2007), The Great Wall. From Beginning to End, Sterling Publishing, New York.
Yokota, J. (2000), Understanding Amida Buddha and the Pure Land Buddhism, Horota, D. (Eds), State University of New York, Albany.
Zhang, T. (1974), Ming dynastic history, 28 vols. Beijing: Xinhua.

CHAPTER 4

The Tokugawa Period (1600–1868): Isolation and Change

Introduction

The Edo Period is also known as the Tokugawa Period in which the Tokugawa family continued to rule Japan, side lining the imperial household and the Emperor, through its control of the Shogunate. Ieyasu Tokugawa managed with his armies to subdue the line of powerful regional feudal lords who had emerged after the end of the Shogun rule in the fifteenth century and had subjected Japan to a state of continuous civil war for a period of 150 years. The rule of Japan by a Shogun had been associated with the delegation of the powers of running the country on a day-to-day basis from the Emperor to a Shogun or Regent. In this case, the Emperor, albeit prisoner in Kyoto with the imperial household, had been relegated to a religious and ritualistic function in Japan, and the Tokugawa Shogun in Edo (later to be named Tokyo in the Meiji Period) held the real power and authority over Japan.

As the European powers were starting on their way to lay claims to lands already inhabited by peoples from the Americas to Africa, India and other parts of Asia, the Tokugawa Shogunate acted to shield Japan from foreign influence. This was done by closing Japan's territories to foreigners in the 1630s at which time all foreign missionaries and traders were expelled from Japanese soil.[1] Through the actions of the Tokugawa

[1] Iwata, M. (1964), Okubo Toshimichi: The Bismarck of Japan, University of California Press, Berkeley.

S. Ramesh, *China's Economic Rise*,
https://doi.org/10.1007/978-3-030-49811-5_4

Shogunate, Japan escaped the fate of the Indian sub-continent whose declining empires and their rulers were more hospitable to the foreign barbarians. The British in India followed the same strategy they used to establish colonies in other parts of the world. It was a strategy which other European powers also followed. The strategy involved establishing a factory, which the British in India did in Masulipatnam in 1613, and then consolidating power and acquiring more territory through trade, deception and military power. So successful were the British in this strategy that the whole of the Indian sub-continent came under the control of the British Crown by 1858.[2] The British continued to rule over India until 1947 at which time it became a sovereign independent nation.[3] However, for over 313 years before 1947, the British stripped India and Indians of their wealth, their dignity and their lives. Stolen wealth provided the resources which were used to facilitate the transition of a feudalistic England into the first country in the world to undergo industrialisation. Thus, had it not been due to the actions of the Tokugawa Shogunate in the third decade of the seventeenth century, Japan may also have suffered a similar fate at the hands of the western barbarians. However, while Shogunate policy may have prevented the colonisation of Japan by the western powers, it may also have constrained Japan's rise as a power.[4] This is because at the time of the implementation of the isolationist policy, Japan had its own trading settlements in the Philippines, Java and Siam.[5] As a result, the Japanese trading settlements in these locations could not develop to the point at which Japan could become a colonial power as did the western powers. The lack of colonies and an empire restricted the potential market for Japanese goods, and thus, there was no stimulus for Japanese industrialisation. Moreover, although proto-industrialisation had occurred in Japan centuries before its occurrence in eighteenth century England, the stimulus for the transition to industrialisation was not present due to the lack of a market for goods as well as a lack of raw materials from those markets. Whereas, in the case of Great Britain there were overseas colonies which provided a market for British goods as well as acting as a source for raw materials from which those goods could be

[2] Tharoor, S. (2018), Inglorious Empire: What the British Did to India, Penguin, UK.

[3] Ibid.

[4] Iwata, M. (1964), Okubo Toshimichi: The Bismarck of Japan, University of California Press, Berkeley.

[5] Ibid.

produced. This incentivised profiteering and the accumulation of wealth by merchants which was a conducive breeding ground for innovation and enterprise. However, the Shogunate's isolationist policies benefited Japan economically by stemming the outflow of gold and allowing domestic industries to develop without the threat of foreign competition.[6] Moreover, Shogunate isolationist policies also allowed the Japanese to develop their own scholarship, art, thought, customs and societal behaviours.[7] Nevertheless, isolationist policies meant reduced trade as well as a lack of foreign stimulus to domestic industries and Japanese thought and culture. As a result, the Shogunate may have entered a period of stagnation, underdeveloped and technologically backward. A state from which it did not wake up from until the mid-nineteenth century when the western powers arrived at its ports, with their military might, demanding that Japan end its isolationism and open itself up to trade. Thus, isolationism, the lack of stimulation for innovation and development as well as the increasing poverty of the samurai may have directly led to the end of the Shoguns in 1867. Moreover, by the end of the Tokugawa period, Japan's military capacity was no match for that of the western powers. Therefore, the Tokugawa Shogunate faced the choice of either being colonised by the British or the Americans or reforming and building up military capacity through a process of industrialisation and modernisation. The end of the shoguns and the Tokugawa period was followed by the restoration of the power and authority, over Japan and the Japanese people, of the Emperor with the crowning of Prince Mutsuhito as the Emperor Meiji in 1868. The Meiji period can be characterised as one in which Japan rapidly industrialised as well as modernised its armed forces and overtime became the first Asian nation to be able to rank itself as being comparable to other western nations. On the other hand, the fate which befell Japan's giant neighbour, Qing China, was much different. Like Tokugawa Japan, Ming China had begun to exhibit isolationist policies in the fifteenth century.[8] However, in the mid-nineteenth century, the ships of the British arrived in China to challenge its hegemony in the region and to open it to trade. At about the same time the Americans arrived off the coast of Japan demanding that Japan also open its borders for trade. But trade was not only what the

[6] Ibid.

[7] Ibid.

[8] Finlay, R. (2008), The Voyages of Zheng He: Ideology, State Power, and Maritime Trade in Ming China, The Journal of the Historical Society, Vol. VIII, No. 3.

British and the Americans wanted, they wanted to exercise a mercantilist resource grab as the British had done all over the world. This was more notable in India, the Americas, Australia and New Zealand. However, the mercantilist resource grab policy did not work with Japan, but it nearly did with Qing China. Power in Tokugawa Japan had become nationally integrated but remained decentralised in comparison to Qing China. This may have saved Japan from the fate that befell Qing China, foreign occupation, social disintegration over a period of a century, culminating in a civil war and the declaration of the establishment of the People's Republic of China by Chairman Mao in 1949. The divorce of political power from the religious power of the Emperor allowed for a quick change of regime at a time when the very sovereignty of Japan was at risk. Nevertheless, in Qing China the political and administrative structures were much bigger and more centralised than in Tokugawa Japan. In the case of the latter, there was a realisation that it was a case of reform or be colonised, while in the case of Qing China, there was a slow denigration of imperial power by the western powers, notably the British, such that it collapsed in 1912.[9]

Early Tokugawa

The stability of the Shogunate system had ended in 1408 with the death of the third Ashikaga Shogun, Yoshimitsu.[10] The latter constrained the powers of the governors of provinces and improved the applicability of the law as well as the stability of the land.[11] Moreover, Yoshimitsu also reinvigorated trade with Ming dynasty China following the mistrust which had arisen between China and Japan because of the Mongol invasions of the Yuan Dynasty.[12] In return, the Ming court bestowed the title of 'King of Japan' upon Yoshimitsu.[13] Trade with Ming China was very important for the Japanese economy at the time. Due to a shortage of its own coinage, Japan had a great need for the importation, amongst other things, of Chinese currency.[14] However, it was the Dutch through the Dutch East India Company who proved to be the conductor for trade between Tokugawa Japan and Ming China. In this case, while the Dutch established

[9] Gascoigne, B. (2003), The Dynasties of China: A History, Carroll & Graf Publishers.

[10] Perez, L. (2013), Japan at War, An Encyclopedia, ABC-CLIO, Oxford, UK.

[11] Ibid.

[12] Ibid.

[13] Ibid.

[14] Ibid.

a factory at Hirado, Japan, in 1609, but it was not until the 1620s that the factory produced the high level of profits which so excited and impressed the directors of the Company in the Netherlands.[15] The Hirado factory's increased profits in the 1620s resulted because it was only at this time that the Dutch began to receive access to China's silk market facilitating them to produce and provide the luxury goods in which the Japanese were interested in.[16] However, the Dutch were not making as much money as were the Portuguese and the Spanish who were selling Chinese goods in Japan. In order to take a bigger share of this lucrative market, the Dutch attacked the Portuguese trading port at Macau in China. However, the attack failed and so the Dutch established a trading port on the island of Taiwan in 1624.[17] This port proved to be a suitable intermediary for the Dutch to facilitate trade between China and Japan. China's Zheng family monopolised indirect Chinese trade with Japan by sending ships laden with Chinese goods to the Dutch port in Taiwan, through which the Dutch East India Company were able to channel Chinese goods to Japan at a time when the Chinese were banned, by their own rulers, from trade with Japan.[18] However, Ieyasu as Shogun proclaimed that Chinese merchant ships would be welcome at Nagasaki. But Japan did not attempt to establish formal diplomatic relations with Ming China. This differential commercial and political strategy was followed in order to ensure that Japan economically benefited from trade with China, but that it did not become a vassal state in a Ming Chinese-dominated world.[19] This policy continued when the Qing took control of China from the Ming dynasty in 1644. While the Qing dynasty also banned Chinese trade with Japan, Ieyasu granted red-seal licences for Japanese and foreign merchants to trade with south-east Asia, the so-called Nanyang trade. Nevertheless, by 1616 the Shogunate only allowed the Japanese merchants to trade with Tonkin, Cambodia, Cochin China, Siam, Luzon and Taiwan.[20] But by 1636 the Shogunate had reduced Japanese trade to only the Chinese and

[15] Laver, M. (2011), The Sakoku Edicts and the Politics of Tokugawa Hegemony, Cambria Press, Amherst, New York.

[16] Ibid.

[17] Ibid.

[18] Ibid.

[19] Ibid.

[20] Gungwu, W., and Chin-keong, N. (2004), Maritime China in Transition 1750–1850, Harrassowitz Verlag, Wiesbaden.

the Dutch, although Siam and Annam continued to send ships to Japan until the end of the Tokugawa period.[21]

The profits made from Japanese trade for the Dutch grew significantly in the 1630s, especially after the Portuguese were banned from trade with Japan in 1639.[22] Using their factories in south-east Asia, the Company was also able to supply the Japanese with a range of luxury goods which the Japanese paid for using the precious metals extracted from their mines. However, when the Shogunate limited the quantity of precious metals which could leave Japan, the fortunes of the Dutch East India Company began to decline in Asia.[23] Moreover, the Shogunate was also asserting more control over Japanese foreign trade, by for example dictating where foreign ships could dock and how foreign merchandise was sold. Nevertheless, foreign trade was becoming more and more important in Tokugawa Japan as the middle class grew in response to the increasing urbanisation due to the rise of castle towns. These were mandated by the Shogunate to be one per domain and in which the Samurai and the daimyo would live, when the latter was not resident in the Shogun's castle in Edo for six months of the year.[24] The increasing concentrations of populations meant that there was also a concentration of those who provided services to the residents. But urban society could only function when the exchange of goods and services for denominations of rice could be replaced by the exchange of goods and services for coinage.[25] This was facilitated by the merchant class who collected the rice and then converted into coinage which could then be used by the daimyo to pay the samurai. However, although wealthy, the merchant class were at the bottom of the Shinokosho hierarchy of samurai-peasants-artisans-merchants.[26] The Shinokosho hierarchy emerged at a time in the sixteenth century when Japan became unified. It was established and maintained through either the use of force or the threatened use of force.[27] Due to the belief that civil conflict and wars had ended, it was felt that only the Samurai ruling class should be allowed

[21] Ibid.

[22] Laver, M. (2011), The Sakoku Edicts and the Politics of Tokugawa Hegemony, Cambria Press, Amherst, New York.

[23] Ibid.

[24] Ibid.

[25] Ibid.

[26] Sheldon, C. (1983), Merchants and Society in Tokugawa Japan, Modern Asian Studies, Vol. 17, No. 3, pp. 477–488.

[27] Ibid.

to carry weapons and all other classes should just produce the means to sustain life as well as to pay the taxes.[28] However, in the sixteenth century, the main preoccupation of those governing Japan was the needs of the Samurai and the peasants who contributed more to the Japanese economy at the time due to its agrarian nature than the merchants did.[29] Nevertheless, each class had its duties and obligations to society, and within a specific class, people's status was determined by their circumstances.[30] Mobility from one class to the other was not possible as it was forbidden.[31] However, as the Japanese economy transitioned from an agrarian one to a partially monetised economy, the merchants were able to improve their class status by making money and providing complex distributional and financial services to the samurai.[32] But the samurai could not fall into debt to the merchants, and courts would often not hear any debt cases brought by merchants against the samurai.[33] Interest rates on loans from merchants to samurai were also artificially kept low, and the state was able to penalise merchants' perceived over-consumption by for example confiscating their property.[34] Moreover, due to the fact that the samurai were banned from trade themselves, the merchants had a monopoly over trade.[35] But during the Tokugawa period, the ability of merchants to trade was restricted by the Shogunate.[36] For example, Japanese merchants were only able to trade with the Dutch trading post at Dejima, with Chinese merchants at Nagasaki, and on a limited basis with the Ryukyu Islands and Korea.[37]

The castle towns became monetised simply because the daimyo and the samurai lived in the castle towns.[38] The high level of output of precious metals, particularly silver, by Japanese mines and the use of European smelting techniques allowed for coinage to be possible. In fact, it has been estimated that in the sixteenth century, Japanese mines produced one-

[28] Ibid.

[29] Ibid.

[30] Ibid.

[31] Ibid.

[32] Ibid.

[33] Henderson, D. (1952), Some Aspects of Tokugawa Law, Washington Law Review, Vol. 21, No. 1, pp. 96, 98–102,

[34] Sheldon, C. (1983), Merchants and Society in Tokugawa Japan, Modern Asian Studies, Vol. 17, No. 3, pp. 477–488.

[35] Ibid.

[36] Ibid.

[37] Ibid.

[38] Ibid.

third of the world's silver output.[39] Monetisation also made it easier for the wealthy samurai and merchant classes to purchase western goods as well as textiles made from Chinese silk, made in Japan by Japanese weavers.[40] Japanese bullion which the Company gained in exchange for the goods it sold either via China or from its factories in other parts of Asia allowed it to become free of the need to use bullion from Europe in order to buy goods to sell in Japan.[41]

Following the death of Yoshimitsu, the stability of the tenure of the Shoguns was short lived, and rival clans such as the Hosokawa and the Yamana turned to open military conflict in order to claim the title of Shogun for themselves.[42] The result was the Onin War of 1467. The Onin War also ended the domination of Japanese economic, political, cultural and religious life by the Gozan Zen branch of Buddhism.[43] The Gozan Zen had become the dominant Buddhist institution in Japan by the end of the fourteenth century.[44] However, after the Onin War at the behest of the towns' people and daimyo of the towns of Kyoto and Sakai, other branches of Buddhism such as the Daitokuji and the Myoshinji were in rivalry to replace Gozan Zen as the dominant Buddhist institution in Japan.[45] After the Onin War, Japan would know no stability until the Battle of Sekigahara.

The Battle of Sekigahara took place in September 1600 near the village of Sekigahara in Mino province, between the forces of Ieyasu and the forces of the daimyos, a coalition of feudal chiefs.[46] Tokugawa Ieyasu was a seventeenth century Japanese military leader who ended more than hundred years of civil war in Japan.[47] By defeating the forces of the daimyos at the Battle of Sekigahara, Ieyasu was able to restore the role of Shogun or military dictator upon himself as well as for the future generations of his family for over 250 years.[48] Some view Ieyasu's victory at Sekigahara in

[39] Ibid.

[40] Ibid.

[41] Ibid.

[42] Perez, L. (2013), Japan at War, An Encyclopedia, ABC-CLIO, Oxford, UK.

[43] Collcutt, M. (1981), Five Mountains: The Rinzai Zen Monastic Institution in Medieval Japan, Council on East Asian Studies, Harvard University, Cambridge, Massachusetts.

[44] Ibid.

[45] Ibid.

[46] Jansen, M. (2000), The Makings of Modern Japan, The Belknap Press of Harvard University Press, Cambridge, Massachusetts.

[47] Turnbull, S. (2012), Tokugawa Ieyasu (Command), Osprey Publishing.

[48] Ibid.

1600 as being the most pivotal one in the history of Japan,[49] while others see Ieyasu's victory at the Battle of Osaka in 1615 as being the most important in the making of a modern Japan.[50] In the Battle of Osaka in 1615, Ieyasu fought and defeated the last of the daimyos who had remained undefeated at the Battle of Sekigahara but were still opposed to Ieyasu as Shogun.[51] From 1467 until Ieyasu reunified Japan under his rule as the restored Shogun, Japan experienced civil war in the context of military conflict between rival chieftains of daimyos.[52] In fact, the period from 1467 AD to 1600 AD in Japan[53] and the early fifth century BC to the early third century BC in China[54] can be both referred to as the 'Warring States' period in which no de facto central state existed.

Tokugawa Political Structure and Institutions

The Tokugawa period was one in which Japan was governed by declining political institutions which also lacked fiscal integrity.[55] However, the newly unified Japan of the Tokugawa period was one which possessed a monopoly on the use of force anywhere within Japanese territory.[56] Nevertheless, in an institutional context there are several features which characterise the Tokugawa period.[57] Firstly, even though the economy was growing alongside the increase in population, the revenues of the Shogunate were declining. Secondly, because there had been relative peace in Japan for over 200 years, there had been no need to develop and maintain military potential. In contrast to the Japanese military of the Tokugawa period, the contemporary military power of the European powers and the Americans was much more advanced. When American, British and Russian

[49] Ibid.

[50] Jansen, M. (2000), The Makings of Modern Japan, The Belknap Press of Harvard University Press, Cambridge, Massachusetts.

[51] Turnbull, S. (2012), Tokugawa Ieyasu (Command), Osprey Publishing.

[52] Ibid.

[53] Ibid.

[54] Lawton, T. (1983), Chinese Art of the Warring States Period: Change and Continuity, 480–222BC, Freed-Hardeman College.

[55] White, J. (1988), State Growth and Popular Protest in Tokugawa Japan, The Journal of Japanese Studies, Vol. 14, No. 1, pp. 1–25.

[56] Weber, M. (1947), The Theory of Social and Economic Organization, University Press, New York.

[57] White, J. (1988), State Growth and Popular Protest in Tokugawa Japan, The Journal of Japanese Studies, Vol. 14, No. 1, pp. 1–25.

warships began to appear off the Japanese coast in the early 1850s, Japan was not prepared militarily to defend itself from occupation and colonisation. Lastly, economic power shifted from the traditional merchant class to newly setting up entrepreneurs. This would have been particularly common in a city such as Hamamatsu, in western Shizuoka prefecture. This is because unlike other parts of Japan which were under the jurisdiction of a feudal lord, Hamamatsu had special protectorate status during the Tokugawa period and therefore under the direct rule of the central government.[58] Hamamatsu was governed by governors from other regions of Japan who were centrally appointed for a period of fourteen years at a time.[59] Central control and externally appointed governors ensured that the people in Hamamatsu were socially mobile in contrast to other parts of Japan in which a rigid social structure had been put in place with a feudal lord at the top followed by the samurai, the peasants, the artisans and the merchants in descending order. However, village and peasant life were organised in such a way that it would not have been recognisable as part of this strict social hierarchy. In the Tokugawa period, villagers were divided into households such that each group of households could bear part of the share of the tax burden.[60] As long as the village paid its allocated tax to the domain it was situated in, the domain was prohibited by the Shogunate from interfering in the affairs of the village.[61] Tokugawa scholars had seen the potential for the military use of the peasants.[62] Towards the end of the Tokugawa period, it had become recognised that suitably trained peasants could form a coastal militia to defend Japan from the foreigners who had begun to appear off its coasts.[63] However, in the period before the Tokugawa, peasants had been disarmed so that peasant revolts such as those which occurred in the Muromachi period would not

[58] Aoyama, Y. (2009), Entrepreneurship and Regional Culture: The Case of Hamamatsu and Kyoto, Japan, Regional Studies, Vol. 43, No. 3, pp. 495–512, https://doi.org/10.1080/00343400902777042.

[59] Ibid.

[60] Varner, R. (1977), The Organised Peasant. The Wakamonogumi in the Edo Period, Monumenta Nipponica, Vol. 32, No. 4, pp. 459–483.

[61] Aoki, M. (2012), The Five Phases of Economic Development and Institutional Evolution in China, Japan and Korea, IN Institutions and Comparative Economic Development, Aoki, M., Kuran, T., and Roland, G. (Eds), Palgrave Macmillan, New York.

[62] Norman, E. (1943), Soldier and Peasant in Japan: The Origins of Conscription, Pacific Affairs, Vol. 16, No. 1, pp. 47–64.

[63] Ibid.

challenge the power of the feudal ruler, the daimyo, of the domain.[64] It was the process of separating those who could bear arms from those who could not which gave rise to the samurai class.[65] The process was known as *nohei-bunri*.[66] Nevertheless, during the Tokugawa period, there was a process by which wealthy peasants and merchants could enter the lower ranks of the samurai by becoming goshi.[67] This status could be granted by clan chiefs for those who reclaimed land under contract or *ukeoi*.[68] Towards the end of the Tokugawa period, it would be the goshi who would lead local militias in fighting the forces of the Shogunate.[69]

Village life was driven not by the rigid social hierarchy imposed by the Tokugawa Shogunate but by the agrarian way of life shared by all of the villagers.[70] The villagers, those with land and those without land, were nevertheless dependent on one another because of the nature of the agricultural work which was done. And the division of labour required for all work to be completed as required by the seasons. The Wakamonogumi was the organisational structure of peasants within the village. It was originally thought to have arisen as a primitive form of marriage, although during the Tokugawa period, the Wakamonogumi was an organisational structure composed of the males of the village who would schedule and organise the work needed to be done by the village.[71] Within the Wakamonogumi, leadership determination was based on variable local criteria and roles differentiated by age.[72] Village life and the Wakamonogumi were highly integrated due to the nature of the latter. The strict social hierarchy imposed on the people during the Tokugawa period as well as the structure of village life meant that a hierarchy of loyalties had also developed in Japanese society.[73] This set of loyalties was based on the family–daimyo–shogun nexus.[74] A hierarchy of loyalties ensured that in

[64] Ibid.

[65] Ibid.

[66] Ibid.

[67] Ibid.

[68] Ibid.

[69] Ibid.

[70] Varner, R. (1977), The Organised Peasant. The Wakamonogumi in the Edo Period, Monumenta Nipponica, Vol. 32, No. 4, pp. 459–483.

[71] Ibid.

[72] Ibid.

[73] Schooler, C. (1990), The Individual in Japanese history: Parallels to the Divergences from the European Experience, Sociological Forum, Vol. 5, No. 4.

[74] Ibid.

Tokugawa Japan, contract enforcement was much stronger than it was in contemporary Qing China.[75] Furthermore, while the political structure of Qing China was huge, in contrast in Tokugawa Japan, it was restricted to only 300 semi-autonomous domains.[76] The smaller scale of the political structure of Tokugawa Japan compared to Qing China meant that political and economic change could be effected more quickly and robustly in Japan than it could be in China. Therefore, the differences in the political structure of Tokugawa Japan and Qing China would explain why the former was able to industrialise in a more structured manner than the latter which faced years of civil war and invasion from the beginnings of the end of the Qing dynasty in the early part of the nineteenth century to the Communist victory in 1949. On the other hand, in contrast to the emerging ideals of individualism in contemporary European society, in Japan, there was more emphasis on mutual dependency as well as group loyalty.[77] However, some aspects of individualism remained in Japan. For example, entrepreneurship requires at least some level of individualism. In this case, in Hamamatsu, craftsmen and artisans were also brought in from outside the region.[78] The social mobility which was characteristic of Hamamatsu, unlike other parts of Japan, would have facilitated 'new blood' entering the region resulting in increased innovation and entrepreneurship. Nevertheless, overall Japanese group loyalty as it emerged during the Tokugawa period was at odds with the emerging individualism of western society.

Japan owed much to China for the development of its culture and civilisation.[79] Nevertheless, Japanese economic development shared several features which were also true of European economic development but not necessarily true of Chinese economic development. Firstly, both Japan and Europe shared the institution of feudalism. And, secondly, both Japan and

[75] Aoki, M. (2012), The Five Phases of Economic Development and Institutional Evolution in China, Japan and Korea, IN Institutions and Comparative Economic Development, Aoki, M., Kuran, T., and Roland, G. (Eds), Palgrave Macmillan, New York.

[76] Ibid.

[77] Hamaguchi, E. (1985), A contextual model of the Japanese: Toward a methodological innovation in Japan studies, Journal of Japanese Studies, Vol. 11, pp. 289–321.

[78] Aoyama, Y. (2009), Entrepreneurship and Regional Culture: The Case of Hamamatsu and Kyoto, Japan, Regional Studies, Vol. 43, No. 3, pp. 495–512, https://doi.org/10.1080/00343400902777042.

[79] Sanderson, S. (1994), The Transition from Feudalism to Capitalism: The Theoretical Significance of the Japanese Case, Review (Fernand Braudel Center), Vol. 17, No. 1, pp. 15–55.

Europe shared the transition from feudalism to capitalism.[80] The roots of the development of Japanese feudalism may have been in the period of the Kamakura Shogunate in 1185.[81] However, its complete development did not take place until the Ashikaga Shogunate in 1338.[82] The period of classical feudalism in Japan has often been identified as being from 1338 to 1603, while the Tokugawa period is known as the late feudal period.[83] Japan's isolationist policies from the start of the Tokugawa period to the mid-eighteenth century helped develop its internal markets and institutions such that the transition from feudalism to capitalism during the Meiji period was stronger.[84] However, when China became isolationist from the fifteenth century, it did not have the ingredients to develop the strong institutions which Japan would develop during the period of its isolation.[85] Most fundamental of these strong institutions would have been an expanding market economy.

The Tokugawa Shogunate banned Christianity in 1614.[86] The Jesuits had been the first European Christians to enter Japan, with the first bishop arriving in 1549.[87] Although Hideyoshi the predecessor of Ieyasu banned Christianity in Japan in 1587, the ban was not regularly enforced because Franciscans were able to enter Japan with a warm welcome in 1593.[88] Hideyoshi banned Christianity because of a fear that Japanese people would realign themselves with another religion and peoples. The English East India Company had been active in Japan from 1613 to 1626.[89] As a

[80] Jacobs, N. (1958), The Origin of Modern Capitalism and Eastern Asia, Hong Kong University Press, Hong Kong.

[81] Sanderson, S. (1994), The Transition from Feudalism to Capitalism: The Theoretical Significance of the Japanese Case, Review (Fernand Braudel Center), Vol. 17, No. 1, pp. 15–55.

[82] Reischauer, E. (1956), Japanese Feudalism, IN Coulborn, R. (Ed), Feudalism, Princeton University Press, Princeton.

[83] Sanderson, S. (1994), The Transition from Feudalism to Capitalism: The Theoretical Significance of the Japanese Case, Review (Fernand Braudel Center), Vol. 17, No. 1, pp. 15–55.

[84] Ibid.

[85] Ibid.

[86] Krieger, L., Neill, K., and Reynolds, E. (1997), World History: Perspectives on the Past, McDougal Littell.

[87] Benham, R., and Barton, A. (1996), Alternative Dispute Resolution: Ancient Models Provide Modern Inspiration, 12 Ga. St. U.L.rev.623.

[88] Ibid.

[89] Screech, T. (2012), The English and the Control of Christianity in the Early Edo Period, Japan Review, No. 24, pp. 3–40.

result, the English tried to bring their brand of Christianity, non-Catholic and free from the control of the Vatican, as opposed to that of the Jesuits to the shores of Japan. The first English ships with printed material and imagery, promoting the English version of Christianity and at the same time undermining the Jesuits and the Catholic church, arrived in Japan in 1616.[90] The printed material and imagery were then passed to Shogunate officials. However, the banning of the Christian faith in 1614 ensured that the English gained no favour from the Shogunate relative to either the Jesuits or the Franciscans.

This intolerance towards this foreign religion was underlined with the execution of 40,000 people following the 1637–1638 religiously associated Shimabara rebellion.[91] In this context, the control over popular dissent was taken away from the feudal lords and put into the hands of the Shogun himself.[92] Like Christianity, Shintoism had been introduced into Japan many centuries before. In this case, Shinto was the original religion of Japan but not indigenous to it, having arrived in Japan with the migrants from Korea and north east Asia in much earlier times.[93] However, Shinto was seen more as a cult than as a religion because it was essentially a combination of many heterogeneous cults and diverse in its origins.[94] Contextually, Shintoism involved the worship of the spirits of the shrines as well as the deities of the heaven and of the earth.[95] While western scholars considered Shinto to be the national faith of Japan, in reality it failed to develop as a national religion because of the differences amongst Japanese people due to regionalism.[96]

Once stability had returned to Japan following the installation of a Tokugawa government with the capacity to control the whole of Japan, there was a rapid increase in commercialisation and monetisation as well as the emergence of credit institutions in Osaka.[97] These credit institutions

[90] Ibid.

[91] White, J. (1988), State Growth and Popular Protest in Tokugawa Japan, The Journal of Japanese Studies, Vol. 14, No. 1, pp. 1–25.

[92] Ibid.

[93] De Bary, T. (1964), Early Shinto, IN Sources of Japanese Tradition, Vol. 1, Tsunoda, R., De Bary, T., and Keene, D. (Eds), Columbia University Press, New York.

[94] Ibid.

[95] Ibid.

[96] Ibid.

[97] Crawcour, S. (1961), The Development of a Credit System in Seventeenth Century Japan, The Journal of Economic History, Vol. 21, No. 3, pp. 347–352.

were on par with European credit institutions of the time.[98] The financial innovations which resulted in the first fifty years of the seventeenth century were put into systematic practice in the latter half of the seventeenth century and may have been responsible for the spurt in Japanese economic growth and development from 1690 to 1740.[99] Although commercial activity increased more in the seventeenth century, the roots of this increase are to be found in the sixteenth century. It was at this time that the existence of the aristocracy as well as a land-owning class who took no part in production allowed for the separation of consumption and production.[100] Furthermore, the commercialisation of the Japanese economy was being driven by the possibilities for new trade with the European powers, first among whom were the Portuguese. Moreover, the abolition of the medieval guilds in the latter quarter of the sixteenth century gave opportunities to landowners who had migrated to urban centres, but had lost links with the land, to take advantage of the situation and become merchants.[101] In this context, in the last fifteen years of the sixteenth century, several factors contributed to spurring commercial activity and facilitating even more rapid increases in economic growth once Japan had become unified under the Tokugawa Shogunate.[102] Firstly, Osaka grew to become a centre of consumption, and all types of goods flowed into Osaka from where it could be redirected to Edo. Secondly, weights and measures became standardised allowing for the ease of monetisation. Lastly, the demands of the wars in Korea in the last decade of the sixteenth century would have facilitated the redirection of resources in the Japanese economy towards production. The most important of the goods to flow into Osaka was rice.[103] The daimyos across Japan collected rice as tax and then had it shipped, often by sea, to Osaka where the rice could be monetised.[104] It was for this reason that the daimyos had facilities in Osaka in order to store large quantities of rice. Osaka was also important for the distribution of imports and exports associated with the port of Nagasaki.[105] By the mid-seventeenth century, the process from production to

[98] Ibid.
[99] Ibid.
[100] Ibid.
[101] Ibid.
[102] Ibid.
[103] Ibid.
[104] Ibid.
[105] Ibid.

consumption through intermediaries had become well established. As commercialisation increased, the specialisation in trade became more clear cut and detailed amongst merchants. This specialisation in trade became more acute after the 1630s when Japan became closed to the outside world and foreign trade was no longer possible. In this case, as the merchants were keen to maintain their market share and reduce competition, the formation of merchant cartels, specifically trade associations, was quite common.[106] These trade associations were also known as either nakama or kabunakama.[107] These associations not only strengthened the commercial power of the merchants within them but also allowed for the emergence of trust amongst merchants within the associations which facilitated them to extend credit to each other.[108] These lines of credit developed between wholesalers in Osaka and Edo and in other urban centres such as Kyoto to a lesser extent.[109] The lines of credit between wholesalers facilitated the development of bills of exchange which eased the development of commerce at a time when monetisation remained underdeveloped. This was because from the tenth to fifteenth centuries, no coins had been minted. Transactions were facilitated by either measured weights of gold or silver or by copper coins which had been imported from Ming dynasty China.[110] It was not until the seventeenth century, when Japan had become more or less unified under the Tokugawa government, that a national monetary system emerged as the government was able to mint a large number of coins which gradually became accepted nationally.[111] But even though a national monetary system emerged in the Tokugawa period, gold currency was used in the Edo region, silver in the Osaka region and copper coins at a national level.[112] Nevertheless, although a unified monetary system did emerge in the Tokugawa period, the use of pre-existing non-standard coins continued; and whereas the Edo region adopted gold for payment, the Osaka region adopted silver.[113] Moreover, there were also other currency substitutes such as bills of exchange, letters of credit, promissory

[106] Ibid.
[107] Ibid.
[108] Ibid.
[109] Ibid.
[110] Ibid.
[111] Ibid.
[112] West, M. (2000), Private Ordering at the World's First Futures Exchange, Michigan Law Review, Vol. 98, No. 8, pp. 2574–2615.
[113] Ibid.

notes and rice.[114] But of the substitute currencies, rice was the most important. This was because rice was the main crop and the one people relied upon for food. Furthermore, the annual Tokugawa annual budget was based on rice as a measure.[115] The currency which the feudal lords used to manage their domains was based on measures of rice which the feudal lords collected as taxes.[116] These rice taxes were then converted into currency using the Komegata ryogae or the rice money changers. Inevitably, in the context of financial transactions, there needed to be an element of enforceability. However, in Tokugawa Japan the legal system was fragmented with government laws only applicable in centrally controlled areas, with daimyos formulating their own laws for their domains.[117] But there was a Tokugawa government edict which stipulated that central government law would predominate over domain laws. While property laws existed at the domain level, dispute resolution was both hierarchical and unpredictable.[118] A codified legal system did not develop in Tokugawa Japan until 1742.[119] Before this time, disputes were managed and directed to the relevant authorities based on the Tokugawa social structure.[120] It was to the backdrop of a weak and primitive legal system as well as falling rice prices that the Dojima rice futures exchange opened in 1730 with the sponsorship of the Shogun Yoshimune.[121] The exchange was able to function simply because the constituent participants were able to draft rules and regulations in order to manage practice. And by doing so, the Dojima became an institution in itself.

Transactions in Osaka were rarely settled by immediate payment, and as transactions were made on credit, they were often settled over a period of months, normally two months. This would suggest that accounting systems were more developed and sophisticated than other parts of Japan because of the need to record monetary values owed by different parties

[114] Ibid.
[115] Ibid.
[116] Ibid.
[117] Ibid.
[118] Ibid.
[119] Ibid.
[120] Crawcour, S. (1961), The Development of a Credit System in Seventeenth Century Japan, The Journal of Economic History, Vol. 21, No. 3, pp. 347–352.
[121] West, M. (2000), Private Ordering at the World's First Futures Exchange, Michigan Law Review, Vol. 98, No. 8, pp. 2574–2615.

over a period.[122] While the credit system emerged in Osaka, no formally organised credit system existed in Japan until 1662 with the emergence of the 'Big 10 Bankers'.[123] However, the first fifty years of the seventeenth century saw the emergence of an informal credit system which only required to be organised from 1662.[124] In the early Tokugawa period, the Japanese financial system consisted of money changers, merchants turned financiers and daimyo financiers.[125] Nevertheless, there was also a developing banking system in a pyramidal structure with the 'Big Ten' banks at the top with an underlying field of smaller banks beneath them. The 'Big Ten' banks of Tokugawa Japan had all the characteristics of what in contemporary times would be the features of a country's central bank.[126] For example, no one would be able to set up in the banking business without the prior approval of the 'Big Ten' or without agreeing to abide by the regulations. Moreover, the 'Big Ten' would act as lender of last resort to the rest of the financial system, manage Tokugawa government finances, control the market for gold and silver as well as taking care of the reserves of the financial system.[127] In addition to the 'Big Ten' and the underlying structure of smaller banks, the Tokugawa financial system had three more categories of money changes including the Zeni-ryogae, the Minami-ryogae and the Komegata-ryogae. The Zeni-ryogae were numerous small-scale money changers. On the other hand, the Minami-ryogae were money changers that took deposits and made loans but were disassociated from the banking system. The Komegata-ryogae were associated with the provision of finance in the rice market in terms of spot and futures transactions in rice.[128]

As Tokugawa finances were becoming constrained by the largesse requirements of the samurai and a declining tax base, Tokugawa bureaucrats in the domains formulated an innovative economic thought called Kokueki thought in the eighteenth century.[129] The Kokueki was a form of

[122] Ibid.

[123] Ibid.

[124] Ibid.

[125] Ibid.

[126] Ibid.

[127] Ibid.

[128] Crawcour, S. (1961), The Development of a Credit System in Seventeenth Century Japan, The Journal of Economic History, Vol. 21, No. 3, pp. 347–352.

[129] Roberts, L. (1998), Mercantilism in a Japanese Domain, The Merchant Origins of Economic Nationalism in 18th century Tosa, Cambridge University Press, Cambridge.

economic thought based on mercantilism which had been adopted by the dominant domains in Japan in the latter part of the eighteenth century, with its origin said to be in 1760.[130] Moreover, Kokueki was the blueprint for a vision of a national system of organisation and which proved to be essential in the establishment of the Meiji period and beyond.[131] Based on the Kokueki, a number of economic initiatives were launched by the Japanese domains in the latter part of the Tokugawa era.[132] Furthermore, this led to some domains developing specific strategies. For example, Tokushima focused on the production of Indigo, Aizu on lacquerware and Matsue on the production of ginseng.[133] Therefore, in the context of the Kokueki and with its slogan of 'Prosperity for the country', there was a high level of domain involvement in the national strategy.[134]

The Tokugawa Economy

It was the merchants who established themselves in the city and the castle towns in trade, distribution and money lending at the start of the Tokugawa period who did much to facilitate Japan's economic growth over the next 100 years.[135] Although the merchants were more concentrated in Kyoto, Edo and Osaka as the Tokugawa period progressed, merchants in other parts of Japan also began to emerge. While Edo and Osaka emerged as centres of population in the sixteenth century. But Kyoto, the old imperial capital, always retained its significance as the heart of Japanese culture. On the other hand, Edo became associated with power and Osaka with money. The characteristics associated with these cities could then be associated with the activities of the merchants who resided there. In Osaka for example, merchants specialised in the provision of money, and once merchants had made a sufficient amount of money themselves, they would retire and pass on the business to the next generation. In retirement, the merchants while being at the head of their class in terms of social status would often spend their time pursuing the arts and culture in a city in which there were

[130] Ibid.
[131] Ibid.
[132] Ibid.
[133] Ibid.
[134] Ibid.
[135] Ibid.

relatively few samurai.[136] However, in China, it was possible for merchants to accumulate wealth, buy land and educate sons who could then pass the imperial exams in order to work for the imperial service. Therefore, in China it was possible for merchants to be able to be socially mobile. On the other hand, in Japan the culture was different. Although at the time of Yoshimune, the eighth Shogun who was in office from 1716 AD to 1745 AD,[137] it had been possible for wealthy merchants to 'buy' samurai status by aligning themselves with samurai families. The general trend was for Japanese merchants to build a business over time and to keep it within the family.[138] Moreover, the principles upon which Japanese merchants would build their businesses would be on the basis of the principles of good will, honesty and credit.[139] Furthermore, merchant family values were based on dedication to the family business, frugality, sincerity and hard work.[140] Osaka merchants were thus motivated and proud to be of the merchant class, easily integrating the principles of morality with that of making money.[141] Nevertheless, Edo merchants were based in a city whose population was half samurai oriented and thus influenced by samurai notions of 'manly entrepreneurship' where money was of secondary importance to managing the business. Edo merchants were also identified as being opulent spenders.[142] However, Osaka merchants were well known for being able to supply goods to the Edo market, although the extent of this fell towards the end of the seventeenth century.[143] At this moment in time, the Shogunate began to experience financial difficulties. This was primarily because the Shogunate's samurai were large in number but underemployed in the execution of their Shogunate duties.[144] Moreover, the samurai had become accustomed to a high standard of living which befitted their status on the upper echelons of Japan's social structure.[145] The increasing poverty of the samurai has been thought of as the reason as

[136] Sheldon, C. (1983), Merchants and Society in Tokugawa Japan, Modern Asian Studies, Vol. 17, No. 3, pp. 477–488.

[137] Goodman, G. (2013), Japan: The Dutch Experience, Bloomsbury, London.

[138] Sheldon, C. (1983), Merchants and Society in Tokugawa Japan, Modern Asian Studies, Vol. 17, No. 3, pp. 477–488.

[139] Ibid.

[140] Ibid.

[141] Ibid.

[142] Ibid.

[143] Ibid.

[144] Ibid.

[145] Ibid.

to why the samurai turned away the Tokugawa Shogunate and facilitated its overthrow in 1868.[146] The samurai class started experiencing increasing poverty in the early eighteenth century, primarily because their wants and needs were growing at a much faster rate than their nominal incomes.[147] For their incomes the samurai depended on the tax collected as a proportion of the annual crops. However, the agricultural yield was not increasing at the same rate as the population which increased by ten million from 1600 to 1700.[148] In contrast, between 1700 and 1868, the population only increased by two million. So, between 1600 and 1700, the Japanese population increase by five times as much as it did between 1700 and 1868. The increasing population consumed more and more of the agricultural produce. Moreover, heavy demands were also being placed on natural forests by the increasing human population. Wood from the trees of the forests was not only used for construction but also for fuel.[149] Furthermore, the woodlands were needed to stabilise the water supply to the arable lowlands in order to maintain its agricultural productivity.[150] By the beginning of the seventeenth century, Japan's increasing population was causing the depletion of Japan's forests.[151] In this case, by the late eighteenth century and the early part of the nineteenth century, a programme of reforestation was started by the Shogunate government and the domains.[152] This was because the natural regrowth of the forest ecosystem was unable to keep pace with the human consumption of wood from forest trees.[153] Due to the fact that by the latter part of the nineteenth century Japan was sourcing wood for consumption from reforestation programmes may suggest that institutional innovations such as the wariyama, nenkiyama and buwakebayashi had a positive impact on Tokugawa Japan's reforestation programme. The nenkiyama was the rental of forest land with the lessee acting as forest warden, planting trees which when grown would be cut

[146] Yamamura, K. (1971). The Increasing Poverty of the Samurai, Journal of Economic History, Vol. XXXI, No. 2, June, pp. 378–406.

[147] Ibid.

[148] Sheldon, C. (1983), Merchants and Society in Tokugawa Japan, Modern Asian Studies, Vol. 17, No. 3, pp. 477–488.

[149] Totman, C. (1984), Land-Use Patterns and Afforestation in the Edo Period, Monumenta Nipponica, Vol. 39, No. 1, pp. 1–10.

[150] Ibid.

[151] Ibid.

[152] Ibid.

[153] Ibid.

and sold by the leaser, with the lessee benefiting from a small commission and whatever was produced by the tree during its lifetime.[154] The wari-yama was the division of a forest amongst villagers for exploitation.[155] And the buwakebayashi was the rent of forest to entrepreneurs or villagers who would share the profit made from whatever was sold and produced on the land.[156]

In addition to depletion of the forest ecosystem, the crop yield was not increasing as much as required because of a lack of technological change and because of a lack of available acreage. Due to overspending the Shogunate began to put into place austerity measures which resulted in the economy slowing.[157] Moreover, the samurai also had to worry about interest charges on debts to merchants as well as the price level of goods which could have acted to reduce their purchasing power.[158] Nevertheless, while the other sectors of the economy were shrinking, only the merchant trade and the banking sectors prospered.[159] The merchants were able to enjoy a higher standard of living than the samurai and even in some cases the feudal lords or daimyos. So, while the samurai were getting poorer, the merchants were getting richer. The increased spending by the state on the upkeep of the samurai during the Tokugawa period without an equal or greater revenue stream often characterises the period as one which lacked fiscal integrity and featured declining political institutions.[160]

Proto-industrialisation in Japan, especially in the silk and cotton industries, began in the second half of the eighteenth century.[161] In this case, there was a shift in production from the high wage urban sector to the low wage rural economy, just as it happened in England.[162] At the same time as production was shifting from the urban economy to the rural economy,

[154] Ibid.

[155] Ibid.

[156] Ibid.

[157] Sheldon, C. (1983), Merchants and Society in Tokugawa Japan, Modern Asian Studies, Vol. 17, No. 3, pp. 477–488.

[158] Ibid.

[159] Ibid.

[160] White, J. (1988), State Growth and Popular Protest in Tokugawa Japan, The Journal of Japanese Studies, Vol. 14, No. 1, pp. 1–25.

[161] Sugihara, K. (2004), The State and the Industrious Revolution in Tokugawa Japan, Working Paper No. 02/04, Graduate School of Economics, Osaka University.

[162] Saito, O. (1985), Age of Proto-industrialisation: A Comparative History of Western Europe and Japan, Nihon Hyoronsha, Tokyo.

there was an increase in the division of labour within the household.[163] The members of the household at this time were able to perform different tasks at the same time such as working in the commercial crop sector, weaving and even working in the urban sector.[164] The employment of an apprentice was also common. A guarantor of apprentice employment during the Tokugawa period was known as a shitauke-nin.[165] In the Tokugawa period, heavy industry such as the manufacture of iron, armaments and ship building did not fully emerge until the end of the period when the western powers began to threaten Japan's independence.[166] In this case, in the late Tokugawa period, the iron, armaments and shipbuilding industries in Japan were oriented towards the military. This laid the foundation for militarism and military expansion after the Meiji Restoration of 1868. However, the ship building industry was owned and managed by the state due to a lack of private enterprise in these areas.[167] In contrast to the latter Tokugawa period, in the early part of the period, the Shogunate had banned ship building in Japan in 1635 AD in order to maintain their hegemony over Japan and prevent other sources of growth and change.[168] The cotton and spinning industries associated with western technology did not also appear until late in the Tokugawa period.[169] In this case, the characteristic of working for wages, working long hours and workers gaining industrial skills did not begin to emerge until the last century of the Tokugawa period.[170] Nevertheless, from the early part of the eighteenth century to the mid-nineteenth century, Japan's economic output grew steadily but slowly, although the population level had stabilised.[171] However, despite slowly rising economic growth, by 1860 AD, it was clear that Japan had not reached the pre-industrial levels of GDP per capita reached by European countries such as England, Sweden and the

[163] Sugihara, K. (2004), The State and the Industrious Revolution in Tokugawa Japan, Working Paper No. 02/04, Graduate School of Economics, Osaka University.

[164] Ibid.

[165] Sato, Y. (1984), The subcontracting production (Shitauke) system in Japan, Keio Business Review, Vol. 21, pp. 1–25.

[166] Smith, T. (1948), The Introduction of Western Industry to Japan During the Last Years of the Tokugawa period, Harvard Journal of Asiatic Studies, Vol. 11, No. 1/2, pp. 130–152.

[167] Ibid.

[168] Ibid.

[169] Ibid.

[170] Ibid.

[171] Ibid.

Netherlands.[172] But by the end of the Tokugawa period, the foundations the country needed for industrialisation to start and be successful in the Meiji period had been established. For example, commercial entities were specialised and larger; and entrepreneurs were numerous as well as being geographically dispersed, workers were literate and more mobile, agriculture was producing a surplus and capital was bountiful.[173] However, the most important factor which facilitated Japanese industrialisation was the new political climate at the end of the Tokugawa period and the start of the Meiji period.[174]

As rural household incomes increased, through the joint occurrence of the commercialisation of agriculture and proto-industrialisation, more food was consumed, and as a result, the population grew rapidly. There was also a transfer of knowledge of agricultural practice from China to Japan at the time. Moreover, from the late 1500 AD and the 1600 AD, there was also the transfer of technology from China to Tokugawa Japan.[175] However, in the context of functional institutional formation, Tokugawa Japan proved to develop more regulatory institutions than did China.[176] Nevertheless, the foundation of economic growth in Tokugawa Japan was due to strong state initiatives.[177] Firstly, the Baku Han system created an echelon of administrative samurai. Secondly, the social order with the samurai at the top of the food chain created a demand for commercial crops such as rice and consumer goods. Lastly, the requirement that the feudal lords reside in Edo and the lords had to spend at least six months of the year in Edo with the rest of the time in their domains meant that the lords have to spend a lot of money. The Sankon Kotai Seido or the alternate attendance system was a key institution which facilitated the transition of a feudal Japan into a modern state. It was formalised by the Tokugawa Shogunate in 1635 AD.[178] It allowed castle towns to become the hub of consumption and production. With the elite residing in the castle towns, there was a requirement for artisans, craftsmen, merchants and servants to

[172] Ibid.

[173] Ibid.

[174] Ibid.

[175] Sugihara, K. (2004), The State and the Industrious Revolution in Tokugawa Japan, Working Paper No. 02/04, Graduate School of Economics, Osaka University.

[176] Ibid.

[177] Ibid.

[178] Nakamura, J. (1981), Human Capital Accumulation in Premodern Rural Japan, The Journal of Economic History, Vol. XLI, No. 2.

also be located within these towns. Furthermore, as the guilds became banned, farmers also began to form a large proportion of the town's folk.[179] The military strength to consolidate territory in Japan increased because of the increase in agricultural productivity during the last years of the Ashikaga Shogunate.[180] This allowed for more taxes to be collected and for more warriors and soldiers to be hired. This led to a consolidation of territories by the Sengoku daimyo, the emergence of castle towns in the latter part of the period before the Tokugawa with a requirement that samurai should move from the rural areas to the castle towns to ensure that there could be no rebellion.[181] The existence and the need for castle towns were further sustained and developed by the arrival in Japan of the cannon and the arquebus in the mid-sixteenth century.[182] The cannon was useful for the defence of fixed locations, like the castle towns, against attack, and the arquebus required group training and fighting in formation.[183] The arquebus, therefore, required that the samurai be located in the castle towns. Twenty-five castle towns were constructed between 1580 and 1610, and each of these was located near and around broad plains so that the castle towns could be readily supplied with agricultural produce.[184] The developing market in castle towns meant that there was a need for the specialisation of labour in order to meet the consumption requirements for goods and for services in the castle towns.[185] Farmers living near the castle towns would produce perishable goods, and those in villages further away would produce staples which were more durable.[186] Castle towns were also located in the midst of agriculturally productive areas; and coupled with an increase in population in the first 100 years of the Tokugawa period, the castle towns were economically significant.[187] However, based on differences in local ecological and environmental factors, some farmers may have had a comparative advantage over others with regard to the nature, type and quantity of products which could be produced. Towards the latter part of the Tokugawa period, however, the population of the

[179] Ibid.
[180] Ibid.
[181] Ibid.
[182] Ibid.
[183] Ibid.
[184] Ibid.
[185] Ibid.
[186] Ibid.
[187] Ibid.

castle towns began to decline, and there was out migration from castle towns to rural areas.[188] However, Edo remained dominant nationally due to be the seat of power of the Shogun and the alternate attendance system.[189] Moreover, Edo was the most populous city in Japan during the last 200 years of the Tokugawa period, reaching its climax in the mid-nineteenth century.

The out migration from castle towns to outlying rural areas meant that there was a diffusion of knowledge from castle towns to rural areas as well as a movement of artisans, craftsmen, businesses and the urban environment. The latter included manufacturing, distribution, retailing and the labour market.[190] There were several reasons for the outward migration of labour from the castle towns back to villages in the rural areas. Firstly, businesses were finding it expensive to be situated in castle towns due to increasing wages, rent and the costs associated with guild membership. Secondly, as the incomes of farmers in rural areas increased, they were not motivated to move to the castle towns and could find waged employment in rural areas where some businesses had relocated. There was also other spill over effects in the country side of the movement of businesses out of castles towns to rural areas.[191] Firstly, landowners in rural areas were able to take advantage of the situation and utilise their entrepreneurial activities to make money. Secondly, workers in rural areas became accustomed to working long hours in order to have the income necessary to purchase the wide range of goods which were becoming readily available in rural areas. During the Tokugawa period, commercial activity became more and more necessary because the alternate attendance system of the ruling elite generated high costs which could only be covered by revenues resulting from greater commercial activity.[192]

The involvement of more and more rural workers in manufacturing and production required increased levels of training and at least a basic education in terms of numeracy and literacy.[193] Thus, there was an increase in

[188] Smith, T. (1973), Premodern Economic Growth: Japan and the West, Past and Present, Vol. 60, pp. 129–131.

[189] Rozman, G. (1974), Edo's Importance in the Changing Tokugawa Society, The Journal of Japanese Studies, Vol. 1, No. 1.

[190] Nakamura, J. (1981), Human Capital Accumulation in Premodern Rural Japan, The Journal of Economic History, Vol. XLI, No. 2.

[191] Ibid.

[192] Ibid.

[193] Ibid.

demand for apprenticeships and schooling in the latter half of the Tokugawa period.[194] Indeed, Shogun Yoshimune who had been Shogun from 1716 AD to 1745 AD had been in favour of knowledge acquisition and scholarly activity.[195] This led to greater human capital accumulation and proved to be sound preparation for the modernisation of the Japanese economy towards the end of the Tokugawa period and during the Meiji era. A typical feature of teaching practice in the Tokugawa period was that no attempt was made to control the learner's external behaviour.[196] Learning was also facilitated during the Tokugawa period because of the flourishing commercial publishing industry.[197]

In order to facilitate travel from other parts of Japan to Edo, required infrastructure such as roads, inns and stables had to be constructed. Pilgrims, to the shrines of Ise, Kannon and Kobo Daishi, as well as Daimyo processions were able to use the five newly constructed highways or Kaido as well as the Waki-Kaido or branch roads connecting the castle towns to the five main highways.[198] Better road infrastructure also facilitated more leisure travel which became easier over time. From the eighteenth century, the guards at the fifty-three checking stations, the Sekisho, along the Gokaido or central transport network were not as strict as they had been before in constraining the movement of travellers.[199] Furthermore, after the mid-eighteenth century, recreational travel for periods of two to four months became more and more common. The trips were associated with visits to hot springs, pilgrimage sites, urban centres as well as places of historical interest.[200]

The hierarchy of the engine of economic growth for Tokugawa Japan was then made up of the state, the han, the towns, the villages and the households. However, the facilitator of economic growth was not

[194] Ibid.

[195] Goodman, G. (2013), Japan: The Dutch Experience, Bloomsbury, London.

[196] Kojima, H. (1986), Japanese concepts of child development from the mid-17th century to the mid-19th century, International Journal of Behavioural Development, Vol. 9, pp. 315–329.

[197] Kazuko, H. (2009), Japanese printed books of the Edo period (1603–1867): history and characteristics of block printed books, Journal of the Institute of Conservation, Vol. 32, No. 1, pp. 79–101, https://doi.org/10.1080/19455220802630768.

[198] Blacker, C. (1984), The Religious Traveller in the Edo Period, Modern Asian Studies, Vol. 18, No. 4, pp. 593–608.

[199] Vaporis, C. (1989), Caveta Viator. Advice to Travellers in the Edo period, Monumenta Nipponica, Vol. 44, No. 4, pp. 461–483.

[200] Ibid.

existence of widespread private property rights but the low transactions costs of merchants and doing business due to the lack of civil strife as well as the trust which people had for each other.[201] Economic activity increased mainly because the Samurai were required to stay in castle towns rather than in rural areas; and trade and craft was prohibited outside towns and castle towns by the Shogunate.[202] However, proto-industrialisation greatly undermined this to an extent in the Tokugawa period; and by the end of the period, the restrictions were lame.[203] Technological change would also have helped to drive economic growth. However, because Japan was closed to the outside world during the Tokugawa period, there was no technological or knowledge diffusion from the outside world and Tokugawa Japan ended up being technologically deficient in comparison to the western powers. However, this was not always the case. For example, in the sixteenth century, Japanese craftsmen designed the flintlock such that a gun could fire in the rain.[204] Moreover, it was the Japanese of the sixteenth century who developed the gun sight which greatly improved the aim as well as the accuracy of the shot; and which was later copied by the Portuguese.[205] The Japanese were also world leaders in the manufacture of paper and higher quality and cheaper copper and steel than was produced in sixteenth century Europe.[206] Moreover, Japanese body armour and swords were also of a high quality for the time as well as being a major contributor to Japanese exports.[207]

Conclusion

Ieyasu Tokugawa united Japan into a loosely knot entity following the victory of his forces over a coalition of feudal lords in 1600 at the Battle of Sekigahara. Similarly, China had been reunified under the Yuan dynasty following the Mongol invasion in 1279 AD. As such Ieyasu was able to

[201] Sugihara, K. (2004), The State and the Industrious Revolution in Tokugawa Japan, Working Paper No. 02/04, Graduate School of Economics, Osaka University.

[202] Smith, T. (1973), Pre-modern Economic Growth: Japan and the West, Past & Present, No. 60, pp. 127–160.

[203] Ibid.

[204] Perrin, N. (1979), Giving Up the Gun: Japan's Reversion to the Sword, 1543–1879, David R. Godine, Boston.

[205] Ibid.

[206] Ibid.

[207] Ibid.

re-establish Shogunate or regency rule over Japan following its demise in the first half of the fifteenth century. However, opposition to his rule amongst the feudal lords or daimyos remained. In this case, it was not until 1615 that Ieyasu was able to cement and consolidate his authority as Shogun, following the victory of his forces over those of the feudal lords at the Battle of Osaka. At around the same time as the Battle of Osaka took place, the British were implementing their land grabbing mercantilist policies in India by establishing a factory at Masulipatnam in 1613. However, by this time the Dutch and the Portuguese had established themselves to a certain extent. Following the arrival of the traders, missionaries followed. At this time the Shogunate was fearful of losing its control over Japan due to the influence of the foreigners. As a result, the Shogunate expelled all foreigners from Japan and closed its borders, starting a policy of isolationism which lasted for over 200 years.

During the period of isolation from the rest of the world, Tokugawa Japan developed a number of distinct features. The first was the implementation of a social structure through which it was difficult but not impossible to move. In this case, the Tokugawa social structure in descending order was composed of the samurai, the peasants, the artisans and the merchants at the bottom. This was also the same in Ming China (1355–1644) where merchants were also seen to be at the bottom of the social scale. They were disruptive to society but necessary parasites who therefore needed to be regulated.[208] Secondly, it was in the Tokugawa period that the institutions and the structures of a market economy began to be laid. In this case, the Shogunate mandated that the families of the feudal lords or daimyos should reside in Edo where the Shogun was based. Moreover, the daimyo himself was mandated to stay in Edo for up to 6 months of the year, with the rest of the year spent in his domain. Edo became a generic 'castle town' in which samurai from rural areas were also expected to reside. The samurai depended on the Shogunate for their income. The castle town elite were becoming more and more urbanised and represented the primary consumers in Tokugawa Japan. As a result, merchants were drawn to the castle towns to provide goods and services which would cater for the needs of the castle town elite. This gave rise to an emergent production and distribution system centred on Osaka which became important in the case of the emergence of a money economy

[208] Yu, Y. (1967), Trade and Expansion in Han China: A Study in the Structure of Sino-Barbarian Economic Relations, University of California Press, Berkeley.

during the Tokugawa period. Osaka supplied the needs of Edo so there was a flow of goods and services from Osaka to Edo and a money flow from Edo to Osaka. The merchants of Osaka were famed for buying rice from farmers and then by a measure converting each quantity of rice into its monetary equivalent which would then be given to the daimyos so that in turn they could pay the samurai. By engaging in production and trade, the merchants would become wealthier than the samurai even though mobility in the social hierarchy of the Tokugawa period was not possible. Thirdly, in the first hundred years of the Tokugawa period from 1600 to 1700, there was a substantial increase in Japan's population. At the same time there was an increase in the production of rice. The tax the daimyos of a domain received was a proportion of the rice harvest in their respective domain. However, the daimyos and domains spent a lot of money on maintaining the upkeep of the commercially unproductive samurai. As spending by the daimyos and the Shogunate outbalanced tax revenue, it became necessary for both to become fiscally responsible and cut back spending. As a result, the samurai became poorer while the merchants got richer. But at the same time prices and wages were rising in urban centres such as Osaka, Kyoto and Edo as well as other relatively smaller castle towns. The result was that there was an outflow of the production of goods and services from these centres to rural areas. In this case, Japan went through the same process of proto-industrialisation which Great Britain went through before it became the first country in the world to undergo industrialisation proper. The rising poverty of the samurai during the Tokugawa period in the face of the western threat to Japan played a strong part in the samurai playing a key role in ending the Tokugawa period and befriending the Meiji period. While Japan turned away from colonisation by choosing to reform its own institutions with the instigation of the Meiji period, the situation was very different in Qing China (1644–1912). In this case, through isolationism the Chinese had become weaker militarily compared to the British who gained commercial and territorial concessions by defeating the Chinese in the Opium wars. Moreover, the influence of foreign religions such as Christianity may have led to internal conflict such as the Taiping rebellion which further weakened the Qing state. The differences in the trajectory of Tokugawa Japan and Qing China may have been due to the differences in their political structure and dimensions of state control. In the case of Qing China, the political and administrative structure needed to govern a very large country with a very large population was itself immense compared to that in Tokugawa Japan.

Furthermore, in Qing China political control through the imperial court was far more centralised than in the way in which the Shogunate governed Tokugawa Japan. Therefore, in Qing China the political institutions and system of governance remained inflexible in the face of changing internal and external conditions. Dissent within the ranks was not possible. However, in Tokugawa Japan the decentralised governance of the state ensured that dissent was possible and able to change the minds of the many to reform the system, end the Tokugawa Shogunate and embrace the Meiji restoration.

References

Aoki, M. (2012), The Five Phases of Economic Development and Institutional Evolution in China, Japan and Korea, IN Institutions and Comparative Economic Development, Aoki, M., Kuran, T., and Roland, G. (Eds), Palgrave Macmillan, New York.

Aoyama, Y. (2009), Entrepreneurship and Regional Culture: The Case of Hamamatsu and Kyoto, Japan, Regional Studies, Vol. 43, No. 3, 495–512, https://doi.org/10.1080/00343400902777042.

Benham, R., and Barton, A. (1996), Alternative Dispute Resolution: Ancient Models Provide Modern Inspiration, 12 Ga. St. U.L.rev.623.

Blacker, C. (1984), The Religious Traveller in the Edo Period, Modern Asian Studies, Vol. 18, No. 4, pp. 593–608.

Collcutt, M. (1981), Five Mountains: The Rinzai Zen Monastic Institution in Medieval Japan, Council on East Asian Studies, Harvard University, Cambridge, Massachusetts.

Crawcour, S. (1961), The Development of a Credit System in Seventeenth Century Japan, The Journal of Economic History, Vol. 21, No. 3, pp. 347–352.

De Bary, T. (1964), Early Shinto, IN Sources of Japanese Tradition, Vol. 1, Tsunoda, R., De Bary, T., and Keene, D. (Eds), Columbia University Press, New York.

Finlay, R. (2008), The Voyages of Zheng He: Ideology, State Power, and Maritime Trade in Ming China, The Journal of the Historical Society, Vol. VIII, No. 3.

Gascoigne, B. (2003), The Dynasties of China: A History, Carroll & Graf Publishers.

Goodman, G. (2013), Japan: The Dutch Experience, Bloomsbury, London.

Gungwu, W., and Chin-keong, N. (2004), Maritime China in Transition 1750–1850, Harrassowitz Verlag, Wiesbaden.

Hamaguchi, E. (1985), A contextual model of the Japanese: Toward a methodological innovation in Japan studies, Journal of Japanese Studies, Vol. 11, pp. 289–321.

Henderson, D. (1952), Some Aspects of Tokugawa Law, Washington Law Review Vol. 21, No. 1, pp. 96, 98–102.
Iwata, M. (1964), Okubo Toshimichi: The Bismarck of Japan, University of California Press, Berkeley.
Jacobs, N. (1958), The Origin of Modern Capitalism and Eastern Asia, Hong Kong University Press, Hong Kong.
Jansen, M. (2000), The Makings of Modern Japan, The Belknap Press of Harvard University Press, Cambridge, Massachusetts.
Kazuko H. (2009), Japanese printed books of the Edo period (1603–1867): history and characteristics of block printed books, Journal of the Institute of Conservation, Vol. 32, No. 1, pp. 79–101, https://doi.org/10.1080/19455220802630768.
Kojima, H. (1986), Japanese concepts of child development from the mid-17th century to the mid-19th century, International Journal of Behavioural Development, Vol. 9, pp. 315–329.
Krieger, L., Neill, K., and Reynolds, E. (1997), World History: Perspectives on the Past, McDougal Littell.
Laver, M. (2011), The Sakoku Edicts and the Politics of Tokugawa Hegemony, Cambria Press, Amherst, New York.
Lawton, T. (1983), Chinese Art of the Warring States Period: Change and Continuity, 480–222BC, Freed-Hardeman College.
Nakamura, J. (1981), Human Capital Accumulation in Premodern Rural Japan, The Journal of Economic History, Vol. XLI, No. 2.
Norman, E. (1943), Soldier and Peasant in Japan: The Origins of Conscription, Pacific Affairs, Vol. 16, No. 1, pp. 47–64.
Perez, L. (2013), Japan at War, An Encyclopedia, ABC-CLIO, Oxford, UK.
Perrin, N. (1979), Giving Up the Gun: Japan's Reversion to the Sword, 1543–1879, David R. Godine, Boston.
Reischauer, E. (1956), Japanese Feudalism, IN Coulborn, R. (Ed), Feudalism, Princeton University Press, Princeton.
Roberts, L. (1998), Mercantilism in a Japanese Domain, The Merchant Origins of Economic Nationalism in 18th century Tosa, Cambridge University Press, Cambridge.
Rozman, G. (1974), Edo's Importance in the Changing Tokugawa Society, The Journal of Japanese Studies, Vol. 1, No. 1.
Sanderson, S. (1994), The Transition from Feudalism to Capitalism: The Theoretical Significance of the Japanese Case, Review (Fernand Braudel Center), Vol. 17, No. 1, pp. 15–55.
Saito, O. (1985), Age of Proto-industrialisation: A Comparative History of Western Europe and Japan, Nihon Hyoronsha, Tokyo.
Sato, Y. (1984), The subcontracting production (Shitauke) system in Japan, Keio Business Review, Vol. 21, pp. 1–25.

Schooler, C. (1990), The Individual in Japanese history: Parallels to the Divergences from the European Experience, Sociological Forum, Vol. 5, No. 4.
Screech, T. (2012), The English and the Control of Christianity in the Early Edo Period, Japan Review, No. 24, pp. 3–40.
Sheldon, C. (1983), Merchants and Society in Tokugawa Japan, Modern Asian Studies, Vol. 17, No. 3, pp. 477–488.
Smith, T. (1948), The Introduction of Western Industry to Japan During the Last Years of the Tokugawa period, Harvard Journal of Asiatic Studies, Vol. 11, No. 1/2, pp. 130–152.
Smith, T. (1973), Pre-modern Economic Growth: Japan and the West, Past & Present, No. 60, pp. 127–160.
Sugihara, K. (2004), The State and the Industrious Revolution in Tokugawa Japan, Working Paper No. 02/04, Graduate School of Economics, Osaka University.
Tharoor, S. (2018), Inglorious Empire: What the British Did to India, Penguin, UK.
Totman, C. (1984), Land-Use Patterns and Afforestation in the Edo Period, Monumenta Nipponica, Vol. 39, No. 1, pp. 1–10.
Turnbull, S. (2012), Tokugawa Ieyasu (Command), Osprey Publishing.
Vaporis, C. (1989), Caveta Viator. Advice to Travellers in the Edo period, Monumenta Nipponica, Vol. 44, No. 4, pp. 461–483.
Varner, R. (1977), The Organised Peasant. The Wakamonogumi in the Edo Period, Monumenta Nipponica, Vol. 32, No. 4, pp. 459–483.
Weber, M. (1947), The Theory of Social and Economic Organization, University Press, New York.
West, M. (2000), Private Ordering at the World's First Futures Exchange, Michigan Law Review, Vol. 98, No. 8, pp. 2574–2615.
White, J. (1988), State Growth and Popular Protest in Tokugawa Japan, The Journal of Japanese Studies, Vol. 14, No. 1, pp. 1–25.
Yamamura, K. (1971). The Increasing Poverty of the Samurai. Journal of Economic History, Vol. XXXI, No. 2, June, pp. 378–406.
Yu, Y. (1967), Trade and Expansion in Han China: A Study in the Structure of Sino-Barbarian Economic Relations, University of California Press, Berkeley.

CHAPTER 5

The Meiji Period (1868–1912): Industrialisation and Democratisation

Introduction

Japan at the time of the Meiji Restoration of 1868 AD was essentially a feudal society stratified into four classes, in descending order, the warriors, the peasants, the artisans and the merchants.[1] At the time, geographically Japan was divided in 260 feudal domains each controlled by a lord who in turn was responsible for managing the people and the land, while they were also answerable to the Shogun.[2] The latter was the head of the Tokugawa family, who resided in a castle in the city of Edo, and whose title was conferred by a titular Emperor who held no real power or authority.[3] However, while the Emperor held on symbolic political authority, he was still seen to hold divine authority at the imperial residence in Kyoto.[4] On the other hand, while the Shogun held political power he had to delegate some of his authority to local feudal lords because of their strength in order to keep central control over the Japanese archipelago.[5] The policies followed by the Shogunate during the Tokugawa period allowed

[1] Hillsborough, R. (2017), Samurai: Assassins, 'Dark Matter' and the Meiji Restoration, 1853–1868, McFarland & Company, Inc., Publishers, Jefferson, North Carolina.

[2] Ibid.

[3] Ibid.

[4] Kohno, M. (2001), On the Meiji Restoration: Japan's Search for Sovereignty, International Relations of the Asia-Pacific, Vol. 1, pp. 265–283.

[5] Ibid.

S. Ramesh, *China's Economic Rise*,
https://doi.org/10.1007/978-3-030-49811-5_5

the Japanese economy to surpass imperial China's GDP per capita.[6] However, the social stratification of Japanese society in the Tokugawa period was such that economic resources were organised in order to benefit the extravagant lifestyle of the elite 6% of the population at the expense of the rest of the population.[7] Moreover, these elites of the population during the Tokugawa period were neither militarily prepared nor strong enough to meet the military challenges posed by the western nations in the nineteenth century.[8] These military challenges were primarily due to the Americans and the British. Indeed, it has been estimated that the consumption of the 6% of the Japanese elite during the Tokugawa period consumed at least 25% of Japan's GDP at the time.[9] The military might visited upon Tokugawa Japan by the US admiral Perry in 1853 and again in 1854 acted as a signal to would be modernisers that unless Tokugawa Japan could be reformed, Japan would always have to be subordinate to western power even to the extent of becoming a colony. Therefore, the only alternative of staving off colonisation by the western powers was to reorganise the political, economic and social structures of Tokugawa Japan such that rapid economic and military development would take place. A politically strong and economically prosperous Japan would mean that it would be also militarily strong and it could defend itself against western aggressors. In this case, the transformation of the Japanese military was the visible evidence for the transition from the Tokugawa period to the Meiji period. In fact, the Japanese military were the first to not only hire the foreign advisors and specialists who had the requisite knowledge to modernise them but also to use western systems of organisation of resources.[10] Furthermore, not only did the Japanese navy and army become the largest organisational forms in Japan in the transition from the Tokugawa period to the Meiji period, but they also acted as a stimulus for the development of new systems mostly associated with a centralised tax system and a system of universal primary education.[11] Education in the Meiji period was centrally controlled by the Ministry of Education, especially in the

[6] Maddison, A. (2006), Asia in the world economy, 1500–2030, Asian Pacific Economic Literature, Vol. 20, No. 2, pp. 1–37.

[7] Ibid.

[8] Ibid.

[9] Ibid.

[10] Westney, D. (1986), The Military, IN Japan in Transition: From Tokugawa to Meiji, Jansen, M., and Rozman, G. (Eds), Princeton University Press, Princeton, New Jersey.

[11] Ibid.

1880s.[12] This central control of the educational system was necessary because in Meiji Japan it was seen that only a uniform educational system would allow for state formation.[13] This is in contrast to the nature of the educational system in the Tokugawa period which was more diversified. However, in contrast to the nation building objectives of the Meiji government, the Tokugawa Shogunate ruled over a politically decentralised country which was held loosely together and would not be a 'nation' in the modern context. In the transition from private to public, Tokugawa to Meiji, Japan's education system allowed for the upward mobility of the commoner through society which had previously been stratified.[14]

While the common perception is that Tokugawa Japan was underdeveloped, and a closed off society, as well as being a feudalistic society, this may not be entirely the case.[15] In fact the Tokugawa Shogunate was selectively able to pick and use foreign expertise as long as its own development strategy could be followed. Moreover, some reports suggest that Commodore Perry was impressed with the Japanese technology he saw on his visit to Japan in 1853 and 1854.[16] Furthermore, there was also indigenous Japanese technological development, from 1850, for its industrialisation and military means with short-term support from specifically selected American and European specialists.[17] However, in general there were three types of foreign workers in Meiji Japan which included labourers, and professional advisors who were either general advisors or specialist advisors.[18] Over 50% of all foreign workers in Meiji Japan were Chinese labourers.[19] Moreover, over 60% of professional advisors were involved in

[12] Rubinger, R. (1986), Education: From One Room to One System, IN Japan in Transition: From Tokugawa to Meiji, Jansen, M., and Rozman, G. (Eds), Princeton University Press, Princeton, New Jersey.

[13] Ibid.

[14] Ibid.

[15] Morris-Suzuki, T. (1994), The Technological Transformation of Japan: From the Seventeenth to Twenty-First Century, Cambridge University Press, Cambridge.

[16] Ibid.

[17] Gooday, G., and Low, M. (1998), Technology Transfer and Cultural Exchange: Western Scientists and Engineers Encounter Late Tokugawa and Meiji Japan, OSIRIS, Vol. 13, Beyond Joseph Needham: Science, Technology, and Medicine in East and Southeast Asia, pp. 99–128.

[18] Ibid.

[19] Ibid.

education and training.[20] Thus, it is clear that the Japanese were firmly in charge of the technological modernisation of their economy, which would also favour rapid industrialisation. However, although initially Meiji Japan relied upon western models for its military (French), banking (American) and for its cotton industry (British), these models were adapted over time for Japanese needs.[21]

Restoration

Although the Meiji Restoration may seem to be the starting point for the integration of medieval Japan into the hierarchy of modern sovereign states, it must be recognised that Japan could still be seen as a sovereign state in the previous Edo or Tokugawa period.[22] Conventional hypotheses suggest that the responsibility for the restoration of the rule of the Emperor in the Meiji period was due to the political decay in the Tokugawa period, the rise of Japanese nationalism led by Katsu Kaishu and Sakamoto Ryoma, or the threat to Japan's sovereignty due to the rise of western imperialism.[23] However, the Meiji restoration may simply have occurred because western nations differentiated between different aspects of Japan's sovereignty, recognising some aspects while not respecting others. This could have constrained the behaviour of the Japanese leaders of the Tokugawa period in how they reacted to the Nanamugi Incident of 1862, causing the Tokugawa period to come to an end in 1868.[24] During the Nanamugi Incident, the armed retinue of the son of the Daimyo of Satsuma killed a British national and seriously assaulted two others, stirring resentment against foreigners living in Japan.[25] Nevertheless, the Nanamugi Incident may simply have been the pivot of the Meiji restoration because the dawn of a modern Japan spans the period 1853–1868.[26] Within this period it is

[20] Burks, A. (1985), The West's Inreach: The Oyatoi Gaikokujin, IN The Modernizers: Overseas Students, Foreign Employees, and Meiji Japan, Burks, A. (Ed), Westview, Boulder, Colorado.

[21] Stern, R., Wright, G., Patrick, H. (2010), The Japanese Economy in Retrospect: Selected Papers by Gary R. Saxonhouse, World Scientific.

[22] Kohno, M. (2001), On the Meiji Restoration: Japan's Search for Sovereignty, International Relations of the Asia-Pacific, Vol. 1, pp. 265–283.

[23] Ibid.

[24] Ibid.

[25] Perez, L. (2013), Japan at War: An Encyclopedia, ABC-CLIO, Oxford, UK.

[26] Hillsborough, R. (2017), Samurai: Assassins, 'Dark Matter' and the Meiji Restoration, 1853–1868, McFarland & Company, Inc., Publishers, Jefferson, North Carolina.

also possible to say that the revolution to overthrow the Tokugawa and reinstate Emperor power began with the assassination of the Shogun's Regent, Ii Naosuke, in 1860.[27] This was then followed up by a reign of terror on the streets of Kyoto, led by the leader of the Tosa Loyalist Party, Takechi Hanpeita.[28] However, the spur for change in Japan came in 1853 when Commodore Perry arrived there with his gunboat, epitomising the supremacy of American military power, demanding that the Tokugawa Shogunate end its isolationist policy for Japan and open up its borders for international trade.[29] The preamble to Perry's expedition was a sign of the times. In mid-nineteenth century America, people were migrating from the east coast to the west coast in large numbers, a Pacific steamship line had been built and America's whaling fleet was reorienting towards the northern Pacific.[30] Perry had heard through acquaintances of the potential wealth which was hidden in trade with the Far East, but had long been dominated by the European powers such as Great Britain and the Netherlands.[31] Moreover, he had set his mind to opening up a Pacific-Asia trade route for America and at the heart of this strategy lay Japan, the trade with which had not been dominated by the European powers principally because Japan under the Tokugawa Shogunate operated a closed border policy with no Japanese involvement in international trade. In this light, Perry took command of the US East India squadron in 1851, and his mission was soon upgraded to opening Japan to international and US trade by President Fillmore and Secretary Graham. The latter ensured that Perry set sail from US shores with the largest naval fleet assembled in US history.[32] However, Perry's first trip to Japan in 1853 only allowed him to deliver President Fillmore's demands to the Japanese Emperor. During this visit, Perry displayed cunning and stealth in getting his message and intentions through to Japanese seniority who only engaged with his party at junior levels at the beginning of the visit. However, by refusing to depart, refusing supplies from the Japanese who would then expect Perry and his ships to leave, and by moving his ships around Uraga and Edo Bay,

[27] Ibid.

[28] Ibid.

[29] Kohno, M. (2001), On the Meiji Restoration: Japan's Search for Sovereignty, International Relations of the Asia-Pacific, Vol. 1, pp. 265–283.

[30] Wittner, D. (2005), Commodore Matthew Perry and the Perry Expedition to Japan, PowerPlus Books, New York.

[31] Ibid.

[32] Ibid.

Perry demonstrated his tenacity.[33] Having been assured of a warm response to President Fillmore's letter, Perry and his squadron left Uraga, vowing to return for a response with more ships. This Perry did in March 1854; and while the Japanese succumbed to all of the demands in President Fillmore's initial letter, Perry wanted more from them in the context of a favourable trade treaty as the one which existed between the United States and China.[34] The Japanese could not withstand Perry's intentions and gave way to these with the signing of the Treaty of Kanagawa at the end of March 1854.[35] Russian warships had also arrived at the port of Nagasaki in 1852 with a letter from the Russian Czar to the Japanese Shogun pressing for greater trade relations between the two countries, a visit repeated in 1854.[36]

The Treaty of Kanagawa allowed for the stationing of an American diplomat in Japan; and duly Townsend Harris arrived in Japan in August 1856 at the port of Shimoda, where he was also given accommodation in a small Buddhist temple by the Japanese authorities in September 1856.[37] It was while Harris was at Shimoda that he demanded a more favourable trade treaty from the Japanese with the United States which would allow US merchants to reside and trade within Japan.[38] The Treaty of Kanagawa only allowed for trade between the United States and Japan. Harris's tenacity paid off, and as a result, the Shimoda Convention was signed between the United States and Japan in June 1857. It was also in 1857 that Donker Curtis of the Netherlands Board of Trade in Deishma[39] warned the Shogunate of not abiding by the terms of the treaties made with foreign powers, using China as an example.[40] China had been defeated by the British in the Opium Wars of the early 1840s.[41] As a consequence, China was forced by the British to open its ports at Amoy, Canton,

[33] Ibid.

[34] Ibid.

[35] Ibid.

[36] Keene, D. (2005), Emperor of Japan: Meiji and His World, 1852–1912, Columbia University Press.

[37] Kshetry, G. (2008), Foreigners in Japan: A Historical Perspective, Xlibris Corporation.

[38] Ibid.

[39] Jones, H. (1974), Bakumatsu Foreign Employees, Monumenta Nipponica, Vol. 29, No. 3, pp. 305–327.

[40] Keene, D. (2005), Emperor of Japan: Meiji and His World, 1852–1912, Columbia University Press.

[41] Fay, P. (1975), The Opium War, 1840–42, The University of North Carolina Press.

Shanghai, Ningpo, Fuchow and Canton.[42] However, the port of Canton resisted opening up to trade with the British, with the British flag at that port being torn apart.[43] As a result, in order to enforce the terms of the treaty, British naval power reduced Canton to rubble.[44] Reports of treaties being imposed on China and the destruction in Chinese cities, through the technologically and militarily superior Europeans, reached the Japanese Shogunate.[45] Furthermore, the fears of the Japanese elite of foreign occupation and dominance of their country were still heightened by the short Russian occupation of Tsushima in 1861 and the competition between the British and the French to provide support for the great lords or Daimyo and the Shogunate, respectively.[46] In this case, the Japanese Shogunate was prepared to appease and kowtow to the Europeans and the Americans until they were at a sufficient military and economic development level to drive the foreigners from their shores.[47]

The Shimoda Convention stipulated how Americans could live in the open ports of Japan, the medium of exchange between Americans in Japan and between the Japanese themselves as well as the legal jurisdiction of Americans and Japanese.[48] However, Harris wanted more from the Japanese, and unlike Perry, he secured a meeting with Shogun Iesada and his ministers in December 1857.[49] Hotta Masayoshi, the senior minister, led the Japanese side in negotiations with the Americans. The Shogunate was very interested in reaching an agreement with the Americans which would also help Japan to modernise and avoid American occupation. By February 1858, a more comprehensive trade agreement between Japan and the United States was ready to be signed. The terms of the new treaty, the Harris Treaty, allowed for the opening up of four additional Japanese ports besides Shimoda and Hakodate, including Kanagawa, Nagasaki,

[42] Keene, D. (2005), Emperor of Japan: Meiji and His World, 1852–1912, Columbia University Press.

[43] Ibid.

[44] Ibid.

[45] Jones, H. (1974), Bakumatsu Foreign Employees, Monumenta Nipponica, Vol. 29, No. 3, pp. 305–327.

[46] Jansen, M. (1995), The Meiji Restoration, IN The Emergence of Meiji Japan, Jansen, M. (Ed), Cambridge University Press, Cambridge.

[47] Jones, H. (1974), Bakumatsu Foreign Employees, Monumenta Nipponica, Vol. 29, No. 3, pp. 305–327.

[48] Kshetry, G. (2008), Foreigners in Japan: A Historical Perspective, Xlibris Corporation.

[49] Ibid.

Niigata and Hyogo.[50] Furthermore, US consular officials were also to be allowed to reside in Edo and US merchants in Edo and Osaka.[51] However, many feudal lords opposed the proposed trade agreement on the basis that too many concessions had been made to the Americans.[52] Due to the open hostility of the feudal lords to the proposed agreement, Hotta Masayoshi arrived in the imperial capital of Kyoto to seek the approval for the proposed trade agreement from Emperor Komei, in March 1858.[53] However, Emperor Komei sided with the feudal lords in opposing the proposed trade agreement especially, in his role as the religious guardian with the divine right to rule. The Emperor's opposition arose because open access to foreigners of Osaka and Hyogo would allow them to be too close to the sacred capital of Kyoto.[54] While Masayoshi did not get the Emperor's approval for the trade agreement, he left Kyoto with the Emperor's order to consider the opinions of the feudal lords, in other words to renegotiate or otherwise nullify the trade agreement. However, to overcome the lack of imperial consent for the agreement, the Shogunate appointed Ii Naosuke as Regent to whom the powers and the authority were forcefully delegated. Naosuke signed the trade agreement, circumventing the need for Emperor Komei's approval in July 1858.[55] Naosuke's actions were on behalf of the national interest and according to the international circumstances of the time.[56] The signing of the Harris Treaty was the only way in which Japan could maintain its independence, until it could prepare to defend itself from foreign powers such as the Americans.[57] Naosuke followed the signing of the Harris Treaty with moves to crush its opponents in the Shogunate, including the execution of pro-Emperor samurai.[58] As Shogun Iesada was dying, Naosuke also ensured that a young weak Shogun, Tokugawa Yoshitomi, Iemochi was selected to succeed him, ignoring the wishes of the pro-Emperor daimyo who had wanted

[50] Ibid.

[51] Ibid.

[52] Ibid.

[53] Ibid.

[54] Ibid.

[55] Cunningham, M., and Zwier, L. (2009), The End of the Shoguns and the Birth of Modern Japan, Twenty-First Century Books, Minneapolis, USA.

[56] Kshetry, G. (2008), Foreigners in Japan: A Historical Perspective, Xlibris Corporation.

[57] Cunningham, M., and Zwier, L. (2009), The End of the Shoguns and the Birth of Modern Japan, Twenty-First Century Books, Minneapolis, USA.

[58] Ibid.

Tokugawa Yoshinobu selected as Shogun.[59] This is because his Tokugawa sect believed that the foreigners should be expelled. More treaties with foreign powers were negotiated and signed by Naosuke. However, it was Naosuke's punishment and treatment of the Lord of Mito, Tokugawa Nariaki, for supporting the Emperor and opposing the Harris Treaty which would end his life by beheading by a samurai of the Mito sect. The killings of pro-western and pro-treaty officials would continue. This is because the low-ranking samurai and the masterless samurai, the ronin, had little to lose from opposing the Shogunate and siding with the Emperor. They had neither the incomes nor the positions of higher-ranking samurai who were by their positions tied to the Shogunate establishment.[60] Furthermore, anti-Shogunate, pro-emperor sentiment amongst the Samurai became consolidated when they met together at swordsmanship schools and were able to discuss their anti-foreigner feelings face to face.[61] These meetings coupled with the teachings of nativist scholars who urged Japan to return to its Shinto, animist past, reflected in a growing violent movement which favoured the restoration of the authority and power of the imperial Emperor and the removal of the Shogunate.

With the advent of foreigners entering Japan after the late 1850s, there was also an economic crisis looming. This was because it was cheaper for foreigners to buy gold in Japan than they could internationally, at a rate of 5 ounces of silver to 1 ounce of gold in Japan compared to 15 ounces of silver to 1 ounce of gold internationally.[62] As foreigners cornered the gold market in Japan, the dramatic outflow of gold caused the Japanese price level to soar, causing the cost of basic food such as rice to soar which was already in short supply due to a poor harvest.[63] This would lead to further heighten social unrest by the samurai acting on behalf of ordinary people. Nevertheless, the Japanese economy was entering the world trade system at a time when the engine of growth of the world economy had initially been the industrial revolution in England in the late eighteenth and early nineteenth centuries, this being superseded by a second industrial revolution in late nineteenth century America. As a result of industrialisation in

[59] Ibid.
[60] Ibid.
[61] Ibid.
[62] Ibid.
[63] Ibid.

Great Britain and in America, a modernising Japanese economy would be bound to grow and prosper.

Emperor Komei was well educated and highly xenophobic.[64] His son, the father of the future Emperor Meiji, was his last surviving child out of five and was born on the 15th October 1851.[65] Of the feudal domains, those most loyal to the Emperor were Satsuma, Choshu, Saga and Tosa. Notably, it had been the retinue of the son of the lord of Satsuma who had been responsible for the Nanamugi Incident in which a foreigner had been killed and anti-foreigner resentment stirred. The domain of Mito was not as effective due to losing its strength through an internal conflict.[66] Together these south western domains of Japan had the resources to buy western guns and ships as well as having a larger number of Samurai than did other regions of Japan.[67] The samurai in Satsuma, Choshu and Tosa also harboured the hate of centuries of resentment of these domains towards Tokugawa rule.[68] This provided a very strong incentive and motive for defeating them. Though there was military conflict between the forces from domains loyal to the Emperor and the forces loyal to the Shogunate, the former proved to be the stronger. The conflict was settled with reforms which saw the reduced primacy of Edo and the Shogunate and the political ascendancy of Kyoto, the imperial court and the power and authority of the Emperor. Central to these reforms was the appointment of loyalist minded Tokugawa people to high positions in the Shogunate. For example, Matsudaira Shungaku was appointed as Supreme Councillor, and Tokugawa Yoshinobu who had lost the Shogunate to the younger Tokugawa Yoshitomi, Shogun Iemochi, was appointed as his guardian.[69] Other reforms included the punishment of government officials who had served in the Shogunate after the killing of Naosuke including those who had negotiated treaties with the foreigners.[70] Moreover, the Naosuke clan lost its role as protector of Kyoto, and the military residence requirement of the Daimyo in Edo was reduced to 100 days within a

[64] Keene, D. (2005), Emperor of Japan: Meiji and His World, 1852–1912, Columbia University Press.

[65] Ibid.

[66] Jansen, M. (1995), The Meiji Restoration, IN The Emergence of Meiji Japan, Jansen, M. (Ed), Cambridge University Press, Cambridge.

[67] Ibid.

[68] Ibid.

[69] Ibid.

[70] Ibid.

three-year period.[71] In this case, the Daimyo set up residences in Kyoto, and the centre of the imperial court was now becoming the dominant political player at the expense of Edo. As a final sign of the decline of the power of the Shogunate and the ascendancy of the Emperor, the young Shogun visited him on a few occasions until the young Shogun Iemochi died in 1866.[72] He was succeeded by Shogun Keiki in 1867 as the fifteenth Tokugawa Shogun, although by November 1867, Keiki agreed to resign as Shogun, thus permanently ending Japan's Shogunate.[73] Authority and power were now back in the hands of the imperial household and the divine Emperor. Nevertheless, the Northern League anti-imperial forces were still engaging and on occasion defeating imperial forces.[74] Furthermore, the law and order situation in Edo was getting worse day by day, and the imperial forces stationed in Edo were unable to get to grips with this worsening situation.[75]

The resignation of the last Shogun followed the death of Emperor Komei from smallpox in February 1867.[76] The people of Japan thought at the time that the deaths of the Shogun and the Emperor at about the same time were due to divine retribution for the signing of the treaties with the western barbarians.[77] Emperor Komei was succeeded by his fifteen-year-old son, Prince Mutsuhito, who was crowned as the Emperor Meiji in 1868, to signify his reign as a period of enlightenment.[78] The presence of the divine Emperor in Edo would be a blow to the rebels of the Northern League, as well as helping to stabilise the situation there.[79] This would be because of the consolidation of power and authority in one place, that of the national government and the imperial household. Thus, for these reasons and at the urging of Okubo Toshimichi, the imperial household and

[71] Ibid.

[72] Ibid.

[73] Hopkins, D. (1983), The Greatest Killer: Smallpox in History, The University of Chicago Press, Chicago.

[74] Steele, M. (2003), Alternative Narratives in Modern Japanese History, RoutledgeCurzon, London.

[75] Ibid.

[76] Hopkins, D. (1983), The Greatest Killer: Smallpox in History, The University of Chicago Press, Chicago.

[77] Ibid.

[78] Ibid.

[79] Steele, M. (2003), Alternative Narratives in Modern Japanese History, RoutledgeCurzon, London.

the Emperor moved from Kyoto to Edo.[80] Okubo Toshimichi, Kido Koin and Saigo Takamori were the three key proponents of the Meiji Restoration.[81] Okubo had served as a minister in the government of the Lord of Satsuma and by fulfilling his needs had become prominent in the polity of the imperial movement going onto serve as minister in the Meiji government following the restoration.[82] On the other hand, Saigo Takamori was well known as the military hero of the imperial restoration movement; and Kido Koin was well known for his liberalism.[83] And, in 1868, Edo was renamed as Tokyo, the capital of a unified Japan, and the Emperor Meiji took up residence in Toyko Castle.[84] At the start of the reign of the Emperor Meiji, Japan was still a feudal society, but within thirty years, it would make the transition to a progressive state with modernised defences, a national educational system, an industrial base and a Parliament.[85]

Political, Economic and Social Reforms

Some might say that the view of Japan's transition from a feudalistic to an industrial one is far too simplistic. In this case, it may be better to think of the emergence of a modern industrial Japan following the Meiji restoration in 1968 as a cumulative one. The implication is that the transition began in the Tokugawa period with a deepening money economy, increasing commercialisation and the denigration of feudal structures due to the rise of a wealthy merchant class.[86] The money economy emerged because the peasants had to transport their agricultural produce to urban centres, but had to first pass through commissioned merchants to whom a Shogunate tax had to be paid in money.[87] But the peasants having no

[80] Ibid.

[81] Iwata, M. (1964), Okubo Toshimichi: The Bismarck of Japan, University of California Press, Berkeley.

[82] Ibid.

[83] Ibid.

[84] Steele, M. (2003), Alternative Narratives in Modern Japanese History, RoutledgeCurzon, London.

[85] Iwata, M. (1964), Okubo Toshimichi: The Bismarck of Japan, University of California Press, Berkeley.

[86] Crawcour, S. (1974), The Tokugawa Period and Japan's Preparation for Modern Economic Growth, The Journal of Japanese Studies, Vol. 1, No. 1, pp. 113–125.

[87] Hirschmeier, J. (1964), The Origins of Entrepreneurship in Meiji Japan, Harvard East Asian Series 17, Harvard University Press.

money to pay the tax had to sell their entire crops to the commissioned merchants.[88] Some might say that a money and commodity economy is a prerequisite for capitalistic state formation and a shift away from feudalism.[89] This situation is very similar to eighteenth-century England that with the industrial revolution there was the rise of the merchant class and the denigration of feudal structures due to this. However, in the case of Japan in the Tokugawa period, the way in which people were making a living through feudalistic subsistence agriculture was increasingly running parallel with the emergence of commercial agriculture and industries. Fiscal concerns, due to increasing defence costs because of Japan's opening up to the world, had stimulated the Shogunate to not only follow commercial and industrial projects, but to also be more acceptable of such activities.[90] The Tempo Reforms of 1841 to 1843 greatly facilitated this shift in policy of the Shogunate away from a dependency on feudalistic subsistence agriculture. As such towards the last few years of the Shogunate, western style factories began to emerge in Japan.[91] This was accompanied by a rise in living standards, due to a decreasing population growth rate and a rise in peasants' incomes.[92] In fact the last one hundred years of the Tokugawa period was only the third time in world history in which rapid economic growth was followed by industrialisation.[93] The other two occasions in which this happened was late eighteenth century England and Song Dynasty China, although industrialisation in the contemporary sense was intense, deeper and sustained in former than it was in the latter. In all three cases, the late Tokugawa period, eighteenth century England and Song Dynasty China, the driving force for economic and social evolution was increasing commercialisation and entrepreneurship.

In the late Tokugawa period, entrepreneurship was becoming increasingly important with entrepreneurs being seen as nationalistic and

[88] Ibid.

[89] Horie, Y. (1937), The Economic Significance of the Meiji Restoration, The Kyoto University Economic Review, Vol. 12, No. 2, pp. 63–81.

[90] Ibid.

[91] Ibid.

[92] Howell, D. (2012), Proto-industrial origins of Japanese Capitalism, IN The Japanese Economy in the Tokugawa Era, 1600–1868, Smitka, M. (Ed), Routledge, New York.

[93] Jones, E.L. (1988), Growth Recurring: Economic Change in World History, The University of Michigan Press, Ann Arbor.

community centred, viewing profit as a by-product of these qualities.[94] However, this was seen more in the case of the Samurai than of the passive traditional merchant class. Unlike their contemporaries in western Europe, the Japanese merchant class did not become powerful enough to bring about change in the economic and social system of the feudalistic Tokugawa Shogunate.[95] Nevertheless, the Guilds in Japan proved to be a stabilising force on domestic, social and economic relations and so were protected by the Shogunate whose primary objective was to promote peace and harmony in order to unify Japan. While the power of the guilds had become eroded by the first decade of the eighteenth century in England, in Japan the Guilds remained vigorous until the time of the Meiji Restoration in 1868[96] although the Shogunate government did abolish the Guild system in 1841–1842 in the face of peasant revolts caused by the high prices for food being charged by the merchants in a time of natural disasters and famines.[97] However, because of economic chaos, the Guilds were resurrected in 1851, but finally being abolished in 1872.[98]

In Japan, the Guilds performed a regulatory function in terms of stabilising price and output of products by controlling membership and by controlling the quality of the product.[99] Moreover, each merchant guild proved to be protective of the groups' interests and thus secured a place in society for each member.[100] The guilds and the merchant class in Japan had by the beginning of the nineteenth century accumulated a lot of wealth, through 200 years of Shogunate protection, but had not contributed to any innovations.[101] In England, the power of the Guilds began to decline from the early seventeenth century simply because the way in which the Guilds organised production in the cities was unable to meet domestic and overseas demand, of an increasing population, for goods such as textiles.[102] There also had been more repression of guilds. In order

[94] Yamamura, K. (1968), A Re-examination of Entrepreneurship in Meiji Japan (1868–1912), The Economic History Review, New Series, Vol. 21, No. 1, pp. 144–158.

[95] Hirschmeier, J. (1964), The Origins of Entrepreneurship in Meiji Japan, Harvard East Asian Series 17, Harvard University Press.

[96] Ibid.

[97] Ibid.

[98] Ibid.

[99] Ibid.

[100] Ibid.

[101] Ibid.

[102] Coleman, D. (1975), Industry in Tudor and Stuart England, Macmillan.

to meet the increased demand and seize the opportunities to make higher profits, individual merchants broke free of the urban-based Guilds and developed a putting out system in which they supplied the tools and raw materials to underemployed agricultural workers in rural households who then produced goods which the merchants sold in cities. This putting out system can be defined as proto-industrialisation. This also occurred in Japan when the commercial treaties made by the Shogunate with the foreign powers in 1858 led to an increased overseas demand for silk and tea and domestic demand for cotton.[103] Moreover, the treaties also allowed foreigners to engage in profitable currency transactions which caused a large influx of gold into Japan.[104] These two factors facilitated the disruption of the traditional commodity economy the Shogunate had been used to and had control over.[105] Peasants could be organised productively in order to meet the extra demand. Thus, in the late Tokugawa period, some small-scale industries were able to grow in size. One such industry was that of herring fishing in southern Hokkaido.[106] In this case, independent fishermen in southern Hokkaido were unable to hire workers from the Ainu ethnic group due to local government mandates. This left them unable to expand their fisheries operations due to a lack of labour. However, a famine in north-eastern Honshu between 1832 and 1838 led to the migration of peasants from Honshu to southern Hokkaido.[107] The southern Hokkaido fishing industry now had a large pool of labour to draw upon and the starving peasants now had access to food. The famine-related migrations from Honshu to southern Hokkaido in the early nineteenth century created a pattern of seasonal and permanent migration which lasted well into the twentieth century.[108] This allowed the Hokkaido fishing industry to draw on both seasonal and permanent labour allowing it to grow over time. As the number of workers used in the industry grew, so did the labour costs of the fishermen and the independent fisheries of Hokkaido. This, therefore, incentivised the fishermen and the independent fisheries to innovate and develop new fishing gear which would not

[103] Kunio, N. (1966), The Reform of the land tax and the government programme for the encouragement of industry, The Developing Economies, Vol. 4, No. 4, pp. 447–471.

[104] Ibid.

[105] Ibid.

[106] Howell, D. (2012), Proto-industrial origins of Japanese Capitalism, IN The Japanese Economy in the Tokugawa Era, 1600–1868, Smitka, M. (Ed), Routledge, New York.

[107] Ibid.

[108] Ibid.

only allow for bigger catches of fish but also for the efficient use of labour.[109] This would increase productivity and revenues while lowering costs. A similar situation occurred in late eighteenth century England when merchants found that rising wage costs were eating into their profits. As a result, the merchants may have been a force for innovation. This was due to the fact that it was in the late eighteenth century that the innovations which would drive England to become the first industrialised country in the world emerged. For example, John Kay invented the flying shuttle, a device which increased the production of cloth by a weaver by 100%, Hargreaves invented the Spinning Jenny which allowed one worker to spin many threads at once, Arkwright invented the water frame which allowed yarn to be produced quickly, in 1769 James Watt patented the steam engine, Whitney invented the Cotton Gin in 1792 and William Perkin invented the first synthetic dye in 1856.[110] Increasing production costs and the accumulation of wealth by merchants facilitated greater innovation by investing wealth in order to fund innovation to reduce costs and increase profits. Similarly, contemporary China having started its economic transformation with the 1978 economic reforms has now transformed itself into a knowledge economy and is competing head on with the United States for technological and global dominance.

Some would argue that it was the poor economic conditions of the Samurai, especially the lower Samurai, who had brought about the Meiji restoration as well as supplying the Meiji government with its first administrators.[111] The Samurai were incentivised to bring down the power of the Tokugawa Shogunate which while maintaining the social and educational advantages of the Samurai had all but economically ruined them by supporting the merchant class and the Guilds.[112] However, increasing poverty incentivised low-ranking Samurai and their families to become more entrepreneurial. While fathers took menial jobs with low incomes, families sustained themselves by undertaking small-scale agricultural activities and sending out children to sell flowers.[113] By gaining experience of buying and selling at a young age, the children would grow into adulthood

[109] Ibid.

[110] Lari, O. (2010), Industrial Sociology – A Comprehensive Approach, Word-Press, Lucknow, India.

[111] Hirschmeier, J. (1964), The Origins of Entrepreneurship in Meiji Japan, Harvard East Asian Series 17, Harvard University Press.

[112] Ibid.

[113] Coleman, D. (1975), Industry in Tudor and Stuart England, Macmillan.

upgrading their skills from selling flowers to becoming money changers and then in some cases building a banking empire.[114] Such entrepreneurs, who were Samurai, would be interested in the general economic progress of the country rather their own self-interest and greed to make profits at the expense of their neighbours.[115] However, by joining the Meiji government in modernising and industrialising Japan, the Samurai were able to secure economic salvation and catch the public mood by being patriotic in nation building.[116] Moreover, the Samurai had two advantages over the merchant class which would facilitate them to be better entrepreneurs than the merchant class could ever be in the Meiji period.[117] Firstly, the Samurai were better educated than the merchant class and would therefore be better in learning new techniques and applying these to Japan's unique environment. Secondly, the Samurai entrepreneurs had better connections to the Samurai officials in the Meiji government than the merchant class and could therefore get things done much more quickly.

Institutionally, the Shogunate was not an ideal political structure which could facilitate national economic growth. This was principally because of its decentralised feudalistic power structure which made Shogunate policies unenforceable uniformly at a national level. However, while the cumulative commercial events which facilitated the transition of the Japanese economy from the Tokugawa period to the Meiji restoration are important, in order to analyse Japan's economic growth trajectory, it is also important to consider the positioning of the Japanese economy in 1868 as well as what happened to it in the next two decades.[118] Nevertheless, the transition phase is noted for the steady dismantling of feudalistic power structures, the growth of traditional Japanese industry such as weaving and the development of hard and soft infrastructure. These can be communications and public utilities but also education, finance and public administration.[119] As a result of the Meiji restoration, not only did the class system become more flexible but prohibitions on occupations by class

[114] Yamamura, K. (1968), A Re-examination of Entrepreneurship in Meiji Japan (1868–1912), The Economic History Review, New Series, Vol. 21, No. 1, pp. 144–158.

[115] Ibid.

[116] Hirschmeier, J. (1964), The Origins of Entrepreneurship in Meiji Japan, Harvard East Asian Series 17, Harvard University Press.

[117] Ibid.

[118] Ibid.

[119] Ibid.

were removed in 1869.[120] And in 1870, common people became entitled to use their family name.[121] The Samurai class became prohibited by 1876, when the Samurai were not only prohibited from bearing arms but also to have found other means of earning an income.[122]

The transition of Japan from a feudal to a modern industrialised state began at the end of the Tokugawa Period with an influx of western knowledge and technology.[123] The diffusion of western technology and knowledge into Japan coincided with the establishment of the Zaibatsu, or traditional western industries in Japan, by the Meiji government in 1870.[124] But at this time traditional Japanese industry such as weaving, in which was used simple handlooms, was also successful alongside the new technologies.[125] However, because indigenous industry was not clustered but sparsely distributed, there was a great variation with regard to the level of technology in use in different parts of Japan.[126] Moreover, there were not only technological differences between industries in different parts of Japan, there were also differential labour requirements.[127] This, therefore, created a big need for technical education in Meiji Japan. Therefore, the Meiji government placed an emphasis on technical education as an avenue for facilitating relatively quick industrialisation, although the requirements for technical education would vary from industry to industry.[128] However, it would seem that trade associations may have played a bigger part in the diffusion of advanced technological knowledge, especially into the traditional weaving industries than business ever did.[129] This was because the trading associations rather than business co-ordinated the dissemination of technological knowledge to the weaving industry in different areas by establishing educational institutes which facilitated the training of workers.

[120] Henshall, K. (2004), A History of Japan: From Stone Age to Superpower, Palgrave Macmillan, Basingstoke.

[121] Ibid.

[122] Ibid.

[123] Hashino, T. (2012), Institutionalising Technical Education: The Case of Weaving Districts in Meiji Japan, Australian Economic History Review, Vol. 52, No. 1.

[124] Ibid.

[125] Ibid.

[126] Ibid.

[127] Ibid.

[128] Ibid.

[129] Hashino, T., and Kurosawa, T. (2011) Beyond Marshallian agglomeration economies: the roles of the local trade association in a Meiji Japan weaving district (1868–1912). Discussion Paper No. 1113, Graduate School of Economics, Kobe University.

However, by the early 1880s the government had begun to set up technical colleges with the specific purpose of providing education and training to the self-employed in traditional industries such as craftwork, dyeing textiles, weaving, metal working and woodwork.[130] And by 1899, there were eighteen government-assisted technical schools in Japan.[131] The stimulation for the establishment of centres of training in the weaving industry had been the production of inferior textiles as well as the inability of indigenous weaving businesses to correctly use synthetic western dyes.[132] The efficient use of synthetic dyes by indigenous weavers would allow for the production of more competitive products.

The transformation of Japanese society and economy continued after the Meiji Restoration of 1868. One of the most sweeping of these transformation reforms was the abolition of the 260 feudal districts and the removal of the powers of their daimyos by the central government in Tokyo in August 1871 through the policy known as Haihan Chiken.[133] The centuries-old strategy used by the Shoguns to maintain their grip on power over Japan by decentralising power to the feudal daimyos and constraining the power of the imperial court and the Emperor was gone. Moreover, the old feudal districts were reduced from 260 to 50, and the rule of the feudal daimyos was replaced by prefectural government and the rule by central government appointed governors.[134] The Haihan Chiken was a political reform aimed at centralising power in Japan to the control of the young Meiji government in Tokyo. However, Japan still needed to learn much from the more prosperous and industrialised countries of the west. To achieve this goal, a special embassy, the Iwakura embassy of 1871–1873, of Japanese commissioners left Japan for the United States, on the first leg of the mission abroad, in December 1871. Japan had been accumulating knowledge of the west through foreign teachers and advisors employed to work in Japan, books and from Japanese abroad.[135] It was felt that further detailed knowledge of the setup of western societies

[130] Hashino, T. (2012), Institutionalising Technical Education: The Case of Weaving Districts in Meiji Japan, Australian Economic History Review, Vol. 52, No. 1.

[131] Ibid.

[132] Ibid.

[133] Umegaki, M. (1986), From Domain to Prefecture, IN Japan in Transition from Tokugawa to Meiji, Princeton University Press, Princeton.

[134] Ibid.

[135] Mayo, M. (1973), The Western Education of Kume Kunitake, 1871–6, Monumenta Nipponica, Vol. 28, No. 1, pp. 3–67.

was needed so that Japan could emulate the policies which had brought rapid economic development and social progress to the west. However, populist government ideology subtly shifted away from enriching the nation and making it stronger to facilitate the nation to achieve enlightenment and civilisation.[136] This also reflected a shift in Japanese perceptions of the west from the barbarian lands of the 1860s to the cultivated lands of the 1870s.[137] While the individual commissioners of the Iwakura embassy were tasked with studying and writing detailed reports of specific aspects of western life, in comparison to previous missions, they seem to be more open to think about the west in their own terms rather than from a Japanese point of view. This was because the Iwakura embassy did not take with it as much of the home comforts which previous missions had.[138] Set apart from the other commissioners was Kume Kunitake, a neo-Confucian scholar from Saga, the capital of Hizen province. Kunitake was tasked by the Chief of mission Iwakura to notarise the activities of the mission apart from state banquets in the countries that it travelled to including the United States, Great Britain and countries in continental Europe.[139] Once the mission returned to Japan from its journey abroad in 1873, Kunitake set to work on editing his voluminous notes from the trip into a coherent publication. This was published in October 1878, with a shortened title of 'Jikki'.[140] Although Kunitake edited and wrote the 'Jikki' in a subjective manner, the publication was not his personal view but the view of the Meiji government under the auspices of Chief of mission Iwakura.[141]

Agriculture, Education and Industrialisation

The year 1878, in which the 'Jikki' was published, coincided with the time period, 1871–1881, which led to the completion of the reform of the Land Tax in 1880.[142] Until this year, the system of land tenure in Japan

[136] Ibid.

[137] Ibid.

[138] Ibid.

[139] Ibid.

[140] Ibid.

[141] Nish, I. (2005), The Iwakura Mission in America and Europe: A New Assessment, Meiji Japan Series, Japan Library, Curzon Press Ltd.

[142] Kunio, N. (1966), The Reform of the land tax and the government programme for the encouragement of industry, The Developing Economies, Vol. 4, No. 4, pp. 447–471.

was under the control of the feudal lords. The reform of the land tax was started in July 1872 after the restructuring of the feudal fiefdoms of the lords and was started just before other reforms such as compulsory education and the conscription ordinance of August and November 1972.[143] The principal goal of Meiji Japan was to match the economic might of the western nations, and education was seen as being important in achieving this goal.[144] However, the transition from a Chinese-oriented learning process to a western one had already begun in the Tokugawa period.[145] In this case, although the Tokugawa Shogun had lifted the ban on western books, it was not until 1771 that it became apparent that western books were more accurate than the Chinese translations of western books.[146] The western books were specifically Dutch, and after 1771, Japanese translations of Dutch books became an important means of learning in the Tokugawa period.[147] The Dutch translations, although limited in number, helped to create a negative image of anything Chinese in the eyes of the Japanese.[148] Learning from the Dutch translations in the Tokugawa period proved to be the intellectual foundation for the 1868 Meiji restoration.[149] Moreover, the 'Dutch learning' proved to be the sustenance for the Japanese western modernisers of the time such as Yukichi Fukuzawa, the founder of Keio University.[150] Learning and education were seen to be important in Meiji Japan.

An educated person can learn new concepts and better be able to learn how to use new technology. In this way work can be carried out much faster, leading to an increase in total factor productivity, with the result that education is a source of economic growth and national income.[151] Indeed, one strand of contemporary economic growth theory, endogenous

[143] Ibid.

[144] Godo, Y. and Hayami, Y. (2002), Catching up in Education in the Economic Catch-up of Japan with the United States, 1890–1990, Economic Development and Cultural Change, Vol. 50, No. 4, pp. 961–978.

[145] Maddison, A. (2006), Asia in the world economy, 1500–2030, Asian Pacific Economic Literature, Vol. 20, No. 2, pp. 1–37.

[146] Ibid.

[147] Ibid.

[148] Ibid.

[149] Ibid.

[150] Ibid.

[151] Godo, Y. and Hayami, Y. (2002), Catching up in Education in the Economic Catch-up of Japan with the United States, 1890–1990, Economic Development and Cultural Change, Vol. 50, No. 4, pp. 961–978.

growth theory, does suggest that human capital is the driver of economic growth.[152] Moreover, the rate of return on human capital investment does stimulate economic growth but only when the market is efficient.[153] However, in Meiji Japan economic thinking was perhaps as not as advanced as it is today, and the call for universal education suffrage was to bring about equality in society.[154] Although the call for universal educational suffrage was in 1872, the shift towards western learning and the importance of the sciences began at the end of the Tokugawa period.[155] This meant that the study of Japanese and Chinese literature was to some extent neglected.[156] However, with the establishment of the University of Tokyo in 1877, there was a resurgence in the study of classical Japanese literature which led to the publication of the first modern versions of the Japanese classics and their history in 1890.[157]

Contemporary China has also placed a great deal of emphasis on reinvigorating its educational system. In this case, since starting its economic reforms and especially over the last thirty years, contemporary China has also carried out educational reforms with a view to improving the skills of its work force as well as to foster economic growth.[158] Prior to the economic reforms of 1978, China had a uniform national educational system.[159] However, as a consequence of the reforms, over time Chinese educational system began to show evidence of local variation.[160] Nevertheless, the testing of students has consistently remained as a feature of education in China for hundreds of years with the Imperial Civil Exam of the Sui Dynasty (580 AD to 618 AD) being substituted for by the

[152] Lee, J., Jeong, H., and Hong, S. (2018), Human Capital and Development Lessons and Insights from Korea's Transformation, Korea Development Institute.

[153] Romer, P. (1990), Endogenous Technological Change, Journal of Political Economy, Vol. 98, No. 5, pp. 71–102.

[154] Henshall, K. (2004), A History of Japan: From Stone Age to Superpower, Palgrave Macmillan, Basingstoke.

[155] Brownstein, M. (1987), Kokugako to Kokubungaku: Canon-Formation in the Meiji Period, Harvard Journal of Asiatic Studies, Vol. 47, No. 2.

[156] Ibid.

[157] Ibid.

[158] Zhao, Y and Qiu, W. (2012) Policy changes and educational reforms in China: decentralization and marketization, On the Horizon, Vol. 20, No. 4, pp. 313–323, https://doi.org/10.1108/10748121211272452.

[159] Zhao, Y. (2007), China and the whole child, Educational Leadership, Vol. 64, No. 8, pp. 70–73.

[160] Ibid.

contemporary College Entrance Examination.[161] The decentralisation of China's education system began with the '1985 Decision to Reform the Education System'. This decentralisation would involve all aspects of the higher education system including financing, administration, the delivery of education as well as its content.[162] The 1985 decision also allowed for the introduction of free market forces into China's educational system with the gradual emergence over time of private education institutions or what become known as Miniban education.[163] The 1985 Decision also allowed for a shift away from the central government funding of education towards multiple levels of government.[164] The next major shift in educational policy in China came with the 1999 Decision which facilitated a shift away from central government control of the curriculum and the textbooks used to teach to the local level.[165] However, although the textbooks to be used in local education could be selected by the local government, the central government still retained control over what books could be published in China.[166] The 2002 Law to Promote Miniban Education further accelerated the marketisation of education with schools now being able to operate enterprises also made prominent by the 1998 Action Plan.[167]

The conscription ordinance facilitated the development of a professional army under the direct control of the Meiji government, which could be used to supress any Samurai uprisings anywhere in the country. The Samurai mainly encompassed the peoples of the Kanto region who were skilled in the use of the bow and the arrow while riding on horseback.[168] The peoples of the Kanto region themselves were drawn from the Japanese colonies on the Korean peninsula which were overrun in the sixth and seventh centuries.[169] However, the true origins of the Samurai may lie further in time as far back as 200 AD when Queen Himiko tried to unify Japan she found that giving swords to farmers was not a militarily viable

[161] Niu, W. (2007), Western influences on Chinese educational testing, Comparative Education, Vol. 43, No. 1, pp. 71–91.

[162] Zhao, Y., and Qiu, W. (2012) Policy changes and educational reforms in China: decentralization and marketization, On the Horizon, Vol. 20, No. 4, pp. 313–323, https://doi.org/10.1108/10748121211272452.

[163] Ibid.

[164] Ibid.

[165] Ibid.

[166] Ibid.

[167] Ibid.

[168] Kure, M. (2002), Samurai: An Illustrated History, Tuttle Publishing.

[169] Ibid.

solution.[170] Instead, professionally trained warriors seemed to be more effective at defeating an enemy. Thus, by 800 AD, warlords and chieftains were relying upon their own professionally trained warriors.[171] The peak period in which the Samurai were popular in Japan was from 1200 AD to 1650 AD.[172] However, after the end of the sixteenth century AD, there was not much fighting, and Japan experienced a few centuries of relative peace. As such, the demand for professional warriors declined significantly, such that the Samurai era came to an end in 1867 AD.[173]

The removal of the control of the system of land tenure from the feudal lords now ensured that peasants who were on land previously controlled by the lord was now able to claim ownership. A land tax was introduced in July 1873, which was fixed in value and taken as a percentage of the assessed value of a plot of land.[174] This replaced the land tax of the Tokugawa period which was based on the value of the harvest and was therefore a variable tax.[175] The ownership of the land rested with the head of the household who had originally paid the tax based on the harvest during the Tokugawa period.[176] But when the harvest had been low, the families had been unable to pay the tax and had to sell their land and become tenants to a landlord. Therefore, the rate of tenancy increased by as much as 40%.[177] And, in most cases land was owned by the landlord who had contractual relations with the tenants on the land.[178] Contracts for the lease of the land could be either made verbally or in writing. But in these contracts, there would have been a stipulation that the landlord could take back the land at any time, in which case the tenant was obliged to vacate the land.[179] The landlord would set the rent for the land at a high level, which would be paid based on the harvest from the land, rice.[180] If the harvest was bountiful, then this would allow the tenant to pay the landlord

[170] Ollhoff, J. (2008), The World of Martial Arts: Samurai, ABDO Publishing Company.

[171] Ibid.

[172] Ibid.

[173] Hanel, R. (2008), Samurai: Fearsome Fighters, Creative Education, USA, Minnesota.

[174] Henshall, K. (2004), A History of Japan: From Stone Age to Superpower, Palgrave Macmillan, Basingstoke.

[175] Ibid.

[176] Ibid.

[177] Ibid.

[178] Kunio, N. (1966), The Reform of the land tax and the government programme for the encouragement of industry, The Developing Economies, Vol. 4, No. 4, pp. 447–471.

[179] Ibid.

[180] Ibid.

the required rent. But if the harvest was poor, it would often mean that the landlords had to accept a lower rent from the tenant farmers. However, the tenants were never in a win–win situation. When the harvest was bountiful, the landlord took most of the rice harvest and the tenants were only left with enough for sustenance.[181] When the harvest was poor, the tenants may have had to return to a partial hunter-gatherer existence. Thus, the tenant farmers of the Meiji period were no better off than the farmers of the Tokugawa period.[182] The essence of the reform of the land tax was to introduce private property rights into Japan, with private property rights being the basis for a capitalistic economy. Following the centralising of power, reform of the land tax and the introduction of compulsory education, the Meiji government instigated the Shokusan Kogyo in the period 1882 to 1891.[183] The Shokusan Kogyo focused on the development of Japanese industry.[184] It was a policy with four different elements.[185] These included the protection of domestic industries, the government giving subsidies to domestic producers, the acquisition of advanced machinery from the west, and the setting up and subsequent transfer of the best state-owned factories to private enterprises.[186] Thus, the transition of the Japanese economy from a feudalistic, agrarian economy to a capitalist, industrial economy was state driven.[187]

The reform of the land tax in Meiji Japan does not have parallels with contemporary China's 1978 agricultural reforms. This is because the initial agricultural reforms in China after 1978 involved a shift in farming from collectives to individual rural households through the Household Responsibility System, incentivising higher agricultural production.[188] This was because any surplus agricultural output which remained after the harvest had been sold to the government, and low fixed prices could be sold

[181] Ibid.

[182] Ibid.

[183] Ibid.

[184] Ibid.

[185] Samuels, R. (1994), Rich Nation, Strong Army: National Security and the Technological Transformation of Japan, Cornell University Press, Ithaca and London.

[186] Ibid.

[187] Allinson, J., and Anievas, A. (2010), The uneven and combined development of the Meiji Restoration: A passive revolutionary road to capitalist modernity, Capital & Class, Vol. 34, No. 3, pp. 469–490.

[188] Li, Z. (2017), Reform and Development of Agriculture in China, Social Sciences Academic Press and Springer Nature Singapore Pte Ltd.

at market prices generating additional income for the household.[189] But in the case of Meiji Japan, reform of the land tax meant that landlords were able to ‘squeeze’ incomes from tenant farmers who had no incentive to produce rice. On the other hand, the Shokusan Kogyo does resemble the industrial strategy embedded in contemporary China’s 1978 economic reforms in the context that foreign MNCs were given preferential treatment in terms of tax rates, the ability to repatriate profits to home countries, property rights and access to infrastructure if they produced goods in China in the Special Economic Zones by bringing in new technology and management techniques and training Chinese workers. The purpose of the Shokusan Kogyo and contemporary China’s economic reforms was to promote rapid economic growth through technology transfer and industrialisation. More interestingly just as small-scale industry and foreign trade were the key drivers of Meiji Japan’s industrial growth and development, so it was with contemporary China with the emergence of the Town and Village Enterprises (TVEs) in the early 1970s. These were small-scale ‘industries’. After the start of China’s economic reforms in 1978, it was the TVEs which played a central role in driving China’s economic growth especially in the 1980s.[190] Both Meiji Japan and contemporary China form high levels of exports by accumulating foreign currency reserves which could be used to buy advanced foreign technology for capital accumulation and industrialisation as well as funds to train domestic workers to use the technology and to train domestic workers.[191] Furthermore, just as the TVEs were behind the momentum for contemporary China’s economic take off, in Meiji Japan, the Zaibatsu or big family-owned businesses were responsible for Japan’s economic take off starting in the latter half of the nineteenth century.[192] The Zaibatsu include names, such as Mitsui, Mitsubishi, Sumitomo, Yasuda, Okura and

[189] Lin, J., Cai, F., Li, Z. (2003), The China Miracle: Development Strategy and Economic Reform, The Chinese University of Hong Kong.

[190] Li, H. (2013), History and Development of Entrepreneurship in China, IN Entrepreneurship and Economic Growth in China, Zhang, T., and Stough, R. (Eds), World Scientific, New Jersey.

[191] Samuels, R. (1994), Rich Nation, Strong Army: National Security and the Technological Transformation of Japan, Cornell University Press, Ithaca and London.

[192] Frankl, J. (1999), An analysis of Japanese corporate structure, 1915–1937, Journal of Economic History, Vol. 59,
pp. 997–1015.

Furukawa,[193] which are still familiar in today's world. Due to the fact that the Zaibatsu were big enterprises, they had the capacity to use the advanced capital-intensive technology which had been available to the west.[194] The Zaibatsu also had other advantages. Firstly, without relying upon equity capital, the Zaibatsu had no shareholders and were thus able to direct the enterprise without any constraints.[195] This may have allowed for the quick implementation of business plans with a focus on long-term growth rather than an eye on short-term profits. Secondly, the Zaibatsu were diversified enterprises which allowed for the spreading of risk of failure over a number of products rather than just on one product.[196] Risks were lowered even further because the Zaibatsu did not have to rely on any external sources of financing, and all investments were financed either from the firms' profits or through family resources.[197] Lastly, the Zaibatsu had sufficient financial resources to employ skilled and educated managers.[198] This allowed for the efficient organisation of the resources of the Zaibatsu and ensured that resources were only used for profitable projects with the long-term growth of the firm in mind. The Zaibatsu had features which would enable them to overcome some of the disadvantages enterprises must have faced in the context of underdevelopment in Meiji Japan. This underdevelopment was particularly associated with a lack of credible and robust institutions such as an established local and national government, a police force, judiciary and courts.[199] Moreover, not only did Meiji Japan suffer from a lack of credible and robust institutions but also a lack of roads, railways, ports and capital markets.[200] The Meiji government, therefore, embarked on a whole scale westernisation of Japanese with the adoption of not only western institutions but also technology.[201] A Japan that was westernised would be respected, and a popular government chant at the time was

[193] Ibid.

[194] Morck, R. and Nakamura, M. (2007), Business groups and the big push: Meiji Japan's mass privatization and subsequent growth, Enterprise and Society, Vol. 8, pp. 543–601.

[195] Ibid.

[196] Ibid.

[197] Ibid.

[198] Ibid.

[199] Gerschenkron, A. (1965), Economic backwardness in historical perspective: a book of essays, Frederick A. Praeger.

[200] Ibid.

[201] Henshall, K. (2004), A History of Japan: From Stone Age to Superpower, Palgrave Macmillan, Basingstoke.

'Oitsuke Oikose' which means 'catch-up, overtake'.[202] Some of the milestones in this process included the instigation of the telegraph in 1869, the postal service in 1871, the compulsory adoption of western dress by government officials in 1872 and the adoption of the Gregorian calendar in 1873.[203] However, the primary railroad lines—the Tokaido line, the Tohoku line and the Shin'etsu line, were not constructed until the late 1880s and the early 1890s.[204]

The lack of robust and credible institutions in Meiji Japan was exactly the same situation faced by contemporary China when it started its economic reforms in 1978. At this time China also had underdeveloped institutions which could not support a market economy, poor infrastructure and an illiquid capital market.[205] Indeed, China's first stock markets did not open until the 1990s.[206] This is why China followed an economic development strategy which involved getting foreign MNCs to set up production in China alongside foreign direct investment. This not only facilitated technology transfer from developed countries to China, but also allowed foreign MNCs to utilise China's supply of cheap and abundant labour as workers in their factories.[207] China's economic development strategy allowed it to accumulate substantial foreign currency reserves through the export of light manufactured goods. But at the same time, it continued its incremental reforms which has allowed it to transform its economy from a purely agricultural and manufacturing economy to a knowledge and services-based economy. Thus, in the case of Meiji Japan, its economic rise would not have been as rapid and as successful without the Zaibatsu, and contemporary China without its TVEs.

[202] Ibid.

[203] Ibid.

[204] Ohsawa, M. (2006), Indignity for the Emperor, Equality for the people: Taisho Democracy and the Transition from Nationalism to Ultra-nationalism in Modern Japan, IN The Dignity of Nations: Equality, Competition and Honor in East Asian Nationalism, Chien, S., and Fitzgerald, J. (Eds), Hong Kong University Press, Hong Kong.

[205] Ramesh, S. (2017), China's Lessons for India: Volume 1 – The Political Economy of Development, Palgrave Macmillan.

[206] Ramesh, S. (2017), China's Lessons for India: Volume 2 – The Political Economy of Change, Palgrave Macmillan.

[207] Ibid.

Conclusion

Just at the time of the Meiji restoration, Japan was putting into place the changes in its institutions and policies which would set the country on a trajectory of rapid industrialisation and economic development. On the other hand, Qing dynasty China was heading towards economic decline, political chaos and a civil war in the first half of the twentieth century. The period of the Qing dynasty China (1644 to 1912) is almost the same as the period of the Tokugawa period (1600–1868) and the Meiji period (1868–1912) in Japan. Moreover, it may not be a coincidence that the end of the Qing dynasty and the end of imperial rule in China had its roots in the nineteenth century just as the roots of Japan's industrialisation and economic development were also to be found. In the case of Qing dynasty China, the long-term impact of three simultaneous processes may have contributed to its decline and ultimate demise.[208] Firstly, the European powers had begun the process of encroachment of other civilisations starting in the fifteenth century with voyages of exploration. This eventually turned into a grab for resources and outright colonialism, a process which reached its zenith in the nineteenth century. While the peoples of the Indian sub-continent had succumbed to British colonial by the mid-nineteenth century, China and Japan were the last 'holdouts' from the European grab for resources and European hegemony. Japan's response to this was to reorganise its economic and political structures such that the organisation of economic resources could be shifted from supporting the lavish lifestyle of the militarily weak Tokugawa elite, which had resulted in an economically underdeveloped Japan, to a form of organisation in which economic resources were directed at making Japan economically, politically and militarily stronger in order to diminish the chances of a potential takeover of the country by the European powers and perhaps by the United States. The combined threat from the United States and Great Britain entwined the fate of Japan and China to such an extent that would never be seen again. Indeed, a Japanese Confucian scholar Iwagaki Gesshu wrote a 7500-word, in 1857–1858, unpublished but circulated essay in which he imagined Japanese military power saving Qing dynasty China from the wrath of the British.[209] Moreover, not only did the Japanese save

[208] Rowe, W. (2009), China's Last Empire – The Great Qing, The Belnap Press of Harvard University Press, Cambridge, Massachusetts.

[209] Wakabayashi, B. (2017), A Bakumatsu 'Greater East Asia War', IN Late Qing China and Meiji Japan: Political and Cultural Aspects, Fogel, J. (Ed), Camphor Press Ltd, Manchester.

Qing dynasty China, but they also went onto conquer Great Britain and partitioned it.[210] In writing the Seisei Kaishin Hen, Iwagaki Gesshu was very critical of the weakness of not only Tokugawa foreign and domestic policy but also of the political institutions of the Tokugawa Shogunate.[211] The latter was seen as weak with regard to giving in to Commodore Perry's demands to open up Japan to trade with the United States. In this case the Tokugawa policy of Sakotu, which ran parallel to the Qing Guangzhou System, began to denigrate albeit slowly. The policy of Sakotu limited Japanese trade to only that with the Chinese and the Dutch and only at the port of Nagasaki.[212] The Qing Guangzhou System focused on limiting foreign access to China's markets, especially tea and silk. In this regard, the monopoly for the importation of tea into British Territories was held by the British East India Company until 1833.[213] In order to facilitate trade in tea with the British East India Company, Qing China developed a policy which became to be known as the Guangzhou System.[214] According to this, authorised foreign enterprises were allowed to trade with Chinese merchants in specially designated areas known as 'factories', located outside the city of Guangzhou.[215] However, trade in tea between the British East India Company and Qing China resulted in huge profits for the former but generated a big trade deficit with China for Great Britain because China did not purchase any British goods.[216] Moreover, the British East India Company was paying for Chinese tea in gold and in silver bullion. This represented a source of loss of bullion which the British economy would not be able to withstand for long without severe economic repercussions. The British East India Company's solution was to grow Opium in India, ship it to the factories in Guangzhou and exchange Opium for Chinese tea, and gold and silver bullion.[217] Merchants would also have been able to buy Opium in India to sell on in

[210] Ibid.

[211] Ibid.

[212] Ibid.

[213] Miller, J. (2006), The Opium of the People: Religion, Science and Modernity, IN Chinese Religions in Contemporary Society, Miller, J. (Ed), ABC-Clio, Santa Barbara, California, USA.

[214] Ibid.

[215] Ibid.

[216] Ibid.

[217] Ibid.

China. By 1839, the trade balance had pivoted in Great Britain's favour as the consumption of Opium in China had increased dramatically.[218] As a result in addition to having to trade tea, the Chinese found that because greater quantities of Opium had to be imported than the amount of tea exported, China was increasingly having to use its gold and silver bullion reserves to trade with Great Britain. Opium proved to not only be addictive and destructive to Chinese society. Attempts by the Qing court to stop the Opium trade ensured that Great Britain declared war on China in 1839 with open hostilities in 1840 which the British won because of their superior military arsenal.[219] The British having won, Qing China was forced into accepting the terms of the Treaty of Nanjing in 1842. China's weakness following its defeat at the hands of the British allowed for the other powers of the time such as France, Germany, Russia and the United States to take advantage of it by negotiating treaties in their favour which allowed for trade on low tariffs as well as the right to establish settlements under their own jurisdiction.[220] The western powers were able to win further concessions from Qing China when the imperial court failed to ratify the 1858 Treaty of Tianjin. This failure led to French and British forces invading China again and burning down the Summer Palace in the Forbidden city. A further weakened Qing China acquiesced to further western demand such as the rite of passage of Christian missionaries in China, as well as the superiority of diplomatic immunity to Chinese law.[221] The western missionaries would also come to establish western style learning institutions through which western thought would enter Chinese minds, most notably through the Chinese educated in these institutions who would then go on to become the revolutionary leaders[222] who would finally bring down thousands of years of imperial rule and the Qing dynasty. However, it was not only western intrusion into China which weakened it, but perhaps the impact of western religion which further caused internal conflict within China. In this case, Hong Xiuquan established the Taiping Heavenly Kingdom with its capital as the city of Nanjing. He was a convert to Christianity and a self-proclaimed brother to Jesus Christ. The result of the establishment of the Taiping Heavenly Kingdom

[218] Ibid.
[219] Ibid.
[220] Ibid.
[221] Ibid.
[222] Ibid.

was that there was civil war between it and the Qing Empire from 1850 to 1864, a civil war in which it is estimated that perhaps 30 million people died.[223] Furthermore, at the end of the civil war, the Qing Empire did not have much control of the provinces as it had before, with provincial as opposed to imperial armies becoming more common.[224] Western imperialism not only led to the economic and institutional weakening of the Qing state but also gave momentum to the reformers in Tokugawa Japan to either change to a better form of governance which would lead to economic prosperity and military upgrading or risk becoming a colony of a western power. Thus arose the stimulus for the urgent reorganisation of Japanese governance to facilitate economic prosperity and military upgrading, and the beginning of the start of the Meiji Restoration of 1858.

The demise of the Qing dynasty was in contrast to its emergence. The Qing dynasty had reached its zenith over the course of the eighteenth century.[225] This was because of the efficient management of the state's resources, stability in society and the cumulative territorial advances under its most distinguished emperors, Kangxi (1662–1722), Yongzheng (1723–1735) and Qianlong (1736–1795).[226] It was the dynamism and tenacity of Kangxi which not only allowed for the south-west of China to be fully integrated into imperial control, but also for the imperial conquest of Mongolia and Taiwan by 1700.[227] Cumulative territorial expansion allowed markets to grow, resulting in increased commercial activity. This allowed merchants and traders to accumulate wealth and for towns to become increasingly urbanised. This imposed a requirement on the state to increase agricultural production through innovation. This was specifically with regard to improvements in the way in which rice was cultivated.[228] Furthermore, every available space on hills and mountains was also utilised to grow crops such as maize, peanuts and sweet potatoes.[229]

[223] Meyer-Fong, T. (2013), What Remains: Coming to Terms with Civil War in 19th Century China, Stanford University Press, Stanford, California.

[224] Ibid.

[225] McMahon, D. (2014), Rethinking the decline of China's Qing Dynasty: Imperial activism and borderland management at the turn of the nineteenth century, Routledge, New York.

[226] Ibid.

[227] Perdue, P. (2005), China Marches West, The Qing Conquest of Central Eurasia, The Belknap Press of Harvard University Press, Cambridge, Massachusetts.

[228] McMahon, D. (2014), Rethinking the decline of China's Qing Dynasty: Imperial activism and borderland management at the turn of the nineteenth century, Routledge, New York.

[229] Ibid.

Improved diets and access to greater quantities of food ensured that the population of China doubled from 150 million to 300 million in the hundred years to 1800.[230] Western encroachment of the Qing Empire started in 1832 when British ships sailed into restricted Chinese waters carrying a cargo of mostly opium and textiles to trade with the Chinese.[231] Jardine, Matheson & Co owned three of the ships and its cargo.[232] While Qing dynasty China had not been closed to the outside world unlike Japan which had been by the Tokugawa Shogunate, access to China by foreigners was tightly regulated and restricted to one point on China's coastal region.[233] However, after 1842, the Qing system of regulating the entry of foreigners into China became weaker, and as a result from this time, settlements of foreigners began to develop in China's coastal cities.[234] Moreover, just at the time that the western powers were encroaching on its territories, China also faced several social and economic challenges which had been accumulating due to a third factor, political dysfunction in the country ensured that economic resources were not effectively targeted towards allowing the country to technologically and economically develop faster than the western powers. This situation must be seen in the context of the situation of the previous Ming dynasty in terms of the land area of China and its population. In this case, compared to the Ming dynasty, the Qing dynasty doubled the land area of China to include not only Han peoples but also other ethnic minority groups such as the Burmese, Tibetans, Uighur Muslims, Tais and the Mongols, and by doing increasing China's population to 500 million people.[235]

References

Allinson, J., and Anievas, A. (2010), The uneven and combined development of the Meiji Restoration: A passive revolutionary road to capitalist modernity, Capital & Class, Vol. 34, No. 3, pp. 469–490.

[230] Ibid.

[231] Bickers, R. (2016), The Scramble for China: Foreign Devils in the Qing Empire, 1832–1914, Penguin Books.

[232] Ibid.

[233] Ibid.

[234] Ibid.

[235] Rowe, W. (2009), China's Last Empire – The Great Qing, The Belnap Press of Harvard University Press, Cambridge, Massachusetts.

Bickers, R. (2016), The Scramble for China: Foreign Devils in the Qing Empire, 1832–1914, Penguin Books.
Brownstein, M. (1987), Kokugako to Kokubungaku: Canon-Formation in the Meiji Period, Harvard Journal of Asiatic Studies, Vol. 47, No. 2.
Burks, A. (1985), The West's Inreach: The Oyatoi Gaikokujin, IN The Modernizers: Overseas Students, Foreign Employees, and Meiji Japan, Burks, A. (Ed), Westview, Boulder, Colorado.
Coleman, D. (1975), Industry in Tudor and Stuart England, Macmillan.
Crawcour, S. (1974), The Tokugawa Period and Japan's Preparation for Modern Economic Growth, The Journal of Japanese Studies, Vol. 1, No. 1, pp. 113–125.
Cunningham, M., and Zwier, L. (2009), The End of the Shoguns and the Birth of Modern Japan, Twenty-First Century Books, Minneapolis, USA.
Denney, J. (2011), Respect and Consideration, Radiance Press, Leicester, UK.
Fay, P. (1975), The Opium War, 1840–42, The University of North Carolina Press.
Frankl, J. (1999), An analysis of Japanese corporate structure, 1915–1937, Journal of Economic History, Vol. 59, pp. 997–1015.
Gerschenkron, A. (1965), Economic backwardness in historical perspective: a book of essays, Frederick A. Praeger.
Godo, Y. and Hayami, Y. (2002), Catching up in Education in the Economic Catch up of Japan with the United States, 1890–1990, Economic Development and Cultural Change, Vol. 50, No. 4, pp. 961–978.
Gooday, G., and Low, M. (1998), Technology Transfer and Cultural Exchange: Western Scientists and Engineers Encounter Late Tokugawa and Meiji Japan, OSIRIS, Vol. 13, Beyond Joseph Needham: Science, Technology, and Medicine in East and Southeast Asia, pp. 99–128.
Hanel, R. (2008), Samurai: Fearsome Fighters, Creative Education, USA, Minnesota.
Hashino, T. (2012), Institutionalising Technical Education: The Case of Weaving Districts in Meiji Japan, Australian Economic History Review, Vol. 52, No. 1.
Hashino, T., and Kurosawa, T. (2011) Beyond Marshallian agglomeration economies: the roles of the local trade association in a Meiji Japan weaving district (1868–1912). Discussion Paper No. 1113, Graduate School of Economics, Kobe University.
Henshall, K. (2004), A History of Japan: From Stone Age to Superpower, Palgrave Macmillan, Basingstoke.
Hillsborough, R. (2017), Samurai: Assassins, 'Dark Matter' and the Meiji Restoration, 1853–1868, McFarland & Company, Inc., Publishers, Jefferson, North Carolina.
Hirschmeier, J. (1964), The Origins of Entrepreneurship in Meiji Japan, Harvard East Asian Series 17, Harvard University Press.
Hopkins, D. (1983), The Greatest Killer: Smallpox in History, The University of Chicago Press, Chicago.

Horie, Y. (1937), The Economic Significance of the Meiji Restoration, The Kyoto University Economic Review, Vol. 12, No. 2, pp. 63–81.
Howell, D. (2012), Proto-industrial origins of Japanese Capitalism, IN The Japanese Economy in the Tokugawa Era, 1600–1868, Smitka, M. (Ed), Routledge, New York.
Iwata, M. (1964), Okubo Toshimichi: The Bismarck of Japan, University of California Press, Berkeley.
Jansen, M. (1995), The Meiji Restoration, IN The Emergence of Meiji Japan, Jansen, M. (Ed), Cambridge University Press, Cambridge.
Jones, E.L. (1988), Growth Recurring: Economic Change in World History, The University of Michigan Press, Ann Arbor.
Jones, H. (1974), Bakumatsu Foreign Employees, Monumenta Nipponica, Vol. 29, No. 3, pp. 305–327.
Keene, D. (2005), Emperor of Japan: Meiji and His World, 1852–1912, Columbia University Press.
Kohno, M. (2001), On the Meiji Restoration: Japan's Search for Sovereignty, International Relations of the Asia-Pacific, Vol. 1, pp. 265–283.
Kshetry, G. (2008), Foreigners in Japan: A Historical Perspective, Xlibris Corporation.
Kunio, N. (1966), The Reform of the land tax and the government programme for the encouragement of industry, The Developing Economies, Vol. 4, No. 4, pp. 447–471.
Kure, M. (2002), Samurai: An Illustrated History, Tuttle Publishing.
Lari, O. (2010), Industrial Sociology – A Comprehensive Approach, Word-Press, Lucknow, India.
Lee, J., Jeong, H., and Hong, S. (2018), Human Capital and Development Lessons and Insights from Korea's Transformation, Korea Development Institute.
Li, H. (2013), History and Development of Entrepreneurship in China, IN Entrepreneurship and Economic Growth in China, Zhang, T., and Stough, R. (Eds), World Scientific, New Jersey.
Li, Z. (2017), Reform and Development of Agriculture in China, Social Sciences Academic Press and Springer Nature Singapore Pte Ltd.
Lin, J., Cai, F., Li, Z. (2003), The China Miracle: Development Strategy and Economic Reform, The Chinese University of Hong Kong.
Maddison, A. (2006), Asia in the world economy, 1500–2030, Asian Pacific Economic Literature, Vol. 20, No. 2, pp. 1–37.
Mayo, M. (1973), The Western Education of Kume Kunitake, 1871–6, Monumenta Nipponica, Vol. 28, No. 1, pp. 3–67.
McMahon, D. (2014), Rethinking the decline of China's Qing Dynasty: Imperial activism and borderland management at the turn of the nineteenth century, Routledge, New York.

Meyer-Fong, T. (2013), What Remains: Coming to Terms with Civil War in 19th Century China, Stanford University Press, Stanford, California.

Miller, J. (2006), The Opium of the People: Religion, Science and Modernity, IN Chinese Religions in Contemporary Society, Miller, J. (Ed), ABC-Clio, Santa Barbara, California, USA.

Morck, R. and Nakamura, M. (2007), Business groups and the big push: Meiji Japan's mass privatization and subsequent growth, Enterprise and Society, Vol. 8, pp. 543–601.

Morris-Suzuki, T. (1994), The Technological Transformation of Japan: From the Seventeenth to Twenty-first Century, Cambridge University Press, Cambridge.

Nish, I. (2005), The Iwakura Mission in America and Europe: A New Assessment, Meiji Japan Series, Japan Library, Curzon Press Ltd.

Niu, W. (2007), Western influences on Chinese educational testing, Comparative Education, Vol. 43, No. 1, pp. 71–91.

Ollhoff, J. (2008), The World of Martial Arts: Samurai, ABDO Publishing Company.

Ohsawa, M. (2006), Indignity for the Emperor, Equality for the people: Taisho Democracy and the Transition from Nationalism to Ultra-nationalism in Modern Japan, IN The Dignity of Nations: Equality, Competition and Honor in East Asian Nationalism, Chien, S., and Fitzgerald, J. (Eds), Hong Kong University Press, Hong Kong.

Perdue, P. (2005), China Marches West, The Qing Conquest of Central Eurasia, The Belknap Press of Harvard University Press, Cambridge, Massachusetts.

Ramesh, S. (2017a), China's Lessons for India: Volume 1 – The Political Economy of Development, Palgrave Macmillan.

Ramesh, S. (2017b), China's Lessons for India: Volume 2 – The Political Economy of Change, Palgrave Macmillan.

Romer, P. (1990), Endogenous Technological Change, Journal of Political Economy, Vol. 98, No. 5, pp. 71–102.

Rowe, W. (2009), China's Last Empire – The Great Qing, The Belnap Press of Harvard University Press, Cambridge, Massachusetts.

Rubinger, R. (1986), Education: From One Room to One System, IN Japan in Transition: From Tokugawa to Meiji, Jansen, M., and Rozman, G. (Eds), Princeton University Press, Princeton, New Jersey.

Samuels, R. (1994), Rich Nation, Strong Army: National Security and the Technological Transformation of Japan, Cornell University Press, Ithaca and London.

Steele, M. (2003), Alternative Narratives in Modern Japanese History, RoutledgeCurzon, London.

Stern, R., Wright, G., Patrick, H. (2010), The Japanese Economy in Retrospect: Selected Papers by Gary R. Saxonhouse, World Scientific.

Umegaki, M. (1986), From Domain to Prefecture, IN Japan in Transition From Tokugawa to Meiji, Princeton University Press, Princeton.

Wakabayashi, B. (2017), A Bakumatsu 'Greater East Asia War', IN Late Qing China and Meiji Japan: Political and Cultural Aspects, Fogel, J. (Ed), Camphor Press Ltd, Manchester.

Westney, D. (1986), The Military, IN Japan in Transition: From Tokugawa to Meiji, Jansen, M., and Rozman, G. (Eds), Princeton University Press, Princeton, New Jersey.

Wittner, D. (2005), Commodore Matthew Perry and the Perry Expedition to Japan, PowerPlus Books, New York.

Yamamura, K. (1968), A Re-examination of Entrepreneurship in Meiji Japan (1868–1912), The Economic History Review, New Series, Vol. 21, No. 1, pp. 144–158.

Zhao, Y. (2007), China and the whole child, Educational Leadership, Vol. 64, No. 8, pp. 70–73.

Zhao, Y and Qiu, W. (2012) Policy changes and educational reforms in China: decentralization and marketization, On the Horizon, Vol. 20, No. 4, pp. 313–323, https://doi.org/10.1108/10748121211272452.

CHAPTER 6

The Taisho Period (1912–1926): Transition from Democracy to a Military Economy

Introduction

The start of the twentieth century was one in which Japan and its people entered the world stage with an air of confidence and positivity following the Japanese victory over the Qing imperial court of China in the Chinese-Japanese War of 1894 to 1895.[1] This war was mainly about which country, China or Japan, should have greater influence over the peoples of the Korean Peninsula. The latter had been the source of conflict between the two countries over the course of the last several hundred years. But on previous occasions such as the Japanese invasion of Korea at the end of the sixteenth century, the forces of the Ming Court of China and the Koreans had been able to beat back the Japanese. However, nearly 300 years later, and following a period of modernisation, the Japanese had been victorious. As a result of its victory, Japan placed in front of Qing China a great list of demands.[2] These demands included the opening up of several interior Chinese ports as treaty ports; the handing over to Japan of Taiwan, Port Arthur and the Liaodong Peninsula; as well as the payment of a huge financial indemnity. Until the financial indemnity was to be paid, Japan

[1] Minichiello, S. (1998), Introduction, IN Japan's Competing Modernities: Issues in Culture and Democracy, 1900–1930, Minichiello, S. (Ed), University of Hawai'I Press, Honolulu.

[2] Paine, S. (2003), The Sino-Japanese War of 1894–1895: Perceptions, Power and Primacy, Cambridge University Press, Cambridge.

S. Ramesh, *China's Economic Rise*,
https://doi.org/10.1007/978-3-030-49811-5_6

would occupy the Chinese port of Weihaiwei.[3] China was also obliged to renegotiate commercial treaties with Japan as well as giving it favourable tax breaks.[4] Japan's treatment of China in the aftermath of the war was essentially because of Ito Hirobumi's, the Japanese Prime Minister, admiration of Otto Von Bismark.[5] The latter had not only internally united Germany but had also raised its profile internationally by defeating the French in the war of 1870–1871.[6] Moreover, at the end of this war, Bismarck pressed for greater German demands against the French in the Treaty of Frankfurt, which Hirobumi mirrored in his demands against the Chinese in the Treaty of Shimonoseki. However, the Triple Intervention of 1895 by Russia, France and Germany required Japan to return the Liaodong Peninsula to China because Japan's possession of it would not only threaten Korean independence but also the capital of China itself.[7] Moreover, Russia not only demanded a lease on Port Arthur for twenty-five years but also to build the China Eastern Railway Line in Manchuria.[8] The other European powers also made their claims, the British in the Valley of the Yantz and the Germans in Shandong.[9] Furthermore, following the damage to the Russian built railway in Manchuria, the Chinese handed over all of their military bases in Manchuria to Russia.[10] A naval base was also established in Port Arthur by the Russians.[11] The Japanese were not militarily strong enough to fight France, Germany and Russia and were forced to accept the terms of the 'Triple Intervention'. The Japanese military and the Japanese public were outraged by a humiliation which would surface in both the long term as well as in the short term. However, in 1902 Japan and Great Britain signed a treaty which would pit both countries together as military allies, with the British recognising Japan's special interest in Korea through the treaty.[12] And as a result of the

[3] Ibid.

[4] Ibid.

[5] Ibid.

[6] Ibid.

[7] Rao, B. (2005), History of Asia, From Early Times to the Present, New Dawn Press, Slough, Berkshire.

[8] Jae-Hyung, L. (2003), China and the Asia-Pacific Region, iUniverse, Lincoln, NE.

[9] Ibid.

[10] Ibid.

[11] Lobanov-Rostrovsky, A. (1965), Russia and Asia, The George Wahr Publishing Company, Ann Arbor, Michigan.

[12] Westwood, J. (1986), Russia Against Japan, 1904–05: A New look at the Russo-Japanese War, State University of New York Press, Albany.

treaty, when war broke out between Great Britain and Germany in 1914, Japan also declared war against Germany and its allies.[13] In the meantime, Japan felt that the Russian presence in Manchuria was a threat to its influence in Korea.[14] As a result, the Russian-Japanese War erupted in 1905, and the Japanese won. The Russian Far Eastern Fleet was destroyed by the naval forces of Admiral Togo[15] at the Battle of Tsushima.[16] The latter has been hailed as one of the top five naval battles in human history, ranking with Leponte, Trafalgar, Jutland and Midway whilst acknowledging Admiral Togo as equal to the genius of Horatio Nelson.[17] Moreover, the Battle of Tsushima in the Korean Straits was the first battle in history which was fought by ships with steel hulls rather than wooden ones, as well as the first naval battle in which wireless telegraphy was in use.[18] The impact of the results of the Battle of Tsushima was so severe that Tsar Nicholas was brought to the negotiating table within three months of its end.[19] The lasting effect of the Battle on the two countries was that it gave hegemony to Japan over East Asia, particularly over Korea and China, until the end of World War 2.[20] However, to Russia the aftermath of the Battle was the onset of the beginnings of the revolution which would bring an end to the Romanov's and the establishment of the Soviet Union. As at sea, the Russians were also facing defeat on land. The Russian Army was pushed back as far as Northern Manchuria.[21] The Japanese victory at the Battle of Mukden ended the conflict in February–March 1905, and until that point in time, it had been one of the most notable land battles between two armies in world history.[22] It was the first battle in which both sides were evenly matched in terms of military technology and perhaps the first time such technology was being used for warfare.[23] Moreover, the number of casualties for both sides was also staggering, with Russians

[13] Ibid.

[14] Ibid.

[15] Ibid.

[16] Lardas, M. (2018), Tsushima 1905: Death of a Russian Fleet, Bloomsbury Publishing.

[17] Pleshakov, C. (2002), The Tsar's Last Armada, The Epic Voyage to the Battle of Tsushima, Best Books, New York.

[18] Ibid.

[19] Jukes, G. (2002), The Russo-Japan War 1904-05, Osprey Publishing.

[20] Ibid.

[21] Riasanovsky, N. (2000), A History of Russia, 6th Edition, Oxford University Press, Oxford.

[22] Ivanov, A., and Jowett, P. (2007), The Russo-Japanese War 1904–05, Osprey Publishing.

[23] Ibid.

having 85,000 and the Japanese 70,000.[24] The conflict between Russia and Japan was finally ended with the signing of the Treaty of Portsmouth in New Hampshire, United States, where it had been negotiated, in September 1905.[25] Under the terms of the Treaty, Russia gave away the southern half of Sakhalin Island to Japan while also recognising its hegemony over the Korean Peninsula as well as withdrawing from Manchuria.[26]

The Taisho Period from 1912 to 1926 was named after the then reigning Emperor. The period 1900 to 1930 which encompasses the end of the Meiji Period, the Taisho Period as well as the start of the Showa Period was a time in which Japan was transitioning to a world power in its own right.[27] This is a very similar situation faced by a contemporary China in the first two decades of the twentieth century. Just as in the first decade of the twentieth century Japan was awed by the new inventions of the time at the 1900 Paris Universal Exposition,[28] which included electricity, the motor car and the aeroplane, China today is facing and embracing a period of rapid technological innovation in its own time. At the start of the twentieth century, Japan was also free to think about experimenting with different political thought, economic systems and overseas expansion.[29] The same can also be said to be true of China over the last forty years, from the start of its economic reforms in 1978. Just as China faced a serious pollution problem in the first decade of the twenty-first century, so did Japan at the start of the twentieth century due to the heavy industrialisation policy followed during the Meiji Era.[30] The question faced by those governing Japan at the time was how to resolve social problems while maintaining a balance between individual freedom and human rights.[31] However, this must be seen from the perspective that at the time of the Meiji Period, the

[24] Nish, I. (1998), The Origins of the Russo-Japanese War, Routledge, London.

[25] Lukoianov, I. (2008), The Portsmouth Peace, IN The Treaty of Portsmouth and its legacies, Ericson, S., and Hockley, A. (Eds), Dartmouth College Press, Hanover, New Hampshire.

[26] Ibid.

[27] Minichiello, S. (1998), Introduction, IN Japan's Competing Modernities: Issues in Culture and Democracy, 1900–1930, Minichiello, S. (Ed), University of Hawai'I Press, Honolulu.

[28] Ibid.

[29] Minichiello, S. (1998), Introduction, IN Japan's Competing Modernities: Issues in Culture and Democracy, 1900–1930, Minichiello, S. (Ed), University of Hawai'I Press, Honolulu.

[30] Ibid.

[31] Ibid.

Japanese constitution was drafted by Ito Hirobumi in such a fashion that it was very similar to the constitution drawn up by Bismarck for a newly reunited Germany.[32] Hirobumi was also very much against the governance of Japan based on a constitutional system of democratic parties.[33] Nevertheless, such a question was pertinent at that time as the first three decades of the twentieth century was a time at which not only was the western democratic model under threat but also its economic system, capitalism, following the Wall Street Crash of 1929.[34] Furthermore, Japan also faced an economic setback of its own with the banking crisis of 1927.[35] This banking crisis arose because of the public remarks made by the then Japanese Finance Minister regarding a particular bank's financial sustainability.[36] However, there also had been concerns about other banks which had not only accumulated debt from loans to rebuild following the Kanto Earthquake of 1923, but also accumulated other non-performing loans.[37] Although the bank run caused by this was eventually stymied by the passing of the Earthquake Legislation Bill, a further bank run occurred when the government was forced to rescue the Bank of Taiwan.[38] Nevertheless, the resulting banking crash in Japan caused an economic downturn which became prolonged and deeper following the Wall Street Crash of October 1929, which tended to exacerbate the effects of the initial downturn on the Japanese economy.[39] This set forth tidal waves of negative disturbances in the Japanese economy which conjoined with negative political waves. One such wave was set forth when the then Japanese Prime Minister, Hamaguchi Osachi, agreed to limiting Japanese construction of heavy cruisers such that Great Britain and the United States would have a numerical advantage over Japan.[40] The agreement by Osachi led to a

[32] Ibid.

[33] Ibid.

[34] Ibid.

[35] Ibid.

[36] Amyx, J. (2004), Japan's Financial Crisis, Institutional Rigidity and Reluctant Change, Princeton University Press, Princeton.

[37] Teranishi, J. (2005), Evolution of the Economic System in Japan, Edward Elgar, Cheltenham, UK.

[38] Teranishi, J. (2005), Evolution of the Economic System in Japan, Edward Elgar, Cheltenham, UK.

[39] Tamaki, N. (1995), Japanese Banking: A History, 1859-1959, Cambridge University Press, Cambridge.

[40] Minichiello, S. (1998), Introduction, IN Japan's Competing Modernities: Issues in Culture and Democracy, 1900–1930, Minichiello, S. (Ed), University of Hawai'I Press, Honolulu.

chorus of nationalist criticism in Japan which would lead to his assassination and eventual death in 1931.[41] Thence there also followed an end to civilian and bipartisan political government in Japan with the start of fifteen years of government featured by militarism and right wing nationalism which would only end with Japan's defeat by the United States in World War II in 1945.

The Taisho Emperor was born in 1879 and died in 1926 at the age of forty-seven, his personal name being Yoshihito.[42] The latter was the third son of the Meiji Emperor and the imperial concubine Yanagihara Naruko, reigning from 1912 to 1926.[43] Yoshihito was raised by his great grandfather and did not know until he was much older that the Empress Haruka, the wife of the Meiji Emperor, was not his real mother.[44] While Yoshihito was tutored at home during his time of learning, the only subject which he enjoyed and showed a passion for was composing Chinese poetry.[45] However, Yoshihito had a brain disease, and the Prime Minister was informed of this in 1919.[46] At this time the World War 1 had come to an end, revolutions were rocking European capitals and political agitation was on the rise in Japan. At this time, it was feared that revolution would also spread to Japan resulting in the overthrow of the imperial household and the instigation of a socialist cum communist government. As a result when this Yoshihito's brain condition worsened, his son Crown Prince Hirohito was appointed regent in 1921.[47] It was also around this time that Prime Minster Hara Kei was assassinated.[48] Hirohito was one of four sons born to Yoshihito and his wife, the Empress Sadako who lived between 1884 and 1951.[49] Sadako introduced modernity into the imperial Japanese family in two ways.[50] Firstly, she ended the system of having concubines in the imperial household by giving birth to four sons. Concubines were

[41] Ibid.

[42] Takeshi, H. (2008), Taisho: An Enigmatic Emperor and His Influential Wife, IN The Emperors of Modern Japan, Shillony, B. (Ed), BRILL, Boston.

[43] Ibid.

[44] Ibid.

[45] Ibid.

[46] Ibid.

[47] Takeshi, H. (2008), Taisho: An Enigmatic Emperor and His Influential Wife, IN The Emperors of Modern Japan, Shillony, B. (Ed), BRILL, Boston.

[48] Ibid.

[49] Ibid.

[50] Ibid.

then not required to propagate the imperial line by giving birth to males. Secondly, she accompanied her husband, the Emperor, on his official visits. This was something which no other Japanese Emperor may have done. Moreover, in the light of her husband's illness and in the years following his death, the Emperor Sadako shifted in belief from Nichiren Buddhism to a belief in Shintoism.[51] She also softened her attitude towards Christianity.[52]

The Japanese state was highly centralised and bureaucratic, especially during the Tokugawa and Meiji Periods.[53] However, there was a shift away from the centralisation of power from the Emperor towards bourgeois politicians during the Taisho Period between 1912 and 1926.[54] The Taisho Period also witnessed the emergence of the first attempts in Japan to organise labour unions as well as political parties, although this was suppressed by the police.[55] This democratic movement had very little similarity with the Anglo-Saxon political systems and parties which were implemented in Japan following the end of World War 2.[56] However, only the Communist and the Socialist parties which were instigated after this time bore any connection with the political parties which had existed during the period of the Taisho Democracy.[57]

Taisho Democracy

It was during the late Meiji period that individualism emerged in Japan, going on to develop further and flourish during the Taisho Period.[58] The development of individualism was accompanied by the emergence of daily newspapers and monthly journals.[59] These allowed individual opinions to form and for people to be better informed, a prerequisite for democratic

[51] Ibid.
[52] Ibid.
[53] Herzog, P. (1993), Japan's Pseudo-Democracy, Routledge, New York.
[54] Ibid.
[55] Ibid.
[56] Ibid.
[57] Ibid.
[58] Nolte, S. (1984), Individualism in Taisho Japan, Journal of Asian Studies, Vol. XLIII, No.4
[59] Ibid.

efficiency. However, some publications such as the Kokumin Shimbun acted as an unofficial mouthpiece for the government.[60]

The emergence of individualism during the late Meiji Period was facilitated by the removal of occupational and residential constraints on individuals as well as the removal of hereditary restrictions.[61] These changes allowed for greater social mobility. Moreover, these changes, to Japanese culture, in conjunction with education and a rising urban middle class, associated with industrialisation, allowed for individualism to develop. This is in contrast to periods in Japan prior to the Meiji Restoration when individualism would have been out of place because status by class and gender would have defined societal behaviour.[62] Furthermore, new experiences associated with the ability to move from one region to another, the shift in culture caused by the dominance of the nuclear family over the extended family and access to western literature and news allowed for the newly emerging Japanese middle class to examine individualism and its implications for and on Japanese civil society.[63] However, while individualism was emerging in Japan, it competed for survival with state power and ideology. This imposed constraints to the extent to which individuals could freely express their thought.[64] Nevertheless, the Japanese state was able together with government and ideology to coalesce individualism to meet Japan's needs. Foremost of these needs was to accumulate overseas territories through colonisation, and this became an official policy of the Japanese state after the acquisition of Taiwan in 1895.[65] The new Japanese identity was viewed as essential for the actioning and implementation of the policy of colonisation by the Japanese state.[66] In order to further the development of the new Japanese identity, the Japanese state implemented the use of progressive educational techniques in Japanese schools in order to facilitate the development of initiative and more activity by the

[60] Pierson, J. (1980), Tokutomo Soho, 1893–1957: A Journalist for Modern Japan, Princeton University Press.

[61] Nolte, S. (1984), Individualism in Taisho Japan, Journal of Asian Studies, Vol. XLIII, No.4.

[62] Ibid.

[63] Ibid.

[64] Ibid.

[65] Ibid.

[66] Nakano A. (1975), On the Taisho free education Movement, Reimei, Tokyo.

children.[67] The progressive educational techniques favoured by the Japanese state were those developed by Johann Pestalozzi, the Swiss teaching and learning professional of the time.[68] The development of individualism in Japan was not a single identity but a development of three strands of thought. In the first case, the development of individualism in Japan was needed for the development of the state and the projection of the power of the state to other countries. Secondly, individualism could co-exist with the state and its ideology in a private sphere.[69] Finally, a valuation of state development should be based on the extent to which individualism had developed. Of the three strands of thought related to individualism in the emergence of the Japanese state, the last one was interpretated as the most liberal of the three by western scholars.[70] This liberal type of individualism only emerged in Japan following the end of the Russo-Japanese War.[71] This third interpretation and identification of individualism in Japan belonged to those who thought that the traditional class and gender structure of Japanese civil society stood in the way of the country's economic, political and cultural development. In this case, class structure and gender restrictions had to be abolished in order for the Japanese state to develop. The presence of liberal individualism in the Taisho Period shows the extent to which Japanese society had advanced in its thinking, leading to a society which was heading towards a pluralist type of governance.

The Taisho democratic period in pre-war Japan spanned from 1905 to 1932.[72] In this case, the Taisho Democracy began a few years before the Meiji Emperor died and overlapped with the end of the Taisho Period and the start of the Showa Period.[73] The main feature of Taisho Democracy, in its purest form, is that it rejected not only the idea of the sovereignty of the Emperor but also notions of imperialism.[74] However, because neither

[67] Nolte, S. (1984), Individualism in Taisho Japan, Journal of Asian Studies, Vol. XLIII, No.4

[68] Ibid.

[69] Ibid.

[70] Ibid.

[71] Ibid.

[72] Gordon, A. (1991), Labor and Imperial Democracy in Pre-War Japan, University of California Press, Berkeley.

[73] Ibid.

[74] Gordon, A. (1991), Labor and Imperial Democracy in Pre-War Japan, University of California Press, Berkeley.

was challenged in the 1920s or the 1930s, Taisho Democracy is seen as having been unsustainable and not rooted deeply enough in Japanese culture, institutionally. Nevertheless, the Taisho democratic movement can be seen as a quest for civil and political freedom under a constitutional system of government.[75] The essential feature of a constitutional system of government is that elected politicians are the representatives of the people having superiority over all other state apparatus.[76] In this case, the overarching objective of the Taisho democratic movement was to establish a constitutional system of governance in pre-war Japan.[77]

Even though the Taisho Democracy is said to have lasted between 1905 and 1932, this involves the merger of two viewpoints as to the historical time period of its existence.[78] The first viewpoint suggests that the Taisho Democracy spanned the years 1918 to 1932, while the second viewpoint suggests that it spanned the years 1905 to 1925.[79] In the case of the former time span, it begins with the formation of the cabinet under Prime Minister Hara and ends with the dissolution of the cabinet of Prime Minister Inukai.[80] The other feature of this time period was that the driving force for constitutional change was from political parties. This was thought to be a necessary characteristic of Taisho Democracy.[81] On the other hand, the second time period from 1905 to 1925 is seen as encompassing Taisho Democracy because of Japan's quest for better peace terms with regard to the settling of the Russo-Japanese War at the start of the period and ending it with Prime Minister Kato's political reforms. These reforms were explicitly begun after the 'Second Campaign for the Defence of the Constitution'.[82] The differentiating feature between the categorisation of the Taisho Period as falling between 1905 and 1925 rather than between 1918 and 1932 is the active participation of common people calling for political change rather than political parties. In this context, the political parties either opposed the so-called peoples campaigns or they

[75] Takayoshi, M. (1966), The Development of Democracy in Japan: Taisho Democracy, Its Flowering and Breakdown." *Developing Economies* 4.4:612–37.

[76] Ibid.

[77] Ibid.

[78] Ibid.

[79] Ibid.

[80] Gordon, A. (1991), Labor and Imperial Democracy in Pre-War Japan, University of California Press, Berkeley.

[81] Ibid.

[82] Ibid.

took advantage of them to further their objectives.[83] However, the part of the Taisho Period which can be best recognised as a democratic system of governance akin to the American and the European model occurred between 1924 and 1932.[84] At this time, two main political parties, the Seiyukai and the Minseito, provided Japan with its Prime Ministers.[85] Between this time, even the political rights and views of all were protected except those of the most radical opponents of the state.[86]

The Taisho Democracy movement for political change in pre-World War 2 Japan had a predecessor in the form of the 'Liberty and Popular Rights Movement', the LPRM, of the Meiji Period.[87] The LPRM had a number of objectives.[88] Firstly, representation of the people by an elected parliament which would embody the political structure of the constitution. The establishment of a parliament was the main political demand of the LPRM. The second demand was more economically orientated and revolved around the abolition of the feudal ownership of the land as well as a reduction in land taxes. The third demand, diplomatic in nature, revolved around the assertion of Japan's sovereignty with regard to amending treaties with terms which would be more beneficial to Japan. On the other hand, the principles of the Taisho Democracy, TD, were similar in nature but different in some ways from those of the LPRM. In this regard, the TD firstly sought the establishment of a sovereign parliament which enshrined the principles of free association, the ability of meetings to be held without restrictions as well as freedom of speech. This required the denigration of the power of the Emperor. Secondly, the TD required the abolition of the feudal tax system as well as a reduction in the inequality of power between capitalists and workers as well as between landowners and peasants.[89] The last demand of the TD movement was the repudiation of Japan's imperialistic ambitions.[90] While both the LPRM

[83] Gordon, A. (1991), Labor and Imperial Democracy in Pre-War Japan, University of California Press, Berkeley.

[84] Smethurst R.J. (1995) Japan's First Experiment with Democracy, 1868–1940. In: Andrews G.R., Chapman H. (eds) The Social Construction of Democracy, 1870–1990. Palgrave Macmillan, London.

[85] Ibid.

[86] Ibid.

[87] Gordon, A. (1991), Labor and Imperial Democracy in Pre-War Japan, University of California Press, Berkeley.

[88] Ibid.

[89] Ibid.

[90] Ibid.

and the TD focused their demands on the assertion of individual freedom and the protection of human dignity, the differences between the two movements arose primarily because they were omnipresent at different stages of Japan's economic development.[91] The LPRM was a force for political change at an early stage of Japan's economic development when the economy was dominated by the capitalist system.[92] Moreover, the challenge to the capitalists arose from farmers and those who had belonged to the Samurai class. These people represented the driving force of the LPRM. However, during the TD movement, the driving force for political change arose from the rising middle classes who had benefited from the industrial policies which Japan had followed in the Meiji Period.[93] Finally, the LPRM movement was driven by political parties whilst the TD movement was driven by ordinary citizens.[94]

During the Taisho and early Showa Periods, Japan was undergoing painful social, political and economic changes.[95] These changes were negatively impacting on people's lives and pushing them in the search for a solution either to the politics of the left wing Marxists or the right to the politics of the right wing nationalists.[96] As the economic recession deepened, labour strikes became a feature of the economy, their increasing frequency signalling the grip of the Marxists on the labour unions.[97] At this time, although Japanese governance had evolved to the multi-party democratic stage, there still existed in parallel the organs of dictatorial power.[98] These organs included the Privy Council, the Emperor system as well as the influence on these of the military faction.[99] It was the existence and functionality of these organs of dictatorship which facilitated the usurping of democracy following a period of instability over a five-year period during which Japan had numerous cabinets.[100] The political instability had two paths, one of which could only be taken. For the Marxists

[91] Gordon, A. (1991), Labor and Imperial Democracy in Pre-War Japan, University of California Press, Berkeley.

[92] Ibid.

[93] Ibid.

[94] Ibid.

[95] Hoston, G. (1984), Marxism and National Socialism in Taisho Japan: The Thought of Takabatake Motoyuki, Journal of Asian Studies, Vol. XLIV, No.1

[96] Ibid.

[97] Ibid.

[98] Ibid.

[99] Ibid.

[100] Ibid.

and the left there could only be a path to revolution.[101] On the other hand, to right wing nationalists, the path away from economic, political and social stagnation lay with imperialistic overseas expansion.[102]

The seeds of the downfall of Taisho Democracy had been laid during the Meiji Period just as was its seeds of bloom. In this context, during the Meiji Period the use of private capital and government support had been espoused and courted by the Meiji Oligarchs, although the educational system was based on an anti-capitalist ethic.[103] This dichotomy resulted in a movement which called for the restoration of traditional Japan in the late 1920s and the 1930s. And, it was this movement which led to the collapse of the Taisho Democracy and its business-dominated political parties.[104] This new reformist movement focused on the control of the Oligarchs, the business leaders and the wage earners by removing the free market mechanism's role in the allocation and the distribution of social goods.[105] The politics of 1930s' Japan was then characterised by the replacement of the market mechanism for the allocation of scarce resources and the output of the production with a bureaucratic one.[106] The transition of politics in Japan from the Taisho Democracy Period to the bureaucratic fascism of the 1930s mirrored the rise of the same process in Europe, particularly in Germany and Italy. The transition was a shift to control the wastefulness of the free market and business decision making rather than as an attack on individual utility and private property.[107] Other reasons for the shift from the Taisho Democracy to a fascist bureaucratic regime in Japan in the 1930s may have because of the constraints and the limitations placed on Japanese military capability and overseas territorial ambitions by the so-called Versailles-Washington Consensus of the western powers.[108] The reformists of the time felt that the impact of Japan adhering to this consensus would forever condemn it to be a backward country.[109] The

[101] Hoston, G. (1984), Marxism and National Socialism in Taisho Japan: The Thought of Takabatake Motoyuki, Journal of Asian Studies, Vol. XLIV, No.1.

[102] Ibid.

[103] Duus, P., and Okimoto, D. (1979), Fascism and the History of Pre-War Japan: The Failure of a Concept, Journal of Asian Studies, Vol.XXXIX, No.1.

[104] Ibid.

[105] Ibid.

[106] Ibid.

[107] Ibid.

[108] Woodall, B. (2014), Growing Democracy in Japan, The Parliamentary Cabinet System Since 1868, University Press of Kentucky.

[109] Ibid.

situation in which Japan was in during the late 1920s and the early 1930s compares well with the situation in which Great Britain is in today in trying to make a clean break from its relationship with the European Union. The latter, in collusion with some UK politicians, seems to be intent to preventing Great Britain from either leaving on favourable terms or from leaving at all.

World War 1 and Territorial Expansion

Following the Meiji Restoration, Japan attempted to renegotiate the unequal treaties which had been imposed upon it during the Tokugawa Period. However, by 1889 this general renegotiation strategy did not bear fruit, and the Japanese government began to take a singular approach to treaty renegotiation.[110] It was the difficulty of achieving an agreement with the western powers about amending previously negotiated unfavourable treaties to more favourable terms for Japan which resulted in negative feelings arising amongst the Japanese public against the western powers. The period following the late 1890s witnessed the rise of Japanese nationalism which in some cases resulted in acts of political violence.[111] Moreover, negative public opinion over the new treaties also arose because the new treaties were unfavourable to Japan.[112] As a result, in 1890 Japan's first elected parliament failed to ratify the treaties.[113] However, it was realised by senior people in the government that it would be easier for Japan to receive favourable terms from the western powers, if its institutions were modelled on western ones.[114] Nevertheless, once Japan was able to behave on equal terms with the western powers, having re-negotiated unequal treaties imposed on it by them, it immediately became a colonial power.[115] However, the rise of Japanese imperialism perhaps can be attributed to the centralisation of power as well as to its consolidation in the hands of the government following the Meiji Restoration of 1868.[116] The late 1880s

[110] Cullen, L. (2003), A History of Japan, 1582–1941; Internal and External Worlds, Cambridge University Press, Cambridge.

[111] Ibid.

[112] Ibid.

[113] Ibid.

[114] Ibid.

[115] Beasley, W. (1987), Japanese Imperialism 1894–1945, Clarendon, Oxford.

[116] Eskildsen, R. (2019), Transforming Empire in Japan and East Asia: The Taiwan Expedition and the Birth of Japanese Imperialism, New Directions in East Asian History, Springer, Singapore.

and the 1890s therefore saw not only the rise of Japanese nationalism but also Japanese colonialism. The peaceful Japanese state which had existed for two and a half centuries was coming to an end. One signal that this was happening was the rise of the embryonic Japanese military in the 1870s.[117] It was in 1872 that the Imperial Japanese Navy split from the control of the Army and became a national military service in its own right. At this time the people of Japan viewed the South Seas as its empire in waiting. As such the only way in which Japanese interests could be protected in this vast region was by having a powerful navy. It was for this purpose and to seek Japanese government support for an expanded navy that officers of the Imperial Japanese Navy adopted a doctrine for Japan's strategic expansion into the South Seas.[118]

In 1895, China had ceded Taiwan to Japan under the terms of the Treaty of Shimonoseki. Moreover, following the end of the Russian-Japanese war of 1905, Russia ceded the southern part of Sakhalin to Japan.[119] In the same year, Japan acquired a lease over Liaotung upon which there was not only the naval base of Port Arthur but also the commercial port of Dairen.[120] Liaotung is in the southern part of Manchuria. In due course, Chinese Liaotung became Japanese Kwantung, and it remained this way until Japan was defeated in World War 2 in 1945. However, before this time Japan had also annexed Korea in 1910.[121] Further opportunities for Japanese territorial expansion occurred with the start of World War 1. In this case, the Japanese benefited by acquiring territory from Germany having declared war upon it, conforming with the requirements of the Anglo-British Alliance.[122] In this case, the Japanese acquired German assets in the Chinese province of Shantung as well as German territories in the western Pacific.[123] However, while Japan kept some economic interests in Shantung, the rights to the territory returned

[117] Cullen, L. (2003), A History of Japan, 1582–1941; Internal and External Worlds, Cambridge University Press, Cambridge.

[118] Schencking, J. (1999), The Imperial Japanese Navy and the Constructed Consciousness of a South Seas Destiny, 1872–1921, Modern Asian Studies, 33, 4, pp.769–796.

[119] Cullen, L. (2003), A History of Japan, 1582–1941; Internal and External Worlds, Cambridge University Press, Cambridge.

[120] Ibid.

[121] Ibid.

[122] Ibid.

[123] Ibid.

to China in 1922 under the terms of the Washington Conference.[124] Moreover, Japan held onto the German territories it had acquired in the Pacific, such as the Mariana, Palau, Caroline and Marshall Islands even after World War 1 had ended under the auspices of the mandate of the then League of Nations.[125]

Japan contributed to the allied efforts during World War 1 in a number of ways.[126] Firstly, German forces were removed from their Chinese enclave in Qingdao as well as from the parts of Micronesia which the Germans controlled. Secondly, convoys of allied troops were escorted by Japanese ships and submarines for protection; and German submarines were hunted and destroyed. And lastly, Japan supplied the allies with home-produced military equipment, resources and financial assistance. In this case, increased foreign trade meant that Japan's balance of payments reflected a surplus for the first time in the country's history.[127] However, mainland Japan remained far from the conflict and its peoples not familiar with the war at all.[128] While this was a visible effect, the impact of the war on the Japanese nation state was far less so. In this case, Japan's involvement in World War 1 marked its transformation from an agricultural regional state into an industrialised world power.[129] At a global level, the Great War also marked the transition from a world centred on European power to an emergent world based on rising American power.[130] In this light it would have seemed that Japan's future at the end of World War 1 was laden with great opportunities for the economy, the people as well as for the country rather than a future of ashes, death and destruction.[131] Moreover, it would have seemed that the transformation which Japan went through from the start to the end of World War 1 laid the foundations of Japanese prosperity and greater global interconnectedness rather than to serve as the roots for

[124] Ibid.

[125] Cullen, L. (2003), A History of Japan, 1582–1941; Internal and External Worlds, Cambridge University Press, Cambridge.

[126] Baldwin, K. (1921), A Brief Account of Japan's Part in the World War, 6, Stanley K. Hornbeck Papers, Box 255, War, Costs and Contributions, The Hoover Institution on War, Revolution and Peace.

[127] Dickinson, F. (2013), World War 1 and the Triumph of a New Japan, 1919–1930, Cambridge University Press, Cambridge.

[128] Ibid.

[129] Ibid.

[130] Ibid.

[131] Dickinson, F. (2015), The World War 1, Japan and a Global Century, IN Japan and the Great War, Frattolillio, O., and Best, A. (Ed), Springer.

the rise of fascism and military expansionism.[132] This paradoxical situation can only be resolved by assessing the behaviour and actions of Japanese policy makers of the time. In 1914, there were two notable and influential characters in Japanese politics. The first was Field Marshal Yamagata Aritomo, and the second was Foreign Minister Kato Takaaki. The former was the architect of the birth, structure and the organisation of the Imperial Japanese Army.[133] Yamagata was known to be schemer as well as being a key proponent of Japanese military expansionism, favouring China and central China in particular.[134] However, Yamagata also took the view that the war in Europe was a racial one and that Japan should keep out of it, favouring on improving ties with China in order to ensure its survival.[135] Nevertheless, at the same time Yamagata also took the view that Japan would be better off on the side of Germany rather than aligning itself with Great Britain.[136] And at the same time, Yamagata had modelled the Imperial Japanese Army on the Prussian Army. In fact the defeat of the German military by the allies stunned the officers of the Imperial Japanese Army, some of whom conducted a study into why it had happened.[137] It was quickly concluded that the German Army was defeated because it could not be consistently supplied with the military supplies it needed to keep going due to allied blockades which prevented resources reaching German factories.[138] In order to prevent this happening to Japan, the Imperial Japanese Army concluded that Japanese territory should expand to encompass areas which held the resources required for military and industrial production.[139] Moreover, Japan should develop a substantial industrial base which could be converted to war time production when required.[140] Nevertheless, in the first two decades of the twentieth century, Japan and Great Britain were bed fellows. In this case, at the time Foreign Minister Kato favoured and did implement the alliance with Great Britain,

[132] Ibid.

[133] Dickinson, F. (1999), War and National Re-invention: Japan in the Great War, 1914–1919, Harvard University Asia Center, Cambridge, Massachusetts.

[134] Ibid.

[135] Ibid.

[136] Ibid.

[137] Barnhart, M. (1981), Japan's Economic Security and the Origins of the Pacific War, Journal of Strategic Studies, 4, 2.

[138] Ibid.

[139] Ibid.

[140] Ibid.

which was substantiated with the use of 29,000 and 2800 Japanese and British troops respectively expelling the Germans from their Chinese enclave of Qingdao.[141] In 1915, Kato would present the Chinese government headed by Yuan Shih-k'ai with a list of twenty-one demands. These demands reiterated perceived Japanese supremacy over the Chinese with regard to preferential rights to Chinese territory and some form of control over other Chinese assets at the expense of other nations.[142] However, if China had accepted the Japanese demands, then China would have become a dependent territory of Japan.[143] But although China rejected the Japanese demands, these demands did stoke the levels of Chinese nationalism to higher levels.[144] China's ability to reject the Japanese demands was made easier by the publicity generated by the Shih-k'ai governments information sharing with western legations in Beijing as well as with the Chinese press. The latter helped to increase the level of national unity amongst the Chinese in opposing the Japanese demands while the former increased western government's support of the Chinese against the Japanese.[145] This made it easier for China to reject the Japanese demands because if the Japanese retaliated with military force against China, then the western powers may have intervened on its behalf.

At the start of the twentieth century, Japan's goal was to become the 'Great Britain' of the far east, through territorial expansion as well as an expansion of its markets through international trade.[146] This was mainly in the context of south-east Asia. However, Japan was forced to return territories it had taken from China as well accepting to voluntarily limit the size of its navy at the Washington Conference of late 1921. The Washington Conference was an attempt by the world's leading powers of the time, which included Great Britain and the United States, to promote stability in East Asia by putting in place an agreement to limit the capacity as well

[141] Dickinson, F. (1999), War and National Re-invention: Japan in the Great War, 1914–1919, Harvard University Asia Center, Cambridge, Massachusetts.

[142] Chaurasia, R. (2003), History of Japan, Atlantic Publishers and Distributors, New Delhi.

[143] Ibid.

[144] Fairbank, J., Reischauer, E., and Craig, A. (1989), East Asia: Tradition and Transformation, revised edition, Houghton Mifflin, Boston.

[145] Luo, Z. (1993), National Humiliation and National Assertion: The Chinese Response to the Twenty-One Demands, Modern Asian Studies, 27, 2.

[146] Fisher, C. (1950), The Expansion of Japan: A Study of Oriental Geopolitics: Part 1, Continental and Maritime Components in Japanese Expansion, The geographical Journal, Vol.115, No1/3, pp.1–19.

as the potential of each country's navies.[147] As an international arms limitation and conflict prevention mechanism, the Washington Conference was a failure because within ten years Japan had invaded Manchuria.[148] Moreover, the Conference outcome also prevented Great Britain and the United States from re-arming quickly enough in order to contain belligerent Japanese territorial expansion in the 1930s.[149] The Japanese may also have resented the tone and the terms of the agreement reached at the Washington Conference because while the capacity of the countries' navies was limited, the Imperial Japanese Navy was more limited with regard to the number and types of ships it could have compared to the navies of Great Britain and the United States.[150] Following the Washington Conference, there was a decade in which many would have thought that Japan was following a liberal, trade-based expansion of its role in the world having shed itself of militaristic, aggressive territorial tendencies.[151] However, what was probably happening was a period in which Japanese leaders and peoples were inwardly examining their role in the world.[152] This was a world which was very different from that which Japan faced as it embarked on the political, economic and industrial reforms of the Meiji restoration. In this case, by the 1920s the Qing Dynasty of China had been overthrown and had become a Republic, similarly the Russian monarchy had been overthrown and a Soviet government put in place Russia and its dominions, and the outcome of the World War 1 had cemented the dominant political and economic ascendancy of the United States in world affairs. Indeed, Japan's role in the world had also changed, and Japan's true intentions did not become clear to the world until the Manchurian Incident of September 1931. This was a bomb explosion on a railway line in Manchuria, instigated by the soldiers of the Japanese Kwantung Army, which had been in Manchuria since 1905, to create a

[147] Goldstein, E., and Maurer, J. (Eds), (1994), The Washington Conference, 1921–22: Naval Rivalry, East Asian Stability and the Road to Pearl Harbor, Routledge, London.

[148] Ibid.

[149] Goldstein, E., and Maurer, J. (Eds), (1994), The Washington Conference, 1921–22: Naval Rivalry, East Asian Stability and the Road to Pearl Harbor, Routledge, London.

[150] Fisher, C. (1950), The Expansion of Japan: A Study of Oriental Geopolitics: Part 1, Continental and Maritime Components in Japanese Expansion, The geographical Journal, Vol.115, No1/3, pp.1–19.

[151] Ibid.

[152] Ibid.

scenario for the complete takeover of Manchuria by Japan.[153] The pretext used by the Japanese to seize Manchuria, a Chinese territory with the combined land area of France and Germany as well as a population of 30 million Chinese, was that Japanese lives and property were at risk from the activities of Chinese revolutionaries.[154] The Japanese had good reason to seize Manchuria as it was agriculturally fertile and possessed natural resources which Japan needed.[155] Indeed, Manchuria was designated as Japan's bread basket in the region's First Five Year Plan of 1937.[156]

The Manchurian Incident as well as subsequent events would change the course of modern Chinese history because the Communists gained at the expense of Chiang Kai-Shek's nationalists. The latter had made good progress in attempting to modernise China with regard to laws, regulations, infrastructure, the military and retrieving control of setting China's tariffs on imports from the foreigners upon whom such power had been bestowed by unequal treaties imposed on China.[157] However, the problem for the nationalists was that their reach of power was only limited to the cities and not to rural areas where millions lived in abject poverty. The Manchurian Incident was only the beginning of Japanese militarism and nationalism with an emphasis on territorial expansion to create a Japanese Empire. The full context of this policy was set out in the Tanaka Memorial of 1927. The authenticity of this document has been questioned, sometimes being considered to be Chinese counter propaganda. Nevertheless, the document singles out the occupation and the economic development of Manchuria and Mongolia as being pivotal for Japan to win world mastery.[158] However, the policy which the Japanese had put in place was different from the one perceived by western governments and diplomats. They perceived that the Japanese would be content with Manchuria, and no further aggression would follow. However, the transition of Chinese Manchuria to Japanese Manchukuo was followed by the Amau Declaration,

[153] Mitter, R. (2013), Forgotten Ally, Houghton Mifflin Harcourt Publishing, New York.

[154] Ibid.

[155] Fisher, C. (1950), The Expansion of Japan: A Study of Oriental Geopolitics: Part 1, Continental and Maritime Components in Japanese Expansion, The geographical Journal, Vol.115, No1/3, pp.1–19.

[156] Ibid.

[157] Mitter, R. (2013), Forgotten Ally, Houghton Mifflin Harcourt Publishing, New York.

[158] Crow, C. (2013), Japan's Dream of World Empire – The Tanaka Memorial, Read Books Ltd.

the China Incident, the Monroe Doctrine for East Asia, the Greater East Asia Prosperity Sphere and then the war in the Pacific.[159]

Economic Development

An understanding of the economic events during the Taisho Period is crucial for understanding the nature of Japan during the preceding Meiji Period as well as in the subsequent Showa Period.[160] In this case, the Taisho Period is an important constituent of the one-hundred-year time span which encompasses Japan's industrialisation.[161] The economic system which functioned in Japan from the mid-1900s to the early 1920s was a three-tiered system.[162] In this case, there was a government–market interface, perhaps through its role in the regulation of the economy. This existed in association with a government–private sector interface due to government support for the Zaibatsu as well as a private sector interface.[163] The Meiji-Taisho economic system was a fully functioning and coherent system by the first decade of the twentieth century, but was replaced by a military economic system in the 1930s.[164] The three-tiered Meiji-Taisho economic system was implemented in the aftermath of the Sino-Japanese War of 1894–1895 and the Russo-Japanese War of 1904–1905 as a high-growth economic system. This was in the context of Japan as a unified national market, the implementation of the Meiji constitution of 1889 and the management of the economy having been split between the government and the private sector.[165] The Russo-Japanese War gave additional momentum for the industrialisation of Japan.[166] A requirement for more

[159] Fisher, C. (1950), The Expansion of Japan: A Study of Oriental Geopolitics: Part 1, Continental and Maritime Components in Japanese Expansion, The geographical Journal, Vol.115, No1/3, pp.1–19.

[160] Smitka, M. (1998), The Interwar Economy of Japan, Colonialism, Depression and recovery, 1910–1940, Garland Publishing Inc, New York.

[161] Smitka, M. (1998), The Interwar Economy of Japan, Colonialism, Depression and recovery, 1910–1940, Garland Publishing Inc, New York.

[162] Ibid.

[163] Ibid.

[164] Ibid.

[165] Teranishi, J. (2005), Evolution of the Economic System in Japan, Edward Elgar, Cheltenham, UK.

[166] Tsuzuki, C. (2000), The Pursuit of Power in Modern Japan 1825–1995, Oxford University Press, Oxford.

steel resulted in the expansion of Yawata Steel in 1906.[167] And in 1907, seventeen private railway companies were nationalised bringing them within state-owned management.[168] Lastly, Japan acquired the ability to set its own customs duties in 1911, and as a result it was able to protect its industries, enabling them to grow faster, by imposing high tariffs on cheaper imports.[169] These factors facilitated an increase in the pace of industrialisation in Japan.[170] However, the financing of industrialisation and the Russo-Japanese War had caused Japan to increase its foreign debt levels.[171] Nevertheless, the levels of Japan's foreign debt began to be brought down with the start of World War 1 during which Japan was able to sell industrial, manufactured and agricultural goods to the combatants at inflated prices. At this time, in 1915, although Japan was still technically at war with Germany due to the Japanese-British alliance, Japanese industry benefited a great deal from the outbreak of hostilities.[172] This is because Japan was located outside the main theatre of the war in Europe and its supply chain was much closer to home resulting from little if any disruption to its industry. As a result, Japanese industry was in a position to supply the belligerents in the war, except Germany. Therefore, there was significant growth in Japanese exports of manufactured goods, specifically in its pre-war markets of the United States and China.[173] Furthermore, the volume of Japanese cotton exports doubled from 1913 to 1918, and the country's textile exports gained a foothold in the non-traditional markets of the Asian colonies of the Dutch and the British.[174] The expansion of Japanese industry and the significant growth of its exports generated a requirement for more raw materials and capital goods to be used for production.[175] The increased demand for raw materials was met by Japan's colonies—Korea, southern Sakhalin, Taiwan, Kwantung Leased Territory and the ex-German possessions in the Pacific.[176] Moreover, Japan's newly

[167] Ibid.
[168] Ibid.
[169] Ibid.
[170] Ibid.
[171] Ibid.
[172] Lockwood, W. (1954), Economic Development of Japan: Growth and Structural Change, Princeton University Press, Princeton, New Jersey, USA.
[173] Ibid.
[174] Ibid.
[175] Ibid.
[176] Ibid.

found colonies were also a good market to export goods manufactured in Japan.[177] However, the countries which supplied the capital goods were those involved in the main theatre of war in Europe in which case productive capacity had been diverted to produce armaments to support the military. In this case, these other countries had wartime controls in place with regard to what items could be produced in order to sustain their war effort. The result was that Japanese exports exceeded its imports with the result that the country had a significant current account and foreign asset surplus.[178] Japan's strong export base meant that firms' profit levels were rising as were household incomes. The result was that increasing aggregate demand in the economy was pushing up the average level of prices in the Japanese economy. And so inflation was accelerating, and securities' and commodities' markets were experiencing increased levels of speculative activity.[179] However, as aggregate demand was increasing, the Japanese economy was also experiencing increasing levels of national output as well as an increase in productive capacity and gains in technical experience.[180] Nevertheless, some factories which had been established to increase production during the war years did not survive for long once the war had ended, world trade returned to its normal pattern and as prices began to fall.[181] Furthermore, the increased productive capacity during the war years had left Japanese industry overcapitalised.[182] And after the war as prices and profits began to fall, bad debt levels in the Japanese economy began to increase. The increasing bad debt levels negatively affected the Japanese banking sector for ten years after the end of the war. Moreover, following an earthquake in Japan in the early 1920s, Japanese banks increased loans to facilitate a construction boom but the loans turned bad and this exercise also tapered into a banking crisis in 1927.[183] However, the corporate sector had taken advantage of the expansionary monetary policy adopted by the government to increase investment and rationalise the production process by using improved technology.[184] In this case,

[177] Ibid.

[178] Ibid.

[179] Ibid.

[180] Lockwood, W. (1954), Economic Development of Japan: Growth and Structural Change, Princeton University Press, Princeton, New Jersey, USA.

[181] Ibid.

[182] Ibid.

[183] Ibid.

[184] Ibid.

there was a marked increase in technological progress in Japanese industry especially after 1927.[185] However, resource extractive industries such as the mining sector faced increasing costs of production in the 1920s because this sector did not benefit from the rationalisation and technical upgrading which other sectors of Japanese industry had experienced.[186] Nevertheless, there had also been expansion in the cotton manufacturing sector, but increase in the productivity of this sector was made possible by better organisation, better equipment and improved technical skills.[187] In the 1920s the economic boom had also allowed the Japanese silk industry to flourish, while other sectors of Japanese industry remained mediocre. The earning of girls working in Japanese silk factories was an important source of income for rural families.[188] And, even at the end of the 1920s, Japan's agricultural sector remained dominant with half of the working population being employed in this sector. The implication of this is that any jobs which had been created in the war and in the interwar years had been in the non-agricultural sector.[189]

In the 1920s, the United States was Japan's biggest export market just as it is China's today. Although the Japanese economy had become integrated into the global economy, Japanese industry was not able to generate sufficient jobs to cater for those who were entering the job market as Japan's population grew.[190] This experience is becoming more evident in contemporary China today with its slowing economy unable to create enough jobs to cater for those entering the jobs market. In the Japan of the 1920s, at the same time as the middle class grew, so did the size of urban centres, there was a developing trend towards more liberal and democratic ideals in Japanese society which exhibited itself in education, the newspapers as well as in Japanese politics.[191] However, while in the years between World War 1 and World War 2, Japan enjoyed a western style, constitutional multi-party democracy, it still revolved around a system of feudal heritage and the corporate sector had an influence on politicians in the

[185] Ibid.

[186] Ibid.

[187] Ibid.

[188] Ibid.

[189] Lockwood, W. (1954), Economic Development of Japan: Growth and Structural Change, Princeton University Press, Princeton, New Jersey, USA.

[190] Ibid.

[191] Ibid.

context of formulating national policy.[192] Nevertheless, the constitutional democracy of interwar years Japan allowed for a wide ranging public discussion of various social issues ranging from the advantages and disadvantages of birth control to workers' safety and factory standards.[193] While the discussion of social issues became a feature of life in the Japanese Diet, successive Japanese governments in the 1920s were not successful at formulating economic policy which would have allowed the economy to stabilise and to be able to cope with the coming future economic crises. This perhaps may have been due to the need to placate different interest groups and compromise in order to formulate economic policy with the result that it was too diluted with little or no long-term impact on the economy.[194] The ineffectual policy making of the 1920s became evident as the Japanese economy felt its chilling winds from 1930 to 1931.[195] However, in the first three decades of the twentieth century, the Japanese industrial sector had expanded at significant levels. And in a historical context, this can only be matched with the rise of modern China from 1978 to 2011. During this period, modern China became an industrialised, manufacturing export-based country having undergone a similar process that the Japanese economy had gone through from 1868, by following successive incremental economic reforms. But there are two big experiences between Japan's industrialisation experience and that of China's. Firstly, Japan also included governance reforms by adopting western-style democracy, whereas China had continued with its one-party system. Secondly, in the case of Japan, the Zaibatsu, industrial conglomerates exercising control over large sectors of the economy, were responsible for the Japanese accumulation of capital and technological know-how. The growth of the Zaibatsu allowed the Japanese economy to benefit from economies of scale.[196] However, in the case of contemporary China, FDI and the policies necessary to attract it were crucial in facilitating China's economic rise.

For Japan, the 1930s were a big contrast to the 1920s in terms of economic and industrial performance as well as governance. In the case of the former, Japan's exports of goods to the US and the European markets were much cheaper than the goods produced by domestic firms in those

[192] Ibid.

[193] Ibid.

[194] Ibid.

[195] Ibid.

[196] Lockwood, W. (1954), Economic Development of Japan: Growth and Structural Change, Princeton University Press, Princeton, New Jersey, USA.

regions. The result was that European countries and the United States, Japan's biggest export market, placed tariffs on Japanese goods after 1932 in order to give domestically produced goods a competitive advantage. However, this reversed the trend in Japanese trade with the United States, such that by 1936, the United States had a surplus in trade against Japan.[197] Also from the early 1930s, right wing groups in Japan were assassinating liberal reformist politicians such as Hamaguchi Osachi and Inukai Tsuyoshi.[198] The former had been responsible for implementing the 1930 London naval Treaty and enraging the Japanese military by doing so.[199] Osachi had also been the leader of the Minseito grouping in the Diet, as well as being Prime Minister from 1929 to 1931.[200] On the other hand, Tsuyoshi had been Prime Minister at the time of the Manchurian Incident in 1931 as well as being the leader for the Protection of Constitutional Government.[201] Despite the threat of assassination, the elements of democracy continued to try and constrain the Japanese military's quest for new adventures abroad.[202] However, by the mid-1930s, the Japanese military had taken control of the government, and it became impossible for the elements of democracy in Japan to do anything to quell their aggression.[203]

The developmental economic system of the early Meiji Period had been put in place in order to facilitate economic and industrial 'catch-up' with the western powers who were threatening Japan's independence from the middle of the eighteenth century.[204] In contrast, the economic system in place in Japan during the 1930s and the early 1940s was one which focused on the needs of a militarised economy managed by the military as well as by bureaucrats.[205] However, before the emergence of the Meiji-Taisho economic system, the management of the economy was left in the hands of bureaucrats and politicians who acted on the basis of their loyalty to a

[197] Ibid.

[198] Benson, J., and Matsumura, T. (2001), Japan, 1868–1945, From Isolation to Occupation, Routledge, London.

[199] Ibid.

[200] Ibid.

[201] Benson, J., and Matsumura, T. (2001), Japan, 1868-1945, From Isolation to Occupation, Routledge, London.

[202] Alexander, A. (2008), The Arc of Japan's Economic Development, Routledge, London.

[203] Ibid.

[204] Teranishi, J. (2005), Evolution of the Economic System in Japan, Edward Elgar, Cheltenham, UK.

[205] Ibid.

particular ruling power structure which revolved around low-level samurai. But in this political-economic apparatus, landlords, farmers and taxpayers were outside the decision-making process.[206]

The industrialisation policies which had been implemented during the Meiji Period resulted in economic growth between 1890 and 1905, and in conjunction with the increase in industrial output as a result of World War I, Japan had become an industrialised economy during the Taisho period.[207] Moreover, it was during the Taisho Period that the Japanese economy experienced increasing industrial output as well as economic recession during the 1920s.[208] While increasing industrial output was a feature of the Taisho Period so was increasing international trade.[209] However, Japan's terms of trade were not good, and the accumulated gold reserves which had been accumulated as a result of increased industrial output during the World War 1 were quickly dissipated once Europe had become peaceful.[210] During the war, Japanese industrial goods could be sold at inflated prices.[211] However, once the war had ended, rapid inflation and rising costs of production in Japan made Japanese goods too expensive for the European market.[212] This was more evident because European countries had devalued their currencies, which contributed to further making Japanese goods expensive in comparison to European ones. The negative terms of trade for Japanese goods was an obvious problem in the context of keeping the Japanese economy competitive. As a result, under the guidance of the Japanese government, the latter half of the Taisho Period was characterised by deliberate attempts at deflation as well as the rationalisation of production in order to lower the costs of production in Japan.[213] Developments in Japan's agricultural sector mirrored those in its industrial sector. During the war, Japanese agricultural produce was able to command high prices throughout the world,

[206] Ibid.

[207] Rosovsky, H., and Ohkawa, K. 91965), A Century of Japanese Economic Growth, IN The State and Economic Enterprise in Japan, Lockwood, W. (Ed), Princeton, New Jersey.

[208] Ibid.

[209] Smitka, M. (1998), The Interwar Economy of Japan, Colonialism, Depression and recovery, 1910–1940, Garland Publishing Inc, New York.

[210] Smitka, M. (1998), The Interwar Economy of Japan, Colonialism, Depression and recovery, 1910–1940, Garland Publishing Inc, New York.

[211] Ibid.

[212] Ibid.

[213] Ibid.

particularly in Europe. However, once the war had ended and especially in the 1920s, the Japanese agricultural sector experienced stagnation.[214] In this case, while Japanese agricultural incomes peaked in 1920, they declined from then and did not return to similar levels until the late 1940s and 1950s.[215] Moreover, between 1920 and 1940, there was no significant increase in rice yields and rice production increased by less than 1% a year.[216] Furthermore, it seemed to be the case that all attempts at technological innovation in order to increase rice yields had been exhausted and that landlords had become happy to reap surplus rents with no need for further innovation.[217] The decreasing activity in the Japanese industrial sector also caused further problems for its agricultural sector as rising unemployment meant that there was no possibility for the absorption of underutilised farm labour. Moreover, after 1917 rising unemployment in Japan stimulated further labour unrest.[218] And by 1920, the government had begun to suppress labour union militancy using the police, further radicalising the politics of labour union activists.[219]

It was during the Taisho Period that the Japanese economy was evolving into its dual structure in the context of cartelisation and oligopolisation.[220] In this case, during the Taisho Period, the economic power in Japan became concentrated through the Zaibatsu, remaining the same into contemporary times,[221] while the dual structure of the Japanese economy which had emerged during the Taisho Period was reflected by the concentration of workers in a few sectors of the economy. Nevertheless, in the newly emerging industries of machinery, chemicals and metals because

[214] Ibid.

[215] Ryoshin, M. (1967), The Turning Point in the Japanese Economy, Yale Growth Discussion Paper, No.2, 18.

[216] Barker, R., Herdt, R., and Rose, B. (1985), The Rice Economy of Asia, Resources for the Future, Washington DC

[217] Ibid.

[218] Smitka, M. (1998), The Interwar Economy of Japan, Colonialism, Depression and recovery, 1910–1940, Garland Publishing Inc, New York.

[219] Smitka, M. (1998), The Interwar Economy of Japan, Colonialism, Depression and recovery, 1910–1940, Garland Publishing Inc, New York.

[220] Tsunehiko, W. (1968), Industrialisation, Technological Progress and Dual Structure, IN Economic Growth, the Japanese Experience since the Meiji Era, Klein, L., and Ohkawa, K. (eds), Connecticut, New Haven.

[221] Smitka, M. (1964), Zaibatsu, Pre-war, and Zaibatsu, Post-war, The Journal of Asian Studies, XXIII.

of their scale these industries tended to be more capital intensive.[222] The concentration of economic power was not confined just to the industrial sector but also to the banking sector in which Zaibatsu also emerged during the Taisho Period.[223]

Conclusion

Situated between the Meiji Period and the Showa Period, the Taisho Period represents a time in which the Japanese state transitioned from a newly modernising industrial economy and a potential global powerhouse to a nationalistic, militaristic colonial power. At the start of the Meiji Restoration in 1868, Japanese military power would not have been strong enough to defeat the might of China or the might of Russia. Yet within for decades of the Meiji Restoration, the Japanese military had beaten both China and Russia in two independent wars. At first China was defeated by Japan in the war of 1894–1895, within twenty-six years of the Meiji Restoration. This war was fought as a prelude to the Japanese annexation of the Korean Peninsula in 1910. The threat from Chinese defence of the Koreans had to be removed, and an all-out war against China and its defeat was one way in which this scenario could be averted. However, Japanese belligerence and demands against the Chinese after the war were mitigated by the intervention of France, Russia and Germany in 1895. This placed limitations on Japanese demands and forced the Japanese to return the Liaodong peninsula to China. Japan was made to return the Liaodong Peninsula to China, due to the possibility that the Japanese would use the peninsula has a platform to invade China and Korea in the future. The other threat to Japanese expansion in Asia was due to Russia; and so, it also had to be contained by a successful war. This the Japanese pursued in 1905, resulting in the defeat of the Russian Far Eastern Fleet at the Battle of Tsushima at sea and the Battle of Mukden on land. The Battle of Tsushima was the first sea battle of the twentieth century in which ships with steel rather than wooden hulls engaged in battle and the first in which wireless technology was used for communication between the commanders of ships. As a result of the Japanese victory,

[222] Yoshinoya, Y. (1968), Patterns of Industrial Development, IN Economic Growth: The Japanese Experience Since the Meiji Era, Klein, L., and Ohkawa, K. (Eds).New Haven, Connecticut.

[223] Smitka, M. (1998), The Interwar Economy of Japan, Colonialism, Depression and recovery, 1910–1940, Garland Publishing Inc, New York.

the Russians were forced to recognise Japanese power over the Korean Peninsula, as well as having to surrender the southern half of Sakhalin Island to the Japanese. Moreover, the Russians were also forced to repatriate all of their assets from Manchuria. The military defeat of both Russia and China allowed Japan to prepare to lay claim to both the Korean Peninsula and Manchuria in the future.

Japan also achieved a military alliance with Great Britain in 1902. This signalled Japan's arrival on the world stage as a technologically, economically and politically modern state in the context of the United States and the European nations. And within seventy-one years, Japan would be engaged in a World War, in a role which would cast it as one of the main aggressors. So how was it that a country which had been relatively underdeveloped, politically, technologically, culturally and economically, and had fought only one war with China and Korea in its history in the sixteenth century, become an industrialised, militaristic, nationalistic, colonial power? Perhaps, it was its backwardness which kept Japan from becoming an aggressive military power. Until 1868, the Japanese state was decentralised and was governed by the Tokugawa Shogun and the Tokugawa Bakufu for over 200 years. Power to the regional Daimyo's was delegated too by the Shogun; and the Daimyo's ruled their regions according to their needs and preferences. Nevertheless, after 1868 Japanese governance began to more and more resemble the western democratic system. Indeed, Ito Hirobumi, who was Japan's first post-Meiji Prime Minister, invoked Japan's first constitution as a modern state based on the Prussian constitutional model. A western style parliamentary system called the 'Diet' was also established, with the first elected 'Diet' convening in 1890. The emergence of a 'democratic' system enabled the Japanese to allocate economic resources more efficiently than had ever been possible through a centralised decision-making system enshrined in the 'Diet'. However, the policy direction of the country was very much dependent on public attitude and the power of the military, a nationalistic and military synergy, whose attractiveness and electability were determined by economic circumstance. In this case, economic crises which negatively impacted on Japanese society and people facilitated an increase in the support for nationalism which enhanced the role of the military in the governance of Japan.

Antagonism against the western powers amongst Japan and its people began in the late Tokugawa Period when the great powers of the time, particularly the United States and Great Britain, began to impose unfair treaties on the Japanese at the barrel of a gun. This antagonism began to embed itself into the hearts and minds of the newly formed national Japanese army and navy of the 1870s. This antagonism only deepened when the United States and Great Britain imposed constraints on Japanese military capacity, in particular naval capacity to below that of the United States and Great Britain, following the Washington Conference of 1922. Antagonism towards the foreign powers, restrictions on what Japan could do in its own 'back yard' vis-à-vis against China and Korea and a worsening economy in the late Taisho Period provided a fertile ground for a political revolution. This was furthered by the dichotomy between the Japanese economic system and its educational system. The latter was based on traditional Japanese values with an anti-capitalistic leaning. However, the economic system was founded on the basis of a marriage between free market forces, the use of private capital and government support for the Zaibatsu oligarchs. The impact of this economic system was that there was an inefficient allocation of social goods and the divide between the rich and the poor was strong. Japanese soldiers and sailors may have been from a poor background. As a result of the increased social divide and deprivation as the Japanese economy industrialised and grew, the individualism and the respect for the democratic system which had been growing since the Meiji Restoration of 1868, despite antipathy from powerful people such as Ito Hirobumi, began to decline towards the end of the 1920s and the early 1930s. In order to more efficiently allocate social goods, there was a drift of popular belief towards the idea that the marriage of free market forces, private capital and government interference would not be able to bring about social equity. Therefore, what was needed to deliver a more efficient allocation of social goods was the bureaucratic fascism which had also been sweeping through the countries of Europe, notably Spain, Germany and Italy. Moreover, this could only be delivered by a nationalistic military government which came to be in the mid-1930s. Furthermore, this alternative government and resource allocation mechanism was promoted by ineffectual government economic policy making in the 1920s and the 1930s which would have helped to stave off a deepening economic situation in Japan. This really began at the end of WW1 when Japanese exports began to fall, with an earthquake in the 1920s followed by a banking crisis and then the imposition of tariffs on Japanese goods by the US and the European powers. Tariffs were imposed on Japanese exports as these were more competitive in price than were domestically produced goods. However, a number of import restrictive regimes emerged in the 1930s throughout the world, mostly from the United States and Europe. This led not only to a decrease in global trade but also to its regionalisation.[224] The United States was the first country to impose an import restrictive regime with the passing of the Smoot–Hawley Tariff Act of 1930.[225] Britain then implemented its own Import Duties Act in 1931, which gave tariff exemption on imports from the Empire as long as 25% of the content of the good was made within the Empire, but adding a 10% tariff on imports from outside the Empire.[226] This was followed by the Ottawa Agreements of 1932 and the US Reciprocal Trade Agreements Act of 1934.[227] The Ottawa Agreements of 1932 established preferential trading arrangements within the British Empire at the expense of foreign powers such as Japan.[228] As a result, by the late 1930s, Japan's trade balance and foreign reserves compared to the other economic powers of the time were in a relatively poor state. In this case, there was a significant drop in the volume of goods traded in Asia; and Japan's balance of trade with the rest of the world fell by 50%.[229] Moreover, while the volume of Japanese exports fell, the corresponding fall in the price of exports meant that Japan's workers and peasants felt the economic impact severely.[230] This is because a fall in the price of exports could lead to workers being laid off in order to minimise costs as firms' profits fell. From this analysis, it becomes clear that deepening economic crises which are not resolved in time by the appropriate economic policies lead to a drift towards nationalism and militarism. In other words, at times of severe economic crisis and

[224] Eichengreen, B., and Irwin, D. (1993), Trade Blocs, Currency Blocs and the Disintegration of World Trade in the 1930s, NBER Working Paper Series, Working Paper No.4445.

[225] Ibid.

[226] Miners, N. (2008), Industrial Development in the Colonial Empire and the Imperial Economic Conference at Ottawa 1932, The Journal of Imperial and Commonwealth History, 30, 2.

[227] Eichengreen, B., and Irwin, D. (1993), Trade Blocs, Currency Blocs and the Disintegration of World Trade in the 1930s, NBER Working Paper Series, Working Paper No.4445.

[228] Miners, N. (2008), Industrial Development in the Colonial Empire and the Imperial Economic Conference at Ottawa 1932, The Journal of Imperial and Commonwealth History, 30, 2.

[229] Paul, E. (2012), neoliberal Australia and US Imperialism in East Asia, Palgrave Macmillan, London.

[230] Schlichtmann, K. (2009), Japan in the World – Shidehara Kijuro Pacifism, and the Abolition of War: Volume 1, Rowman & Littlefield Publishers, Inc, Plymouth, UK.

distress, democracy is hijacked by the forces of the far right. The beliefs associated with this political spectrum delve deep into the dark side of humanity and into an evil with no matching parallel. When an individual is expressing economic hardship, it becomes easier to blame others for their predicament. In the case of Japan, a resurgent nationalism and militarism overcame the bastion of democracy setting in play terrible events as Japan unleashed its relatively new military might on the peoples of Asia. The brunt of this viciousness was born by the people of China. Japan's militarism and nationalism led to the brief downfall of western empires in the east, reconquering peoples for Japan amongst those who had already been conquered and subjugated by the British, the Dutch, the French and the Americans. However, unlike Japan, historically China has not been a global instigator of war on other nations. Nevertheless, China has acted to expand, maintain and integrate its own national territory over thousands of years establishing its own Han majority identity. But this did involve military incursions into lands which today can be identified as present-day Vietnam and Korea. Moreover, in the mid-twentieth century, China also gave military support to North Korea during the Korean War to stop it being defeated by American forces. This support was provided in order to support an ideological soulmate. However, in the contemporary world, China's militarisation of islands in the South China Sea represents an outlier in its behaviour with other nation states at a historical level. This is also because these very same islands are claimed by several countries which are China's neighbours in the region. In this case, the Permanent Court of Arbitration in the Hague ruled in July 2016 that China had no historic claim to 90% of the waters of the South China Sea it claimed possession to and which extended hundreds of miles to the east and to the south of its Hainan Province.[231] At the same time, China and the United States have clashed with each other with regard to freedom of navigation for ships and planes in the South China Sea.[232] This has often been characterised by US ships and planes being buzzed by Chinese ships and planes in association with stern warnings to US ships and planes by radio from the Chinese military on islands in the South China Sea.

Besides political reform, the Meiji Restoration also objectified the turning of the Japanese economy into a modern industrial one on the basis of

[231] Hunt, K. (2016), South China Sea: Court Rules in Favour of Philippines Over China', https://edition.cnn.com/2016/07/12/asia/china-philippines-south-china-sea/

[232] Ibid.

a mixed market economy. However, there was an emphasis on strong government support for the private sector in order to ensure that the Zaibatsu or industrial conglomerates acted as the dynamos of industrialisation. The formation of a market economy had been achieved to such an extent that by the time of the Taisho Period, the Japanese economic system was tiered into three levels of interface. The first was the government–private interface because it was government support for the large industrial conglomerates, the Zaibatsu, which facilitated rapid Japanese industrialisation. The second interface which characterised the Japanese economy of the time was the government–market interface with the last one being the private sector interface. Japan also wrested the control for setting its own tariffs from other countries in 1911. As a result, the pace of Japanese industrialisation increased during the Taisho Period because the government was able to use import substitution policies to facilitate the growth of the various industrial sectors by imposing tariffs on imports. In effect this made imports more expensive compared to domestically produced goods. As a result, Japanese domestically produced goods had a competitive advantage over imported goods. World War 1 also caused a spurt in the growth of Japanese industrial capacity because of the increased demand for Japanese manufactured goods from the United States, Europe and China. However, increased industrial capacity and increasing industrial production resulted in an increased need for raw materials. This increased need was met by drawing on the resources of Japan's new colonies in the German colonies of the Pacific which had been taken by Japan at the start of World War 1; Japanese annexed Korea, Taiwan, which had been ceded to Japan by China as a result of the 1894–1895 war which China lost; Southern Sakhalin which had been ceded to Japan by Russia as a result of losing the war of 1905; and the leased Kwantung Territory.

References

Alexander, A. (2008), The Arc of Japan's Economic Development, Routledge, London.

Amyx, J. (2004), Japan's Financial Crisis, Institutional Rigidity and Reluctant Change, Princeton University Press, Princeton.

Baldwin, K. (1921), A Brief Account of Japan's Part in the World War, 6, Stanley K. Hornbeck Papers, Box 255, War, Costs and Contributions, The Hoover Institution on War, Revolution and Peace.

Barker, R., Herdt, R., and Rose, B. (1985), The Rice Economy of Asia, Resources for the Future, Washington DC.

Barnhart, M. (1981), Japan's Economic Security and the Origins of the Pacific War, Journal of Strategic Studies, 4, 2.

Beasley, W. (1987), Japanese Imperialism 1894–1945, Clarendon, Oxford.

Benson, J., and Matsumura, T. (2001), Japan, 1868–1945, From Isolation to Occupation, Routledge, London.

Chaurasia, R. (2003), History of Japan, Atlantic Publishers and Distributors, New Delhi.

Crow, C. (2013), Japan's Dream of World Empire – The Tanaka Memorial, Read Books Ltd.

Cullen, L. (2003), A History of Japan, 1582–1941; Internal and External Worlds, Cambridge University Press, Cambridge.

Dickinson, F. (1999), War and National Re-invention: Japan in the Great War, 1914–1919, Harvard University Asia Center, Cambridge, Massachusetts.

Dickinson, F. (2013), World War 1 and the Triumph of a New Japan, 1919–1930, Cambridge University Press, Cambridge.

Dickinson, F. (2015), The First World War, Japan and a Global Century, IN Japan and the Great War, Frattolillio, O., and Best, A. (Ed), Springer.

Duus, P., and Okimoto, D. (1979), Fascism and the History of Pre-War Japan: The Failure of a Concept, Journal of Asian Studies, Vol.XXXIX, No.1.

Eichengreen, B., and Irwin, D. (1993), Trade Blocs, Currency Blocs and the Disintegration of World Trade in the 1930s, NBER Working Paper Series, Working Paper No.4445.

Eskildsen, R. (2019), Transforming Empire in Japan and East Asia: The Taiwan Expedition and the Birth of Japanese Imperialism, New Directions in East Asian History, Springer, Singapore.

Fairbank, J., Reischauer, E., and Craig, A. (1989), East Asia: Tradition and Transformation, revised edition, Houghton Mifflin, Boston.

Fisher, C. (1950), The Expansion of Japan: A Study of Oriental Geopolitics: Part 1, Continental and Maritime Components in Japanese Expansion, The geographical Journal, Vol. 115, No 1/3, pp.1–19.

Goldstein, E., and Maurer, J. (Eds), (1994), The Washington Conference, 1921–22: Naval Rivalry, East Asian Stability and the Road to Pearl Harbor, Routledge, London.

Gordon, A. (1991), Labor and Imperial Democracy in Pre-War Japan, University of California Press, Berkeley.

Herzog, P. (1993), Japan's Pseudo-Democracy, Routledge, New York.

Hoston, G. (1984), Marxism and National Socialism in Taisho Japan: The Thought of Takabatake Motoyuki, Journal of Asian Studies, Vol. XLIV, No.1

Hunt, K. (2016), South China Sea: Court Rules in Favour of Philippines Over China', https://edition.cnn.com/2016/07/12/asia/china-philippines-south-china-sea/

Jae-Hyung, L. (2003), China and the Asia-Pacific Region, iUniverse, Lincoln, NE.

Ivanov, A., and Jowett, P. (2007), The Russo-Japanese War 1904–05, Osprey Publishing.

Jukes, G. (2002), The Russo-Japan War 1904–05, Osprey Publishing.

Lardas, M. (2018), Tsushima 1905: Death of a Russian Fleet, Bloomsbury Publishing.

Lobanov-Rostrovsky, A. (1965), Russia and Asia, The George Wahr Publishing Company, Ann Arbor, Michigan.

Lockwood, W. (1954), Economic Development of Japan: Growth and Structural Change, Princeton University Press, Princeton, New Jersey, USA.

Lukoianov, I. (2008), The Portsmouth Peace, IN The Treaty of Portsmouth and its legacies, Ericson, S., and Hockley, A. (Eds), Dartmouth College Press, Hanover, New Hampshire.

Luo, Z. (1993), National Humiliation and National Assertion: The Chinese Response to the Twenty-One Demands, Modern Asian Studies, 27, 2.

Miners, N. (2008), Industrial Development in the Colonial Empire and the Imperial Economic Conference at Ottawa 1932, The Journal of Imperial and Commonwealth History, 30, 2.

Minichiello, S. (1998), Introduction, IN Japan's Competing Modernities: Issues in Culture and Democracy, 1900–1930, Minichiello, S. (Ed), University of Hawai'I Press, Honolulu.

Mitter, R. (2013), Forgotten Ally, Houghton Mifflin Harcourt Publishing, New York.

Nakano A. (1975), On the Taisho free education Movement, Reimei, Tokyo.

Nish, I. (1998), The Origins of the Russo-Japanese War, Routledge, London.

Nolte, S. (1984), Individualism in Taisho Japan, Journal of Asian Studies, Vol. XLIII, No.4

Paine, S. (2003), The Sino-Japanese War of 1894–1895: Perceptions, Power and Primacy, Cambridge University Press, Cambridge.

Paul, E. (2012), Neoliberal Australia and US Imperialism in East Asia, Palgrave Macmillan, London.

Pierson, J. (1980), Tokutomo Soho, 1893–1957: A Journalist for Modern Japan, Princeton University Press.

Pleshakov, C. (2002), The Tsar's Last Armada, The Epic Voyage to the Battle of Tsushima, Best Books, New York.

Rao, B. (2005), History of Asia, From Early Times to the Present, New Dawn Press, Slough, Berkshire.

Riasanovsky, N. (2000), A History of Russia, 6th Edition, Oxford University Press, Oxford.

Rosovsky, H., and Ohkawa, K. 91965), A Century of Japanese Economic Growth, IN The State and Economic Enterprise in Japan, Lockwood, W. (Ed), Princeton, New Jersey.

Ryoshin, M. (1967), The Turning Point in the Japanese Economy, Yale Growth Discussion Paper, No.2, 18.

Schencking, J. (1999), The Imperial Japanese Navy and the Constructed Consciousness of a South Seas Destiny, 1872–1921, Modern Asian Studies, 33, 4, pp.769–796.

Schlichtmann, K. (2009), Japan in the World – Shidehara Kijuro Pacifism, and the Abolition of War: Volume 1, Rowman & Littlefield Publishers, Inc, Plymouth, UK.

Smethurst R.J. (1995) Japan's First Experiment with Democracy, 1868–1940. In: The Social Construction of Democracy, 1870–1990, Andrews, G.R., and Chapman, H. (Eds), Palgrave Macmillan, London.

Smitka, M. (1964), Zaibatsu, Pre-war, and Zaibatsu, Post-war, The Journal of Asian Studies, XXIII.

Smitka, M. (1998), The Interwar Economy of Japan, Colonialism, Depression and recovery, 1910–1940, Garland Publishing Inc, New York.

Takayoshi, M. (1966), The Development of Democracy in Japan: Taisho Democracy, Its Flowering and Breakdown. Developing Economies 4.4:612–37.

Takeshi, H. (2008), Taisho: An Enigmatic Emperor and His Influential Wife, IN The Emperors of Modern Japan, Shillony, B. (Ed), BRILL, Boston.

Tamaki, N. (1995), Japanese Banking: A History, 1859–1959, Cambridge University Press, Cambridge.

Teranishi, J. (2005), Evolution of the Economic System in Japan, Edward Elgar, Cheltenham, UK.

Tsunehiko, W. (1968), Industrialisation, Technological Progress and Dual Structure, IN Economic Growth, the Japanese Experience since the Meiji Era, Klein, L., and Ohkawa, K. (eds), Connecticut, New Haven.

Tsuzuki, C. (2000), The Pursuit of Power in Modern Japan 1825–1995, Oxford University Press, Oxford.

Westwood, J. (1986), Russia Against Japan, 1904–05: A New look at the Russo-Japanese War, State University of New York Press, Albany.

Woodall, B. (2014), Growing Democracy in Japan, The Parliamentary Cabinet System Since 1868, University Press of Kentucky.

Yoshinoya, Y. (1968), Patterns of Industrial Development, IN Economic Growth: The Japanese Experience Since the Meiji Era, Klein, L., and Ohkawa, K. (Eds). New Haven, Connecticut.

CHAPTER 7

The Showa Period (1926–1989): War and the Emergence of a Modern Japan

Introduction

The Showa Period began in 1926 with Prince Hirohito becoming Emperor of Japan following the death of his father, the Emperor Taisho.[1] The name of the period was formulated from the Chinese Classics, with a recognition of the time to come as being one of good government and peace.[2] Indeed, commentators spoke of the need for the Showa Period to evolve and progress further from the economic, political and cultural developments which had transformed Japan during the Meiji Period into a modern economy.[3] But although Japan was passing its coming of age during the Showa period, there was a need for the reform of the corrupt politics of the time.[4] And, some argued at the time that Japan should remain oriental at a time in which it was being compared to the three great powers of the world.[5] However, as a nation the country had a policy with regard to its international direction, namely maintaining its hegemony over Korea. And in this context, Japan had already been to war with China and Russia over this very issue. And, in its sixty-three years, the Showa Period witnessed Japanese economic expansion following WW1, the economic

[1] Morris-Suzuki, T. (2012), Showa: An Inside History of Hirohito's Japan, Bloomsbury, London.
[2] Gluck, C. (1990), The Idea of Showa, Daedalus, Vol.119, No.3, pp. 1–26.
[3] McNeill, W. (1986), Mythistory and Other Essays, University of Chicago Press, Chicago.
[4] Gluck, C. (1990), The Idea of Showa, Daedalus, Vol.119, No.3, pp. 1–26.
[5] Ibid.

S. Ramesh, *China's Economic Rise*,
https://doi.org/10.1007/978-3-030-49811-5_7

crisis of the 1920s and the early 1930s followed by the takeover of government by a military bureaucracy, a disastrous war, occupation by America and an economic resurgence after the 1950s.

And so, Japan entered an age in which it would brutally confront the nations which had threatened its existence in the mid-nineteenth century leading to the Meiji Restoration of 1868 and Japan becoming the aggressor. In this case, Japan transitioned from a peaceful seclusion from the world which had lasted over 200 years under the Tokugawa Shogunate to a period of industrialisation, rapid economic development, militarisation, colonisation and nationalism. The last three features would become ascendant in 1930s' Japan, incentivised by a deepening economic crisis made worse by the regionalisation of global trade and tariff initiatives. The first attempted military takeover of the government in Japan occurred in 1932 and is better known as the May 15th Incident.[6] The second such military takeover of the government in Japan occurred in 1936, and this became known as the February 26 Incident.[7] At the same time Japan had begun showing increased belligerence to China, in effect using the September Incident as a prelude to annexing Manchuria in 1931 before retitling the region to Japanese Manchukuo in 1932.[8] To stop the League of Nations interfering to constrain and prevent its belligerence, Japan left the League of Nations in 1933.[9] This acted as a prelude to the outbreak of full scale war between Japan and China in 1937 following the Marco Polo Bridge Incident.[10] By this time, the mid to the late 1930s, the Japanese economy was being managed as a militaristic bureaucratic centrally planned economy. In other words, the sole purpose of economic activity was to aid Japan's war efforts. Finally, Japan positioned itself to enter the war in Europe, which had started in 1939 with the German invasion of Poland, by signing the Axis Treaty with Italy and Germany in 1940.[11] Japan's attack on the US naval base at Pearl Harbor on 7 December 1941 heralded the onset of World War II. In Asia this would end with the deaths of hundreds of thousands of people, the destabilisation of empires and the atomic bombing of the Japanese cities of Hiroshima and Nagasaki in

[6] Morris-Suzuki, T. (2012), Showa: An Inside History of Hirohito's Japan, Bloomsbury, London.

[7] Ibid.

[8] Ibid.

[9] Ibid.

[10] Ibid.

[11] Ibid.

1945. After which the United States would formally occupy Japan, not relinquishing control until a formal peace treaty was signed in 1951, ending the US occupation.[12] By the late 1980s the Japanese economy would have grown to become the second largest in the world and the country being the largest holder of foreign assets. However, after the late 1980s, the bursting of the property bubble led the Japanese economy to stagnate as it experienced deflation and low economic growth over the next two decades. In fact, economic growth rates fell to under 2% annually in the 1990s and to even lower figures in the first decade of the twenty-first century.[13] Nevertheless, following the commencement of economic reforms in China in 1978 and the country's accession to the World Trade Organisation in 2001, the economy began to grow rapidly. Such was the case that by February 2011, the Chinese economy had overtaken the Japanese economy as the second largest in the world.[14]

Economic Crisis and a Mild Recession

The Japanese economy faced a spiralling downward economic crisis in the 1930s because of two specific economic events in the 1920s. These two events were the financial crisis of 1927 and the depression of the early 1930s.[15] The financial crisis of 1927 resulted because of accumulated bad debts by financial institutions.[16] The economic situation faced by Japan in the 1920s was in stark contrast to that which it faced during the years of WW1 when industrial capacity and production increased in order to meet the demands of the countries which were at war, mainly in the European front. At the same time company profits must also have increased as national income and national output grew. However, when WW1 ended Japan was left with productive over capacity. Expectations by investors that an economic downturn was on the way because Japanese firms had over

[12] Ibid.

[13] Wakatabe, M. (2015), Japan's Great Stagnation and Abenomics: Lessons for the World, Palgrave Macmillan, UK.

[14] Moore, M. (2011), China is the world's second largest economy, https://www.telegraph.co.uk/finance/economics/8322550/China-is-the-worlds-second-largest-economy.html.

[15] Shizume, M. (2009), 'The Japanese Economy during the Interwar Period: Instability in the Financial System and the Impact of the World Depression,' Bank of Japan Review Series 09-E-2, Bank of Japan.

[16] Ibid.

invested in productive capacity during the war years led to a dramatic fall in stock prices in Japan in March 1920.[17] Around this time the sources of investment finance were getting scarce because of monetary austerity followed by the BoJ to combat inflation.[18] And although Japan's international payments balance was also in deficit due to the high costs of imports, Japanese commercial enterprises continued to engage in speculative activities and production expansion.[19] Following the plunge in the stock market, a bank transactions intermediary, the Masuda Bill Broker Bank collapsed in April 1920.[20] After this commodity markets collapsed, and there were also further steep drops in the stock markets of Osaka and Tokyo.[21] This sparked a run on regional banks in Japan, and as a result, the Bank of Japan had to issue 'special loans' to stabilise the financial system as well as suspending operations in several banks for a few months to stem the crisis.[22] The collapse of the Masuda Bill Broker Bank proved to be the start of widespread instability in the Japanese financial system. Next, a speculative lumber company Ishii Corporation went bankrupt in February 1922 causing further regional bank runs.[23] In the last three months of 1922, the bank runs became more widespread. Some banks were either temporarily or permanently closed while others were injected with fresh liquidity in the early months of 1923. The Great Kanto Earthquake also indirectly damaged Japan's financial system in the context of the physical and financial assets of the banks.[24] Furthermore, loan repayments to banks would either be paid late or not paid at all resulting in the banks accumulating debt.[25] Moreover, some firms had to write off losses, such as productive capacity or inventory loss, in quake-devastated areas as there was

[17] Ibid.

[18] Takafusa, N. (1998), Depression, Recovery, and War, 1920–1945, IN Showa japan: Political, economic and social history 1926–1989, Large, S. (Ed), Routledge, London.

[19] Ibid.

[20] Shizume, M. (2009), 'The Japanese Economy during the Interwar Period: Instability in the Financial System and the Impact of the World Depression,' Bank of Japan Review Series 09-E-2, Bank of Japan.

[21] Von Staden, P. (2008), Business-Government Relations in Pre-war Japan, Routledge, New York.

[22] Shizume, M. (2009), 'The Japanese Economy during the Interwar Period: Instability in the Financial System and the Impact of the World Depression,' Bank of Japan Review Series 09-E-2, Bank of Japan.

[23] Ibid.

[24] Ibid.

[25] Ibid.

no other choice.[26] However, in order to stabilise the situation, the government and the BoJ through a co-ordinated policy postponed loan repayments, provided special loans as well as indemnifying the BoJ for losses up to a maximum amount.[27] Loan repayment dates were later finally set to be 30 September 1927.[28] The seeds of the 1927 financial crisis had thus been sown in the preceding years, firms over investment in productive capacity during WW1, instability of the financial system characterised by bank runs and deferred, delayed or non-payment of loans to banks which had been made as a result of the earthquake. However, the final trigger for the crisis may have occurred in January 1927 during a Diet debate into legislation which would have allowed the government to issue new bonds to exchange with previously issued Earthquake Casualty Bills.[29] At the time, the Finance Minister may have let falsely slip that the Tokyo Watanabe Bank had failed setting in motion a run on the banks.[30] The bank was owned by the Watanabe family, and during the boom of WW1, it had ventured to the financial support and management of over forty enterprises of which only a handful turned out to be profitable.[31] And following the dramatic fall in share prices in 1920, debts owed to the bank could not be repaid.[32] Further national bank runs occurred when debates were held in the Diet regarding the financial health of two other Japanese banks, the Bank of Taiwan and Suzuki & Co.[33] The Bank of Taiwan ceased operations in Japan, although it remained functional in Taiwan.[34] However, quick government and BoJ action was enough to calm the situation. Whereas the Showa Financial

[26] Sawai, M. (1999), Noda Shoichi and Roku-Roku Shoten, a machine tool manufacturer, Social Sciences Japan Journal, Vol.2, No.1, pp. 107–122.

[27] Shizume, M. (2009), 'The Japanese Economy during the Interwar Period: Instability in the Financial System and the Impact of the World Depression,' Bank of Japan Review Series 09-E-2, Bank of Japan.

[28] Ibid.

[29] Ibid.

[30] Ibid.

[31] Yukio, C. (1999), Exposing the incompetence of the bourgeoisie: The financial panic of 1927, IN Banking in Japan: The evolution of Japanese banking, 1868–1952, Tsutsui, W. (Ed), Routledge, New York.

[32] Ibid.

[33] Shizume, M. (2009), 'The Japanese Economy during the Interwar Period: Instability in the Financial System and the Impact of the World Depression,' Bank of Japan Review Series 09-E-2, Bank of Japan.

[34] Tamaki, N. (1995), Japanese Banking – A History, 1859–1959, Cambridge University Press, Cambridge.

Crisis resulted because of structural problems within the Japanese financial system as discussed, the Showa Depression of the early 1930s was of a different nature. The Showa depression lasted between 1930 and 1932.[35] The depression was caused by a series of bank failures which followed as a result of Japan reintroducing the use of the gold standard in January 1930 at a level of parity to its currency which was too high.[36] However, other external macroeconomic factors such as imported deflation, an appreciating currency and falling overseas demand for Japanese goods also contributed to triggering the Showa Depression.[37] The severe economic contraction of the Japanese economy continued until Japan subsequently left the gold standard in December 1931.[38] However, the economic damage was intense with over 112 banks failures resulting in severe financial losses to ordinary Japanese as the central bank did not operate any type of insurance to compensate bank depositors.[39] This banking crisis in conjunction with the impact of the Great Depression and the imposition of tariffs on Japanese goods by other countries led to a deep and prolonged downturn in Japanese economic activity. The British Empire decided at the imperial economic conference at Ottawa in 1932 to impose punitive tariffs on Japanese manufactured goods because they were displacing British and Canadian manufacturers due to their relative cheapness.[40] However, by December 1931, Korekiyo Takahashi had become Finance Minister in the government of the Seiyo-Kai party which had assumed power when the government of the Minseito Party had collapsed.[41] The Minseito Party championed liberal values which were at odds with the proto-fascist

[35] Akiyoshi, F. (2009), Banking Panics, Bank Failures, and the Lender of Last Resort: The Showa Depression of 1930–1932, Oxford Economic Papers, 61, 776–800.

[36] Ibid.

[37] Shizume, M. (2009), 'The Japanese Economy during the Interwar Period: Instability in the Financial System and the Impact of the World Depression,' Bank of Japan Review Series 09-E-2, Bank of Japan.

[38] Akiyoshi, F. (2009), Banking Panics, Bank Failures, and the Lender of Last Resort: The Showa Depression of 1930–1932, Oxford Economic Papers, 61, 776–800.

[39] Ibid.

[40] Miners, N. (2002), Industrial development in the colonial empire and the imperial economic conference at Ottawa 1932, 30:2, 53–76, DOI: https://doi.org/10.1080/03086530208583141.

[41] Shizume, M. (2009), 'The Japanese Economy during the Interwar Period: Instability in the Financial System and the Impact of the World Depression,' Bank of Japan Review Series 09-E-2, Bank of Japan.

Japanese military who feared budget cuts by a Minseito government.[42] But his appointment had originally been blocked by the Japanese Army who had initially refused to support the government of Prime Minister Okada who had replaced Prime Minister Saito in 1934.[43] Takahashi put in place a Keynesian economic policy designed to boost aggregate demand through an expansionary monetary and fiscal policy in conjunction with an exchange rate depreciation.[44] The expansionary monetary policy was to be associated with an interest rate cut associated with lending by the BoJ to Japanese commercial banks. The expansionary fiscal policy, essentially increased government expenditure, was associated with insuring bonds issued by the BoJ. And the exchange rate depreciation was associated with making Japanese exports cheaper and imports into Japan more expensive, positively affecting Japan's trade balance. However, Takahashi was keenly aware of the unsustainability of a large government budget deficit. It was because Takahashi fought to keep the budget deficit small, if not reduce it, this meant that he would have to fight the military's demands for increased spending on Japan's military means. The Finance Ministry had become the only vocal opposition to the military in government having even been at odds with the military over the 1933 and 1934 budgets.[45] Moreover, it was the Finance Ministry which also resisted attempts by the military to steer economic activity in the Japanese economy, in 1934.[46] It was perhaps because of this conflict between Takahashi and the military that he was assassinated by militarists in February 1936.[47] This was in the aftermath of a general election in which the ruling Seiyukai Party lost the election and the opposition Minseito won by a landslide.[48] Troops had seized Tokyo at the behest of junior officers and Takahashi and ex-Prime Minister Saito

[42] Snyder, J. (1991), Myths of Empire – Domestic Politics and International Ambition, Cornell University Press, Ithaca.

[43] Young, A. (2011), Imperial Japan: 1926–1938, Volume 54, Routledge, New York.

[44] Shizume, M. (2009), 'The Japanese Economy during the Interwar Period: Instability in the Financial System and the Impact of the World Depression,' Bank of Japan Review Series 09-E-2, Bank of Japan.

[45] Barnhart, M. (2013), Japan Prepares for Total War: The Search for Economic Security, 1919–1941, Cornell University Press, Ithaca.

[46] Barnhart, M. (1995), Japan and the World Since 1868, Edward Arnold Publishing.

[47] Shizume, M. (2009), 'The Japanese Economy during the Interwar Period: Instability in the Financial System and the Impact of the World Depression,' Bank of Japan Review Series 09-E-2, Bank of Japan.

[48] Kamii, Y. (1937), Industrial Recovery in Japan: Its causes and Social Effects, international Labour Review, 35, pp. 31–52.

had been killed by them.[49] From this time, the Japanese economy moved into a military command economy mode which reflected fiscal irresponsibility rather than fiscal caution.[50] However, although the Japanese economy faced its own crises during the 1920s and the 1930s, it did not enter into an economic depression as did the economies of European countries and the United States.[51] In this case, it is possible to say that in the early 1930s the Japanese economy experienced a mild recession but that on the whole between 1925 and 1938, the Japanese economy grew on average by 4%.[52] This was due to the diligence of the government and the BoJ of being able to see off crises such as the financial crisis of 1927 and the depression of 1930–1932. Moreover, in an external economic environment in which the demand for Japanese products was falling, the economic policies of Takahashi and military demand in the 1930s stimulated economic growth in Japan.[53] Nevertheless, the distribution of income in Japan in the 1920s as well as in the 1930s was unfair.[54] This may have led to the undermining of the democratic system of governance and the imposition of the command economy by the military. Like Japan in the decades following the Meiji Restoration of 1868, China in its first steps to economic modernisation implemented the market oriented reforms of 1978. Since then China has industrialised in the context of manufactured goods, to become the world's second largest economy. But this has, like the Japan of the 1920s and the 1930s, been at the expense of growing income inequality between China's regions and its peoples.[55] It is, therefore, important that the Chinese government instigate and implement policies to mitigate the unequal distribution of income in Chinese society to prevent the political and social instability which Japan experienced in the 1920s and the

[49] Kirshner, J. (2007), Appeasing bankers: Financial Caution on the Road to War, Princeton University Press, Princeton.

[50] Shizume, M. (2009), 'The Japanese Economy during the Interwar Period: Instability in the Financial System and the Impact of the World Depression,' Bank of Japan Review Series 09-E-2, Bank of Japan.

[51] Lincoln, E. (1990), The Showa Economic Experience, Daedalus, Vol.119, No.3, pp. 191–208.

[52] Ibid.

[53] Ibid.

[54] Minami, R. (1998), Economic development and income distribution in Japan: an assessment of the Kuznets hypothesis, Cambridge Journal of Economics, 22, pp. 39–58.

[55] Shi, L., Sato, H., and Sicular, T. (2013), Rising Inequality in China, IN Rising Inequality in China: Challenges to a Harmonious Society, Shi, L., Sato, h., and Sicular, T. (Eds), Cambridge University Press, Cambridge.

late 1930s. Moreover, China's economic growth is also experiencing a downturn, but time can only tell how severe that will be or not. Although Japan's economy grew between 1925 and 1938, World War 2 devastated the Japanese economy, and as a result, Japan had lost 50% of its GNP by 1945.[56]

Rise of Militarism and World War II

Between the early 1930s and until the end of World War 2, there was a shift in political power in Japan from the established political parties and the nobility towards a civilian–military–Zaibatsu coalition.[57] This had been mainly because the established democratic political system had been unable to satisfactorily resolve the potential security and economic threats Japan had faced at the time. The Army was aware of threats to Japan's position in Manchuria from rising Chinese nationalism as well as the Soviet military build-up in Siberia.[58] However, at the London Conference, Japan had been forced to accept limitations on its military capacity.[59] On the other hand, government economic policy emphasised contractionary monetary and fiscal policy, a return to the gold standard in 1930 and deflation.[60] However, the economic policies implemented by the Minseito government were unable to remedy the growing poverty and distress in Japan's agricultural sector as well as the growing disparity between the rich and the poor in Japanese society.[61] Despite the fact that the economic challenges faced by the Minseito government were international in origin, unfortunately it was unable to resolve the resulting social, economic and political problems which resulted.

The Japanese Army and Navy were subjected to cuts in government expenditure in the early 1920s.[62] However, because of public perceptions that the cuts in expenditure were not big enough, further cuts in military

[56] Lincoln, E. (1990), The Showa Economic Experience, Daedalus, Vol.119, No.3, pp. 191–208.

[57] Berger, G. (1988), Politics and Mobilisation in Japan, 1931–1945, IN The Cambridge History of Japan, Vol.6, The Twentieth Century, Duus, P. (Ed), Cambridge University Press, Cambridge.

[58] Ibid.

[59] Ibid.

[60] Ibid.

[61] Ibid.

[62] Kitaoka, S. (1993), The Army as a Bureaucracy: Japanese Militarism Revisited, The Journal of Military History, Vol.57, No.5.

personnel were authorised by War Minister Ugaki Kazushige in 1924.[63] Nevertheless, the money which was saved was not transferred into other types of government expenditure, but instead used to modernise the Army.[64] The expenditure cuts and the diversion of savings made into expenditure on the modernisation of the Japanese Army by War Minister Ugaki were not favoured by some senior military personnel such as Field Marshal Uyehara Yusaku (1856–1933), for a number of reasons.[65] These reasons included the fact that the Japanese economy was in a weak condition, that countries such as China and Russia were themselves in turmoil and therefore posed no threat to Japan, and that Japan did not have sufficient natural resources to sustain a war.[66] It was because of the latter that cuts to the numbers of military personnel were objected to as it would prevent Japan winning a war relatively quickly. However, if Japan did not modernise its military whereas other countries were doing, then it would fall behind to the extent that it would not be able to defend its economic and political interests in its own back yard.[67] In this case, the Japanese Supreme War Council accepted War Minister Ugaki's budgetary proposals and objectives for the Japanese military by August 1924, but only by a slender margin.[68] Nevertheless, the modernisation of the Japanese military proceeded at a relatively small pace given the weak condition of the Japanese economy.[69] The human and capital cost imposed on Japan by the Kanto Earthquake of 1923 also proved to be non-conducive to any faster economic growth. At the same time as the slow pace of modernisation of the Japanese military, the army of the Soviet Union had recovered strength from the chaos of the revolution and the Chinese Nationalists were posing a threat to Japan in Manchuria.[70] This cast doubts on the potential effectiveness of the modernisation of Japan's military in defending the country's interests abroad. In this case, the General Staff revitalised the strategy of a quick mobilisation of the military in order to quickly engage and defeat the enemy, in 1928. Japanese Chinese specialists also argued that

[63] Ibid.

[64] Kitaoka, S. (1993), The Army as a Bureaucracy: Japanese Militarism Revisited, The Journal of Military History, Vol.57, No.5.

[65] Ibid.

[66] Ibid.

[67] Ibid.

[68] Ibid.

[69] Ibid.

[70] Ibid.

modernisation at the expense of manpower was a bad idea, because Manchuria would directly be ruled by Japan and its military, rather than through a Chinese warlord.[71] Araki Sadao was appointed as War Minister in 1931. In 1928, a new rule book called the 'Tosui Koryo' had been adopted by the Imperial Japanese Army, remaining its rule book until 1945.[72] The new rule book featured two main features. The first was the recognition of the importance of the superiority of morale over material. This was in recognition of Japan's limited resources.[73] And secondly, the non-existence of negative terms such as 'surrender', 'retreat' and 'defence' in the rule book because of the negative psychological impact on soldier's morale when used.[74] As the new War Minister, Araki Sadao felt that military conflict with China and Russia was inevitable because of the reliance upon Marxist ideology by the rulers of these countries. In this case, the Japanese state should be made to be stronger and the people loyal to the government and to the Emperor. One way in which this could be done was by spending more money on the agricultural sector of the economy.[75] Nevertheless, those in the Japanese military who had become disillusioned with the approach taken by Araki now turned to Nagata Tetsuzan who wanted to continue the dialogue with other states to prevent war. But at the same time the Japanese military should be rearmed in terms of quality and quantity. In order to achieve this, Nagata wanted to mobilise Japan's resources, economic, political and social incrementally over time in order to achieve the objective of total war planning.[76] But the only problem was that the Kodo-ha faction in the Japanese Army, the Imperial Way Faction, wanted total war at once.[77] In this case, Nagata Tetsuzan and the head of the anti-Kodo-ha faction in the Army, Hayashi Senjyuro, were intent on

[71] Kitaoka, S. (1993), The Army as a Bureaucracy: Japanese Militarism Revisited, The Journal of Military History, Vol.57, No.5.

[72] Humphreys, L. (1995), The Way of the Heavenly Sword; The Japanese Army in the 1920's, Stanford University Press, Stanford, California.

[73] Ibid.

[74] Ibid.

[75] Kitaoka, S. (1993), The Army as a Bureaucracy: Japanese Militarism Revisited, The Journal of Military History, Vol.57, No.5.

[76] Berger, G. (1988), Politics and Mobilisation in Japan, 1931–1945, IN The Cambridge History of Japan, Vol.6, The Twentieth Century, Duus, P. (Ed), Cambridge University Press, Cambridge.

[77] Takenaka, H. (1998), The Collapse of the Semi-Democratic Regime in Pre-War Japan, Stanford University Press, Stanford, California.

expelling the members of the Kodo-ha faction.[78] They were successful in this endeavour when in July 1935, they were able to expel the head of the Kodo-ha faction, Mazaki Jinzaburo, from the post of Inspector General of Military Education.[79] In the Army this was considered to be one of the three most prominent posts.[80] In pushing for incremental preparation for war, Nagata looked upon a growing meritocracy which was founded on the development of strong links between the bureaucracies of the civilian arm of government and the military as well as with the Zaibatsu.[81] However, the young officers who were in the Kodo Faction were opposed to the ideas and actions of Nagata Tetsuzan, and he was subsequently assassinated in August 1935. But the death of Nagata was only a temporary setback, and his reforms for developing a strong link based on meritocracy between the civilian bureaucracy of government, military bureaucracy and the Zaibatsu to foster long-term industrial and military development became the Army's accepted strategy to prepare in the long term for total war.[82]

Factionalism was rife in the Imperial Japanese Army, particularly between the Tosei-ha (Control Group) and the Kodo-ha (Imperial Way Faction).[83] The former faction was oriented towards the ideology of Nazi Germany while the latter were oriented towards the principles of Kokutai.[84] It was the general perception of the time that the Kodo-ha, led by General Araki and General Mazaki, were putting Japan and its military on to a disastrous course.[85] However, the February 26 Incident facilitated the removal of the Kodo-ha faction by the Tosei-ha faction.[86] This shift from one faction to the other allowed the Imperial Japanese Army to gain more

[78] Ibid.

[79] Takenaka, H. (1998), The Collapse of the Semi-Democratic Regime in Pre-War Japan, Stanford University Press, Stanford, California.

[80] Ibid.

[81] Ibid.

[82] Berger, G. (1988), Politics and Mobilisation in Japan, 1931–1945, IN The Cambridge History of Japan, Vol.6, The Twentieth Century, Duus, P. (Ed), Cambridge University Press, Cambridge.

[83] Crowley, J. (1962), Japanese Army Factionalism in the Early 1930's, Journal of Asian Studies, xxi, 72–91.

[84] Ibid.

[85] Yagami, K. (2006), Konoe Fumimaro and the Failure of Peace in Japan, 1937–1941: A Critical Appraisal of the Three-Time Prime Minister, McFarland & Company Inc, Publishers, London.

[86] Ibid.

political influence than it ever had, allowing it to take Japan in any direction it wanted to.[87] Unfortunately for Japan and as evident from a historical perspective, the dominance of the Tosei-ha faction over the Kodo-ha ensured that Japan would enter World War 2 with its attack on the US base of Pearl Harbor on the main island of Hawaii on 7 December 1941. The February 26 Incident was essentially the result of the social discontent and malaise of Japanese society having diffused into the Imperial Japanese Army whose lower ranks and junior officers were made of common stock. In contrast to the senior officers in Army Headquarters, junior officers were in daily contact with the common soldier whose families had directly experienced the economic crises Japan had gone through since the early 1920s. The February 26 Incident, therefore, served as notice of the need for social justice in Japanese society as opposed to a reaction against fascist military planners.[88] The junior and regimental officers considered the central staff planners to be elitist as well as being part of the 'Establishment'.[89] Most of the radical young officers were based in the First Division of the Imperial Japanese Army which in January 1936 was based in Tokyo. While the young officers had been primed to act against the 'Establishment' following the sacking of General Mazaki and the court martial of General Aizawa, it was the proposed move of the First Division from Tokyo to Manchukuo which acted as the trigger for the young officers to stage an attempted coup d'etat in February 1936.[90] Nevertheless, the February 26 Incident was not a popular revolt against the 'Establishment', but more associated with a 'Palace Coup' because of a reliance for its success on the Emperors approval.[91] However, in the aftermath of the coup and the purported claim by the junior officers to the Emperor that the coup was a purge of the evil in his administration, the Emperor did not approve of it after all.[92] Moreover, the Emperor actually requested the government to take action against those who had been responsible for the coup as well as those who had also taken part in it. Perhaps the Emperor's actions could be explained by the fact that the coup plotters had no popular support

[87] Ibid.

[88] Sims, R. (2001), Japanese Political History Since the Meiji Renovation 1868–2000, Hurst & Company, London.

[89] Ibid.

[90] Ibid.

[91] Banno, J. (2014), Japan's Modern History, 1857–1937, A New Political Narrative, Routledge, London.

[92] Ibid.

amongst the electorate. Just six days before the attempted coup, 12 million Japanese electors had voted in overwhelming numbers for an 'anti-fascist' government of the Minseito Party.[93] Moreover, the 'Social Masses Party' also won eighteen seats, and it was a party closely aligned to the Tosei-ha faction of the Imperial Japanese Army.[94] Furthermore, the Social Masses Party also did not have any links with those responsible for the attempted coup, the Kodo-ha faction of the Japanese Army.[95] The resurgence of the Social Masses Party was another indication that the Japanese electorate favoured those parties which had an anti-fascist gaunt.[96]

The February 26 Incident of 1936 and its aftermath worried senior Japanese Army Generals as to the scale of the damage on the functioning and independence of the Army.[97] Moreover, because of the purge of officers belonging to the Koda-ha faction, the Japanese military lost a large number of its experienced officers. However, ultimate power over Japan's military lay with the War Minister, and this represented the most important characteristic of the relationship between the Japanese State and its military. But due to the purge of military personnel, less experienced officers were able to move into senior positions. One of these relatively inexperienced officers was a certain Tojo Hideki who having been War Minister for under two years was appointed as Prime Minister in September 1941.[98] Tojo Hideki had only been a Lieutenant General when he had become War Minister. However, before Hideki had assumed office, Konoe Fumimaro, a Prince of the Imperial Court, had become Prime Minister in June 1937.[99] By that time all Prime Ministerial appointments had become subject to the approval of the Japanese Army and Navy, without whose consent appointment would not have been possible.[100] In this case, while Konoe had knowledge and experience of the Western powers, he was also acceptable to the Army and the Navy. It would seem that Prince Konoe

[93] Ibid.

[94] Ibid.

[95] Banno, J. (2014), Japan's Modern History, 1857–1937, A New Political Narrative, Routledge, London.

[96] Ibid.

[97] Kitaoka, S. (1993), The Army as a Bureaucracy: Japanese Militarism Revisited, The Journal of Military History, Vol.57, No.5.

[98] Ibid.

[99] Sims, R. (2001), Japanese Political History Since the Meiji Renovation 1868–2000, Hurst & Company, London.

[100] Flath, D. (2000), The Japanese Economy, Oxford University Press, Oxford.

Fumimaro's appointment as Prime Minister at this time was one of the reasons as to Japan's highly probable trajectory to World War 2. This is because Konoe felt the dominant Anglo-American hegemony was controlling global resources at the expense of Japan under the guise of pacifism and democracy.[101] The other factor which would put Japan on an inevitable trajectory to World War 2 would be its military involvement on the Chinese mainland. This had begun in 1932 with the annexation of Manchuria, which had been renamed Manchukuo, in 1932.[102] By 1936, Japanese central planning had failed to deliver the benefits of Manchukuo's resources. At this time, the Japanese Army invited the private sector, the new Zaibatsu which included the forerunners of Nissan and Fuji Heavy Industries to set up business in Manchukuo with the insurance of government guarantees.[103] Chinese nationalism was on the rise, and the Chinese wanted back their territory. Tensions were on the rise, and in July 1937, Japanese and Chinese troops exchanged fire in Beijing at the Marco Polo Bridge. This incident would be the trigger for the second Sino-Japanese War which raged between 1937 and 1945. There was now no time left for Japan to incrementally mobilise its resources through building relationships between civilian and military bureaucracies and the Zaibatsu. Therefore, the time had come to implement the long-term plan of implementing a military central command economy befitting total war.[104] Nevertheless, it was still recognised that Japan did not have enough resources to fight a sustained long-term war with a number of belligerents.[105] The implication of this was that while Japan was waging war against China, it would engage in diplomacy to ensure that other countries did not enter the war against it.[106] At the same time, the Japanese were finding that by 1939 the war in China had reached a stalemate because while the Japanese controlled the majority of cities and roads, the countryside where the bulk of the population lived were in the hands of either the Chinese Nationalists or the Chinese Communists. At the same

[101] Ibid.
[102] Flath, D. (2000), The Japanese Economy, Oxford University Press, Oxford.
[103] Ibid.
[104] Ibid.
[105] Ibid.
[106] Ibid.

time, in Japan leftist politicians and writers were being persecuted with some even being tortured and killed by the police.[107]

In the context of gaining allies and mitigating its defences, the Japanese signed a Tripartite Pact with Italy and Germany in September 1940, while signing a neutrality pact with the USSR in April 1941.[108] And in July 1941, Japanese forces had begun to move into southern Indo-China.[109] This caused the United States to impose embargoes on all exports to Japan. For the Americans, Japanese incursions into Indo-China represented the last straw following Japanese militarism in China. Once the American oil embargo began to hurt its economy, the Japanese would have no option but to take the Dutch West Indies for its oil resources by military force.[110] However, this would put Japan on a war trajectory with Great Britain and with the United States.[111] Moreover, over time negotiations between Japan and the United States were proving to be unfruitful. As a result, when Tojo Hideki became Japanese Prime Minister in the latter half of 1941, he ramped up preparations for Japan to go to war with the United States.[112] In sum the Japanese military had lost a number of its most experienced soldiers through a purge, following the February 26 Incident, while others as well as civilian politicians and business leaders had been assassinated by right wing radicals.[113] The implication of this would have been that co-operation with politicians would have become more difficult as would have been the control of the army. And, inevitably Japan was on the road to World War II.

[107] Shimazu, N. (2003), Popular Representations of the Past: The Case of Post-War Japan, Journal of Contemporary History, Vol.38 (1), pp. 101–116.

[108] Flath, D. (2000), The Japanese Economy, Oxford University Press, Oxford.

[109] Ibid.

[110] Flath, D. (2000), The Japanese Economy, Oxford University Press, Oxford.

[111] Ibid.

[112] Ibid.

[113] Large, S. (2001), Nationalist Extremism in Early Showa Japan: Inoue Nissho and the 'Blood Pledge Corps Incident' 1932, Modern Asian Studies, 35, 3, pp. 533–564.

American Occupation and Economic Renewal

Japan's post Taisho Period history can be divided into three distinctive phases.[114] The first which has been discussed for the fifteen years in which Japan was governed under military domination for a planned military economy. This lasted from the early 1930s to Japan's surrender to the allies in 1945. On the other hand, the other two phases depict Japan rising from its ashes. Thus, the second phase was the one which incorporated the American occupation of Japan from 1945 until 1952. During this phase, Japan was demilitarised, and democracy was re-introduced. The third phase was the one in which the Japanese economy experienced very high economic growth rates in the 1960s, such that it became an acknowledged economic superpower by the early 1970s.[115]

Emperor Hirohito could have ended the war for Japan as far back as March 1943, but any attempt by him to do so would have not been whole hearted because of military promises of victory against the United States.[116] In this case, Japan's unconditional surrender and acceptance of the allies' Potsdam Terms of July 1945 were dependent on two convergent factors which weighed heavily on Emperor Hirohito's insistence that the war be ended immediately.[117] The first factor was the use of atomic bombs against the Japanese cities of Hiroshima and Nagasaki on 6 and 9 August 1945. These two bombs dropped on two separate Japanese cities killed tens of thousands of people within seconds with many more thousands dying from radiation-related illnesses in the future. Initial reports of the effects of the bombs on the cities to Emperor Hirohito, who was a trained marine Biologist, raised his worst fears that if Japan did not surrender soon then the whole country would become a wasteland of atomic ashes. It was just as the Americans had expected, the dropping of the bombs would strengthen the hand of the doves while weakening the hands of the hawks. The doves encompassed the so-called party of peace, which included Emperor Hirohito; the Keeper of the Privy Seal, Kido Koichi, Togo Shigenori, the Foreign Minister; and Yonai Mitsumasa, the Navy

[114] Dower, J. (1990), The Useful War, Daedalus, Vol.119, No.3, Showa: The Japan of Hirohito, pp. 49–70.

[115] Ibid.

[116] Bix, H. (1995), Japan's Delayed Surrender: A Reinterpretation, Diplomatic History, 19, pp. 197–225.

[117] Asada, S. (1998), The Shock of the Atomic Bomb and Japan's Decision to Surrender: A Reconsideration, Pacific Historical Review, Vol.67, No.4, pp. 477–512.

Minister.[118] On the other hand, the hawks were represented by the military chiefs which included the staunchest critic of peace, Anami Korechika, the Army Minister; Umezu, the Chief of the Army General Staff; and Toyoda Soemu, Chief of the Naval General Staff.[119] It was these military men who insisted that Japan could still be victorious and defeat the United States once it had invaded the mainland. In this context, the General Military Staff represented the biggest obstacle to Japan's unconditional surrender. The second convergent factor which again gave the doves or the party of peace the upper hand against the hawks in the Japanese government was the entry of the Soviet Union into the war against Japan on 9 August 1945.[120] On this date, the Soviet Union declared war against the Empire of Japan, and the military forces of the Soviet Union entered the annexed Japanese territory of Manchuria, clashing with the Japanese Kwantung Army who were not expected to last for longer than two weeks against the Soviet onslaught. Moreover, Japan now faced the threat of a two-pronged assault against the main Japanese islands—by the military forces of the Soviet Union as well as by the military forces of the United States on two fronts. In conjunction with the American possession of the atomic bomb, the weight of probability was in favour of an immediate and unconditional Japanese surrender. On the morning of 9 August 1945, the Lord of the Privy Seal, Kido Koichi, spoke with Prime Minister Suzuki who finally acknowledged that Japan should unconditionally surrender immediately.[121] A conversation with the same consensus later took place between Kido Koichi and the Emperor at his underground bunker at the Imperial Palace.[122] The Supreme War Council then went into session. The primary purpose of the Supreme War Council was to determine war policy as well as the policy of the military services.[123] However, the Supreme War Council, which included the Prime Minister, the Foreign Minister as well as senior military personnel, came to a deadlock with regard to whether Japan should surrender or not.[124] And the deadlock was only broken at

[118] Ibid.

[119] Ibid.

[120] Ibid.

[121] Asada, S. (1998), The Shock of the Atomic Bomb and Japan's Decision to Surrender: A Reconsideration, Pacific Historical Review, Vol.67, No.4, pp. 477–512.

[122] Ibid.

[123] Chaurasia, R. (2003), History of Japan, Atlantic Publishers & Distributors, New Delhi.

[124] Asada, S. (1998), The Shock of the Atomic Bomb and Japan's Decision to Surrender: A Reconsideration, Pacific Historical Review, Vol.67, No.4, pp. 477–512.

2.30 am on 10 August 1945 by the intervention of the Emperor, in favour of Japan's unconditional surrender to the allies and thus accepting the terms of the Potsdam Declaration of July 1945.[125] The Potsdam Declaration asked for the total and unequivocal surrender of Japan's armed forces.[126] However, the Potsdam Declaration did not call for the abolition of the Emperor system in which case Emperor Hirohito and the Japanese monarchy were saved in the midst of Japan's defeat.[127] But when Japan did surrender, the Japanese government stipulated that the country would only do so if the Emperor's position was safe. In this case, the response received from the Americans was ambiguous and Japan's surrender was in doubt until the Emperor intervened for a second time on 14 August 1945 to ensure that the Japanese government did unconditionally surrender to the United States and its allies.[128]

President Harry Truman informed the waiting press at the White House on 14 August 1945 that the Empire of Japan had surrendered unconditionally and in full acceptance of the terms of the Potsdam Declaration.[129] And, the document of surrender was signed on board the USS Missouri on 2 September 1945.[130] This had been followed by the atomic bombing of Hiroshima on 6 August 1945 using 'Little Boy'.[131] However, in order to ensure that the Japanese fully understood the American and allied intent on ending the war immediately, another atomic bomb, known as 'Fat Man', was dropped on the ship building city of Nagasaki on 9 August 1945.[132] The dropping of the bomb on Nagasaki killed 70,000 people instantly out of the city's total pre-bombing population of 240,000.[133] However, thousands died in the ensuing months and years of illnesses resulting from exposure to the nuclear radiation which

[125] Ibid.

[126] Hasegawa, T. (2005), Racing the Enemy: Stalin, Truman, And the Surrender of Japan, The Belknap Press of Harvard University Press, Cambridge, Massachusetts.

[127] Kataoka, T. (1991), The Price of a Constitution: The Origin of Japan's Postwar Politics, Taylor & Francis, New York.

[128] Asada, S. (1998), The Shock of the Atomic Bomb and Japan's Decision to Surrender: A Reconsideration, Pacific Historical Review, Vol.67, No.4, pp. 477–512.

[129] Spector, R. (2007), In the Ruins of Empire: The Japanese Surrender and the Battle for Post-War Asia, Random House Trade Paperbacks, New York.

[130] Hannah, K. (2016), Trust and Deception, ebookIt.com.

[131] Eiji, T. (2002), The Allied Occupation of Japan, Continuum, London.

[132] Poolos, J. (2008), The Atomic Bombings of Hiroshima and Nagasaki, Chelsea House Publishers, New York.

[133] Ibid.

had resulted from the blast. Although 'Fat Man' was a more powerful bomb than was 'Little Boy', it did less damage because the city of Nagasaki was buttressed by hills which reduced the impact of the bomb on the city's population and infrastructure.[134] On 30 August 1945, General Douglas MacArthur landed at Atsugi Air Base in Tokyo.[135] Before the end of World War 2, MacArthur had been to Japan briefly on four occasions.[136] On one of these occasions, MacArthur met the military men who had been instrumental in Japan's victory in the Sino-Russian War. Perhaps, this in itself signified the economic and the military might of the United States which had defeated Japan in Asia and had contributed to the defeat of Germany and Italy in Europe.[137] Indeed, the United States was the most powerful country in the world, the only one with the atomic bomb at the time. MacArthur's landing at Atsugi also signified the beginning of American hegemony in the world, the beginning of a truly global Pax Americana.[138] Nevertheless, it was also an uncertain time and a brave action for MacArthur to take when millions of Japanese soldiers still remained armed on the Japanese mainland. This is because MacArthur arrived in Japan before the bulk of the US military arrived. However, Japan's surrender had been made at the express request of Emperor Hirohito to the Japanese military and to the Japanese government. The first few days, weeks and months for MacArthur represented a steep learning curve because he had to learn from the Japanese about their situation and become better acquainted on how the occupation could successfully ensure peace was brought about. In this case, MacArthur would learn a lot from men such as Yoshida Shigeru who would go on to become Japanese Prime Minister; Mamoru Shigemitsu, the former Japanese foreign minister; and Emperor Akihito himself.[139] However, initial preparations had begun for the American occupation of Japan on 14 August 1945 with an American request to the Japanese government that they send an advanced party to meet MacArthur in Manila, Philippines.[140] Following this, on 28 August 1945, 200 US

[134] Ibid.

[135] Eiji, T. (2002), The Allied Occupation of Japan, Continuum, London.

[136] Finn, R. (1992), Winners in Peace, MacArthur, Yoshida and Post-war Japan, University of California Press, Berkeley.

[137] Eiji, T. (2002), The Allied Occupation of Japan, Continuum, London.

[138] Ibid.

[139] Eiji, T. (2002), The Allied Occupation of Japan, Continuum, London.

[140] Schaller, M. (1985), The American Occupation of Japan: The Origins of the Cold War in Asia, Oxford University Press, Oxford.

army technical experts were dispatched to Atsugi Air Base, Tokyo, in order to prepare for MacArthur's arrival.[141]

MacArthur had the chance to reshape Japan in America's eyes. In this case, he would focus on specific areas. First and foremost would be the need to ensure that Japan's military capabilities were neutered so that it would never again be able to launch another war. This was to be achieved by writing into the new constitution a prohibition on Japan having armed forces as well as permanently stationing US troops in Japan.[142] This would negate the need for Japan to have its own armed forces and allow Japan to act as a forward base should war break out with the Soviet Union.[143] The other objectives which MacArthur had in mind were a stable, just and civil Japanese society which espoused political freedom, press freedom, a liberal education, the enfranchisement of women, a free market, the inclusion of labour unions and an independent judiciary and police force.[144] At the end of World War 2, the Japanese legal system was an amalgam of legal developments of the Tokugawa and the Meiji Periods. The Tokugawa Period espoused Confucianism which necessitated a need for social harmony.[145] The implication of this was that those who engaged in legal disputes were causing disharmony, and for this reason, such disputes were frowned upon.[146] In this case because of an emphasis on ensuring social harmony, there was no recognition of individual rights in the Tokugawa legal code.[147] Indeed, there was no vocabulary in the Japanese language to give a recognition for 'individual rights'.[148] Even during the Meiji Period, which espoused a totally different governance structure for Japan from the previous period, individual rights were slow to develop, emerging not till the early part of the twentieth century. Nevertheless, the new Meiji Constitution did impose upon Japan's growing economy, western legal concepts and institutions, such as an elected Parliament (Diet) for example.[149] However,

[141] Ibid.

[142] Ibid.

[143] Ibid.

[144] Ibid.

[145] Uchtmann, D., Blessen, R., Maloney, V. (1987), The Developing Japanese Legal System: Growth and Change in the Modern Era, 23 Gonz. L. Rev. 349.

[146] Uchtmann, D., Blessen, R., Maloney, V. (1987), The Developing Japanese Legal System: Growth and Change in the Modern Era, 23 Gonz. L. Rev. 349.

[147] Ibid.

[148] Ibid.

[149] Henderson, D. (1952), Some Aspects of Tokugawa Law, 27 Wash. L Rev. 85, 91.

during the Meiji Period the Tokugawa methods for solving legal disputes survived the new constitution.[150] Even following the American occupation, the reconstruction, post-war Japanese constitution and the Americanisation of the Japanese legal system, it remained a hybrid of the Tokugawa legal system, the changes introduced during the Meiji Period as well as the changes of the post-1945 era.[151]

The Post-war Economy (1952–1989)

Many of the features which had been required for Japan's economic renewal had in fact been laid during the years of militarism in the 1930s.[152] Japan was not rebuilt in the context of an 'old' Japan or a 'New' Japan because the American occupation following Japan's surrender in 1945 maintained the pre-war elite and the American reforms were implemented by those who remained of Japan's pre-war bureaucracy.[153] Furthermore, the political-economic doctrine used as the philosophy for rebuilding Japan after World War 2 was termed the Yoshida Doctrine, named after the first Japanese Prime Minister Yoshida Shigeru.[154] There were three facets of the Yoshida Doctrine.[155] Firstly, Japan's economic revival based on a close political and economic cooperation with the United States. Secondly, Japan's military expenditure was to be kept at a minimal level so that financial resources and people's energies could be diverted into the productive capacity of the economy. The last facet of the Yoshida Doctrine was to ensure that the United States would guarantee the long-term security of the Japanese nation which would provide military bases on Japanese soil for the United States.[156] This last aspect of the Yoshida Doctrine was supported by domestic Japanese pacifism and pressure against

[150] Ibid.

[151] Uchtmann, D., Blessen, R., Maloney, V. (1987), The Developing Japanese Legal System: Growth and Change in the Modern Era, 23 Gonz. L. Rev. 349.

[152] Dower, J. (1990), The Useful War, Daedalus, Vol.119, No.3, Showa: The Japan of Hirohito, pp. 49–70.

[153] Garon, S. (1984), The Imperial Bureaucracy and Labour Policy in Post-war Japan, Journal of Asian Studies, Vol. XLIII, No.3.

[154] Man, T. (2007), Japan's Grand Strategic Shift from Yoshida to Koizumi: Reflections on Japan's Strategic Focus in the 21st Century, Akademika, 70, pp. 117–136.

[155] Ibid.

[156] Pyle, K. B, (1996), The Making of Modern Japan, 2nd Ed, D. C. Heath and Co, Lexington, Massachusetts.

militarisation from its war time victims, most notably Korea and China.[157] Moreover, in the aftermath of the end of the war, the United States had become the source of much needed monetary and food assistance for the Japanese.[158] The latter had a resource scarcity problem at a time when there were still six million members of the Japanese military personnel as well as civilian personnel in various parts of Asia.[159] The Yoshida Doctrine had become so successful that by 1955, the majority of Japan's economic indicators had risen above their pre-war levels.[160] For example, real GNP had risen to its pre-war levels by 1951, real per capita consumption by 1953 and per capita GNP by 1955.[161]

The militarisation of Japan in the 1930s and the subsequent resurgence of its economy after 1945 have a similarity with the last fifteen years of the Tokugawa Period and the emergence of political, economic and social reforms of the Meiji Period.[162] In the case of the transition from the Tokugawa Period to the Meiji Period, this was in particular due to the fear of colonisation by an European power or by the American's themselves. However, following the surrender in 1945, there was now a need to rebuild the country and reclaim sovereignty. Both situations were one's of crisis for Japan, but crises which brought about change.[163] Nevertheless, even though there was change in Japan at these two junctures of history in the nineteenth and twentieth centuries, the linkages between one period to the next remained in place.[164] These linkages were mainly associated with personnel, institutions, bureaucracy, technology and culture and beliefs. In this case, although the purge of ultra-nationalists and militarists began at the start of the American occupation, this had little impact on military men and those with deep national beliefs being involved in either the public sector, the private sector or multi-party politics once Japan had

[157] Man, T. (2007), Japan's Grand Strategic Shift from Yoshida to Koizumi: Reflections on Japan's Strategic Focus in the 21st Century, Akademika, 70, pp. 117–136.

[158] Ibid.

[159] Ibid.

[160] Ibid.

[161] Uchino, T, (1983), Japan's Post-war Economy: An Insider's View of Its History and Its Future, Kodansha International Ltd, Tokyo.

[162] Dower, J. (1990), The Useful War, Daedalus, Vol.119, No.3, Showa: The Japan of Hirohito, pp. 49–70.

[163] Ibid.

[164] Dower, J. (1990), The Useful War, Daedalus, Vol.119, No.3, Showa: The Japan of Hirohito, pp. 49–70.

become re-democratised.[165] Moreover, the continuity of personnel from Japan's pre-war period to its post-war period had been made possible because of organisational changes which had been made in the past and the resulting institutions.[166] For example, in post-war Japan, the Emperor remained as a constitutional monarch, the political beliefs and parties of the Taisho Period re-emerged under the democratisation of the American occupation, and the Ministry and Finance and the Bank of Japan continued their functions.[167] However, while these institutional continuities are transparent, there are others whose emergence cannot be so easily discerned. This is the case with the Economic Planning Agency which had been established in 1955, the Ministry of International Trade and Industry, the Federation of Economic Organisations, national newspapers as well as industrial conglomerates.[168] In other words, these institutions did not have to be built from scratch but evolved from or emerged from previous institutional re-incarnations. Moreover, while Japan lost the tangible assets which had been created in the decade before 1945, it still had human capital in abundance.[169] Furthermore, it is also important to recognise that Japan was not totally in ashes following its surrender in 1945. In this case, the Japanese economy was growing at an average of 5% of GNP throughout the 1930s.[170] But on the other hand, the US economy had been struggling to regain the levels of economic growth it had experienced until the Wall Street Crash of 1929.[171] Therefore, it would suffice to say that even through political instability, the Japanese economy experienced economic growth in the 1930s as well as in the years following the attack on Pearl Harbor in December 1941.[172] However, this national growth masked the

[165] Pempel, T.(1987), The Tar Baby Target: 'Reform' of the Japanese Bureaucracy, IN Democratizing Japan: The Allied Occupation, Ward, R. and Sakamoto, Y (Eds), University of Hawaii Press, Honolulu.

[166] Dower, J. (1990), The Useful War, Daedalus, Vol.119, No.3, Showa: The Japan of Hirohito, pp. 49–70.

[167] Ibid.

[168] Ibid.

[169] Ibid.

[170] Patrick, H., and Rosovsky, H. (1976), Japan's Economic Performance: An Overview, IN Asia's New Giant: How the Japanese Economy Works, Patrick, H., and Rosovsky, H. (Eds), Brookings Institution, Washington, DC, 8–9.

[171] Dower, J. (1990), The Useful War, Daedalus, Vol.119, No.3, Showa: The Japan of Hirohito, pp. 49–70.

[172] Johnson, C. (1982), MITI and the Japanese Miracle: The Growth of Industrial Policy, 1925–1975, Stanford University Press, Stanford.

growth of individual sectors in the Japanese economy ranging from consumption goods, investment goods, metals, engineering and chemicals.[173] Moreover, by 1937 Japan had become self-sufficient in the production of basic chemical products, scientific instruments and in the construction of its own factories.[174] Furthermore, Japan had become a major exporter of manufactured goods, although half of this represented textiles, as well as a major importer of raw materials such that its industrial capacity was greater than the whole of Asia but not including the Soviet Union.[175] In this case, at the time Japan ranked fourth amongst the major exporting countries after the United States, United Kingdom and Germany, while its merchant marine shipping was the third largest in the world.[176] These features of the Japanese economy in the 1930s and the early 1940s are not inclusive of the economic performance of Japan's colonies which included the rapidly industrialising puppet state of Manchukuo, annexed Korea and formerly Chinese Taiwan.[177] The reason why Japan's economy was growing so rapidly towards the late 1930s was that the military bureaucracy had intensified its controls on all types of economic activity especially after the outbreak of war with China in July 1937 and the allied powers in 1941 following the Japanese bombing of Pearl Harbor.[178] As a result of improved organisation of the allocation of resources, Japan's economy experienced significant growth at a national level but also within specific sectors such as manufacturing, steel production, machinery production and non-ferrous metal production.[179] Moreover, there was also increase in fixed capital investment as well as an increase in the labour force. The manufacturing and construction labour force increased from 5.8 million in 1930 to 9.5 million in 1944, but at the same time, there was an increase in the number of workers in heavy industry as a proportion of the total labour force from 1937 to 1942.[180] It would seem that the transition from the

[173] Dower, J. (1990), The Useful War, Daedalus, Vol.119, No.3, Showa: The Japan of Hirohito, pp. 49–70.

[174] Ibid.

[175] Allen, G. (1958), Japan's Economic Recovery, Oxford University Press, London.

[176] Dower, J. (1990), The Useful War, Daedalus, Vol.119, No.3, Showa: The Japan of Hirohito, pp. 49–70.

[177] Ibid.

[178] Ibid.

[179] Ibid.

[180] Cohen, J. (1949), Japan's Economy in War and Reconstruction, University of Minnesota Press, Minneapolis.

plural democratic system of the Taisho Period to the military bureaucratic economy of the 1930s necessitated a second industrial revolution in pre-war Japan which caused changes in the country's labour and capital.[181] This may be associated with improving the skill levels of Japanese workers and using technologically advanced machinery for production. However, Japan's economic dividend did not match the boom in the US economy which resulted because of the war.[182] In this case, Japan's defeat by America may have led to long-term benefits for the Japanese economy especially in the context of gaining access to American technology which had been developed because of the war and the rebuilding of Japanese factories using such advanced technology.[183] Furthermore, in an international environment which strongly favoured decolonisation, including the loss of its own colonies, Japan developed an industrial and economy strategy which was based on the manufacture and export of light technological goods by transposing war time technological innovations into post-war trade advantages.[184] The institutional continuity also assisted this strategy as firms which had engaged in war time production such as Toyota, Nissan and Isuzu would continue production in the same specialism during peacetime.[185] These firms had been manufacturers of vehicles for the military during the war and had benefited when Ford and GM left the Japanese market due to government regulation in 1936.[186] The Japanese Automobile Manufacturers Association (JAMA) emerged in 1948 from two control associations which had been in place in 1941 and in 1942.[187] The JAMA had pushed the government to impose tariffs on imports of cars into Japan in order to protect the development of the Japanese car manufacturing industry as well as persuading the government to provide low cost loans in the 1950s and in the 1960s.[188] Other contemporary Japanese organisations also evolved during the period of war and militarisation. For example,

[181] Dower, J. (1990), The Useful War, Daedalus, Vol.119, No.3, Showa: The Japan of Hirohito, pp. 49–70.

[182] Ibid.

[183] Ibid.

[184] Ibid.

[185] Ibid.

[186] Ibid.

[187] Ibid.

[188] Odaka, K., Ono, K., and Adachi, F. (1988), The Automobile Industry in Japan: A Study of Ancillary Firm Development, Kinokuniya Company and Oxford University Press, Tokyo.

Nomura had been founded in 1925 to conduct business in the bond market.[189] However, it expanded into trading in stocks in 1938 and operating investment trusts in 1941.[190] Furthermore, Hitachi and Toshiba, well-known manufacturers of electrical equipment, were established in 1910 and 1904 respectively with the formative years of both forms being in the 1930s operating under a military bureaucracy. Moreover, the Japanese economy was on the brink of peacetime technologically achievements principally because of certain things which had occurred under the military bureaucracy. For example, the number of technical schools providing technical training, in order to produce skilled workers, had increased to 400 in 1945 from only 11 in 1935.[191] Furthermore, those students who had been studying Science and Engineering subjects at Japanese universities had been exempted from military service, and the number of graduates in these fields was three times as many in the four years before Japan's surrender compared to a decade earlier.[192] These graduates would have been able to find work in the firms which had resulted from the dissolution of the wartime Zaibatsu. Despite the dissolution of the Zaibatsu, the firms which had once formed their core remained close through formal and informal relationships.[193] Indeed, the 'big six' business and financial groupings of post-war Japan were formed from three historical Zaibatsu groupings.[194] Furthermore, the key role played by Japan's national oligopolistic banking sector in the post-war years has its origins in the pre-war years when the Japanese government designated specific banks to receive funds from the Bank of Japan and the government in return for providing loans to over 600 firms which were engaged in essential war time production.[195] Post-war Japanese work practices also emerged from changes which had been implemented by the military government. For example, because staff turnover was high in essential war time industries, following the commencement of war with China in July 1937 and with the allies after December 1941, the Japanese government restricted labour

[189] Dower, J. (1990), The Useful War, Daedalus, Vol.119, No.3, Showa: The Japan of Hirohito, pp. 49–70.

[190] Dower, J. (1990), The Useful War, Daedalus, Vol.119, No.3, Showa: The Japan of Hirohito, pp. 49–70.

[191] Ibid.

[192] Ibid.

[193] Ibid.

[194] Ibid.

[195] Ibid.

movement in 1939 and 1942 through legislation.[196] Furthermore, between 1939 and 1943, legislation was passed to ensure a stable wage structure in which wage levels increased incrementally over time due to length of service.[197] These changes to working practice in Japan which were implemented in Japan in the war years led to the popular idea of life-long employment in Japanese firms and high salary levels of older workers due to their seniority.[198] The third feature of Japanese employment practice, a fruitful co-operation between firms and unions, did not emerge until later the post-war period. The overall success of the Japanese economy in the post-war period was essentially due to the military strengthening the bureaucratic organisation of economic activity in the 1930s and its subsequent reinforcement during the seven years of the American occupation of Japan.[199] In the post-war period Japanese bureaucrats were engaged in long-term planning in order to build a healthy and a modern state in the context of a world order in which a Pax Americana was at its heart. In this case Japan benefited at this time because of the emerging Cold War in East Asia.[200]

The long-term focus of politicians and bureaucrats in post-World War 2 Japan was in sharp contrast to their counterparts during late Taisho and the early Showa Period. In this case, the politicians and political parties of this time were seen to look out for only their vested interests, campaign funds and re-election by bringing benefits to their constituencies.[201] The implication is that the politicians of the late Taisho Period and the early Showa Period were only interested in the short term and not in the welfare of Japanese society over the long term. This is in the context of increasing disparities in the income levels of the rural inhabitants of Japan and its urban inhabitants, which the military was concerned about.[202] It was this which led to greater military involvement in Japan's governance. Spurred in part by a lack of qualifications, the young leaders of the Japanese military

[196] Ibid.

[197] Dower, J. (1990), The Useful War, Daedalus, Vol.119, No.3, Showa: The Japan of Hirohito, pp. 49–70.

[198] Ibid.

[199] Ibid.

[200] Shimazu, N. (2003), Popular Representations of the Past: The Case of Post-War Japan, Journal of Contemporary History, Vol.38 (1), pp. 101–116.

[201] Kosaka, M. (1990), The Showa Era (1926–1989), Daedalus, Vol.119, No.3, Showa: The Japan of Hirohito.

[202] Ibid.

sought recognition, and politics was one way to achieve this.[203] Typically, these young leaders of Japan's military had risen through the ranks, having attended a military academy but were consequently less educationally qualified than were there peers.[204]

In order to remedy the increasing income disparity between Japan's rural and urban inhabitants, the military's strategy was to build a colonial sphere in China, Korea, Taiwan and in the Pacific in order to control natural resources needed for its industry but were scarce in Japan. In this case, just as Great Britain had benefited economically from its colonies, so could Japan from its colonies. But the American empire was not based on the accumulation of overseas colonies. Rather it was based on a set of ideas encompassing the imposition of the notions of justice and righteousness on other countries.[205] However, the problem was that the United States objected to Japan's strategy, and the only way for Japan to beat the United States was a quick military victory and then negotiate favourable peace terms.[206] The land and sea battles of Guadalcanal between August 1942 and February 1943 were the first to be lost by the Japanese military to the forces of the United States and its allies.[207] As a result the short-term strategy of a military defeat for Japan against the United States was abandoned, and production increased across Japan's economy in order to boost military action against the Americans. But unfortunately, this came too late and the military and civil infrastructure required to support a sustained long-term military campaign was not available.[208] The result was a Japanese defeat, American occupation and a subsequent economic renewal. Had the military and its sympathisers listened to Emperor Hirohito, who wanted peace, Japan would not have been plunged into war and its subsequent defeat.[209]

[203] Yamazaki, M. (1990), The Intellectual Community of the Showa Era, Daedalus, Vol.119, No.3, Showa: The Japan of Hirohito.

[204] Ibid.

[205] Kitaoka, S. (1990), Diplomacy and the Military in Showa Japan, Daedalus, Vol 119, No.3, Showa: The Japan of Hirohito, pp. 155–176.

[206] Morgan, A. (1950), Japan's Economy in War and Reconstruction, *The Economic Journal*, Volume 60, Issue 237, Pages 145–150, https://doi.org/10.2307/2227225.

[207] Bartsch, W. (2014), Victory Fever on Guadalcanal – Japan's First Land Defeat of WWII, Texas A&M University Press, College Station.

[208] Morgan, A. (1950), Japan's Economy in War and Reconstruction, *The Economic Journal*, Volume 60, Issue 237, Pages 145–150, https://doi.org/10.2307/2227225.

[209] Large, S. (1991), Review: Emperor Hirohito and Early Showa Japan, Monumenta Nipponica, Vol. 46, No.3, pp. 349–368.

Following its defeat and surrender, the process of stabilising the Japanese economy was a slow one, and in 1950, the Japanese economy was still unstable and in the doldrums.[210] Nevertheless, American orders as a result of the Korean War proved to be a boon for Japanese manufacturing which slowly began to recover as did Japan's negative trade balance.[211] Increased Japanese manufacturing as a result of the Korean War may have led to the modernisation of Japanese industry through the 1950s as well as an expansion in global demand for Japanese manufactured goods.[212] As a result, the Japanese economy began to grow by 10% per year from 1960.[213] By 1988, the Japanese economy had grown by nine times its size in 1955.[214] However, the US economy had only grown by 2.67 times its 1955 size by 1988.[215] Although Japan had become the world's second largest economy by 1988, behind the United States, its GNP per capita was higher than that of the United States at $23,382 compared to $19,813 respectively.[216] A number of reasons have been put forward to explain the rapid economic growth experienced by Japan in the forty-three years from its defeat and surrender in 1945 to the penultimate year of the Showa Period. Firstly, a high level of savings and investments could have led to the accumulation of a greater amount of fixed capital over time.[217] Secondly, the job for life relationship between the worker and the firm could have led to the accumulation of firm specific skills which could have led to positive externalities for the firm over time.[218] Thirdly, the organisation of Japanese industry into competing enterprise groups could have led to incentivise long-term planning.[219] This would have allowed firms to gain strategic advantage through innovation by more efficiently organising resources. Fourthly, the use of appropriate monetary and fiscal policy would have allowed for greater economic stability which would have fostered greater long-term investments by firms due to decreased uncertainty.

[210] Forsberg, A. (2000), America and the Japanese Miracle: The Cold War Context of Japan's Postwar Economic Revival, 1950–1960, The University of North Carolina Press.

[211] Ibid.

[212] Forsberg, A. (2000), America and the Japanese Miracle: The Cold War Context of Japan's Postwar Economic Revival, 1950–1960, The University of North Carolina Press.

[213] Ibid.

[214] Ito, T. (1992), The Japanese Economy, The MIT Press, Cambridge, Massachusetts.

[215] Ibid.

[216] Ibid.

[217] Ibid.

[218] Ibid.

[219] Ibid.

Moreover, the use of appropriate fiscal policy would have allowed for greater spending on infrastructure which would have facilitated the expansion of markets for Japanese producers as well as lower transport costs which would have facilitated firm's production experiencing economies of scale. Lastly, whereas the Americans favoured the diffusion of advanced technology to Japanese firms via market forces, joint ventures, the Japanese were more restrictive of foreign direct investment and the ownership of Japanese firms by foreign ones.[220] Therefore, in the case of Japan, technology acquisition was under the control of the Ministry of International Trade and Industry and not left just to the private sector.[221]

Conclusion

The Showa Period began in 1926 at a time of economic crisis in Japan which was doing nothing to address the widening disparities of income between the rural poor and the urban rich. Economic crisis was a common feature of the Japanese economy in the few years before the start of the Showa period and for the first few years after it began. For example, stock prices fell sharply in March 1920, and as a result, there was widespread panic amongst investors. This caused the Bank of Japan to be more relaxed about the lending practices of Japan's commercial banks, causing an increase in lending.[222] However, later on the Bank of Japan had to follow a constrained monetary policy in order to combat inflation. This resulted in the scarcity of the sources of finance. As a result, bank runs followed in 1922. Before this could be adequately resolved, the Tokyo area was struck by an earthquake of 7.9 magnitude in 1923, killing over 120,000 people and destroyed nearly half of Tokyo and all parts of Yokohama.[223] While the earthquake was a national calamity, the bureaucratic elite saw it as an opportunity to rebuild Tokyo to modern standards.[224] However, others saw the devastation of the earthquake as an opportunity to build a new

[220] Forsberg, A. (2000), America and the Japanese Miracle: The Cold War Context of Japan's Post-war Economic Revival, 1950–1960, The University of North Carolina Press.

[221] Ibid.

[222] Hamada, K. (1999), Bubbles, bursts and bailouts: a comparison of three episodes of financial crises in Japan, IN Banking in Japan, Tsuisui, W. (Ed), Routledge, London.

[223] Schencking, J. (2013), The Great Kanto Earthquake and the Chimera of National Reconstruction of Japan, Columbia University Press, New York.

[224] Ibid.

social consensus for regeneration between the rich and the poor.[225] Yet the Kanto earthquake also damaged Japan's financial sector as bank and firm assets were destroyed, records lost and borrowers became unable to repay loans. As a result, debts amongst banks began to accumulate, resulting in the Showa Financial Crisis of 1927. Had the Bank of Japan been more conservative about commercial banking lending practices in 1919–1920, then the Showa Financial Crisis may not have been so severe as the accumulated debts of the commercial banks would not have been as large.[226] Ironically, the earthquake also proved to be an opportunity for nations to share their humanity. In this case, the United States donated supplies for earthquake relief, and the US Navy delivered the supplies to Japan for distribution. Yet eighteen years later the two countries would be at war.

The Showa Financial Crisis of 1927 had resulted because of accumulated debts within the Japanese banking system which could not be settled. However, the Showa Depression of 1931–1932 occurred because Japan reintroduced the gold standard in January 1930. But the economic problems resulted because the parity level of the currency to gold was set too high. Nevertheless, other factors also converged to trigger the Showa Depression. These factors included an appreciating currency, imported inflation as well as a reduction in the international demand for Japanese goods. The Japanese economy continued to contract until Japan left the gold standard in December 1931. As a result of Japan having re-joined the gold standard, over 112 banks had collapsed causing economic hardship and financial losses to customers. The gold standard fiasco, the Great Depression and the imposition of tariffs on Japanese goods led to a severe downturn in Japanese economic activity in the early 1930s. However, at the time of the Showa Depression, Korekiyo Takahashi had been Minister of Finance in the Seiyo-Kai Party. In this case, in order to boost aggregate demand at a time when consumption expenditure was falling, Takahashi put in place expansionary monetary and fiscal policies as well as depreciating the exchange rate in order to make Japanese produced goods relatively cheap. Nevertheless, Takahashi was not a believer in the profligate spending by the state. In this case, he fought to maintain a small government budget deficit if not to also reduce it. However, this put him at odds with Japan's military who wanted the government to increase military

[225] Ibid.

[226] Hamada, K. (1999), Bubbles, bursts and bailouts: a comparison of three episodes of financial crises in Japan, IN Banking in Japan, Tsuisui, W. (Ed), Routledge, London.

spending. But in the face of increasing demand from the military, the Ministry of Finance was the main opposition in government to its requests for additional funding especially in the 1933 and in the 1934 budgets. It also opposed the military's greater role in directing Japan's economy. It may have been due to the Ministry of Finance's opposition to the military on two fronts that Takahashi was assassinated by militarists in February 1936. Indeed, the 1930s was a period of time in which neonationalists murdered politicians, business people and even members of the military who were obstacles to their goals. Principally, this was a greater role for the military in Japan's economic, political and social affairs. Between the early 1930s and until the end of World War 2, there was a shift in political power in Japan from the established political parties and the nobility towards a civilian–military–zaibatsu coalition. This had been mainly because the established democratic political system had been unable to satisfactorily resolve the potential security and economic threats Japan faced. Politicians seemed to be corrupt and only interested in being re-elected to allow them to maintain their wealth and position in society. Commercial interests were furthered by political connections which made the apparent corruption worse. In this case, Japanese politicians were not interested in improving the welfare of Japanese society. The implication was that politicians sought short-term policies to resolve Japan's economic, social and political problems but a long-term strategy was needed in order to ensure that the income disparity between the rural poor and the urban rich could be reduced. This was at the heart of military concerns, and the military was filled with men from rural Japan. Moreover, factionalism was highly prevalent in the Japanese military. This was particularly between the Tosei-ha (Control Group) and the Koda-ha (Imperial Way faction). The Tosei-ha believed in the ideology of Nazi Germany, while the Kodo-ha believed in the principles of Kokutai. The demise of the Kodo-ha faction resulted because of its involvement in the 26 February 1926 Incident. As a result, this faction was crushed by the Tosei-ha faction. Due to this factional shift, there was greater involvement of the military in Japanese politics, facilitating it to influence the direction which Japan took both domestically and internationally.

Those who engineered the February 26 Incident wanted to use it as a signal for the need for social justice in Japanese society. A society in which income and wealth disparities between the rich and the poor were increasing. In this case, the elections clearly indicated a resurgent left suggesting a signal by democracy for social justice. Many military men lacked a formal education, and the only basic education was at the military academy. As a result, many of Japan's military leaders were less educated than their peers and far less educated than the scholars and politicians of the Meiji Period. The rational and scientific thinking[227] which had characterised the Meiji Period and the Taisho Period had been replaced in the early Showa Period by an ideology associated with neonationalism. This led Japan into governance by a military bureaucracy which had the strategy of a colonial Japan which would be able to accumulate wealth as had been done by the British Empire. However, American ideals of justice and righteousness were in the way. The only way in which Japan could succeed was a quick military defeat of America followed by negotiations in Japan's favour. In order to achieve this end, Japan sought allies in Germany and Italy and signed a Tripartite Treaty with these countries in September 1940. It also signed a neutrality pact with the USSR in April 1941. Unfortunately, unlike its earlier wars with China (1894–1895) and Russia (1904–1905) which it had won, the Japanese were convincingly defeated on the land and on the sea by the American military on Guadalcanal. This therefore necessitated a shift in Japanese strategy from a short-term campaign to one which would require increased levels of production across all sectors in order to support the Japanese war machine. However, the infrastructure in terms of maritime shipping had not been put into place, and as a result, increased supply of military materials was of no use if they could not be shipped to wherever it was needed. Nevertheless, Japan's economic growth rates in the 1930s had been positive, whereas America was struggling to retrieve its economic growth rate before the Wall Street Crash of 1929. Furthermore, the military bureaucracy of the 1930s served to strengthen the way in which the Japanese economy was able to organise and allocate resources more efficiently.

Japan's unconditional surrender and acceptance of the conditions of the allies' Potsdam Declaration of July 1945 had been dependent upon two convergent factors. These factors weighed heavily on Emperor Hirohito's insistence that the war be ended immediately. The first factor had been the use of atomic bombs by the Americans on the Japanese cities of Hiroshima and Nagasaki on 6 and 9 August 1945. The second convergent factor which gave the Emperor and the other doves the upper hand

[227] Ishii, K., & Jarkey, N. (2002), The Housewife Is Born: The Establishment of the Notion and Identity of the Shufu in Modern Japan, Japanese Studies, 22:1, 35–47, DOI: https://doi.org/10.1080/103713902201436732.

against the hawks was the entry of the USSR into the war against Japan on 9 August 1945. President Harry Truman broke the news to the world through the White House Press Corps on 14 August 1945 that Japan had unconditionally surrendered and in full acceptance of the terms of the Potsdam Declaration. The subsequent American occupation only served to strengthen the bureaucratic mechanism behind the organisation of resources in Japanese society because the Americans maintained the pre-war Japanese elite and its bureaucrats to help with the demilitarisation and democratisation of Japanese society. However, the process of stabilising the Japanese economy was a slow one, and in 1950, the Japanese economy was still unstable and in the doldrums.[228] Nevertheless, American orders as a result of the Korean War proved to be a boon for Japanese manufacturing which slowly began to recover as did Japan's negative trade balance.[229] Increased Japanese manufacturing as a result of the Korean War may have led to the modernisation of Japanese industry through the 1950s as well as an expansion in global demand for Japanese manufactured goods.[230] As a result, the Japanese economy began to grow by 10% per year from 1960.[231] By the end of the 1980s the Japanese economy had become the second largest in the world behind the United States, but had a GNP per capita which was higher than the GNP per capita of the United States.[232] Furthermore, at the same time while the United States had become world's largest debtor nation, Japan had become the world's biggest holder of foreign assets.[233] However, despite the resurgence of the Japanese economy after 1945 to its becoming the second largest economy in the world towards the late 1980s, the divide between the rich and the poor remained as Japan entered the last decade of the twentieth century.[234] In this case Japanese workers worked longer hours than did American workers, workers paid higher prices and the price of land had reached exorbitant levels by the late 1980s.[235] It is this economic feature which sets the

[228] Forsberg, A. (2000), America and the Japanese Miracle: The Cold War Context of Japan's Postwar Economic Revival, 1950–1960, The University of North Carolina Press.

[229] Ibid.

[230] Ibid.

[231] Ibid.

[232] Ito, T. (1992), The Japanese Economy, The MIT Press, Cambridge, Massachusetts.

[233] Ibid.

[234] Ibid.

[235] Ibid.

economic backdrop for the start of the Heisei Period following the death of Emperor Hirohito in 1989.

References

Akiyoshi, F. (2009), Banking Panics, Bank Failures, and the Lender of Last Resort: The Showa Depression of 1930–1932, Oxford Economic Papers, 61, 776–800.

Allen, G. (1958), Japan's Economic Recovery, Oxford University Press, London.

Asada, S. (1998), The Shock of the Atomic Bomb and Japan's Decision to Surrender: A Reconsideration, Pacific Historical Review, Vol.67, No.4, pp.477–512.

Banno, J. (2014), Japan's Modern History, 1857–1937, A New Political Narrative, Routledge, London.

Barnhart, M. (1995), Japan and the World Since 1868, Edward Arnold Publishing.

Barnhart, M. (2013), Japan Prepares for Total War: The Search for Economic Security, 1919–1941, Cornell University Press, Ithaca.

Bartsch, W. (2014), Victory Fever on Guadalcanal – Japan's First Land Defeat of WWII, Texas A&M University Press, College Station.

Berger, G. (1988), Politics and Mobilisation in Japan, 1931–1945, IN The Cambridge History of Japan, Vol.6, The Twentieth Century, Duus, P. (Ed), Cambridge University Press, Cambridge.

Bix, H. (1995), Japan's Delayed Surrender: A Reinterpretation, Diplomatic History, 19, pp.197–225.

Chaurasia, R. (2003), History of Japan, Atlantic Publishers & Distributors, New Delhi.

Cohen, J. (1949), Japan's Economy in War and Reconstruction, University of Minnesota Press, Minneapolis.

Crowley, J. (1962), Japanese Army Factionalism in the Early 1930's, Journal of Asian Studies, xxi, 72–91.

Dower, J. (1990), The Useful War, Daedalus, Vol.119, No.3, Showa: The Japan of Hirohito, pp.49–70.

Eiji, T. (2002), The Allied Occupation of Japan, Continuum, London.

Finn, R. (1992), Winners in Peace, MacArthur, Yoshida and Post-war Japan, University of California Press, Berkeley.

Flath, D. (2000), The Japanese Economy, Oxford University Press, Oxford.

Forsberg, A. (2000), America and the Japanese Miracle: The Cold War Context of Japan's Post-war Economic Revival, 1950–1960, The University of North Carolina Press.

Garon, S. (1984), The Imperial Bureaucracy and Labour Policy in Post-war Japan, Journal of Asian Studies, Vol. XLIII, No.3.

Gluck, C. (1990), The Idea of Showa, Daedalus, Vol.119, No.3, pp.1–26.

Hamada, K. (1999), Bubbles, bursts and bailouts: a comparison of three episodes of financial crises in Japan, IN Banking in Japan, Tsuisui, W. (Ed), Routledge, London.

Hannah, K. (2016), Trust and Deception, ebookIt.com.

Hasegawa, T. (2005), Racing the Enemy: Stalin, Truman, And the Surrender of Japan, The Belknap Press of Harvard University Press, Cambridge, Massachusetts.

Henderson, D. (1952), Some Aspects of Tokugawa Law, 27 Wash. L Rev. 85, 91.

Humphreys, L. (1995), The Way of the Heavenly Sword; The Japanese Army in the 1920's, Stanford University Press, Stanford, California.

Ito, T. (1992), The Japanese Economy, The MIT Press, Cambridge, Massachusetts.

Johnson, C. (1982), MITI and the Japanese Miracle: The Growth of Industrial Policy, 1925–1975, Stanford University Press, Stanford.

Kamii, Y. (1937), Industrial Recovery in Japan: Its causes and Social Effects, international Labour Review, 35, pp. 31–52.

Kataoka, T. (1991), The Price of a Constitution: The Origin of Japan's Postwar Politics, Taylor & Francis, New York.

Kirshner, J. (2007), Appeasing bankers: Financial Caution on the Road to War, Princeton University Press, Princeton.

Kitaoka, S. (1990), Diplomacy and the Military in Showa Japan, Daedalus, Vol 119, No.3, Showa: The Japan of Hirohito, pp.155–176.

Kitaoka, S. (1993), The Army as a Bureaucracy: Japanese Militarism Revisited, The Journal of Military History, Vol.57, No.5.

Kosaka, M. (1990), The Showa Era (1926–1989), Daedalus, Vol.119, No.3, Showa: The Japan of Hirohito.

Ishii, K., & Jarkey, N. (2002), The Housewife Is Born: The Establishment of the Notion and Identity of the Shufu in Modern Japan, Japanese Studies, 22:1, 35–47, DOI: https://doi.org/10.1080/10371390220143673 2.

Large, S. (1991), Review: Emperor Hirohito and Early Showa Japan, Monumenta Nipponica, Vol. 46, No.3, pp.349–368.

Large, S. (2001), Nationalist Extremism in Early Showa Japan: Inoue Nissho and the 'Blood Pledge Corps Incident' 1932, Modern Asian Studies, 35, 3, pp.533–564.

Lincoln, E. (1990), The Showa Economic Experience, Daedalus, Vol.119, No.3, pp.191–208.

Man, T. (2007), Japan's Grand Strategic Shift from Yoshida to Koizumi: Reflections on Japan's Strategic Focus in the 21st Century, Akademika, 70, pp.117–136.

McNeill, W. (1986), Mythistory and Other Essays, University of Chicago Press, Chicago.

Minami, R. (1998), Economic development and income distribution in Japan: an assessment of the Kuznets hypothesis, Cambridge Journal of Economics, 22, pp.39–58.

Miners, N. (2002), Industrial development in the colonial empire and the imperial economic conference at Ottawa 1932, 30:2, 53–76, DOI: https://doi.org/10.1080/03086530208583141.

Moore, M. (2011), China is the world's second largest economy, https://www.telegraph.co.uk/finance/economics/8322550/China-is-the-worlds-second-largest-economy.html.

Morgan, A. (1950), Japan's Economy in War and Reconstruction, *The Economic Journal,* Volume 60, Issue 237, Pages 145–150, https://doi.org/10.2307/2227225.

Morris-Suzuki, T. (2012), Showa: An Inside History of Hirohito's Japan, Bloomsbury, London.

Odaka, K., Ono, K., and Adachi, F. (1988), The Automobile Industry in Japan: A Study of Ancillary Firm Development, Kinokuniya Company and Oxford University Press, Tokyo.

Patrick, H., and Rosovsky, H. (1976), Japan's Economic Performance: An Overview, IN Asia's New Giant: How the Japanese Economy Works, Patrick, H., and Rosovsky, H. (Eds), Brookings Institution, Washington, D.C, 8–9.

Pempel, T. (1987), The Tar Baby Target: 'Reform' of the Japanese Bureaucracy, IN Democratizing Japan: The Allied Occupation, Ward, R. and Sakamoto, Y (Eds), University of Hawaii Press, Honolulu.

Poolos, J. (2008), The Atomic Bombings of Hiroshima and Nagasaki, Chelsea House Publishers, New York.

Pyle, K. B, (1996), The Making of Modern Japan, 2nd Ed, D. C. Heath and Co, Lexington, Massachusetts.

Sawai, M. (1999), Noda Shoichi and Roku-Roku Shoten, a machine tool manufacturer, Social Sciences Japan Journal, Vol.2, No.1, pp.107–122.

Schaller, M. (1985), The American Occupation of Japan: The Origins of the Cold War in Asia, Oxford University Press, Oxford.

Schencking, J. (2013), The Great Kanto Earthquake and the Chimera of National Reconstruction of Japan, Columbia University Press, New York.

Shi, L., Sato, H., and Sicular, T. (2013), Rising Inequality in China, IN Rising Inequality in China: Challenges to a Harmonious Society, Shi, L., Sato, h., and Sicular, T. (Eds), Cambridge University Press, Cambridge.

Shimazu, N. (2003), Popular Representations of the Past: The Case of Post-War Japan, Journal of Contemporary History, Vol.38 (1), pp.101–116.

Shizume, M. (2009), 'The Japanese Economy during the Interwar Period: Instability in the Financial System and the Impact of the World Depression,' Bank of Japan Review Series 09-E-2, Bank of Japan.

Sims, R. (2001), Japanese Political History Since the Meiji Renovation 1868–2000, Hurst & Company, London.

Snyder, J. (1991), Myths of Empire – Domestic Politics and International Ambition, Cornell University Press, Ithaca.

Spector, R. (2007), In the Ruins of Empire: The Japanese Surrender and the Battle for Post-War Asia, Random House Trade Paperbacks, New York.
Takafusa, N. (1998), Depression, Recovery, and War, 1920–1945, IN Showa japan: Political, economic and social history 1926–1989, Large, S. (Ed), Routledge, London.
Takenaka, H. (1998), The Collapse of the Semi-Democratic Regime in Pre-War Japan, Stanford University Press, Stanford, California.
Tamaki, N. (1995), Japanese Banking – A History, 1859–1959, Cambridge University Press, Cambridge.
Uchino, T, (1983), Japan's Post-war Economy: An Insider's View of Its History and Its Future, Kodansha International Ltd, Tokyo.
Uchtmann, D., Blessen, R., Maloney, V. (1987), The Developing Japanese Legal System: Growth and Change in the Modern Era, 23 Gonz. L. Rev. 349.
Von Staden, P. (2008), Business-Government Relations in Pre-war Japan, Routledge, New York.
Wakatabe, M. (2015), Japan's Great Stagnation and Abenomics: Lessons for the World, Palgrave Macmillan, UK.
Yagami, K. (2006), Konoe Fumimaro and the Failure of Peace in Japan, 1937–1941: A Critical Appraisal of the Three-Time Prime Minister, McFarland & Company Inc, Publishers, London.
Yamazaki, M. (1990), The Intellectual Community of the Showa Era, Daedalus, Vol.119, No.3, Showa: The Japan of Hirohito.
Young, A. (2011), Imperial Japan: 1926–1938, Volume 54, Routledge, New York.
Yukio, C. (1999), Exposing the incompetence of the bourgeoisie: The financial panic of 1927, IN Banking in Japan: The evolution of Japanese banking, 1868–1952, Tsutsui, W. (Ed), Routledge, New York.

CHAPTER 8

The Heisei Period (1989–2019): Economic Stagnation and the Rise of China

Introduction

Japan's wartime Emperor Hirohito died in 1989 and with his death ended the Showa Period. Hirohito's son Akihito then became Emperor ushering in the Heisei Period in modern Japanese history, the name symbolising the achievement of 'full peace'.[1] The practice of assigning a specific name with its unique meaning to the time period associated with each Emperor's reign was started after the Meiji Restoration.[2] The purpose of the practice was to better associate the Emperor of a particular period with the peoples of the time.[3] The meaning of the 'Heisei' Period may have been indicative of the idea that the nation had been rebuilt and that the time had come for the people of Japan to enjoy the fruits of their hard work.[4] Another major difference between the Heisei Period and other periods in Japanese history was that Emperor Akihito married the Empress for love and the

[1] Henshall, K.G. (2012), A Superpower Adrift: The Heisei Years. In: A History of Japan: From Stone Age to Superpower, Palgrave Macmillan, London.

[2] Morris-Suzuki, T. (1989), The Meaning of Heisei, Japanese Studies, Vol. 9, No. 1, pp. 23–24, DOI: 10.1080/10371398908522088

[3] Ibid.

[4] Henshall, K.G. (2012), A Superpower Adrift: The Heisei Years. In: A History of Japan: From Stone Age to Superpower, Palgrave Macmillan, London.

S. Ramesh, *China's Economic Rise*,
https://doi.org/10.1007/978-3-030-49811-5_8

marriage broke tradition by not being 'brokered' by third parties according to the status of the couple.[5]

Unfortunately for Japan, 1989 was not only the beginning of the Heisei Period but also the beginning of a prolonged economic crisis which would last well into the twenty-first century.[6] However, although economic crisis provided the fabric of the Heisei period, there were also political and social changes as well as natural events which fell under its wings. Two damaging earthquakes featured during the Heisei Period.[7] The first was the Kobe Earthquake of 1995 in which 6000 people were killed and infrastructure severely damaged.[8] The second was the Tohoku region earthquake and Tsunami in March 2011 which caused 20,000 deaths and the meltdown of the Fukushima Dai-Ichi nuclear facility.[9] This necessitated the mass evacuation of the surrounding areas. Both disasters evidenced the ineptitude and inefficiency of the Japanese government in relieving and supporting the afflicted areas within a reasonable period of time.[10] On the other hand in the socio-economic context divorce rates were rising during the Heisei period, and marriage and family life was falling out of fashion. As Japan entered the twenty-first century, divorce rates reached levels not seen since the start of the twentieth century, but not the high levels of divorce seen in the last two decades of the nineteenth century.[11] People were embracing their jobs and had little time left for leisure activities during which they could meet their potential partners.[12] As a result of fewer marriages, fewer babies were being born and the population growth rate began to decline.[13] The same thing in contemporary China is happening today. Despite the increase in divorce rates during the Heisei Period, there

[5] Lebra, T. (1997), Self and Other in Esteemed States: The Changing Culture of the Japanese Royalty from Showa to Hesei, The Journal of Japanese Studies, Vol. 23, No. 2, pp. 257–289.

[6] Ibid.

[7] Dunscomb, P. (2018), The Reign of Emperor Akihito 1989-2019: A History in Five Words, Education About Asia, Vol. 23, No. 3.

[8] Ibid.

[9] Dunscomb, P. (2018), The Reign of Emperor Akihito 1989-2019: A History in Five Words, Education About Asia, Vol.23, No.3.

[10] Ibid.

[11] Fuess, H. (2004), Divorce in Japan: Family, Gender, and the State, 1600–2000, Stanford University Press, Stanford, California.

[12] Dunscomb, P. (2018), The Reign of Emperor Akihito 1989-2019: A History in Five Words, Education About Asia, Vol. 23, No. 3.

[13] Ibid.

was also an increase in the trend of other socio-economic phenomena such as single parent families, the abuse of children, suicide and domestic violence.[14]

The economic crisis in Japan began in 1989 when the Bank of Japan started to increase interest rates in order to control rapidly rising inflation.[15] As a result of the increase in interest rates, the property bubble burst, and this would send the economy into a recession for over two decades.[16] The economic contraction was severe with land prices falling and rapidly rising bankruptcies, bad debts, crime rates and suicides.[17] The latter may have resulted because due to the lack of economic growth, falling profits and inability to repay corporate debts, Japanese firms were simply abandoning 'jobs for life' which the Japanese had taken for granted.[18] The fall in corporate profits increased towards the late 1990s as the Japanese economy went into deflation.[19] Yet another feature of the economic crisis which began in 1989 was a prolonged fall in the value of corporate stock, in other words a stock market slump.[20] The result was rising unemployment and rising homelessness especially amongst the generation who had been accustomed to the job for life. Unemployment meant that men lost their dignity and could not face their families, ending up homeless and on the street. Day labourers were the category which was most affected as they relied upon government spending on public works for employment. If government did not release funds for public works, day labourers would not be able to earn an income resulting in homelessness.[21]

During the Heisei Period, Japan developed further as America's ally and key strategic local partner to counter threats from North Korea and the People's Republic of China.[22] In the case of North Korea, this alliance

[14] Kingston, J. (2013), Contemporary Japan: History, Politics and Social Change Since the 1980's, 2nd Edition, John Wiley & Sons, Chichester, West Sussex.

[15] Henshall, K.G. (2012), A Superpower Adrift: The Heisei Years. In: A History of Japan: From Stone Age to Superpower, Palgrave Macmillan, London.

[16] Ibid.

[17] Ibid.

[18] Ibid.

[19] Henshall, K.G. (2012), A Superpower Adrift: The Heisei Years. In: A History of Japan: From Stone Age to Superpower, Palgrave Macmillan, London.

[20] Ibid.

[21] Gill, T. (1994), Sanya Street Life under the Heisei Recession. Japan Quarterly, Vol. 41, pp. 270–86

[22] Rozman, G. (2008), Internationalism and Asianism in Japanese Strategic Thought from Meiji to Hesei, Japanese Journal of Political Science, Vol. 9, No. 2, pp. 209–232.

between Japan and the United States was against its nuclear programme, which in recent years has become more advanced and threatening to both Japanese and US security. The mistake had been made in 1994 when diplomatic negotiations had removed the threat of a military strike on North Korea's emergent plutonium complex at Yongbyon.[23] This had allowed North Korea to deepen its nuclear programme by developing ballistic missiles and uranium enrichment capabilities and other locations.[24] Moreover, the United States was the guarantor of Taiwanese independence.[25] With US military bases on Japanese soil, any attack by China on Taiwan would lead to war with not only the United States but also Japan. Finally, in the context of the Association of Southeast Asian Nations (ASEAN), the United States wanted Japan to be more international in its approach by allowing for countries outside the region such as India and Australia to join, whereas China's strategy has been a regional one.[26]

Economic Crisis

There were essentially four economic features which lent themselves to facilitating the stagnation of the Japanese economy after 1990.[27] Firstly, there was the higher Yen syndrome. This arose through the Plaza Accord[28] which facilitated the appreciation of the Yen making Japanese exports expensive and imports cheaper, creating an environment suitable to generating negative trade balances. The Plaza Accord of 1985 was essentially a macroeconomic level agreement under which the currencies of Germany and Japan were objectively allowed to increase in value relative to the value of the US dollar.[29] The need for the Plaza accord arose because of the

[23] Volpe, T. (2017), The Unravelling of North Korea's Proliferation Blackmail Strategy, IN North Korea and Nuclear Weapons: Entering the New Era of Deterrence, Kim, S., and Cohen, M. (Eds), Georgetown University Press, Washington, DC.

[24] Ibid.

[25] Hickey, D. (2013) U.S. Policy Toward Taiwan: Time For Change?, Asian Affairs: An American Review, Vol. 40, No. 4, pp. 175–198, DOI: 10.1080/00927678.2013.847747

[26] Rozman, G. (2008), Internationalism and Asianism in Japanese Strategic Thought from Meiji to Hesei, Japanese Journal of Political Science, Vol. 9, No. 2, pp. 209–232.

[27] Wakatabe, M. (2015), Japan's Great Stagnation and Abenomics: Lessons for the World, Palgrave Macmillan, New York.

[28] Ibid.

[29] Holroyd, C. (2002), International Trade, and Laissez-Faire Capitalism, Canada, Australia, and New Zealand's Relations with Japan, McGill-Queen's University Press, Montreal.

American's argument that the Japanese trade surplus with the United States was essential because the value of the Yen was undervalued in comparison to the US dollar.[30] In the contemporary world a similar situation exists with regard to the size of the US–China trade balance which has been in China's favour for a few years. This has led to a trade war between the two countries, with the Trump administration first imposing tariffs on Chinese exports to the United States. In retaliation, the Chinese then imposed tariffs on US exports to China with negotiations between the two sides to remedy the ongoing situation. However, as with Japan, the United States also asserts that China is manipulating its currency in order to undervalue it, giving Chinese exports a competitive advantage over American goods. In this case, during the period 1994 to 2005, China pegged the value of the Yuan to the US dollar at 8.3.[31] The People's Bank of China (PBC) would then buy or sell either US dollars or dollar-denominated deposits in order to maintain the desired value of the Yuan to the US dollar. Under this fixed exchange rate regime, it is clear to see that there is the possibility that the Yuan–US dollar value could have been undervalued by as much as 40%.[32] As a result, America's products would be too expensive, America would suffer a trade deficit with China and America's unemployment rate will have increased.[33] On the other hand, the Chinese counter the American argument by citing the need to maintain economic stability with a managed currency.[34] However, maintaining an undervalued currency and building up a surplus of foreign reserves necessitate the use of monetary policy to control inflationary pressures in the economy.[35] But the problem is that overtime, this may cause imbalances in the Chinese economy.[36] In July 2005, the fixed exchange rate regime was abandoned by the PBOC and replaced by a 'managed float' regime.[37] This involved free market forces in the determination of the

[30] Ibid.

[31] Salitan, C. (2010), China's Currency Regime: The Perceived Threat to the US Economy, International Affairs Review, Vol. XIX, No. 1.

[32] Sanford, J. (2006), China's Currency: US Options, IN China's Currency and Economic Issues, Morrison, W., Labonte, M., and Sanford, J. (Eds), Novinka Books, New York.

[33] Ibid.

[34] Ibid.

[35] Ibid.

[36] Ibid.

[37] Ibid.

value of the currency alongside state intervention to reduce volatility.[38] Nevertheless, despite the move to a managed economy, it was still felt that China was undervaluing its currency to give its exports a competitive advantage. A further change to China's exchange rate regime occurred in August 2015 when the PBOC announced that the exchange rate would be determined by market forces.[39] However, to all intents and purposes, this was still a 'managed float' in which case the RMB–Dollar exchange rate was allowed to move within a 2% trading band around a rate which had been set by the PBOC on each morning.[40] However, in the case of the Plaza Accord of 1985, the strengthening Yen did cause a recession in Japan until late 1986.[41] So in the short term the impact on the Japanese economy was negative. But in the long term, there were two effects at play which ensured that despite the doubling of the value of the Yen compared to the US dollar between 1985 and 1987, the visible impact on Japan's trade balance with the United States was not noticeable.[42] The first effect was that the Yen increased in value, and Japanese imports of raw materials became cheaper by as much as 50% in value.[43] The second effect was because Japanese firms were willing to operate at either minimal profit levels or even to suffer losses in order to maintain market share.[44] This was possible because Japanese firms knew that they could rely upon financial assistance from the Japanese government.[45] This was particularly beneficial to the Japanese economy as Japan did not have the natural resources to power an industrial economy.[46] Secondly, the policies towards dealing with the asset price bubble were not able to mitigate the problem. In order to mitigate the negative effects of the appreciation of the Yen, the government and the BoJ then instigated policies which facilitated asset price

[38] Ibid.

[39] Prasad, E. (2017), Gaining Currency: The Rise of the Renminbi, Oxford University Press, Oxford.

[40] Ibid.

[41] Holroyd, C. (2002), International Trade, and Laissez-Faire Capitalism, Canada, Australia, and New Zealand's Relations with Japan, McGill-Queen's University Press, Montreal.

[42] Ibid.

[43] Ibid.

[44] Ibid.

[45] Ibid.

[46] Nafziger, E. (2006), Economic Development, Fourth Edition, Cambridge University Press, NY, USA.

inflation.[47] Thirdly, in the face of economic volatility, macroeconomic policies remained uncoordinated. Lastly, asset price deflation should have been met with an expansionary monetary policy but was instead met with deregulation and liberalisation.[48] As the Japanese economy moved out of recession in late 1986, following the implementation of the 1985 Plaza Accord, the economy began to expand over the subsequent years such that by mid-1990, a bubble economy had emerged.[49] In the process there had been substantial increases in capital spending by firms as well as in increase in consumption expenditure by households, financed by cheap borrowing. The features of the bubble economy were particularly visible in the over pricing of real estate and stock.[50] These were being used as collateral for loans from banks such as Sumitomo, Fuji and the Industrial Bank of Japan in order to buy more real estate.[51]

The Nikkei hit a peak average of Yen 38,915 in the last session of trading on 29 December 1989.[52] Nevertheless, the first symptoms of economic crisis began with the crash of the Nikkei Stock Exchange in 1990.[53] This began the bursting of the stock market and the real estate bubble leading to a wave of bad debts for firms as well as corporate in individual bankruptcies.[54] By October 1990, the Nikkei average had fallen to below Yen 20,000.[55] And in March 1990, the Ministry of Finance implemented a regulation regarding the control of the size of the volume of loans to financial institutions.[56] It was this new regulation which is widely perceived as the single biggest reason for the land price collapse in Japan and the

[47] Wakatabe, M. (2015), Japan's Great Stagnation and Abenomics: Lessons for the World, Palgrave Macmillan, New York.

[48] Ibid.

[49] Holroyd, C. (2002), International Trade, and Laissez-Faire Capitalism, Canada, Australia, and New Zealand's Relations with Japan, McGill-Queen's University Press, Montreal.

[50] Ibid.

[51] Ibid.

[52] Komine, T. (2018), A Retrospective View of the Heisei Economy, Asia-Pacific Review, Vol. 25, No. 1, pp. 19–37, DOI: 10.1080/13439006.2018.1475705

[53] Carroll. M. (2018), Production, reproduction, and crisis in Heisei Japan, The Japanese Political Economy, DOI: 10.1080/2329194X.2018.1466180

[54] Holroyd, C. (2002), International Trade, and Laissez-Faire Capitalism, Canada, Australia, and New Zealand's Relations with Japan, McGill-Queen's University Press, Montreal.

[55] Komine, T. (2018) A Retrospective View of the Heisei Economy, Asia-Pacific Review, Vol. 25, No. 1, pp. 19–37, DOI: 10.1080/13439006.2018.1475705

[56] Ibid.

prime cause of the bad debt problems of Japanese financial institutions.[57] This in turn led to a monetary contraction in the Japanese economy which denigrated the efficiency of financial intermediation between financial institutions and the real economy.[58] The bursting of the stock market and real estate bubble in 1990 led to over twenty years of economic stagnation during which the holy grails of Japanese company practice such as life time employment came to an end, replaced by a more flexible labour market.[59] The economic and social costs of Japan's economic stagnation have been very high.[60] For the next twenty years, the inflation-adjusted rate of annual economic growth was only 1.1%, lower by 1.4% in comparison to the inflation-adjusted economic growth rate of the United States.[61] Economically, Japan's public debt is at a level which is an all-time high.[62] Socially, Japan's population is shrinking at an alarming level as fewer and fewer babies are being born as both men and women turn away from the traditional life cycle associated with a nuclear family.[63] Japan's falling birth rate has created labour shortages. This has necessitated both women to fill labour shortages as well as carrying on with their traditional gender-biased roles of being mothers and bringing up children in order to reduce the fall in birth rates.[64]

Japan's post-war economic miracle began in an unsettled economic, political and social environment after Japan's surrender to the United States and its allies in 1945. However, as the economy progressed through the 1950s, the export-oriented economy began to take off as economic growth took hold. The take-off of Japan's economy in the 1950s can be

[57] Ibid.

[58] Hamada, K. (2003), The Heisei Recession: An Overview, The ESRI International Forum, The Social and Economic Research Institute, Cabinet Office of Japan.

[59] Osawa, M., Kim, M and Kingston, J. (2013), Precarious work in Japan, American Behavioral Scientist, Vol. 57, No. 3, pp. 309–334.

[60] Carroll. M. (2018), Production, reproduction, and crisis in Heisei Japan, The Japanese Political Economy, DOI: 10.1080/2329194X.2018.1466180

[61] Lincoln, E. (2011), The Heisei Economy: Puzzles, Problems, Prospects, The Journal of Japanese Studies, Vol. 37, No. 2, pp. 351–375.

[62] Carroll. M. (2018), Production, Reproduction, and Crisis in Heisei Japan, The Japanese Political Economy, DOI: 10.1080/2329194X.2018.1466180

[63] Nemoto, K. (2008), Postponed Marriage: Exploring Women's Views of Matrimony and Work in Japan, Gender and Society, Vol. 22, No. 2, pp. 219–37.

[64] Kawai, Y (2009), Neoliberalism, Nationalism, and Intercultural Communication: A Critical Analysis of Japan's Neoliberal Nationalism Discourse Under Globalization, Journal of International and Intercultural Communication, Vol. 2, No. 1, pp. 16–43.

associated with a partnership between stable and consistent government over a period of time by the Liberal Democratic Party, the Ministry of International Trade and Industry (MITI) and the way in which firms were organised in the Japanese economy through the Keiretsu.[65] This tripartite partnership facilitated the double-digit growth of the Japanese economy in the late 1950s and in the 1960s, although this had slowed to an economic growth rate of 4% in the 1970s and the 1980s.[66] However, relative to world economic growth during these years, the economic growth rate experienced by the Japanese economy was the best.[67] The reason for this was that the Japanese corporate system was flexible enough to adapt to the volatile and changing global economic environment.[68] In this case, while avoiding large scale layoffs, Japanese firms nevertheless reduced labour costs by terminating the positions of part-time workers and temporary female workers.[69] But at the same time the profits of Japanese firms were falling while the Japanese government was using contractionary monetary and fiscal policy in order to contain inflation.[70] In a country such as the United Kingdom, entrenched trade union practice would have meant that workers had to be kept on for fear of industrial action. Nevertheless, at the heart of post-war Japanese expansion was high level of profitability and economic growth which resulted from the combination of imported advanced technology with relatively low-cost labour.[71] However, the economic and institutional model from which the high levels of economic growth occurred was no match for the global economy of the 1990s and beyond. In this case, there were a number of structural and institutional flaws with Japan's post-1990 economic model.[72] Firstly, financial intermediation was mainly through the banks rather than through the stock and the bond markets. There was also a lack of competition in the banking sector which was effectively protected by the government. The close

[65] Carroll. M. (2018), Production, Reproduction, and Crisis in Heisei Japan, The Japanese Political Economy, DOI: 10.1080/2329194X.2018.1466180

[66] Itoh, M. (2000), The Japanese Economy Reconsidered, Houndmills, Basingstoke, UK.

[67] Shibata, T. (1998), An Evolutionary Interpretation of the Japanese Depression in the 1990's, Journal of Economic Issues, Vol. 32, No. 2, pp. 411–418.

[68] Ibid.

[69] Ibid.

[70] Ibid.

[71] Lincoln, E. (2011), The Heisei Economy: Puzzles, Problems, Prospects, The Journal of Japanese Studies, Vol. 37, No. 2, pp. 351–375.

[72] Ibid.

association between financial institutions and the Ministry of Finance ensured that there was a lack of government oversight regarding the efficacy of bank lending. Moreover, government would grant loans to firms from government-controlled banks, and this would be a signal to other commercial banks to also lend to these firms.[73] Firms also lacked accountability to shareholders as well as a lack of oversight by them. In this case, firms would increase investment in capital expenditure leading to overcapacity and a decrease in their profitability.[74] The labour market was also inflexible as workers enjoyed the security of knowing that they had a job for life, denigrating the motivation to be productive. Firms were also protected from competition in an oligopolistic market structure by regulations preventing the entry into the market of new firms. Lack of competition and the vertical integration of firms through Keiretsu allowed for the costs of production of Japanese firms to rise.[75] The lack of a competitive market for high tech start-up firms also contributed to established manufacturing firms losing global market share because of the lack of the diffusion of technological innovation in the Japanese economy. To some extent the economic system was plagued by moral hazard as both firms and financial institutions knew that whatever actions they took, they could always rely upon government support.

In the case of Japan, economic growth continued until the Plaza Accord of 1985 after which the Japanese economy went into recession, not picking up growth until towards the end of 1986.[76] In fact the period between December 1986 and January 1991 was known as the 'Hesei Boom' in which firms increased investment in fixed capital and households increased consumption expenditure.[77] In contrast to the other economic booms of post-war Japan, the 'Hesei Boom' was the second longest after the 'Izanagi Boom'.[78] The latter occurred between October 1965 and July 1970.[79] Although the 'Hesei Boom' was facilitated by increased fixed capital investment and increased consumption expenditure by 1992, both had

[73] Ibid.

[74] Ibid.

[75] Ibid.

[76] Shibata, T. (1998), An Evolutionary Interpretation of the Japanese Depression in the 1990's, Journal of Economic Issues, Vol. 32, No. 2, pp. 411–418.

[77] Ibid.

[78] Ibid.

[79] Bird, A. (2002), Encyclopedia of Japanese Business and Management, Routledge, London.

begun to decline.[80] Both declines could be attributed to the bursting of the stock market bubble and the real estate bubble. The decline in fixed capital investment by firms would have occurred due to a decline in the under usage of existing fixed capital as well as a decline in firms' profit/sales ratio.[81] The decline in consumption expenditure on durable goods, which became negative in 1992, occurred due to decline in the growth rate of household income as well as a decline in household wealth due to the bursting of the property and equity bubble.[82] To make matters worse the Japanese government followed a contractionary fiscal policy in 1997 in order to reduce the budget deficit by increasing sales tax from 3% to 5% and terminating a personal tax income allowance.[83] Both strands of policy had the effect of decreasing consumption expenditure further by making goods more expensive and reducing available disposable income to spend. The overseas demand for Japanese goods also became negative after 1993.[84]

Japan's pattern of economic growth has been very similar to that experienced by the Chinese economy. In fact between 1978 and 2000, the average economic growth rate of the Chinese economy was 9.7%; between 2000 and 2010, it was 10.5%; and between 2010 and 2016, it was 7.7%.[85] Over the same period, China's average yearly population growth rate also began to decline.[86] Between 1978 and 2000, China's average yearly population growth rate was 1.3%; between 2000 and 2010, it was 0.6%; and between 2010 and 2016, it had fallen to 0.5%.[87] This pattern of decline in China's economic growth rate and its population growth rate bears a historical resemblance to the fall in Japan's economic growth rate and the fall in its population growth rate in the seventy-three years following the end of World War 2. While this tripartite partnership may have facilitated the resurgence of the post-war Japanese economy, it may also have acted as a constraint to the remodelling of the Japanese economy in the years of

[80] Shibata, T. (1998), An Evolutionary Interpretation of the Japanese Depression in the 1990's, Journal of Economic Issues, Vol. 32, No. 2, pp. 411–418.

[81] Ibid.

[82] Ibid.

[83] Ibid.

[84] Higuchi, Y. (1997), Trends in Japanese Labour Markets, IN Japanese Labour and Management in Transition, Sako, M., and Sato, H. (1997), Routledge, London.

[85] China Statistical Yearbook 2017, China Statistical Press, http://www.stats.gov.cn/tjsj/ndsj/2017/indexeh.htm

[86] Ibid.

[87] Ibid.

economic stagnation following the post-1989 economic crisis.[88] In this case, economic stagnation may have resulted because of an imbalance between its productive economy and its social reproduction.[89] But the policies required to facilitate the re-emergence of capital accumulation are quite different from those required to stimulate social reproduction.[90] However, this did not prevent Japanese politicians from trying to bring about change. This was associated with both domestic market reform as well as Japan's interactions with the global economy. At the domestic level, in order to improve financial intermediation in the Japanese economy, a number of reforms were facilitated.[91] In 1996, legal and regulatory measures were introduced to better integrate Japan's stock and bond market with the role of the banking sector and to promote Tokyo as an international financial centre.[92] And in 1998, oversight of the Japanese financial institutions was taken away from the Ministry of Finance and placed in the hands of a new Financial Services Agency.[93] And sixteen large financial institutions were merged into four, disrupting the traditional horizontal lineage of firms and financial institutions.[94] At the start of the Heisei Period, the first of these policies was the Takeshita Doctrine which spanned from 1987 to 1996.[95] The Takeshita Doctrine had a number of Macroeconomic aspects.[96] These included, firstly, more macroeconomic policy co-ordination with the United States, Western European countries and Canada. Secondly, a focus on expanding domestic Japanese demand at a target GNP growth rate of 4%. Thirdly, structural changes to the Japanese

[88] Ibid.

[89] Miura, M. (2012), Welfare through Work: Conservative Ideas, Partisan Dynamics, and Social Protection in Japan. Cornell University Press, New York.

[90] Carroll. M. (2018), Production, reproduction, and crisis in Heisei Japan, The Japanese Political Economy, DOI: 10.1080/2329194X.2018.1466180

[91] Lincoln, E. (2011), The Heisei Economy: Puzzles, Problems, Prospects, The Journal of Japanese Studies, Vol. 37, No. 2, pp. 351–375.

[92] Shirai, S. (2009), Promoting Tokyo as an International Financial Centre,' IN Competition among Financial Centres in Asia Pacific, Young, S., Choi, D., Seande, J., and Shirai, S. (Eds), (Singapore: Institute of Southeast Asian Studies.

[93] Lincoln, E. (2011), The Heisei Economy: Puzzles, Problems, Prospects, The Journal of Japanese Studies, Vol. 37, No. 2, pp. 351–375.

[94] Ibid.

[95] Sudo, S. (2003), Evolution of ASEAN-Japan Relations, Flipside Digital Content Company Inc.

[96] Pringsheim, K. (1989), The Takeshita Doctrine and the advent of the Hesei Era, American Foreign Policy Newsletter, Vol. 12, No. 1, pp. 1–10.

economy which would facilitate a reduction in the export surplus. Fourthly, Japan should contribute positively to global prosperity by making better use of the finances arising from its trade surpluses. Fifthly, Japan would advance debt reducing policies to African countries. Lastly, the 1988 fiscal year defence expenditure would increase by 5.2% so that Japan could pay its contribution towards the cost of keeping the US military on Japanese soil. Nevertheless, as a result of a political crisis, Prime Minister Takeshita was forced to resign in April 1989, before the commencement of the Heisei Period. Furthermore, between 1987 and 1991, the period encompassing a phase of economic growth following the Plaza Accord and the beginning of the stagnation of the Japanese economy, Japan had four Prime Ministers. The political instability could have resulted in the mismanagement of the economy, and politicians not being able to spot and effectively deal with the symptoms of the emerging economic crisis. However, despite the political instability the Takeshita Doctrine seemed to have prevailed until 1996, when in 1997 it was supplanted by the Hashimoto Doctrine which itself lasted until 2003.[97] The Hashimoto Doctrine was international in orientation with a focus on recognising the Association of Southeast Asian Nations (ASEAN) as an equal partner and on encouraging greater exchanges between the private sectors of Japan and ASEAN.[98] Moreover, there were also to be cultural exchanges between Japan and ASEAN as well as greater co-operation between the two countries in international forums associated with counter-terrorism, drug trafficking, climate change as well as food security.[99] Nonetheless, Prime Minister Hashimoto did not only develop policies for Japan's international role. In this case, Hashimoto instigated the Heisei Reforms which would continue under successive Prime Ministers from Obuchi to Koizumi.[100] The Heisei Reforms were intended to improve the efficiency and productivity of the Japanese economy through reforms associated with the disclosure of information, the management of firms and the equality of the sexes in the work place. The objective of the reforms associated with improving the disclosure of information was associated with elevating the levels of

[97] Sudo, S. (2003), Evolution of ASEAN-Japan Relations, Flipside Digital Content Company Inc.

[98] Hashimoto, R. (1997), Reforms for the New Era of Japan and ASEAN: For a Broader and a Deeper Partnership, Institute of Southeast Asian Studies, Singapore.

[99] Ibid.

[100] Rose, C. (2006), The Battle for Hearts and Minds; Patriotic Education in Japan in the 1990's and Beyond, IN Nationalism in Japan, Shimazu, N. (Ed), Routledge, London.

accountability and transparency.[101] Furthermore, the part of the Heisei Reforms associated with the management of the firms focused on better protecting shareholders' interests as opposed to the interests of institutional investors and employees as it had been.[102] The third aspect of the Heisei Reforms focused on gender equality in the work place so that women could join the work force in order to compensate for the decline in the number of workers due to the rapidly ageing population.[103]

The Japanese Ministry of Finance and the Japanese government have also been taking action to try and mitigate the bad debt problems of Japanese financial institutions.[104] This involved the establishment of a new financial structure to mitigate bank failures as well as the instigation of a mechanism to recapitalise banks with bad debts, in October 1998.[105] However, it would seem that the practices of Japanese banks could be more transparent then they actually are.[106] Nonetheless, the other major problems associated with the Japanese economy are the high levels of bureaucracy and regulation, which have a tendency to reduce productivity, innovation and entrepreneurship in the economy.[107] This kind of high-level deregulation of the Japanese economy is essential because it has been recognised that despite the productivity of Japan's export sector, the overall productivity of the Japanese economy tends to be low in comparison.[108] Increasing the productivity of the Japanese economy as a whole is important at a time when the population is ageing rapidly and more workers are required to support those who have retired. Nevertheless, despite the productivity of Japan's export sector, it is itself burdened with low profit margins and over capacity. In an entrepreneurial economy, this would not exist. It is therefore clear that while Japan's economy has been

[101] Uga, K. (2007). Development of the Concepts of Transparency, and Accountability in Japanese Administrative Law' IN Law in Japan: A Turning Point, Foote, D. (Ed), University of Washington Press.

[102] Okuno-Fujiwara, M.(1999), Japan's Present-Day Economic System: Its Structure and Potential for Reform, IN The Japanese Economic System and Its Historical Origins, Okazaki, T., and Okuno-Fujiwara, M. (Eds), Oxford University Press, Oxford.

[103] Osawa, M. (2000), Government Approaches to Gender Equality in the Mid-1990s, Social Science Japan Journal, Vol. 3, pp. 3–5.

[104] Gilpin, R. (2002), The Challenge of Global Capitalism: The World Economy in the 21st Century, Princeton University Press, Princeton.

[105] Ibid.

[106] Ibid.

[107] Ibid.

[108] Ibid.

over-regulated to maintain the social harmony of the nation, the result has been that innovation and entrepreneurship are being stifled.[109] Furthermore, too many regulations result in a lack of incentives for initiative, low worker productivity in non-export-oriented sectors of the economy as well as the inefficient allocation of capital and labour in general.[110] In this case, introducing free market reforms to deregulate the Japanese economy would allow for the more efficient allocation of labour and capital and increases in productivity through greater entrepreneurship.[111] But nonetheless, the kind of deregulation required to kick-start the Japanese economy may not happen because this may threaten the wealth, the privilege and the positions of those who hold the reins of political and corporate power. In this case, it is necessary to wonder whether Japan has entered the late stage of economic development whereby the political system has not been resilient and robust enough to facilitate a dynamic economic which is in tune with both its external and internal environments. So perhaps, like Britain, Japan is at a late stage of economic development where economic growth rates are at low levels, and the economy is no longer seen to be dynamic.[112] However, two decades of economic stagnation did result in a shift from the thinking that rural areas should depend for their economic development on the central government to a line of thinking which necessitated the idea that the actions of local government were more important to local development.[113] In order to cut costs, services were rationalised through the merger of rural municipalities, but this also led to a loss of local identity.[114] The transition from a state-led development philosophy to a neoliberal agenda in Japan meant that between 2000 and 2010, the number of municipalities fell from 3000 to 1800.[115] However, in Japan's modern history, the Heisei Period municipal mergers

[109] Gilpin, R. (2002), The Challenge of Global Capitalism: The World Economy in the 21st Century, Princeton University Press, Princeton.

[110] Ibid.

[111] Ibid.

[112] Karan, P. (2005), Japan in the 21st Century, Environment, Economy and Society, The University Press of Kentucky.

[113] Rausch, A. (2009), Japanese Revitalization: The Reality and Potential of Cultural Commodities as Local Brands, Japanstudien, Vol. 20, No. 1, pp. 223–245, DOI:10.1080/09386491.2009.11826981

[114] Rausch, A. (2014), Japan's Heisei Municipal Mergers and the Contradictions of Neoliberal Administrative Planning, Asia Pacific Journal of Public Administration, Vol. 36, No. 2, pp. 135–149, DOI: 10.1080/23276665.2014.911490

[115] Ibid.

were the third such mergers. In this case, the first series of mergers occurred after the Meiji Restoration between 1888 and 1889.[116] During this period 71,314 settlements were merged into 15,859 cities, towns and villages.[117] The second phase of mergers occurred in the period 1953 to 1956 when 9868 cities, towns and villages were merged to form 4668 municipalities.[118]

The evidence that the Japanese economy still has not recovered from the economic stagnation which began in 1989 is clear and incontrovertible. Even in January 2019, the annualised rate of economic growth for the last three months of 2018 was only 1.8%.[119] In addition to the low rates of economic growth experienced by the Japanese economy, the government is expected to increase Japan's consumption tax from 8% to 10% in order to finance increasing social costs associated with an ageing population.[120] Nevertheless, in January 2019, Japan's industrial production had fallen by 3.7% on a year-on-year basis, while retail sales had only increased by 0.6% on the same basis.[121] This is in contrast to retail sales growth of 1.3% in December 2018 and 0.5% lower than the level of growth which had been forecast.[122] These economic data are evidence for the fact that if the Japanese government goes ahead with increasing consumption tax in October 2019, this may again send the Japanese economy into recession. This is the same policy mistake which the Japanese government made in the 1990s, that by increasing the rate of the consumption tax and effectively decreasing income tax thresholds, consumer expenditure was negatively affected. So, the chances are high of the Japanese economy going

[116] Rausch, A. (2012), A Framework for Japan's New Municipal Reality: Assessing the Heisei Gappei Mergers, Japan Forum, Vol. 24, No. 2, pp. 185–204, DOI: 10.1080/09555803.2012.671845

[117] Ibid.

[118] Ibid.

[119] White, E., and Harding, R. (2019), Japan's economy returns to growth despite trade worries, The Financial Times, https://www.ft.com/content/80fc68ea-2fe7-11e9-8744-e7016697f225

[120] Kyodo Staff Report. (2018), Abe Says He's Going Ahead with Japan's Consumption Tax Hike in October 2019, https://www.japantimes.co.jp/news/2018/10/15/business/economy-business/abe-says-hes-going-ahead-japans-consumption-tax-hike-october-2019/#.XIVzlUx2uUl

[121] Woodhouse, A. (2019), Japan industrial production records largest fall in a year, The Financial Times, https://www.ft.com/content/092e4fac-3af2-11e9-b72b-2c7f526ca5d0

[122] Ibid.

into recession after October 2019 if the government goes ahead with the increase in the rate of the consumption tax.

Japan, China and Globalisation

Over the last thirty to forty years, the economies of countries have become more and more connected through increased trade and technological innovations associated with travel, shipping and telecommunications. In this case, the economic and political institutions of countries had to be dynamic and flexible in embracing the global environment in order to allow economies to thrive and prosper. Early scholarly works on the Political Economy of Japan, in particular institutional stability, investigated the linkages and co-operation between the economic actors of the Japanese economy which had facilitated Japan's 'co-ordinated market economy', CME.[123] The CME had facilitated the double-digit growth of the Japanese economy in the 1950s and the 1960s.[124] And although economic growth continued into the 1970s and the 1980s, it was not at lower levels in comparison to the 1950s and the 1960s.[125] However, with the development of a world order, with neoliberalism as its foundation, towards the beginning of the 1990s, the Japanese CME was no longer the best institutional structure to deliver prosperity and economic growth for Japan. In other words, while the CME had been fine tuned to function effectively in an environment which fostered control, co-operation and incremental change, it could no longer do so in a neoliberal global environment in which innovation, competition and market openness were the ingredients which would accommodate economic success.[126] Therefore, in order to bring about institutional change in the Japanese economy which would facilitate economic growth and prosperity in the new global environment, some public policy reforms were started in the 1990s as well as in the twenty-first century.[127] However, even though Japanese politicians and business leaders recognised that labour market inflexibility, market access, distortions in the financial system and dense linkages between firms were making the Japanese economy less competitive compared to the US

[123] Suzuki, M. (2016), Globalisation and the Politics of Institutional Reform in Japan, Edward Elgar Publishing Limited, Cheltenham, UK.

[124] Ibid.

[125] Ibid.

[126] Ibid.

[127] Ibid.

economy, which was more competitive, there was little mood for change. Therefore, instead of shifting the Japanese economy from CME to the US competitive model, existing institutions were either reinforced or modified instead of being replaced.[128]

Government reforms were associated with the postal service, the labour market and the financial system.[129] The reforms in the labour market were intended to lower firms' labour costs by allowing for more labour market flexibility. However, while this may be the perception with the rise of temping and the end of life-time employment, the opposite was the case. This is because the Japanese government's overall strategy encompassed the goal of preserving employment rather than making it easier for firms to sack workers.[130] In this case, the Japanese government would boost spending on public works projects in outlying areas so that small businesses and construction companies would be protected from the adverse economic climate.[131] Moreover, the government also made slow progress with labour market deregulation because it was seen that non-competitive practices would allow for job protection which would not have happened with the market competition that deregulation would bring specifically to protected sectors such as retail and distribution.[132] Nevertheless, there was some easing of labour standards.[133] This included the passing of the Temporary Worker Law of 1999 which abolished restrictions on the occupations which could be staffed by temporary workers.[134] Furthermore, in order to protect small businesses, the government did not put in place measures to ensure that the non-performing loans held by banks should be liquidated.[135] This evidences the fact that both the Japanese government and

[128] Gronning, T. (1998), Whither the Japanese Employment System? The Position of the Japan Employers Federation, Industrial Relations Journal, Vol. 29, pp. 295–303.

[129] Suzuki, M. (2016), Globalisation and the Politics of Institutional Reform in Japan, Edward Elgar Publishing Limited, Cheltenham, UK.

[130] Vogel, S. (2006), Japan Remodeled: How Government and Industry are Reforming Japanese Capitalism, Cornell University Press, Ithaca and London.

[131] Ibid.

[132] Vogel, S. (2006), Japan Remodeled: How Government and Industry are Reforming Japanese Capitalism, Cornell University Press, Ithaca, London.

[133] Ibid.

[134] Weathers, C.(2004), Temporary Workers, Women and Labour Policymaking in Japan, Japan Forum, Vol. 16, No. 3, pp. 423–447, DOI: 10.1080/0955580042000257918

[135] Vogel, S. (2006), Japan Remodeled: How Government and Industry are Reforming Japanese Capitalism, Cornell University Press, Ithaca and London.

Japanese financial institutions did not fully embrace market forces.[136] The reforms in the financial system were meant to allow for better financial intermediation between financial institutions and the commercial sector so that savings could be more efficiently translated into investments in the real economy. To this end there was a liberalisation of financial flows.[137] Japan's economic malaise may have been caused by the misallocation of capital to industries and sectors of the economy which were not competitive in the global context. In this case, the traditional means of allocation of capital to industries was through the bank associated with that industry. This was due to the Keiretsu form of industrial organisation in post-war Japan. Traditionally, industries in Japan had been selected for capital allocation and government support based on an analysis by MITI using a criteria reflecting technological innovation, comparative advantage and increasing returns to scale.[138] On the other hand, industries which were seen to be in decline and experiencing decreasing returns to scale were to be deprived of government support.[139] However, the problem is that it is not so clear cut as to how the analysis carried out by MITI would have been able to recognise long-term trends in successful technologies and which industries this would encompass in a dynamic and fluid global market environment.[140] The identification of an industry which would not be globally competitive in the long term would mean that capital and government support would be misallocated. Therefore, it is important that the allocation of capital and government support should not be based on institutionalised government bureaucracy but in the context of free market forces. Moreover, the allocation of capital through the Keiretsu-based industrial structure in which banks are associated with specific industries also leads to the inefficient allocation of capital. An efficient allocation of capital occurs when international and domestic investors decide to invest in a venture based on the criterion that investment in the venture will deliver the highest rate of return in the future.[141] The marketisation of

[136] Malcolm, J. (2001), Financial Globalisation and the Opening of the Japanese Economy, RoutledgeCurzon, Abingdon, Oxon, UK.

[137] Vogel, S. (2006), Japan Remodeled: How Government and Industry are Reforming Japanese Capitalism, Cornell University Press, Ithaca, London.

[138] Beason, D., and Patterson, D. (2004), The Japan That Never Was: Explaining the Rise and Decline of a Misunderstood Country, State of New York Press, Albany.

[139] Ibid.

[140] Ibid.

[141] Cerny, P. (2001), Financial Globalisation and the Unravelling of the Japanese Model, IN The Political Economy of Japanese Globalisation, Hook, G., and Hasegawa, H. (Eds),

finance in Japan would allow for the efficient allocation of capital especially in industries which are experiencing rapid and dynamic technological change.[142] This would be difficult to achieve if capital was allocated on a mechanism associated with state planning and a Keiretsu-based industrial structure.[143] However, it may be the case that due to the traditional nature of the state–industry relationship that the Japanese economy may have evolved into a hybrid structure with one part of the economy populated by export competitive industries and the other part populated by declining industries which cannot compete globally, and thus acting as a weight on the entire Japanese economy.[144] Nevertheless, the Japanese economy should be seen as being split in three ways—the competitive export industries, the protected industries and the emerging high tech industries.[145] In the case of the latter, it has been more of a case of providing support for a specific sector of the economy rather than as an industrial policy.[146] Moreover, government expenditure has focused not only on the development of ongoing basic research but also on the award of patents for commercial applications.[147] Furthermore, the government has also provided for the preferential tax treatment of expenditure by the private sector on research.[148] However, Japanese government support for the development of high technology industries is not something that is a recent phenomenon.[149] In this case, it was government support for high technology industries which facilitated the development of the Tomioka Silk Reeling plant in the Meiji Period and the manufacture of Dynamic Random Access Memory (DRAM) silicone semi-conductors in the 1970s following its

Routledge, London.

[142] Ibid.

[143] Cerny, P. (2001), Financial Globalisation and the Unravelling of the Japanese Model, IN The Political Economy of Japanese Globalisation, Hook, G., and Hasegawa, H. (Eds), Routledge, London.

[144] Katz, R. (1998) The System that Soured: Toward a New Paradigm to Guide Japan Policy, Washington Quarterly, Vol. 21, No. 4, pp. 43–78, DOI: 10.1080/01636609809550350

[145] Cerny, P. (2001), Financial Globalisation and the Unravelling of the Japanese Model, IN The Political Economy of Japanese Globalisation, Hook, G., and Hasegawa, H. (Eds), Routledge, London.

[146] Flath, D. (2014), The Japanese Economy, Third Edition, Oxford University Press, Oxford.

[147] Ibid.

[148] Ibid.

[149] Ibid.

invention in America by Intel in 1970.[150] Other reforms focused on experimentation with economic policy in order to revive the economy, lowering interest rates and changing public spending levels and tax levels, a revision of corporate law and the pension system, bank finance rejuvenation and the privatisation of public corporations.[151] On the other hand, Japanese firms focused on corporate governance reforms, updating logistics, attaining a lean corporate structure and sourcing finance from the stock market rather than through the traditional bank method.[152] At the same time, the Japanese government also reorganised itself.[153] However, because of stakeholder interest and the rent seeking behaviour of Japanese politicians, these reforms could not be implemented without difficulty.[154] Moreover, the post-war emphasis on government ministries extending their bureaucratic control over specific sectors of the Japanese economy has become so pervasive and rooted in Japan's political economy that the necessary structural, economic and social required to reinvigorate Japan's economic performance cannot be implemented thoroughly.[155] This is also in the context of the current economic problems which the Japanese economy faces having survived the collapse of the bubble economy, which was followed by negative economic growth rates and deflation.[156] These current economic problems can be associated with a lack of domestic demand, a dependence on exports, the increased vulnerability of the Japanese economy to external shocks in the global economy and decline in the growth potential of firms due to lack of historical investment.[157] In order to revitalise the Japanese economy, the incoming government of Shinzo Abe, in 2013, instigated an economic programme which was termed Abenomics. The latter emphasised an ultra-loose monetary policy to facilitate a target inflation rate of 2% accompanied by rising wages levels,[158] the establishment of Free Trade

[150] Ibid.

[151] Vogel, S. (2006), Japan Remodeled: How Government and Industry are Reforming Japanese Capitalism, Cornell University Press, Ithaca and London.

[152] Ibid.

[153] Ibid.

[154] Ibid.

[155] Carpenter, S. (2016), Why Japan Can't Reform: Inside the System, Palgrave Macmillan.

[156] Aramaki, K. (2019), Japan's Long Stagnation, Deflation and Abenomics: Mechanisms and Lessons, Palgrave Macmillan.

[157] Ibid.

[158] Yoshida, R. (2019), Abenomics Under Heavy Fire after Dodgy Data Hid Apparent Drop in Wages Across Japan in 2018, The Japan Times, https://www.japantimes.co.jp/

Agreements[159] and the promotion of inward-bound Foreign Direct Investment.[160] However, the rate of inflation in Japan was barely above 0% in March 2019,[161] and growth in wage levels remained questionable.[162] With regard to the share of Japanese trade encompassing Free Trade Agreements (FTA), this is expected to rise from 19% in 2013 to 70% in 2018.[163] Contextually, the recent successes of a liberalising Japan under Prime Minister Shinzo Abe include the EU-Japan Free Trade Agreement as well as the Trans-Pacific Partnership Free Trade Agreement.[164] On the other hand, the structural reform component of Abenomics associated with increasing inward-bound Foreign Direct Investment seems to have been less successful due to the bureaucratic and regulatory nature of the Japanese economy which makes it costly for foreign firms to do business with Japan.[165]

Conclusion

Japan's high level of economic growth in the 1950s and in the 1960s was based, as was the case of the rise of the contemporary Chinese economy post 1978, on a combination of the use of imported advanced technology and the abundant availability of low cost labour. Moreover, the co-ordinated market economy featuring intervention in the economy by government departments such as MITI to support industry and the structuring

news/2019/02/06/national/politics-diplomacy/abenomics-heavy-fire-dodgy-data-hid-apparent-drop-wages-across-japan-2018/#.XI1UbHd2vb0

[159] Solis, M., and Urata, S. (2018), Abenomics and Japan's Trade Policy in a New Era, Asian Economic Policy Review, Vol. 13, pp. 106–123.

[160] Hoshi, T. (2018), Has Abenomics Succeeded in Raising Japan's Inward Foreign Direct Investment, Asian Economic Policy Review, Vol. 13, No. 1, pp. 149–168.

[161] Bloomberg. (2019), Japan Inflation Barometer Points to Zero Price Growth by Summer, Weighed Down by Oil and Phones, https://www.japantimes.co.jp/news/2019/03/04/business/economy-business/flat-line-japan-inflation-barometer-points-zero-price-growth-summer/#.XI1Ya3d2vb0

[162] Yoshida, R. (2019), Abenomics Under Heavy Fire after Dodgy Data Hid Apparent Drop in Wages Across Japan in 2018, The Japan Times, https://www.japantimes.co.jp/news/2019/02/06/national/politics-diplomacy/abenomics-heavy-fire-dodgy-data-hid-apparent-drop-wages-across-japan-2018/#.XI1UbHd2vb0

[163] Solis, M., and Urata, S. (2018), Abenomics and Japan's Trade Policy in a New Era, Asian Economic Policy Review, Vol. 13, pp. 106–123.

[164] Porter, S. (2018), A Whole New World for Free Trade? https://www.bbc.co.uk/news/business-46601315

[165] Hoshi, T. (2018), Has Abenomics Succeeded in Raising Japan's Inward Foreign Direct Investment, Asian Economic Policy Review, Vol. 13, No. 1, pp. 149–168.

of industries through Keiretsu allowed for an efficient allocation of resources. The American defence of Japan also ensured that state financial resources could be diverted to industry rather than to military expenditure. Furthermore, there was a diffusion of technology from America to Japan whose industries became technologically advanced manufacturers due to government support. The global economic environment between 1945 and the early 1970s was also conducive to supporting Japan's export-led growth. This was because Keynesian economic ideology, that of supporting aggregate demand, was in favour in the post-war global economies. As western governments supported domestic aggregate demand, this served as a source of demand for Japanese products. However, after the mid-1970s, inflation and unemployment were on the rise, while economic growth was falling. The world economy had encountered stagflation, and governmental economic ideology in the west began to shift away from Keynes and Monetarism. This also marked a shift towards neoliberal, Washington Consensus set of policies which embraced free trade, private property rights, low levels of inflation, little government intervention in the economy and fiscal responsibility. However, neoliberalism was at odds with the function of the Japanese economy which was heavily regulated, relatively closed, featuring high levels of government intervention with industries structured in an oligopoly fashion and, therefore, lacking competition. By the late 1980s, the Japanese economy was no longer competitive in the context of a growing neoliberal global economic environment. Moreover, while in the 1950s and the 1960s Japanese economic growth had been double digits, by the 1970s and the 1980s economic growth had fallen to single figures. Furthermore, while Japan was able to reduce its budget deficit in the early 1980s, this was only because the Americans were increasing their budget deficit.[166] But by the end of the 1980s as America began to reduce its budget deficit, Japan's budget deficit began to grow.[167] At the same time, Japan was also running a very big trade surplus with America by sending it goods and capital.[168] In order to address American concerns regarding its trade imbalance with Japan, the G5 group of countries agreed to a managed decline in value of the US dollar

[166] Katz, R. (1998), Japan, The System That Soured, The Rise and Fall of the Japanese Economic Miracle, M.E Sharpe, London, UK.

[167] Ibid.

[168] Ibid.

as well as an appreciation of the Japanese Yen.[169] As the Japanese Yen appreciated over the short term, this led to a fall in Japanese exports, causing the Japanese economy to go into recession.[170] In order to stimulate the economy, the Japanese government introduced a huge spending package and the BoJ reduced its lending rates to a historic low of 2.5%.[171] The lowering of interest rates in Japan led to an increase in the uptake of loans for stock market and real estate investment.[172] As a result there was a surge in stock market valuations and real estate prices. In this case, between 1985 and 1989, the Nikkei 225 stock market index grew at an annualised rate of 31% reaching a peak of 39,000 on the last day of trading in December 1989.[173] Similarly, between 1985 and 1989, housing loan values doubled in size from Yen 12,800 billion to Yen 28,990 billion.[174] And land became an important part of Japanese companies' assets, and as land prices went up, so did stock prices.[175] However, by May 1989, the Bank of Japan decided to end the era of easy money which had lasted for nearly ten years and started to follow a contractionary monetary policy.[176] Between May 1989 and August 1990, the Bank of Japan had increased the discount rate by five times leaving it at a level higher than it was in 1985 at the time of the Plaza Accord.[177] At the same time, the Japanese Ministry of Finance constrained land transactions by introducing laws and regulations.[178] The effect of this was to restrict the supply of land such that it could not so straight forwardly be sold. So, nearly two decades after the stock market and real estate bubble bursting in 1990–1991, the value of house prices in

[169] Iyoda, M. (2010), Post-war Japanese Economy: Lessons of Economic Growth and the Bubble Economy, Springer.

[170] Ibid.

[171] Ibid.

[172] Ibid.

[173] Kahkonen, J. (1985), Movements in Asset Prices Since the Mid-1980's, IN Saving Behaviour and the Asset Price Bubble in Japan, Analytical Studies, Baumgartner, U., et al. (Eds), Occasional Paper 124, International Monetary Fund.

[174] Renaud, B., Kim, K., and Cho, M. (2016), Dynamics of Housing in East Asia, John Wiley & Sons, Chichester, West Sussex, UK.

[175] Ibid.

[176] Jinushi, T., Kuroki, Y., and Miyao, R. (2000), Monetary Policy in Japan Since the Late 1980's: Delayed Policy Actions and Some Explanations, IN Japan's Financial Crisis and its Parallels to U.S. Experience, Mikitani, R., and Posen, A. (Eds), Special Report 13, Institute for International Economics, Washington, DC.

[177] Ibid.

[178] Ibid.

Japan had fallen by nearly 60% in real terms, whereas the value of household debt had not.[179] In the years that followed 1990, the Japanese economy experienced stagnation and deflation, and even after this economic growth has been moribund. The contemporary explanation for Japan's economic malaise is that its economy has fallen into a liquidity trap in which case the interest rate has fallen so low that it can fall no more so people would prefer to hold cash rather than borrow.[180] However, empirical and theoretical analysis indicates that the stagnation of the Japanese economy is due to a vertical Investment-Savings (IS) curve, with regard to the IS-LM model.[181] This suggests that the interest rate is no longer able to affect any economic variable which implies that national output is independent of the interest rate. Therefore, a vertical IS curve implies that Japan's three decades of economic malaise have been due to the structural features of the economy rather than a conventional economic downturn.[182] These structural features would be associated with a rapidly ageing population, the dependence of regional governments on central government funding and the unwillingness of Japanese banks to lend to Japanese SMEs and MSEs due to the Basel capital requirements.[183]

In order to confront Japan's structural challenges and to lead the Japanese economy into sustained growth, the government has progressed with facilitating Free Trade Agreements with other countries and promoting more foreign investment in Japan. This has been accompanied by a loose monetary policy. But despite government policies and in the wake of Covid-19, the Japanese economy remains struggling to rebound to its pre-1989 robustness. And even in 2018, the Japanese economy only grew in real terms by 0.7%, although this was a consistent increase in the economy's real growth over several years.[184]

[179] Renaud, B., Kim, K., and Cho, M. (2016), Dynamics of Housing in East Asia, John Wiley & Sons, Chichester, West Sussex, UK.

[180] Yoshino, N., and Taghizadeh-Hesary, F. (2017), Japan's Lost Decade: Causes and Remedies, IN Japan's Lost Decade: Lessons for Asian Economies, Yoshino, N., and Taghizadeh-Hesary, F. (Eds), Springer, Singapore.

[181] Ibid.

[182] Ibid.

[183] Ibid.

[184] Japan Times. (2019), Japan's Economy Shows Modest Rebound in October-December Quarter, https://www.japantimes.co.jp/news/2019/02/14/business/economy-business/japanese-economy-rebounded-modestly-October-December-quarter/#.XI6qr7inzb0

References

Aramaki, K. (2019), Japan's Long Stagnation, Deflation and Abenomics: Mechanisms and Lessons, Palgrave Macmillan.

Beason, D., and Patterson, D. (2004), The Japan That Never Was: Explaining the Rise and Decline of a Misunderstood Country, State of New York Press, Albany.

Bird, A. (2002), Encyclopedia of Japanese Business and Management, Routledge, London.

Bloomberg (2019), Japan Inflation Barometer Points to Zero Price Growth by Summer, Weighed Down by Oil and Phones, https://www.japantimes.co.jp/news/2019/03/04/business/economy-business/flat-line-japan-inflation-barometer-points-zero-price-growth-summer/#.XI1Ya3d2vb0

Carpenter, S. (2016), Why Japan Can't Reform: Inside the System, Palgrave Macmillan.

Carroll, M. (2018), Production, Reproduction, and Crisis in Heisei Japan, The Japanese Political Economy, DOI: https://doi.org/10.1080/2329194X.2018.1466180.

Cerny, P. (2001), Financial Globalisation and the Unravelling of the Japanese Model, IN The Political Economy of Japanese Globalisation, Hook, G., and Hasegawa, H. (Eds), Routledge, London.

China Statistical Yearbook 2017, China Statistical Press, http://www.stats.gov.cn/tjsj/ndsj/2017/indexeh.htm

Dunscomb, P. (2018), The Reign of Emperor Akihito 1989–2019: A History in Five Words, Education About Asia, Vol. 23, No. 3.

Flath, D. (2014), The Japanese Economy, Third Edition, Oxford University Press, Oxford.

Fuess, H. (2004), Divorce in Japan: Family, Gender, and the State, 1600–2000, Stanford University Press, Stanford, California.

Gill T. (1994), Sanya Street Life Under the Heisei Recession, Japan Quarterly, Vol. 41, pp. 270–286.

Gilpin, R. (2002), The Challenge of Global Capitalism: The World Economy in the 21st Century, Princeton University Press, Princeton.

Gronning, T. (1998), Whither the Japanese Employment System? The Position of the Japan Employers Federation, Industrial Relations Journal, Vol. 29, pp. 295–303.

Hamada, K. (2003), The Heisei Recession: An Overview, The ESRI International Forum, The Social and Economic Research Institute, Cabinet Office of Japan.

Hashimoto, R. (1997), Reforms for the New Era of Japan and ASEAN: For a Broader and a Deeper Partnership, Institute of Southeast Asian Studies, Singapore.

Henshall, K.G. (2012) A Superpower Adrift: The Heisei Years. IN A History of Japan: From Stone Age to Superpower, Palgrave Macmillan, London.

Hickey, D. (2013), U.S. Policy Toward Taiwan: Time For Change?, Asian Affairs: An American Review, Vol. 40, No. 4, pp. 175–198, DOI: https://doi.org/10.1080/00927678.2013.847747

Higuchi, Y. (1997), Trends in Japanese Labour Markets, IN Japanese Labour and Management in Transition, Sako, M., and Sato, H. (Eds), Routledge, London.

Holroyd, C. (2002), International Trade, and Laissez-Faire Capitalism, Canada, Australia, and New Zealand's Relations with Japan, McGill-Queen's University Press, Montreal.

Hoshi, T. (2018), Has Abenomics Succeeded in Raising Japan's Inward Foreign Direct Investment, Asian Economic Policy Review, Vol. 13, No. 1, pp. 149–168.

Itoh, M. (2000), The Japanese Economy Reconsidered, Houndmills, Basingstoke, UK.

Iyoda, M. (2010), Post-war Japanese Economy: Lessons of Economic Growth and the Bubble Economy, Springer.

Japan Times. (2019), Japan's economy shows modest rebound in October-December quarter, https://www.japantimes.co.jp/news/2019/02/14/business/economy-business/japanese-economy-rebounded-modestly-october-december-quarter/#.XI6qr7inzb0

Jinushi, T., Kuroki, Y., and Miyao, R. (2000), Monetary Policy in Japan Since the Late 1980's: Delayed Policy Actions and Some Explanations, IN Japan's Financial Crisis and its Parallels to U.S. Experience, Mikitani, R., and Posen, A. (Eds), Special Report 13, Institute for International Economics, Washington, DC.

Kahkonen, J. (1985), Movements in Asset Prices Since the Mid-1980's, IN Saving Behaviour and the Asset Price Bubble in Japan, Analytical Studies, Baumgartner, U., et al (Eds), Occasional Paper 124, International Monetary Fund.

Karan, P. (2005), Japan in the 21st Century, Environment, Economy and Society, The University Press of Kentucky.

Katz, R. (1998a) The System that Soured: Toward a New Paradigm to Guide Japan Policy, Washington Quarterly, Vol. 21, No. 4, pp. 43–78, DOI: https://doi.org/10.1080/01636609809550350.

Katz, R. (1998b), Japan, The System That Soured, The Rise and Fall of the Japanese Economic Miracle, M.E Sharpe, London, UK.

Kawai, Y. (2009), Neoliberalism, Nationalism, and Intercultural Communication: A Critical Analysis of Japan's Neoliberal Nationalism Discourse Under Globalization, Journal of International and Intercultural Communication, Vol. 2, No. 1, pp. 16–43.

Kingston, J. (2013), Contemporary Japan: History, Politics and Social Change Since the 1980's, 2nd Edition, John Wiley & Sons, Chichester, West Sussex.

Komine, T. (2018), A Retrospective View of the Heisei Economy, Asia-Pacific Review, Vol. 25, No. 1, pp. 19–37, DOI: https://doi.org/10.1080/13439006.2018.1475705

Kyodo Staff Report. (2018), Abe Says He's Going Ahead with Japan's Consumption Tax Hike in October 2019, https://www.japantimes.co.jp/news/2018/10/15/business/economy-business/abe-says-hes-going-ahead-japans-consumption-tax-hike-october-2019/#.XIVzlUx2uUl

Lebra, T. (1997), Self and Other in Esteemed States: The Changing Culture of the Japanese Royalty from Showa to Hesei, The Journal of Japanese Studies, Vol. 23, No. 2, pp. 257–289.

Lincoln, E. (2011), The Heisei Economy: Puzzles, Problems, Prospects, The Journal of Japanese Studies, Vol. 37, No. 2, pp. 351–375.

Malcolm, J. (2001), Financial Globalisation and the Opening of the Japanese Economy, RoutledgeCurzon, Abingdon, Oxon, UK.

Miura, M. (2012), Welfare through Work: Conservative Ideas, Partisan Dynamics, and Social Protection in Japan, Cornell University Press, New York.

Morris-Suzuki, T. (1989), The meaning of Heisei, Japanese Studies, Vol. 9, No. 1, pp. 23–24, DOI: https://doi.org/10.1080/10371398908522088

Nafziger, E. (2006), Economic Development, Fourth Edition, Cambridge University Press, NY, USA.

Nemoto, K. (2008), Postponed Marriage: Exploring Women's Views of Matrimony and Work in Japan, Gender and Society, Vol. 22, No. 2, pp. 219–237.

Okuno-Fujiwara, M. (1999), Japan's Present-Day Economic System: Its Structure and Potential for Reform, IN The Japanese Economic System and Its Historical Origins, Okazaki, T., and Okuno-Fujiwara, M. (Eds), Oxford University Press, Oxford.

Osawa, M. (2000), Government Approaches to Gender Equality in the Mid-1990s, Social Science Japan Journal, Vol. 3, pp. 3–5.

Osawa, M., Kim, M., and Kingston, J. (2013), Precarious Work in Japan, American Behavioral Scientist, Vol. 57, No. 3, pp. 309–334.

Porter, S. (2018), A Whole New World for Free Trade?, https://www.bbc.co.uk/news/business-46601315

Prasad, E. (2017), Gaining Currency: The Rise of the Renminbi, Oxford University Press, Oxford.

Pringsheim, K. (1989), The Takeshita Doctrine and the Advent of the Hesei Era, American Foreign Policy Newsletter, Vol. 12, No. 1, pp. 1–10.

Rausch, A. (2009), Japanese Revitalization: The Reality and Potential of Cultural Commodities as Local Brands, Japanstudien, Vol. 20, No. 1, pp. 223–245, DOI: https://doi.org/10.1080/09386491.2009.11826981

Rausch, A. (2012), A Framework for Japan's New Municipal Reality: Assessing the Heisei Gappei Mergers, Japan Forum, Vol. 24, No. 2, pp. 185–204, DOI: https://doi.org/10.1080/09555803.2012.671845

Rausch, A. (2014), Japan's Heisei Municipal Mergers and the Contradictions of Neo-Liberal Administrative Planning, Asia Pacific Journal of Public

Administration, Vol. 36, No. 2, pp. 135–149, DOI: https://doi.org/10.1080/23276665.2014.911490.
Renaud, B., Kim, K., and Cho, M. (2016), Dynamics of Housing in East Asia, John Wiley & Sons, Chichester, West Sussex, UK.
Rose, C. (2006), The Battle for Hearts and Minds; Patriotic Education in Japan in the 1990's and Beyond, IN Nationalism in Japan, Shimazu, N. (Ed), Routledge, London.
Rozman, G. (2008), Internationalism and Asianism in Japanese Strategic Thought from Meiji to Hesei, Japanese Journal of Political Science, Vol. 9, No. 2, pp. 209–232.
Salitan, C. (2010), China's Currency Regime: The Perceived Threat to the US Economy, International Affairs Review, Vol. XIX, No. 1.
Sanford, J. (2006), China's Currency: US Options, IN China's Currency and Economic Issues, Morrison, W., Labonte, M., and Sanford, J. (Eds), Novinka Books, New York.
Shibata, T. (1998), An Evolutionary Interpretation of the Japanese Depression in the 1990's, Journal of Economic Issues, Vol. 32, No. 2, pp. 411–418.
Shirai, S. (2009), Promoting Tokyo as an International Financial Centre,' IN Competition among Financial Centres in Asia Pacific, Young, S., Choi, D., Seande, J., and Shirai, S. (Eds), Institute of Southeast Asian Studies, Singapore.
Solis, M., and Urata, S. (2018), Abenomics and Japan's Trade Policy in a New Era, Asian Economic Policy Review, Vol. 13, pp. 106–123.
Sudo, S. (2003), Evolution of ASEAN-Japan Relations, Flipside Digital Content Company Inc.
Suzuki, M. (2016), Globalisation and the Politics of Institutional Reform in Japan, Edward Elgar Publishing Limited, Cheltenham, UK.
Uga, K. (2007). Development of the Concepts of Transparency, and Accountability in Japanese Administrative Law' IN Law in Japan: A Turning Point, Foote, D. (Ed), University of Washington Press.
Vogel, S. (2006), Japan Remodeled: How Government and Industry are Reforming Japanese Capitalism, Cornell University Press, Ithaca, London.
Volpe, T. (2017), The Unravelling of North Korea's Proliferation Blackmail Strategy, IN North Korea and Nuclear Weapons: Entering the New Era of Deterrence, Kim, S., and Cohen, M. (Eds), Georgetown University Press, Washington, DC.
Wakatabe, M. (2015), Japan's Great Stagnation and Abenomics: Lessons for the World, Palgrave Macmillan, New York.
Weathers, C. (2004) Temporary workers, women and labour policymaking in Japan, Japan Forum, Vol. 16, No. 3, pp. 423–447, DOI: https://doi.org/10.1080/0955580042000257918

White, E., and Harding, R. (2019), Japan's Economy Returns to Growth Despite Trade Worries, The Financial Times, https://www.ft.com/content/80fc68ea-2fe7-11e9-8744-e7016697f225

Woodhouse, A. (2019), Japan Industrial Production Records Largest Fall in a Year, The Financial Times, https://www.ft.com/content/092e4fac-3af2-11e9-b72b-2c7f526ca5d0

Yoshida, R. (2019), Abenomics Under Heavy Fire after Dodgy Data Hid Apparent Drop in Wages across Japan in 2018, The Japan Times, https://www.japantimes.co.jp/news/2019/02/06/national/politics-diplomacy/abenomics-heavy-fire-dodgy-data-hid-apparent-drop-wages-across-japan-2018/#.XI1UbHd2vb0

Yoshino, N., and Taghizadeh-Hesary, F. (2017), Japan's Lost Decade: Causes and Remedies, IN Japan's Lost Decade: Lessons for Asian Economies, Yoshino, N., and Taghizadeh-Hesary, F. (Eds), Springer, Singapore.

CHAPTER 9

Conclusion: Lessons for Contemporary China

Ancient Japan was a primitive aboriginal society until 400 AD, due to its isolation from the Asian mainland. But the period 200 BC to 300 AD encompasses the time during which Japan's original aboriginal hunter-gatherer culture, the Jomon culture, transitioned to the Yoyoi culture. This transition was a technological transformation comparable to the Meiji period after 1868 when Japan began to emerge as an industrialised power. Before 712 AD there is no indigenous documentation of Japanese culture and history. However, documentation of pre-712 AD Japan was maintained by scholars of the imperial Chinese courts of the Han and the Wei dynasties. An embryonic Japanese state emerged from the fourth century AD to the eighth century AD. It was in the Nara period that the imperial court established the first permanent imperial capital at Nara, to the south of Kyoto.[1] It was a capital city which was modelled on the Chinese capital.[2] By the sixth century AD, under the hegemony of Prince Shotoku (592 AD to 628 AD), Buddhism diffused into Japan from China and was made the official state religion. In 604 AD, the Prince implemented constitutional government and political reform by publishing a seventeen-page constitution, which was based on Confucian thinking emphasising social harmony, moral and spiritual values. During Shotoku's period of governance, not only was there an inflow of knowledge about Buddhist and Confucian

[1] Ishibashi, K. (2004), Status of historical Seismology in Japan, Annals of Geophysics, Vol.47, No.2/3.

[2] Ibid.

S. Ramesh, *China's Economic Rise*,
https://doi.org/10.1007/978-3-030-49811-5_9

thinking from China to Japan but also Chinese written characters began to enter the Japanese language.

Agricultural techniques had developed during the Yoyoi Culture, the Kofun Period from 300 AD to 700 AD. This period also saw the increased use of iron tools in farming.[3] As a result agricultural productivity increased. This allowed for wealth accumulation, and more food meant that the population increased at the same time. As the population increased, there was more need for better social organisation. And, in this case the Taika Reforms were launched in 645 AD.[4] These reforms would, it was hoped, contribute to Japan becoming a centralised state in the mould of China.[5] In 701 AD a legal system known as the Ritsuryo, which encompassed both civil and criminal code, became established across the whole of Japan except for Hokkaido which had not yet become integral to Japanese territory.[6] Under the Ritsuryo, planning related to agriculture—rezoning of the size of paddy fields, the reclamation of paddy fields or changes to irrigation canals—was all under the control of the central government.[7] However, between 794 AD and 1192 AD as aristocrats and the temples began to own more land, the centrally administered Ritsuryo system began to weaken.[8] Landowners and farmers began to supply their own tools. They also reclaimed swampy land for agriculture at their own initiative. The supply of tools and the reclamation of land had been under the jurisdiction of the central government during the time in which the Ritsuryo legal system was in force.[9] As landowners and farmers became wealthy, they armed themselves and their followers. Over time, under their powerful leaders, these autonomous armed groups came to be known as Samurai.[10] And by the eighth century AD, the Yamato Clan had introduced elements of the indigenous animistic religion, Shintoism, into

[3] Ito, M., and Hiraizumi, K. (2008), Agriculture in Japan, IN Encyclopaedia of the History of Science, Technology, and Medicine in Non-Western Cultures, Selin, H.(ed), 2nd Edition, Springer.

[4] Ibid.

[5] Ibid.

[6] Ito, M., and Hiraizumi, K. (2008), Agriculture in Japan, IN Encyclopaedia of the History of Science, Technology, and Medicine in Non-Western Cultures, Selin, H.(ed), 2nd Edition, Springer.

[7] Ibid.

[8] Ibid.

[9] Ibid.

[10] Ibid.

Buddhism.[11] The Yamato chieftain, claiming descent from the Sun Goddess Amaterasu, became known as 'Emperor' and gave rise to the imperial line from which the current Japanese emperor is also drawn from.[12] So by the twelfth century, the two well-known 'institutions' of Japanese culture had become established, the Samurai and the Emperor.

The shift from the Heian Period to the Kamakura Period represented a major change in the dynamics of Japanese social and political organisation. In this case, this shift represented a shift from an aristocratic society to a feudalistic one with a greater military orientation. The political change was due to a move away from the centralisation of state power to decentralisation in which the Kamakura Bakufu devolved power to local regional war lords or Daimyos. The emergence of feudalism represented the social change in which Japan's society was now stratified into classes. In descending order, these classes included the samurai, the aristocrats, the clergy, the farmers, the peasants, the merchants and outcasts. Due to the fact that there was increasing monetisation, although the merchants were at the lowest level of the social order, they were responsible for facilitating economic activity by converting measured quantities of rice into coinage. In effect, the merchants were acting as the intermediary between the Bakufu, the Daimyo and the farmers. At the same time, the Japanese market was expanding due to increased trade with Japan. Market expansion and increasing monetisation of the economy required the regulation of economic activity through dispute resolution. In order to facilitate this, the Joei Code was implemented in 1232 AD. The Joei Code represented the first indigenous legal code.

The Kamakura Period came to an end in 1333. And once the Kamakura Bakufu had been defeated militarily, the government was transferred back to Kyoto in what became known as the short-lived Kemmu Restoration of 1333 to 1336.[13] However, this was followed by the establishment of two rival courts in the Nambokucho Era from 1336 to 1392 when one of the Emperor's generals rebelled. There then followed the ascendancy of the Ashikaga Shoguns from 1392 to 1568, in a period of stability for Japan in the Muromachi or Ashikaga Period.[14] The Muromachi Period in Japanese

[11] Ibid.

[12] Ibid.

[13] Shackley, M. (1986), Arms and the Men;14th Century Japanese Swordsmanship Illustrated by Skeletons fromZaimokuza, near Kamakura, Japan, World Archaeology, 18:2, pp.247–254.

[14] Ibid.

economic and political history was one in which there were social and political changes which contributed towards the development of institutions in Japan. It was during the early Muromachi Period in 1342 that the Gozan Josselsu System of monastery–temple organisation was firmly established. The Muromachi Period was at its height between 1368 and 1394 during the tenure of the Shogun Yoshimitsu who favoured Buddhism rather than Japan's indigenous Shinto religion. Yoshimitsu also achieved this by bringing together the governance structures and the institutions of the Bakufu and the imperial court. To some extent he achieved this by bringing court officials under his control. At the same time as bringing court officials under his control, Yoshimitsu also extended his power over the nobility by reducing their land holdings to a tenth of what they previously had, making them poorer. This would reduce the capacity of the nobility to wage war against the Bakufu by using their wealth to raise an army. However, following the death of Yoshimitsu in 1408, his son Yoshimochi undid much of his work by making appointments based on merit and tradition. This had the effect of separating the governance structures of the Bakufu and the Court. Nevertheless, the control of land by the nobility through the Shoen System began to decline through the fifteenth century. Such was the case that by the end of the fifteenth century, the nobility as Shoen proprietors of the land had given control of the land to local warriors on a contractual basis. The legal code was also extended during the Muromachi Period by supplementing the Joei Shikimoku from the Kamakura Period. One of the additions made to the Joei Shikimoku was the Kenmu Shikmoku by the Shogun Ashikaga Takauji. The demise of the Kamakura Shogunate lies with the costs which were required and incurred to defend Japan from the Mongols.

The three to four decades of instability during the Azuchi Momoyama Period was brought to an end in 1600 AD with the start of the Tokugawa period and the start of the longest period of stability and economic development in Japanese history. However, it was not until 1615 that Ieyasu was able to cement and consolidate his authority as Shogun, following the victory of his forces over those of the feudal lords at the Battle of Osaka. In the time period approaching the commencement of the Tokugawa period, European ships began arriving in Asia. These ships brought traders and missionaries. At this time the Shogunate was fearful of losing its control over Japan due to the influence of the foreigners. As a result, the Shogunate expelled all foreigners from Japan and closed its borders, starting a policy of isolationism which lasted for over 200 years. During the period of isolation from the rest of the world, Tokugawa Japan developed a number of distinct features. The first was the implementation of a social structure through which it was difficult but not impossible to move. In this case, the Tokugawa social structure in descending order was composed of the samurai, the peasants, the artisans and the merchants at the bottom. Secondly, it was in the Tokugawa period that the institutions and the structures of a market economy began to be laid. In this case, the Shogunate mandated that the families of the feudal lords or daimyos should reside in Edo where the Shogun was based. Moreover, the daimyo himself was mandated to stay in Edo for up to 6 months of the year, with the rest of the year spent in his domain. Edo became a generic 'castle town' in which samurais from rural areas were also expected to reside. The samurai depended on the Shogunate for their income. The castle town elite were becoming more and more urbanised and represented the primary consumers in Tokugawa Japan. Merchants were drawn to the castle towns, and a trading system developed between Edo, Osaka and Kyoto with Osaka at its centre. This was because it was in Osaka that coinage emerged. Due to increasing economic activity and trade, the merchants were becoming wealthier than the Samurai. However, the Samurai depended on the local Daimyo for income. And the local Daimyo collected tax from local farmers as a proportion of the rice harvest in their domains. But as such revenues were less than expenditures, the Daimyo's payments to the Samurais were falling. Consequentially, Samurais were becoming poorer. Thirdly, as a result of an increase in food production, there was a significant increase in Japan's population between 1600 AD and 1700 AD.

By the mid-nineteenth century, the European powers and America were again drawn to Japan for trade. However, Tokugawa Japan had been closed to trade with the outside world except with Korea and China for over 200 years.[15] And as a result, Japan had fallen behind militarily, technologically and economically. It was not in a position to defend itself from attack. And the Tokugawa Bakufu had to make unfavourable agreements with the Europeans and the Americans, to open the country to international trade, in order to merely keep the country's sovereignty. However, unfavourable trade agreements, the fear of European and/or American colonisation in the face of China's experience at the time, drove the lower

[15] Jansen, M. (1992), China in the Tokugawa World, Harvard University Press, Cambridge, Massachusetts.

Samurai to back the reformers who wanted an end to the Tokugawa Bakufu and the restoration of the authority of the Emperor over the country, in association with political, economic and technological modernisation. This became known as the Meiji Restoration of 1868. This encompassed a constitutional government with the Emperor at its head, an elected parliament, industrialisation and the development and strengthening of the country's Army and Navy. However, the policy direction of the country was very much dependent on public attitude and the power of the military, a nationalistic and military synergy, whose attractiveness and electability were determined by economic circumstance. In this case, economic crises which negatively impacted on Japanese society and people facilitated an increase in the support for nationalism which enhanced the role of the military in the governance of Japan. Moreover, Japanese industry was centred on the Zaibatsu with government support and the use of private capital. There was also a close relationship between the politicians and those who controlled Japanese industry, the Zaibatsu Oligarchs. At the same time, there was an increase in the income disparity between the rich and the poor. The military were drawn from the poor. As a result of the increased social divide and deprivation as the Japanese economy indus trialised and grew, the individualism and the respect for the democratic system which had been growing since the Meiji Restoration of 1868 became more and more threatened in the subsequent Taisho Period by the Japanese military. In other words, at times of severe economic crisis and distress, democracy is hijacked by the forces of the far right. The beliefs associated with this political spectrum delve deep into the dark side of humanity and into an evil with no matching parallel. But at the same time, through the Taisho Period increased industrial capacity and increasing industrial production resulted in an increased need for raw materials. As a result, Japan acquired Korea, Manchuria and Taiwan through military power and negotiation.

The Showa Period began in 1926 at a time of economic crisis in Japan which was doing nothing to address the widening disparities of income between the rural poor and the urban rich.

Economic crisis was a common feature of the Japanese economy in the few years before the start of the Showa period and for the first few years after it began. Politicians were seen as corrupt, because of their close association with the Zaibatsu Oligarchs, and ineffective in formulating effective long-term economic policies to reduce the income divide. The Japanese military's solution featured two strands. Firstly, to take control of governing Japan and turn it into a militaristic bureaucratic planned economy. And secondly, in doing so, prepare to challenge American and largely the European hegemony of Asia through military means. Once defeated, as the Chinese and the Russians had been, Japan could then negotiate with the Europeans on what parts of their Asian colonies Japan could keep in order to expand the market for its goods and in order to increase its hegemony. The result of this strategy was Japan's defeat in World War 2 by the allies and its subsequent defeat, surrender and occupation by the United States. After signing a peace treaty with the United States in the early 1950s and regaining its sovereignty, the Japanese economy then grew to become the second largest economy in the world after the United States towards the late 1980s.

Just as the Japanese economy was challenged as it went into recession in the early 1980s by an ascendant American neoliberal order, the same is true of China in 2019. There are also similarities between the economy of Japan in 1989–1990 and that of China in 2019–2020. Firstly, just as Japan's economy featured government intervention, regulation and bureaucracy, so does the Chinese economy. Secondly, just as easy money was made available in Japan following the appreciation of the Yen after the signing of the Plaza Accord by the G5 countries in 1985, credit was made readily available to state-owned enterprises in China following the aftermath of the global financial crisis of 2008. The results were essentially the same. In Japan from 1985 to 1989, the availability of cheap money led to excessive borrowing by investors for speculation in the stock market as well as in real estate. This led to a stock market bubble and a property bubble which 'popped' as the Bank of Japan decided to end a decade of cheap credit by easing up interest rates, incrementally a number of times, from May 1989 to August 1990. At the same time, the Japanese Ministry of Finance implemented laws and regulations which constrained the transfer/sale of land. Land featured heavily in the assets of firms, often serving as collateral for loans, and whose value was linked and rising in tandem to the value of the stock market. In the last day of trading in Japan in December 1989, the Nikkei 225 hit a peak of 39,000, and subsequently, the Nikkei 225 collapsed in value over the subsequent months and years. Similarly, in contemporary China following the global financial crisis of 2008, the Chinese government instigated a fiscal stimulus amounting to US$580 billion in November 2008. This stimulus was exercised by the Chinese government instructing the four state-owned banks to increase 'soft' lending to Chinese state-owned enterprises, particularly in the constructions sector. As a result, a bubble began to form in China's real estate sector and in its stock market. A third similarity between Japan after 1989 and contemporary China is that the population is ageing dramatically. This may lead to labour shortages which could impact on either the agricultural sector or the manufacturing sector. However, in contrast to Japan, the advantage for China is that its base population from which the decline is starting is much higher at over 1.3 billion people. A third similarity between Japan after 1989 and contemporary China is that local Chinese authorities were using land and shares in state-owned companies as collateral for loans.[16] Firms in Japan used land as collateral during the period 1989 to 1989. And as land was firms' assets, land prices and share prices rose in tandem. Similarly, when the Japanese stock market crashed in early 1990, both land prices and share prices crashed in tandem leading to prolonged and sustained economic stagnation. The fourth similarity between the Japan of the late 1980s and contemporary China is that in order to curtail the real estate bubble, property began to be regulated. In Japan, in the late 1980s, the Ministry of Finance implemented laws and regulations which constrained the transfer of property. And this in association with the increases in the discount rate implemented by the Bank of Japan burst the real estate bubble and the stock market bubble sending the Japanese economy into a prolonged stagnation. Similarly, cities in China began to regulate and legislate against the purchase and transfer of real estate in a bid to restrain speculation in the sector.[17] Tighter regulation began in China's big cities where real estate prices are high, but in 2018 medium and smaller cities followed with regulating the real estate market in order to control speculation and stabilise prices.[18] In this case, forty cities released fifty regulations in May 2018 alone.[19] The fifth similarity between the Japan of the late 1980s and contemporary China is that local government is very dependent on central government for fiscal sustenance through tax transfers. Local government in China was given a fixed share

[16] The Economist (2017), What a debt crisis in the provinces says about governing China, https://www.economist.com/china/2017/11/16/what-a-debt-crisis-in-the-provinces-says-about-governing-china

[17] Lingqing, Z. (2018), Shenzhen announces tighter property market regulation, http://www.chinadaily.com.cn/a/201808/01/WS5b61463ea31031a351e91735.html

[18] Xinhua (2018), Economy Watch: China sticks to tight property market regulation, http://www.xinhuanet.com/english/2018-06/12/c_137249459.htm

[19] Ibid.

of taxes on goods and on income in a 5:4 ratio, respectively.[20] However, while local government in China receives half of central government tax revenues, they are responsible for two-thirds of central government spending.[21] This inevitably acted as an incentive for local government to seek unorthodox sources of finance. And as a result, the 'Local Government Financing Vehicle' (LGFV) was created. The LGFV was a shadow unregulated investment company through which local government was able to acquire loans for infrastructure investment using state-owned land and shares in state-owned enterprises as collateral.[22] Moreover, the LGFVs were established as state-owned enterprises, which allowed them to benefit from a soft budget, in that borrowed money would not have to be paid back because central government would take care of it.[23] Furthermore, another advantage of registering the LGFVs as state-owned enterprises was that their valuations could be kept off balance sheet of local government finances and in effect hidden from central government regulatory review and control.[24] By 2013, the central government had become so concerned with LGFVs that it conducted an audit which revealed that there were over 10,000 LGFVs in China with a total borrowing of $1.1 trillion or 13% of Chinese GDP.[25] But by 2015, local government debt in China, most of which was accounted for by LGFV debts, amounted to 24% of GDP.[26] However, in order to control LGFVs in 2014, the central government ordered local governments to issue bonds and then used the money raised to refinance the LGFVs, with the process to be completed by 2018.[27] But, in addition the other purpose of the money raised through the issuance of these special bonds was to finance infrastructure projects and not pay for the general expenditure of local governments.[28] For 2018,

[20] The Economist (2017), What a debt crisis in the provinces says about governing China, https://www.economist.com/china/2017/11/16/what-a-debt-crisis-in-the-provinces-says-about-governing-china

[21] Ibid.

[22] The Economist (2017), What a debt crisis in the provinces says about governing China, https://www.economist.com/china/2017/11/16/what-a-debt-crisis-in-the-provinces-says-about-governing-china

[23] Ibid.

[24] Ibid.

[25] Ibid.

[26] Ibid.

[27] Ibid.

[28] Wildau, G., and Jia, Y. (2018), China floods debt market with new bond to boost infrastructure, https://www.ft.com/content/8e3e2dae-ba58-11e8-94b2-17176fbf93f5

the central government approved the issuance of these special purpose bonds equivalent in value to $197 billion.[29] The central bank also injected more monetary liquidity into the economy so that the sale of the special purpose bonds could be observed.[30] Nevertheless, the special bonds issued by local governments are unattractive to investors compared to other types of bonds because they have a lower yield.[31] Consequentially, local governments have put pressure on the banks, by only depositing money in the banks which purchase the bonds.[32]

In order to stop the dubious financing of local governments, the central government began to include borrowing decisions of local government officials in career profiles, the banning of questionable incentives to entice private investors as well as a new revenue-sharing scheme in the 2016 Five Year Plan.[33] And in order to increase the tax raising potential of local governments, a property tax was proposed in 2013.[34] However, local and central governments have not reached any fiscal transfer agreement, and the imposition of a property tax may cause the real estate market to crash.[35] But government efforts were not working in order to constrain local government borrowing as admitted by President Xi in July 2017 because China's financial and macroeconomic stability was being undermined by mounting local government debt.[36] It is also unlikely that if the LGFVs defaulted, then it is highly unlikely that local governments would be able to bail them out.[37] In addition to local government debt, the other type of debt which is a threat to China's financial and macroeconomic stability is the accumulated debt of state-owned enterprises.[38] In fact, Qinghai Provincial Investment Group, a state-owned company, defaulted on an

[29] Ibid.

[30] Ibid.

[31] Ibid.

[32] Ibid.

[33] The Economist (2017), What a debt crisis in the provinces says about governing China, https://www.economist.com/china/2017/11/16/what-a-debt-crisis-in-the-provinces-says-about-governing-china

[34] Ibid.

[35] Ibid.

[36] Ibid.

[37] Wildau, G., and Jia, Y. (2018), China floods debt market with new bond to boost infrastructure, https://www.ft.com/content/8e3e2dae-ba58-11e8-94b2-17176fbf93f5

[38] The Economist (2017), What a debt crisis in the provinces says about governing China, https://www.economist.com/china/2017/11/16/what-a-debt-crisis-in-the-provinces-says-about-governing-china

$11 million interest payment on a $300 million bond, the first in twenty years.[39]

In 2019, China's economic growth rate is tipped to fall to 6%, the lowest level for nearly thirty years.[40] However, even though the Chinese economy is growing, albeit not in double digits but in single-digit growth, there is growth inequality amongst China's provinces.[41] This may cause the resulting impact of economic growth on local government debt to vary from one region of the country to another. Moreover, at the end of 2017 China's debt as a percentage of its GDP was 260%.[42] At the same time China's trade deficit in future years will be either into small surpluses or even into deficits.[43] This is in contrast to the previous two and a half decades in which China's trade account featured significant surpluses.[44] However, as China transitions from a low-income country to a middle-income country and its economic growth model shifts from an investment, export led one to a domestic consumption-driven model, there has been a shift to greater imports such as soybeans, energy, aircraft and cars.[45] Moreover, China's services component of the trade balance was $230 billion for the first three quarters of 2018.[46] This represented the entire services deficit for 2016.[47] While China was running a trade surplus, the United States was able to benefit because Chinese investors were able to finance US debt by buying US government bonds and corporate bonds. In this case, in January 2019 China held the equivalent of $1.3 trillion of US government and corporate debt as well as US equities, real estate and

[39] Nin, G. (2019), A Chinese government-owned company just defaulted on its debt. It's a worrying sign for the country's economy, https://nordic.businessinsider.com/china-economy-qinghai-first-state-owned-firm-debt-default-since-1998-2019-2/

[40] Lockett, H. (2019), China GDP growth tipped to slow to 6% in Q1:State Paper, https://www.ft.com/content/3051cf8e-2d94-11e9-8744-e7016697f225

[41] Bloomberg (2018), China's Regional Growth Divergence Adds to Debt Policy Dilemma, https://www.bloomberg.com/news/articles/2018-08-09/china-s-regional-growth-divergence-adds-to-debt-policy-dilemma

[42] Bloomberg News (2019), China to Propose Wider 2019 Fiscal Deficit Amid Slowdown, https://www.bloomberg.com/news/articles/2019-01-09/china-is-said-to-propose-wider-2019-fiscal-deficit-amid-slowdown

[43] Campbell, B. (2019), China's appetite for US assets imperilled at worst possible time, https://www.ft.com/content/f2a386b8-495a-11e9-8b7f-d49067e0f50d

[44] Ibid.

[45] Ibid.

[46] Ibid.

[47] Ibid.

assets of a different nature.[48] However, as China's trade surplus begins to decline, Chinese investors will have less financial resources to invest in US debt and assets at a time when the level of US debt financing is growing.[49] In 2019, US treasury issuance will amount to anything between $1.3 trillion and $1.7 trillion, while US firms will need to roll over $700 billion in 2019.[50] The economic situation that the United States and China find themselves in today is similar to the US–Japan economic relationship prior to 1985 when Japan was running a trade surplus with the United States, and the United States was running a budget deficit as well as a trade deficit with Japan.[51] In an effort to reduce the trade deficit with Japan, the United States was going to launch protectionist measures against Japanese imports, just as it has been done with Chinese imports, unless Japan restructured its economy to make it more competitive. However, in order to mitigate this prospect, Japan took immediate steps to comply beginning with the Plaza Accord of 1985 by which it explicitly allowed the Yen to appreciate in value.[52] However, even though the US trade deficit began to decline after 1987,[53] Japan remained a relatively closed economy even until 2007.[54] But the advent of Abenomics in 2013 has ensured that Japan has embraced free trade since then implementing the TPP and EU–Japan free trade agreement in December 2018 and February 2019, respectively.[55] In the context of contemporary, US-Chinese economic and trade relations, both countries have imposed tariffs on each other's goods in an escalating trade war. In this case, just as in the early 1980s, the United States wanted Japan to restructure its economy to make it more competitive so that the United States would not suffer sustained trade deficits, similar demands are being placed on China by the United States in

[48] Ibid.

[49] Ibid.

[50] Ibid.

[51] Hiroshi, N. (2002), Japanese Relations with the US, IN The Golden Age of US, China-Japan Triangle, 1972-1989, Vogel, E., Ming, Y., and Akihiko, T. (Eds), Harvard University Press, Cambridge, Massachusetts.

[52] Hiroshi, N. (2002), Japanese Relations with the US, IN The Golden Age of US, China-Japan Triangle, 1972–1989, Vogel, E., Ming, Y., and Akihiko, T. (Eds), Harvard University Press, Cambridge, Massachusetts.

[53] Ibid.

[54] Lawrence, R. (2007), How Open is Japan? IN Trade with Japan Has the Door Opened Wider? Krugman, P. (Ed), University of Chicago Press, Chicago.

[55] Politi, J. (2019), Robert Lighthizer aims to tackle Japan as US farmers suffer, https://www.ft.com/content/f1ac531e-497a-11e9-8b7f-d49067e0f50d

contemporary times. The Trump administration wants China to prevent enforced transfers of US technology to Chinese firms, and it wants China to make its market more competitive by removing barriers to entries for US firms as well as stopping Chinese government subsidisation of Chinese firms.[56] The EU has also woken up to China's economic power, with countries like Italy joining the 'One Belt, One Road' Project,[57] in viewing the country not as a lucrative market for its goods, but as an economic threat.[58]

In order to stimulate the economy, the government has proposed lifting the budget deficit target to 2.8% for 2019, compared to 2.6% in 2018.[59] This follows a cut in the budget deficit from 3% to 2.6% from 2017 to 2018.[60] The cut in the budget deficit was made in an attempt to cut rising debt levels which had fuelled credit-led investment in the economy.[61] However, with the ongoing downturn in the economy, infrastructure investment needs a boost in order to maintain economic growth.[62] As central government is the key contributor of funds for infrastructure investment, there is a need for an increase in the budget deficit so that infrastructure investment recovery can take hold.[63] However, China's economic future depends on how much economic growth falls, the ability of central government to prevent/bailout local governments and state-owned enterprises defaulting on debt, and what will happen when the

[56] Politi, J., and Mitchell, T. (2019), US-China trade talks: What does the US want? https://www.ft.com/content/a747e98e-1f5c-11e9-b126-46fc3ad87c65

[57] Ghiglione, D., Sevastopulo, D., Peel, M., and Hornby, L. (2019), Italy Set to Formally Endorse China's Belt and Road Initiative, https://www.ft.com/content/17f91d24-3f60-11e9-b896-fe36ec32aece

[58] Peel, M., Hornby, L., and Sanderson, R. (2019), European Foreign Policy: A New Realism in China, https://www.ft.com/content/d7145792-4743-11e9-b168-96a37d002cd3

[59] Bloomberg News (2019), China to Propose Wider 2019 Fiscal Deficit Amid Slowdown, https://www.bloomberg.com/news/articles/2019-01-09/china-is-said-to-propose-wider-2019-fiscal-deficit-amid-slowdown

[60] Reuters (2018), China should tolerate bigger budget deficit in 2019 to boost economy: State media, https://www.reuters.com/article/us-china-economy-fiscal-policy/china-should-tolerate-bigger-budget-deficit-in-2019-to-boost-economy-state-media-idUSKBN1O60EC

[61] Reuters (2018), China should tolerate bigger budget deficit in 2019 to boost economy: State media, https://www.reuters.com/article/us-china-economy-fiscal-policy/china-should-tolerate-bigger-budget-deficit-in-2019-to-boost-economy-state-media-idUSKBN1O60EC

[62] Ibid.

[63] Ibid.

Renminbi is allowed to freely float. When this happens if the Renminbi appreciates in value, the Bank of China may have to cut interest rates. But this will make it easier for firms and households and speculators to borrow money and so risk a further escalation in the valuation of real estate and equities. If interest rates are then raised to cool these sectors, then the result may be that China's property bubble may burst and along with it equities, giving rise to colossal local government debt and state-owned company debt which will trigger Japanese style economic stagnation and deflation. The Covid-19 pandemic of 2020 may be the trigger of significant economic upheavals not only in China but throughout the world.

References

Bloomberg (2018), China's Regional Growth Divergence Adds to Debt Policy Dilemma, https://www.bloomberg.com/news/articles/2018-08-09/china-s-regional-growth-divergence-adds-to-debt-policy-dilemma

Bloomberg News (2019), China to Propose Wider 2019 Fiscal Deficit Amid Slowdown, https://www.bloomberg.com/news/articles/2019-01-09/china-is-said-to-propose-wider-2019-fiscal-deficit-amid-slowdown.

Campbell, B. (2019), China's appetite for US assets imperilled at worst possible time, https://www.ft.com/content/f2a386b8-495a-11e9-8b7f-d49067e0f50d

Ghiglione, D., Sevastopulo, D., Peel, M., and Hornby, L. (2019), Italy Set to Formally Endorse China's Belt and Road Initiative, https://www.ft.com/content/17f91d24-3f60-11e9-b896-fe36ec32aece

Hiroshi, N. (2002), Japanese Relations with the US, IN The Golden Age of US, China-Japan Triangle, 1972–1989, Vogel, E., Ming, Y., and Akihiko, T. (Eds), Harvard University Press, Cambridge, Massachusetts.

Ishibashi, K. (2004), Status of historical Seismology in Japan, Annals of Geophysics, Vol.47, No.2/3.

Ito, M., and Hiraizumi, K. (2008), Agriculture in Japan, IN Encyclopaedia of the History of Science, Technology, and Medicine in Non-Western Cultures, Selin, H.(ed), 2nd Edition, Springer.

Jansen, M. (1992), China in the Tokugawa World, Harvard University Press, Cambridge, Massachusetts

Lawrence, R. (2007), How Open is Japan? IN Trade with Japan Has the Door Opened Wider? Krugman, P. (Ed), University of Chicago Press, Chicago.

Lingqing, Z. (2018), Shenzhen announces tighter property market regulation, http://www.chinadaily.com.cn/a/201808/01/WS5b61463ea31031a351e91735.html

Lockett, H. (2019), China GDP growth tipped to slow to 6% in Q1:State Paper, https://www.ft.com/content/3051cf8c-2d94-11e9-8744-e7016697f225

Nin, G. (2019), A Chinese government-owned company just defaulted on its debt. It's a worrying sign for the country's economy, https://nordic.businessinsider.com/china-economy-qinghai-first-state-owned-firm-debt-default-since-1998-2019-2/

Peel, M., Hornby, L., and Sanderson, R. (2019), European Foreign Policy: A New Realism in China, https://www.ft.com/content/d7145792-4743-11e9-b168-96a37d002cd3

Politi, J. (2019), Robert Lighthizer aims to tackle Japan as US farmers suffer, https://www.ft.com/content/f1ac531e-497a-11e9-8b7f-d49067e0f50d

Politi, J., and Mitchell, T. (2019), US-China trade talks: What does the US want? https://www.ft.com/content/a747e98e-1f5c-11e9-b126-46fc3ad87c65

Reuters (2018), China should tolerate bigger budget deficit in 2019 to boost economy: State media, https://www.reuters.com/article/us-china-economy-fiscal-policy/china-should-tolerate-bigger-budget-deficit-in-2019-to-boost-economy-state-media-idUSKBN1O60EC.

Shackley, M. (1986), Arms and the Men; fourteenth Century Japanese Swordsmanship Illustrated by Skeletons from Zaimokuza, near Kamakura, Japan, World Archaeology, 18:2, pp.247–254.

The Economist (2017), What a debt crisis in the provinces says about governing China, https://www.economist.com/china/2017/11/16/what-a-debt-crisis-in-the-provinces-says-about-governing-china

Xinhua (2018), Economy Watch: China sticks to tight property market regulation, http://www.xinhuanet.com/english/2018-06/12/c_137249459.htm

INDEX[1]

NUMBERS AND SYMBOLS
57AD, 1, 26
700AD, 1
1868, ix, x, xv–xvii, 18n145, 21, 25, 44n80, 45n82, 64, 79n74, 80n79, 101–131, 135–167, 135n1, 138n26, 147n92, 148n94, 149n106, 151n114, 152n129, 183n84, 185n108, 186, 197, 198n198, 198n201, 201–203, 212, 215n31, 217n46, 218, 223n88, 224n99, 281, 286
1978, ix, xv, xvii, 7n49, 11n88, 87n141, 150, 156, 159, 162, 176, 197, 213, 218, 261, 272
1989, xix, 127n199, 190n144, 211–246, 214n18, 238n201, 251–276, 251n2, 252n7, 252n9, 252n12, 262n96, 287, 292n51, 292n52

A
Abe, Shinzo, 271, 275
Abenomics, 213n13, 254n27, 257n47, 271, 271n156, 271n158, 272n159, 272n160, 272n162, 272n163, 272n165, 275, 275n184–186, 276n188, 292
Action Plan, 157
Agreement by Osachi, 177
Akihito, Emperor, 230, 251, 252n7, 252n9, 252n12
Akiie, Kitabatake, 71
Ainu, 25, 45, 149
Altaic, 10
Amami Gunto islands, 44
Amami Islands, 44
Amaterasu, 11, 11n88, 16, 27, 28, 283
Amida, 56, 73, 74n27
Amidist Sect, 56
Anti-Kodo-ha faction, 221

[1] Note: Page numbers followed by 'n' refer to notes.

S. Ramesh, *China's Economic Rise*,
https://doi.org/10.1007/978-3-030-49811-5

Antoku, Emperor, 43
Araki Sadao, War Minister, 221, 222
Aritomo, Field Marshal Yamagata, 189
ASEAN, 254, 262n95, 263, 263n97, 263n98
Ashikaga Period, 62, 67, 283
Asia, 1n5, 2, 2n10, 3n13, 3n17, 3n20, 4n23, 5n35, 5n37, 6n46, 10n73, 12, 13n102, 14n112, 15n116, 18n147, 19n153, 41n53, 47n106, 48n110, 48n111, 52n150, 56n186, 56n187, 58, 58n200, 60n214, 60n219, 60n222, 64n252, 75, 75n41, 95, 101, 105, 106, 108, 113n80, 114, 135n4, 136n6, 137n17, 138n22, 139, 139n29, 155n145, 163n209, 174n7, 174n8, 174n11, 175, 186n116, 189n133, 190, 190n141, 190n144, 193, 200n216, 201, 204, 204n229, 212, 229n129, 230, 230n140, 233, 234n170, 235, 252n7, 252n9, 252n12, 257n52, 257n55, 262n92, 265n114, 274n174, 275n179, 284, 287
Asuka Period, 17–19
Atsugi Air Base, 230, 231
Australia, xix, 4, 104, 204n229, 254, 254n29, 256n41, 257n49, 257n54
Austronesian, 10
Axis Treaty, 212
Azuchi-Momoyama Period, 71–97

B

Bakufu, x, xviii, 36, 37, 42, 45, 47, 49, 51, 54, 60, 62, 64–66, 65n255, 73, 75, 76n46, 77–79, 77n57, 82, 83n113, 87, 91, 93, 94, 202, 283, 285
Banking crisis of 1927, 177
Bank of Taiwan, 215
Battle of Dannoura, 36, 43–45
Battle of Mukden, 175, 201
Battle of Osaka, 109, 129
Battle of Pyokchegwan, 90
Battle of Sekigahara, 108, 128
Battle of Shijo Nawate, 74
Battle of Tsushima, 175, 201
Big 10 Bankers, 118
Black Stream, 12
Board of Enquiry, 54, 84
Bodhisattva, 56, 73
BoJ, 214, 215, 256, 274
British, xi, 102, 136, 163, 164, 194, 216
British East India Company, 164
British Empire, xi, 204, 216, 244
British Territories, 164
Buddhism, 15, 17, 18, 22, 27, 28, 54, 54n170, 55n174, 62n240, 72n6, 73n25, 74, 74n27, 76, 80, 81, 93, 94, 108, 179, 281, 283, 284
Bugyonin, 53
Bushi Code, 83
Bushido, 40n42, 46, 46n93
Buwakebayashi, 121

C

Caesar, Julius, 26
Caroline, 188
Ceylon, vii
Chengliang, General Li, 89
Chengxun, General Zhao, 89
Ch'I dynasty, 80
Chieftains, 1, 2, 45, 109, 158
Child poverty, xiv, xivn21, xx
Ch'in, 39, 40
China, ix, x, xii, xiv, xvii, xviiin28, xviiin29, xix, xx, 2, 3, 8, 9, 12, 14, 17–20, 18n143, 22, 25–27, 26n205, 26n206, 39, 39n32,

39n35, 40n37, 44, 47, 47n106, 48, 51, 52n150, 55–64, 56n188, 57n190, 57n192, 57n194, 58n195, 58n197–199, 59n204, 59n208, 59n211, 66, 75, 76, 80, 84, 86n138, 87, 87n150, 89n164, 89n166, 89n167, 91, 94, 95, 95n199, 95n203, 96n210, 97, 103, 103n8, 104, 104n9, 105n20, 108, 109, 110n61, 112, 112n75, 116, 120, 124, 128, 129, 129n208, 136, 140, 147, 150, 156, 156n158, 156n159, 157n162, 159, 159n188, 160n189, 160n190, 162, 162n205, 162n206, 163, 163n208, 163n209, 166, 166n223, 166n225, 166n227, 166n228, 167n231, 167n235, 173, 174n8, 176, 187, 189, 190, 192, 194, 196, 201–203, 205n231, 206, 211, 212, 213n14, 218, 218n55, 220, 225, 226, 233, 235, 239, 244, 252, 253, 255, 255n31, 255n32, 261, 261n85, 267–272, 281, 282, 285, 285n15, 287, 288n16, 288n18, 289n20, 289n22, 289n28, 290, 290n33, 290n37, 290n38, 291, 291n40–43, 292n51, 292n52, 293, 293n56–61, xiiin10–12
China FDI, 197
China's Lessons for India, ix, 162n205, 162n206
Chinese Classics, 211
Chinese-Japanese War, 173
Chou China, 39
Christianity, 113, 113n89, 114, 130, 165, 179
Chubu, 7
Chu-chien, Ching-sou, 62
Codified legal system, 117
College Entrance Examination, 157
Commercialisation, 61, 63, 66, 114, 116, 124, 146
Confucian, 18, 21, 27, 51, 80, 81, 154, 163, 281
Confucianism, 17, 18, 18n148, 21, 27, 80, 81, 231
Confucius, 46
Constitution, 17, 27, 79, 81, 82, 94, 177, 182, 183, 193, 202, 229n127, 231, 281
Constitutional change, 182
Cotton Gin, 150
Credit, 75, 114, 117, 120, 287, 293
Czech Republic, xiv

D
Daifang, 1
Daimyo, 64, 66, 78n63, 78n70, 82, 83, 85, 90, 91, 94, 127, 138, 141, 144, 202, 283, 285
Daini, 71
Dairen, 187
Debt Relief Law, 64
Decision to Reform the Education System, 157
Deflation, 271
Deishma, 140
Depression of 1930–32, 218
Deregulation, 257, 264, 268
Divine, 11, 21, 81, 135, 142, 145
Dokyo, 20
Domains, 83, 112, 117, 118, 121, 124, 130, 135, 144, 285
Dutch East India Company, 104–106

E
Earthquake Casualty Bills, 215
Earthquake of 1923, 177, 220
Eastern Han, 26, 72
Economic contraction, 216, 253

Economic crisis, xi, xv, xvii, 143, 204, 211–213, 241, 252, 253, 257, 262, 286
Economic growth, 115, 119, 123, 124, 127, 147, 151, 155, 156, 160, 199, 213, 218, 220, 227, 234, 240, 244, 253, 258, 260, 261, 265–267, 271, 272, 291, 293
Economic Planning Agency, 234
Economic reform, ix, xix, 76
Economy, ix, xi, xv–xvii, 8, 37, 41, 48, 51, 58, 60, 63, 64, 66, 91, 95, 104, 107, 109, 113, 115, 122, 127, 129, 136, 136n6, 138, 143, 146, 149, 151, 153, 155n145, 159, 162, 164, 177, 184, 188, 193, 196, 198–201, 203, 205, 211–213, 213n14, 220, 225–227, 231–233, 239–242, 244, 245, 253, 254, 258, 260, 261, 264, 266, 266n119, 266n120, 267, 269, 272, 272n161, 275, 276n187, 276n189, 283, 285–287, 291, 291n39, 293, 293n60, 293n61
Ecosystem, 7, 121, 122
Edo, 20, 65, 101, 106, 110n60, 111n70, 113n89, 115, 119, 121n149, 124, 126, 126n189, 127, 127n197–199, 129, 135, 138, 142, 144, 145, 285
Employment, 123, 126, 238, 253, 258, 268
England, 17, 57, 102, 122, 138n25, 143, 147, 148, 148n102, 150n113, 273n166
Entrepreneurship, 112, 120, 147, 264
Esoteric, 74, 93
EU, xiii, xivn17, xivn19, xx, 272, 292
EU-8, xiii
EU-Japan FTA, 272
Europe, xivn23, xix, 52n150, 84n120, 85n126, 86n138, 91n177, 92n182, 92n185, 96, 108, 112, 122n162, 128, 148, 154, 154n141, 185, 189, 194, 199, 203, 206, 212, 230
Eurozone, xiii, xiiin9, xx

F
Fat Man, 229
February Incident, 243
February 26th Incident, 212, 223, 224, 226
Federation of Economic Organisations, 234
Feudalism, 39, 42, 50, 64, 112, 113, 147, 283
Finance Ministry, 217
Financial crisis of 1927, xii, 213, 218, 287
First Five Year Plan, 192
Five Mountains Zen, 62
Flintlock, 128
Foreign Direct Investment, 272, 272n160, 272n165, 275, 275n186
Forests, 121
France, 12, 165, 174, 201
Free Trade Agreements, 271–272, 275
French, 10, 138, 141, 165, 174, 205
Fuji, 225, 257
Fujiwara, 22, 35, 36, 54, 264n102
Fumimaro, Konoe, 222n85, 224

G
GDP per capita, 123, 136
Gempei War, 36, 37, 39–46
Genghis Khan, 12
Genji, 29, 43
German, 10, 174, 187, 188, 194, 206, 212

Germany, xi, xiv, 165, 174, 177, 185, 187, 189, 192, 194, 201, 203, 212, 222, 226, 230, 235, 243, 244, 254
GNP, 219, 233, 234, 240, 245, 262
Global Financial Crisis, xi, xiv
Godaigo, Emperor, 71
Gokenin, 52
Gold, 103, 116, 118, 143, 149, 164, 199, 216, 219, 242
Gold standard, 216, 219, 242
Gozan Bungaku, 62
Gozan Josselsu, 73, 93, 284
Gozan Zen, 108
Great Britain, ix, x, 42, 102, 130, 139, 144, 154, 163, 174, 177, 186, 189, 190, 202, 226, 239
Great Depression, xi, 95n199, 95n203, 96n210, 216, 242
Great Kanto Earthquake, 214, 241n223
Guilds, 148, 150

H
Haengju, 90
Haihan Chiken, The, 153
Hakata Bay, 12, 61, 66, 85
Hamamatsu, 110, 110n58, 112, 112n78
Han, 1, 9, 10, 14, 26, 26n205, 26n206, 39, 40, 40n37, 72, 124, 129n208, 167, 205, 281
Hanpeita, Takechi, 139
Haruka, Empress, 178
Hashimoto Doctrine, 263
Hawaii, 2n10, 15n116, 22n175, 22n179, 22n182, 26n205, 26n206, 223, 234n165
Heian Period, 22–25, 22n182, 23n184, 23n188, 29, 35, 35n3, 37, 39, 47, 48, 51, 54, 60, 61, 63, 64, 66, 72, 283
Heike, 40, 40n43, 40n44, 41n54, 43, 44n74, 44n77, 55, 55n179, 56n182, 66
Heike Monogatari, 40, 40n43, 40n44, 41, 41n54, 55, 55n179, 56n182, 66
Heisei Period, 246, 251–276
Heishi, 29
Hesei Boom, 260
Hesei Reforms, 263
Hideki, Tojo, 224, 226
Hideyoshi, General Hashiba, 87
Hideyoshi, Toyotomi, 87, 92, 97
Himiko, Queen, 15, 157
Hirado, 105
Hirobumi, Ito, 174, 177, 202, 203
Hirohito, Crown Prince (Emperor), 178, 211, 227, 230, 239, 239n209, 244, 251
Hiroshima, 212, 227, 229, 229n132, 244
Hitachi, 237
Hojo, 36, 38, 49, 53, 60, 65
Hojo Regency, 39, 60
Hojo Regent, 49
Hokkaido, 4, 6, 7, 28, 149, 282
Holocene, 4
Homo Erectus, 2, 3
Homo Sapien, 3
Hongaku, Tendai, 54, 55, 55n174
Honshu, 4, 6, 9, 13, 15, 84, 149
House of Minamoto, the, 43
House of Taira, 43
Huawei, xix, xixn30, xx
Human behaviour, xi
Huizi, 58
Hungary, xiv
Hyogo, 15, 44, 142

I
Imari Bay, 12
Imperial Civil Exam, 156

Imperial Way Faction, 221, 222
Import Duties Act, 204
Income, xi, xvi, xvii, xviin27, xx, 38, 52, 66, 126, 129, 152, 155, 160, 196, 213, 218n54, 238, 239, 241, 243, 253, 261, 266, 285, 286, 289, 291
India, xvi, 17, 39n32, 58, 80, 101, 102n2, 104, 106, 113, 129, 139, 150n110, 164, 254
Individualism, xvi, 112, 179, 180, 203, 286
Industrial Bank of Japan, 257
Industrialisation, x, 9, 76, 102, 122, 122n162, 130, 137, 143, 147, 152, 160, 163, 176, 180, 193, 197, 199, 206, 212, 286
Infrastructure, xix, 58, 95, 127, 151, 160, 162, 192, 230, 239, 241, 244, 252, 289, 289n28, 290n37, 293
Inspector General of Military Education, 222
Instability of the financial system, 215
Institutions, xiii, xvi, 18, 20, 23, 35, 40, 50, 52, 58, 59n204, 72, 77, 78, 81, 93, 94, 109, 113, 114, 122, 124, 129, 157, 161–163, 186, 213, 231, 233, 257, 260, 262, 264, 267, 268, 283–285
Invention, 7, 8, 189n133, 190n141, 270
Iron, 9, 16, 26–28, 57, 88, 123, 282
Ise Bay, 4
Ishii Corporation, 214
IS-LM model, 275
Isolationist policies, 103, 113
Iwakura embassy, 153, 154
Izanagi, 11, 260
Izanami, 11

J

Japan, ix–xi, xv–xvii, xviin27, xix, xx, 1, 1n2, 2n7, 3–6, 3n13, 3n20, 4n29, 5n34–37, 6n43, 6n44, 6n47, 7n48, 7n50, 7n52–55, 8, 8n56, 8n58, 8n60, 8n61, 9n68, 10, 12n94, 12n96, 13–15, 13n102, 13n103, 13n106, 14n109, 14n112–114, 15n116, 15n118, 15n121, 15n124, 16n126–128, 17, 17n134, 17n140, 18n149, 18n150, 19–22, 19n156, 19n157, 20n165, 21n167, 21n170, 21n172, 22n175, 22n179, 22n181, 22n182, 23n184, 23n188, 24n196, 25–27, 26n205, 26n206, 27n208, 27n211, 28n218, 35, 35n1, 35n3, 35n4, 36n6, 36n7, 36n9, 36n11, 37, 37n12, 37n13, 39–42, 39n28, 39n29, 39n31, 41n56, 42n64, 43n68, 44n80, 45, 45n82, 45n85, 45n88, 45n89, 46n90, 46n93, 46n96, 46n98, 47–50, 47n107, 50n128, 50n132, 50n133, 50n135–137, 51n146, 51n147, 52, 52n149, 52n150, 52n153, 52n154, 53n156, 53n163, 53n164, 54, 54n165, 54n167, 56, 58, 58n200, 60, 60n214, 60n219, 60n222, 61, 62n234, 62n238, 63–66, 64n252, 65n255, 65n258, 65n259, 67n260, 67n261, 71n2, 72, 72n6, 72n9, 72n12, 73n17–20, 73n25, 74, 74n33, 74n36, 75n38, 75n41, 75n44, 76, 76n45, 76n46, 77, 77n57, 77n58, 78n62, 78n63, 78n70, 79n73, 79n74, 80n79, 81, 82, 82n96, 83n113, 84n114,

84n116, 84n120, 85, 85n124, 87, 87n144, 87n150, 88n151, 88n157, 89n160, 90, 90n172, 90n173, 90n175, 91, 91n177, 92n182, 92n183, 92n185, 92n189, 93, 93n198, 94, 97, 101, 101n1, 102n4, 104, 104n10, 106, 106n26, 107n34, 108, 108n42, 108n43, 108n46, 109, 109n50, 109n55, 109n57, 110n58, 110n61, 110n62, 112–114, 112n75, 112n77, 112n78, 113n89, 114n91, 114n97, 117, 117n120, 118n128, 119, 120n136, 120n137, 120n138, 121n148, 122, 122n157, 122n160, 122n161, 122n162, 123n163, 123n165, 123n166, 124, 124n175, 124n178, 126n188, 126n190, 127–129, 127n195, 128n201, 128n202, 128n204, 135n4, 136n10, 137, 137n12, 137n15, 137n17, 138, 138n20, 138n22, 138n25, 139n29, 139n30, 140, 140n36, 140n37, 140n40, 141, 141n42, 141n46, 141n48, 142n55–57, 143–146, 144n64, 144n66, 146n81, 146n85–87, 148, 148n94, 148n95, 150n111, 151–154, 151n114, 151n116, 152n120, 152n123, 152n129, 153n130, 153n133, 154n141, 155n144, 155n151, 156, 156n154, 157, 158n174, 159, 159n185, 160n191, 161n194, 161n201, 162, 162n204, 163, 163n209, 167, 173, 173n1, 174n12, 175n19, 176, 176n27, 176n29, 177n36–38, 177n40, 178–188, 178n42, 178n47, 179n53, 179n58, 180n60, 180n61, 181n67, 181n72, 181n74, 182n75, 182n80, 183n83, 183n84, 183n87, 184n91, 184n95, 185n101, 185n103, 185n108, 186n110, 186n116, 187n117, 187n119, 188n125–127, 188n131, 189n133, 189n137, 190, 190n141, 190n142, 190n146, 191n150, 192, 192n155, 192n158, 193, 193n159, 193n160, 193n161, 193n165, 193n166, 194n172, 195n180, 196–202, 196n189, 197n196, 198n198, 198n201, 198n202, 198n204, 199n207, 199n209, 199n210, 200n218, 200n219, 201n223, 204n230, 206, 211–213, 211n1, 212n6, 213n13, 213n15, 214n20–22, 215n26, 215n27, 215n31, 215n33, 216n37, 216n41, 217n43, 217n44–48, 218n50, 218n54, 219, 219n57, 220, 221n76, 221n77, 222, 222n79, 222n82, 222n85, 223n91, 224, 224n95, 226, 226n107, 226n113, 227, 227n114, 227n116, 227n117, 228n121, 228n123, 228n124, 229, 229n126–128, 229n131, 230n135–137, 230n139, 230n140, 231–233, 232n152, 232n153, 232n154, 232n156, 233n157, 233n161, 233n162, 233n164, 234n165, 234n166, 234n170, 234n171, 235n173, 235n175, 235n176, 235n180, 236n181, 236n188, 237n189, 237n190, 238–242, 238n197, 238n200, 238n201, 239n203,

Japan (*cont.*)
239n205–209, 240n210, 240n212, 241n220, 241n222, 241n223, 242n226, 244, 244n227, 245n228, 251–254, 251n1, 251n4, 252n11, 253n14, 253n15, 253n19, 254n27, 254n29, 256n41, 257, 257n47, 257n49, 257n53, 257n54, 258, 258n58–60, 258n62–64, 259n65, 260, 261, 262n89, 262n90, 262n95, 263n97, 263n98, 263n100, 264, 264n101–103, 265n112, 265n114, 266–272, 266n116, 266n119, 266n120, 266n121, 267n123, 268n128–130, 268n132, 268n134, 268n135, 269n137, 269n138, 270n144, 271n151, 271n155, 271n156, 271n158, 272n159–163, 272n165, 273n166, 274n173, 274n176, 275, 275n180, 275n184, 281–287, 281n1, 282n3, 282n6, 283n13, 292, 292n51, 292n52, 292n54, 292n55
Japanese Army, 219, 224
Japanese Automobile Manufacturers Association, 236
Japanese civil society, 180
Japanese CME, 267
Japanese Diet, 197
Japanese Kwantung, 187, 191, 228
Japanese Manchukuo, 192, 212
Japanese merchants, 61, 85, 105, 107, 120
Japanese military, xvii, 90, 108, 109, 136, 163, 174, 185, 187, 189, 198, 201, 203, 217, 220, 224, 226, 230, 233, 238, 239, 243, 286
Japanese Navy, 42, 42n61, 187, 187n118, 191, 219, 224
Japanese Supreme War Council, 220
Japanese trading settlements, 102
Japan's defeat, 229
Japan's economic dividend, 236
Jianwu Restoration, 72
Jikki, 154
Jimmu, 2, 11
Jinshin Revolt, 20
Jito, 38, 51, 54, 65
Joei Code, 49, 50, 65, 283
Jokyu War, 38, 40, 47–56
John, King, 17
Jomon, 2–13, 3n19, 5n36, 6n47, 7n48–50, 7n54–56, 8n58, 8n60, 8n61, 25, 281
Jutland, 175

K

Kagami, Azuma, 62, 63, 66
Kaido, 127
Kamakura, x, 29, 35–67, 37n14, 38n23, 40n42, 42n58, 53n163, 53n164, 54n167, 54n170, 55n174, 62n241, 65n255, 65n258, 67n261, 74, 77n57, 78, 79, 84, 93, 94, 113, 283, 283n13
Kamakura Period, x, 35–67, 42n58, 62n241, 84, 94, 283
Kambun, 40
Kami, 11, 16
Kammu, Emperor, 19
Kana syllabary, 25
Kango trade, 84
Kangxi (1662–1722), 166
Kannami, 93
Kanrei-Yoriai System, 76
Kanto, 4, 5, 7, 36, 42, 43, 45, 49, 52, 157, 177, 214, 220, 241n223, 242
Kawachi Court, 15, 16

Kawashima, 71, 71n2, 72n9
Kay, John, 150
Kazushige, Ugaki, 220
Kei, Prime Minster Hara, 178
Keiki, Shogun, 145
Keiretsu, 259, 269, 273
Kemmu Restoration, 67, 72, 283
Kenka Ryoseibai, 82, 95
Kenmu Shikimoku, 79
Keynesian economic policy, 217
Khubilai Khan, 12
Kinai, 2, 4
Kinai-Yamato, 2
King of Japan, 77, 91, 93, 104
Kiyomori, Taira, 36, 40, 43, 55, 61
Koda-ha, 224, 243
Kodo-ha faction, 221, 222, 243
Kodo Faction, 222
Kofun Period, 13–16, 13n104, 16n125, 27, 282
Koguryo, 14
Kogyo, Shokusan, 159, 160
Koichi, Kido, 227, 228
Ko-ikki disturbance, 75
Koin, Kido, 146
Kojiki, 22, 26
Kokueki, 118
Komegata-ryogae, 118
Komei, Emperor, 142, 144, 145
Korea, 1, 8, 9, 12, 14, 17, 26, 48, 48n117, 75, 87, 87n144, 87n147, 87n150, 90, 90n173, 91, 97, 107, 110n61, 112n75, 114, 115, 156n152, 173, 187, 194, 201–203, 206, 211, 233, 235, 239, 253, 254n23, 285
Korean, 2, 3, 10, 11, 13, 14, 25, 26, 47, 49, 66, 87, 87n148, 90, 91n180, 92n187, 97, 157, 173, 201, 205, 240, 245
Korean emigrants, 48
Korean Straits, 175
Korean War, 205, 240, 245
Korechika, Anami, 228
Kunitake, Kume, 153n135, 154
Kyoto, 5, 15, 20, 22, 27, 35, 37, 43, 46, 61, 65–67, 71, 74, 93, 101, 108, 110n58, 112n78, 116, 119, 130, 135, 139, 142, 144, 146, 147n89, 281, 283, 285
Kyushu, 1, 2, 2n7, 4, 6, 9, 12, 25, 47–49, 61, 71, 75, 84, 87

L
Land Tax, 154
Late Kofun period, 16
Law to Promote Miniban Education, 157
League of Nations, 188, 212
Lelang, 1
Leponte, 175
Liaodong Peninsula, 173
Liberal Democratic Party, 259
Liberalisation, 257
Liberty and Popular Rights Movement, 183
Little Boy, 229
London Conference, 219

M
MacArthur, General Douglas, 230, 230n136, 231
Macron, xv
Maize, 166
Manchuria, 14, 19, 174, 187, 191, 192, 202, 212, 219, 220, 225, 228, 286
Manchurian Incident, 191, 192, 198
Mandokoro, 54, 65, 83
Manila, 6n46, 230
Manufactured goods, x, xi, xvii, 162, 194, 206, 216, 235, 240, 245

Mao, Chairman, 104
Mariana, 188
Marshall Islands, 188
Maruyama, 8, 8n58, 8n61
Masako, Hojo, 36
Masatsura, Kusunoki, 74
Masayoshi, Hotta, 141
Masuda Bill Broker Bank, 214
Mazaki, General, 222
Meiji Period, 9, 42, 46n98, 101, 135–167, 156n155, 176, 179, 180, 183, 185, 193, 198, 199, 201, 211, 231, 233, 244, 270
Meiji Restoration, xi, 42, 45, 131, 138, 146, 150, 151, 155, 163, 191, 266
Meiji-Taisho economic system, 193, 198
Mencius, 46
Micronesia, 188
Middle Kofun period, 16
Midway, 175
Militarism, xi, xvi, xvii, 64, 123, 178, 192, 204, 226, 232
Minami-ryogae, 118
Minamoto Clan, 35, 42–44, 43n66, 43n70, 55, 66, 84
Minamoto Yoritomo, 35n1, 35n4, 36, 36n7, 36n9, 37, 37n13, 40, 45, 49, 51, 52n149, 53n156
Minatogawa, 3, 5
Minatomo, 40, 43, 56
Minatomo Clan, 43, 56
Ming China, 85, 91, 96, 103, 104
Ming Dynasty, 48, 59, 77, 85, 92, 95, 104, 116, 167
Ming Emperor, 86
Ministry of Education, 136
Ministry of Finance, 243, 257, 260, 262, 264, 274, 287
Ministry of International Trade and Industry, 234, 241, 259
Minseito government, 217, 219
Minseito Party, 216, 224
Mito sect, 143
Mitsumasa, Yonai, 227
Miwa Court, 15
Monchuju, 54, 65
Monetary and fiscal policy, 217, 219, 240, 259
Monetary policy, 195, 217, 241, 255, 271, 274, 275
Monetisation, 60, 108
Money, xv, xvii, 59, 59n204, 64–66, 75, 91, 96, 105, 107, 117–119, 124, 126, 129, 146, 151, 220, 274, 287, 294
Mongol, 13, 48n117, 65, 67, 89, 104, 128, 284
Mongolic, 10
Mononofu, 17
Motokiyo, Zeami, 92, 92n190
Muromachi, 50, 62n234, 67, 71–97, 72n12, 75n41, 76n46, 83n113, 110, 283
Muromachi Period, 71–97, 283
Mutiny of Pubei and Liu Dongyang, 89
Mutsuhito, Prince, 103, 145

N

Nagasaki, 105, 107, 115, 140, 141, 164, 212, 227, 229, 229n132, 244
Nanamugi Incident, 138, 144
Nanjing, 90, 95, 165
Nanyang trade, 105
Nara, 15, 19–22, 20n158, 25, 27, 50, 54, 65, 281
Naosuke, Ii, 139, 142
Nationalism, xi, xv–xvii, 19, 27n210, 138, 162n204, 178, 186, 190, 192, 202, 204, 212, 219, 225, 258n64, 286

Nenkiyama, 121
Neolithic, 5, 6
Neo-Marxism, xviii
New Buddhism, 54
New Zealand, xix, 104, 254n29, 256n41, 257n49, 257n54
Nihon Hyoronsha, 122n162
Nihon Shoki, 22, 26–27
Niigata, 142
Nikkei Stock Exchange, 257
Nikkei 225, 274, 287
Ning-Po, 85
Nintoku, 13
Nishigaoka, 71
Nobi, 4, 5
Nomura, 237
Non-performing loans, 177, 268
Northern Manchuria, 175
Northern Zhou Dynasty, 80

O

Oama, Prince, 22
Oitsuke Oikose, 162
Okada, Prime Minister Keisuke, 217
Okayama, 15
Okhotsk Current, 12
Okinawa, 3, 6, 44, 48, 48n114
Omoto, Prince, 22
Onin War, 82, 94, 108
Opium, 130, 140, 140n41, 164, 164n213
ORE, 35, 54
Osaka, 4, 13, 15, 19, 23, 46, 65, 109, 114, 115, 117, 119, 122n161, 123n163, 124n175, 128n201, 129, 142, 214, 284
Osaka Bay, 4
Osachi, Prime Minister Hamaguchi, 177, 198
Ottawa, xi, xin1, xx, 204, 204n226, 204n228, 216, 216n40
Ottawa Agreements of 1932, 204
Ouchi family, 86

P

Pacific, 42, 135n4, 138n22, 139n29, 188, 262n92
Paekche, 14
Palaeolithic, 2–13, 3n13, 3n20, 4n25, 5n35, 5n37, 13n102, 14n112
Palau, 188
Paris Universal Exposition, 176
Pax Americana, 230, 238
Peanuts, 166
Pearl Harbor/Pearl Harbour, xvii, 191n147, 191n149, 212, 223, 234, 235
Peasants, 49, 54, 65, 73, 106, 110, 111, 129, 135, 146, 149, 158, 183, 204, 283, 285
People's Bank of China, 255
Permanent Court of Arbitration, 205
Perry, Matthew, 136, 137, 139, 139n30, 141, 164
Plaza Accord of 1985, 254, 256, 260, 292
Pleistocene, 3, 6
Poland, xiii, 212
Population, xv, 1, 3–5, 7, 8, 13, 28, 61, 109, 119, 121, 123, 124, 130, 136, 147, 148, 167, 192, 196, 225, 229, 252, 258, 261, 264, 266, 275, 282, 285, 288
Port Arthur, 173, 187
Portuguese, 75, 86, 88, 105, 106, 115, 128, 129
Post-Meiji Japan, xv
Potsdam Terms of July 1945, 227
Pottery, 6, 8
Private sector, 193, 206, 225, 233, 241, 270
Privy Council, 184

Productive capacity, 195, 214, 232
Promissory notes, 58
Property, xiii, xvii, xix, xx, 24, 45, 50, 77, 107, 117, 128, 159, 160, 185, 192, 213, 261, 273, 287, 288n17, 288n18, 290, 294, xiiin10–12
Property and equity bubble, 261
Proto-industrialisation, x, 102, 124, 128, 130, 149
Pure Land, 74, 74n27
Pusan, 87

Q
Qianlong (1736–95), 166
Qing, x, 103, 105, 112, 130, 163, 163n208, 163n209, 166, 166n225, 166n227, 166n228, 167n231, 167n235, 173, 191
Qing China, 104, 112, 130, 164, 173
Qingdao, 188
Qing Empire, 166, 167, 167n231
Qing Guangzhou System, 164
Quanzhou, 48, 57

R
Real estate bubble, 257, 261, 274, 288
Referendum, xiv
Regent, 17, 23, 27, 38, 49, 53, 65, 81, 101, 139, 142
Republic, 104, 191, 253
Ritsuryo, 28, 29, 50, 51, 51n143, 81, 282
RMB-Dollar exchange rate, 256
Rudders, 63
Rusong, General Li, 89, 90
Russian Army, 175
Russian Far Eastern Fleet, 175, 201
Russian monarchy, 191
Russo-Japanese War, 174n12, 175n22, 176n24, 181, 182, 193
Ryukyu, 44, 44n74, 44n77, 48, 48n110, 48n111, 48n114, 107
Ryukyu Islands, 48, 48n114, 107

S
Sadako, Empress, 178, 179
Saigo Takamori, 146
Saito Makoto, Prime Minister, 217
Sakai, 85, 108
Sakhalin, 3, 176, 187, 194, 202, 206
Samurai, 12n96, 17n137, 29, 38n25, 39n28, 40n42, 41n56, 42n64, 43n68, 43n71, 43n72, 45n83, 45n85, 45n88, 45n89, 46n90, 46n93, 46n96, 52, 55n179, 56n182, 74, 75n40, 79n71, 83, 83n110, 86n140, 93, 106, 121n146, 128, 135n1, 138n26, 143, 144, 148, 150, 152, 157, 157n168, 158n170, 158n173, 184, 282, 285, 286
Sankon Kotai Seido, 124
Sanna, 8
Sekisho, 127
Sengoku daimyo, 125
Senjyuro, Hayashi, 221
Seto Inland Sea, 61
Shaman Queen, 15
Shantung, 187
Shigenori, Togo, 227
Shigeru, Yoshida, 230, 232
Shih-k'ai, 190
Shimabara rebellion, 114
Shimoda Convention, 140, 141
Shinden-Zukuri, 73, 93
Shinobi, 18
Shinokosho hierarchy, 106
Shintoism, 19, 28, 76, 114, 179, 282
Shitenno-Ji Temple, 19

Shoen, 38, 50, 50n135, 51, 51n146, 51n147, 52n153, 52n154, 78, 94, 284
Shogun, Ashikaga, xvi, xviii, 37, 38, 45, 49, 53, 67, 72, 74–77, 79, 81, 85, 87n141, 91–94, 101, 104, 106, 108, 114, 117, 120, 126, 127, 129, 135, 139, 141, 144, 145, 153, 155, 202, 284
Shogunate, Ashikaga, 84, 113, 125
Shogun Iesada, 141, 142
Shoin-Zukuri, 73, 93
Shotoku, Empress, 17–20, 18n149, 19n156, 27, 79–81, 94, 281
Showa Depression, 216, 216n35, 216n38, 242
Showa Financial Crisis, 215–216, 242
Showa Period, 181, 184, 201, 211–246, 251, 286
Shugo, 38, 51, 54, 65, 75, 76, 84
Shugodai, 84
Siberia, 3, 219
Silla, 14
Silver bullion, 164
Sino-Japanese War of 1894–1895, 173n2, 193
Sino-Russian War, 230
Smoot-Hawley Tariff Act, 204
Social change, 64, 283
Social Masses Party, 224
Social progress, 154
Soemu, Toyoda, 228
Song Dynasty, 56–59, 61, 63, 147
Song merchants, 47, 59
Southern Song, 62, 63
Soviet Union, 175, 220, 228, 231, 235
Specialisation of labour, 9, 26, 125
Spindle, 9, 26
Sub-prime, xii, xiin7, xx
Sui Dynasty, 80, 81, 94, 156
Sumitomo, 160, 257
Supreme Councillor, 144
Suzuki, Prime Minister, 228
Suzuki & Co, 215
Sweet potatoes, 166

T

Taiho Code, 50
Taika Reform, 21, 28, 42, 50, 282
Taiping Heavenly Kingdom, 165
Taira, 35, 36, 40, 43, 43n66, 43n70, 45, 56, 61, 64, 66
Taisho, Emperor, 211
Taisho Democracy, 162n204, 179–186, 182n75
Taisho Period, 173–206, 227, 234, 238, 244, 286
Taiwan, xv, 10, 105, 166, 173, 177, 180, 186n116, 187, 194, 206, 215, 235, 239, 254, 254n25, 286
Takaaki, Foreign Minister Kato, 189
Takahashi, Korekiyo, 216, 242
Takashima, 13
Takauji, Ashikaga, 71, 79, 81, 94, 284
Takeshita Doctrine, 262, 262n96, 263
Takeshita, Prime Minister, 263
Tally trade, 75, 77, 92
Tanaka Memorial, 192, 192n158
Tang, 2, 26, 26n205, 26n206, 47, 48, 51
T'ang Dynasty, 21, 25, 61, 63, 80
Tenjin, Emperor, 22
Tenmu, Emperor, 22
Tao, 80, 81
Tariffs, xi, xiv, xvii, 165, 192, 194, 198, 203, 206, 216, 236, 242, 255, 292
Tax, 24, 52, 58, 64, 66, 78, 85, 96, 110, 115, 118, 121, 130, 136, 146, 149n103, 154n142, 155, 158, 158n178, 159, 174, 183, 261, 266, 266n120, 270, 285, 288, 290

Tea, 58, 74, 149, 164, 165
Temporary Worker Law of 1999, 268
Tempo Reforms of 1841, 147
Tenant farmers, 42, 66, 159, 160
Tendai Sect, 20
Terado, 71
Tetsuzan, Nagata, 221, 222
Textiles, xi, 96, 108, 148, 153, 167, 235
Tiara Clan, 44, 55, 66
Tohoku region earthquake, 252
Tohuku, 7
Tokugawa, x, 25, 46, 50, 72, 75, 78n63, 78n70, 83, 86, 86n140, 87n141, 91, 97, 101–131, 105n15, 106n22, 106n26, 107n33, 107n34, 108n47, 109n51, 109n55, 109n57, 114n91, 120n136, 120n138, 121n148, 122n157, 122n160, 122n161, 123n163, 123n166, 124n175, 126n189, 128n201, 135, 136n10, 137, 137n12, 137n17, 138, 142, 144, 146, 146n86, 147, 147n92, 149–152, 149n106, 153n133, 155, 156, 158, 163, 167, 179, 186, 202, 212, 231, 231n149, 233, 284, 285, 285n15
Tokugawa Ieyasu, 83, 86, 86n140, 87n141, 91, 97, 108, 108n47, 109n51
Tokugawa Period, x, 75, 83, 97, 101–131, 146n86, 152, 186, 202, 231, 233
Tokyo, 87n141, 122n162, 146, 214, 223, 230, 233n161, 236n188, 241, 262, 262n92
Tokyo Bay, 4
Tokyo Castle, 146
Tokyo Watanabe Bank, 215
Tosa Loyalist Party, 139
Tosei-ha faction, 222, 243
Toshiba, 237
'Tosui Koryo,' 221
Town and Village Enterprises, 160
Trafalgar, 175
Trans-Pacific Partnership FTA, 272
Treaty of Frankfurt, 174
Treaty of Kanagawa, 140
Treaty of Nanjing, 165
Treaty of Portsmouth, 176, 176n25
Treaty of Shimonoseki, 174, 187
Treaty of Tianjin, 165
Tribesmen, 26
Triple Intervention of 1895, 174
Truman, President Harry, 229, 245
Trump, President Donald, xiv
Tsushima, 86, 141, 175, 175n16, 175n17, 201
Tsuyoshi, Inukai, 198
Turkic, 10
Turtle ships, 88

U

Ugaki Kazushige, War Minister, 220
Ugi, 16, 27
Uji Chieftain, 16
Uji Kami, 16
UK, xii, xiii, xivn17, xivn22, xvii, xx, 88n151, 88n155, 88n157, 89n160, 90n172, 90n175, 102n2, 104n10, 108n42, 177n37, 177n38, 186, 193n165, 198n204, 204n230, 213n13, 235, 259n66, 267n123, 268n129, 269n136, 274n174, 275n179
United States, xiv, xvii, 87n144, 90n173, 140, 150, 153, 163, 176, 177, 190, 196, 198, 202,

226, 227, 230, 232, 239, 240, 245, 254, 255, 258, 262, 287
University of Tokyo, 156
Uraga, 139
US competitive model, 267–268

V
Vassals, 52, 64, 65
Vatican, 114
Versailles-Washington Consensus, 185
Vietnam, 61, 97, 205

W
Wa, 1, 18n149, 19n156, 26
Wakamonogumi, 110n60, 111, 111n70
Waki-Kaido, 127
Wall Street Crash, xi, 177, 234, 244
War, xix, 22, 29, 36, 40–42, 49, 64, 78, 88, 94, 97, 101, 104, 108, 112, 163, 173, 181, 187, 188, 193, 194, 199, 200n221, 201, 202, 205, 206, 211–213, 214n21, 220, 225–227, 229, 230n136, 231, 232, 232n153, 233n161, 234, 239, 241n220, 242, 244, 254, 255, 258, 260, 261, 269, 273, 274n169, 283, 284, 292
Wariyama, 121
Washington Conference, 188, 190, 191n147, 191n149, 203
Washington Consensus, 273
Wei, 1, 26, 281
Weihaiwei, 174
Wen Ti, Emperor, 80
Western provinces, 43
World Trade Organisation, 213
World War 1 (WW1), xviii, 186–194, 188n127, 196, 203, 206, 211, 213
World War 2, 19, 21, 29, 175, 179, 187, 287
Writing, xxi
Wutsung, 80

X
Xiuquan, Hong, 165

Y
Yamadai, 2
Yamaichi, 2
Yamato, 16, 27, 39, 92, 282
Yamato Court, 16
Yamato Emperor, 28
Yamato Ugi, 16, 27
Yangtze River, 12
Yashiro Heike Monogatari, 40
Yasutoki, 49
Yawata Steel, 194
Yayoi, 2–14, 9n72
Yellow Sea, 14
Yi, Admiral, 88
Yi dynasty, 92
Ying and the Yang, 76
Yingzong, Emperor (1436–1449 AD and 1457–1465 AD), 96
Yokohama, 241
Yongbyon, 254
Yongzheng (1723–35), 166
Yoritomo, 35n1, 35n4, 36n7, 36n9, 37, 37n13, 45, 51, 52n149, 53n156, 54, 63, 65
Yoshida Doctrine, 232
Yoshiharu, Shogun, 85
Yoshimasa, Shogun, 85

Yoshimitsu, 76, 76n48, 77, 77n53, 77n60, 85, 91, 92, 94, 104, 108, 284
Yoshimune, 117, 120, 127
Yoshinori, Shogun, 75, 94
Yoyoi, 1, 9, 9n66, 25, 27, 281, 282
Yoyoi culture, 1, 9, 25, 281
Yoyoi Period, 9, 9n66
Yuan, 12, 39, 56–64, 104, 128, 190, 255
Yusaku, Field Marshal Uyehara (1856–1933), 220

Z

Zaibatsu, 152, 160, 162, 193, 197, 200, 200n221, 201, 203, 206, 219, 222, 225, 237, 286
Zen, 18n148, 62, 62n234, 62n238, 62n240, 72n6, 73n18, 74, 79, 93, 108, 108n43
Zen Buddhism, 74, 93
Zeni-ryogae, 118
Zhoukoudian, 3
Zoshiki, 53

The manufacturer's authorised representative in the EU is Springer
Nature Customer Service Centre GmbH, Europaplatz 3, 69115 Heidelberg,
Germany. If you have any concerns regarding our products, please
contact ProductSafety@springernature.com

Printed and bound by CPI Group (UK) Ltd, Croydon, CR0 4YY
30/09/2026
02225246-0003